A Daily Study Guide to the Entire Bible

This Morning with God

general editor:
Carol Adeney

InterVarsity Press
Downers Grove
Illinois 60515

© 1968, 1970, 1971, 1974, 1978 by Inter-Varsity Christian Fellowship of the United
States of America

InterVarsity Press is the book-publishing division of Inter-Varsity Christian Fellowship,
a student movement active on campus at hundreds of universities, colleges and
schools of nursing. For information about local and regional activities,
write IVCF, 233 Langdon St., Madison, WI 53703.

Originally published in book form in four volumes. Prior to that This Morning with God
appeared in HIS magazine, the monthly publication of Inter-Varsity Christian Fellowship.
These studies are revised and adapted for continuous use.

Distributed in Canada through InterVarsity Press, 1875 Leslie St., Unit 10,
Don Mills, Ontario M3B 2M5, Canada.

ISBN 0-87784-870-X
Library of Congress Catalog Card Number: 68-28080

Printed in the United States of America

18   17   16   15   14   13   12   11   10   9
94   93   92   91   90   89   88

YEAR ONE

	page	date started	date finished
☐ *Year One*	17		
☐ Luke 1—9	18		
☐ Genesis 1—26	30		
☐ Luke 10:1—19:28	36		
☐ Genesis 27—50	45		
☐ Luke 19:29—24:53	50		
☐ Psalms 1—12	55		
☐ Acts 1—12	58		

☐ Exodus 1—20 _____ 65 _____ _____
☐ Acts 13—28 _____ 73 _____ _____
☐ Amos _____ 83 _____ _____
☐ Hosea _____ 85 _____ _____
☐ Psalms 13—29 _____ 87 _____ _____
☐ 1 Thessalonians _____ 92 _____ _____
☐ 2 Thessalonians _____ 94 _____ _____
☐ Joshua _____ 95 _____ _____
☐ Galatians _____ 100 _____ _____
☐ Exodus 21—40 _____ 105 _____ _____
☐ Romans _____ 113 _____ _____

YEAR TWO

☐ *Year Two* _____ 129 _____ _____
☐ Proverbs _____ 130 _____ _____
☐ 1 Corinthians _____ 139 _____ _____
☐ Psalms 30—41 _____ 149 _____ _____
☐ 2 Corinthians _____ 153 _____ _____
☐ Micah _____ 160 _____ _____
☐ 1 Timothy _____ 162 _____ _____
☐ Titus _____ 165 _____ _____
☐ 2 Timothy _____ 166 _____ _____
☐ Leviticus _____ 168 _____ _____
☐ Hebrews _____ 176 _____ _____
☐ Numbers _____ 187 _____ _____
☐ Mark 1—9 _____ 198 _____ _____
☐ Deuteronomy _____ 211 _____ _____
☐ Mark 10—16 _____ 221 _____ _____

☐ Judges —————— 228 ———————— ————————
☐ 1 Peter —————— 235 ———————— ————————
☐ 1 Samuel ————— 239 ———————— ————————

YEAR THREE

☐ *Year Three* ————— 249 ———————— ————————
☐ Ruth ——————— 250 ———————— ————————
☐ Ephesians —————— 252 ———————— ————————
☐ Job ——————— 257 ———————— ————————
☐ Psalms 42—51 ———— 270 ———————— ————————
☐ 2 Samuel ————— 273 ———————— ————————
☐ Psalms 52—72 ———— 280 ———————— ————————
☐ 1 Kings ————— 286 ———————— ————————
☐ John 1—12 ————— 294 ———————— ————————
☐ 2 Kings ————— 306 ———————— ————————
☐ John 13—21 ———— 312 ———————— ————————
☐ Isaiah 1—39 ———— 320 ———————— ————————
☐ 1, 2, and 3 John ——— 332 ———————— ————————
☐ Isaiah 40—66 ——— 336 ———————— ————————
☐ Philippians ———— 346 ———————— ————————
☐ Jonah ————— 349 ———————— ————————
☐ Joel ——————— 351 ———————— ————————
☐ Zephaniah ———— 352 ———————— ————————
☐ Nahum ————— 353 ———————— ————————
☐ Habakkuk ———— 353 ———————— ————————
☐ Obadiah ————— 355 ———————— ————————
☐ Colossians ———— 355 ———————— ————————
☐ Philemon ———— 358 ———————— ————————

YEAR FOUR

☐ *Year Four* —————359 —————— ——————
☐ Jeremiah 1—25 —————360 —————— ——————
☐ Matthew 1—7 —————368 —————— ——————
☐ Jeremiah 26—52 —————373 —————— ——————
☐ Lamentations —————382 —————— ——————
☐ Matthew 8—18 —————385 —————— ——————
☐ Ezekiel 1—32 —————397 —————— ——————
☐ Psalms 73—89 —————408 —————— ——————
☐ Ezekiel 33—48 —————413 —————— ——————
☐ Matthew 19—28 —————418 —————— ——————
☐ Ezra —————427 —————— ——————
☐ Nehemiah —————431 —————— ——————
☐ Psalms 90—106 —————436 —————— ——————
☐ Haggai —————440 —————— ——————
☐ Zechariah —————441 —————— ——————
☐ Malachi —————444 —————— ——————
☐ James —————446 —————— ——————
☐ 1 Chronicles —————448 —————— ——————
☐ Psalms 107—138 —————455 —————— ——————
☐ Esther —————465 —————— ——————
☐ Ecclesiastes —————467 —————— ——————
☐ 2 Chronicles —————471 —————— ——————
☐ Song of Solomon —————482 —————— ——————
☐ 2 Peter —————486 —————— ——————
☐ Jude —————488 —————— ——————
☐ Daniel —————489 —————— ——————
☐ Psalms 139—150 —————493 —————— ——————
☐ Revelation —————497 —————— ——————

	Pages	Author
Genesis	30-36, 45-50	Alice Naumoff
Exodus	65-73, 105-13	Yvonne Vinkemulder
Leviticus	168-76	Edson Peck
Numbers	187-98	JoAnne Fields
Deuteronomy	211-21	Steve Smith
Joshua	95-100	Donald Wade
Judges	228-35	Marion Snyder
Ruth	250-52	Ruth Adeney
1 Samuel	239-48	Virginia Hearn, ed. by Carol Adeney
2 Samuel	273-79	Marilyn Kunz, rev. by Linda Doll
1 Kings	286-94	Larry Sibley
2 Kings	306-12	Martha Reapsome
1 Chronicles	448-55	Margaret Brearley
2 Chronicles	471-82	Margaret Brearley
Ezra	427-31	Lois Bright
Nehemiah	431-35	Lois Bright
Esther	465-67	Gladys Hunt
Job	257-69	Charles Hatfield
Psalms 1—27	55-58, 87-92	Frank Currie
28—51	92, 149-53, 270-73	James Sire
52—72	280-86	Ruth Stoll/Mary Beaton
73—89	408-13	Alice Naumoff
90—94	436-37	Richard Wagner
95—106	437-40	Harish Merchant
107—120	455-60	Richard Wagner
121—150	460-65, 493-97	Ken Radke
Proverbs	130-39	Carol Adeney
Ecclesiastes	467-71	Madelyn Powell
Song of Solomon	482-86	Donald Smith
Isaiah	320-32, 336-46	Fred Woodberry
Jeremiah	360-67, 373-82, 385	Joyce Rigdon
Lamentations	382-85	Peter and B. Northrup
Ezekiel	397-408, 413-18	Fred and Jeanne Woodberry
Daniel	489-93	Bill Weimer
Hosea	85-87	Fred Wagner
Joel	351-52	Fred Wagner
Amos	83-85	Burton Harding
Obadiah	355	Donald Wade

Jonah	349-50	Clayton Lindgren
Micah	160-62	Clayton Lindgren
Nahum	353	Clayton Lindgren
Habakkuk	353-54	Clayton Lindgren
Zephaniah	352	Clayton Lindgren
Haggai	440-41	Carol Adeney
Zechariah	441-44	Frederick Wagner
Malachi	444-46	JoAnne Butts
Matthew	368-73, 385-97, 418-27	Louis Gropp/ Carol Adeney
Mark	198-211, 221-28	Yvonne Vinkemulder/ JoAnne Fields
Luke	18-30, 36-45, 50-55	Ronald Thompson/ Yvonne Vinkemulder/ Carol Adeney
John	294-305, 312-19	Carol Adeney
Acts	58-65, 73-83	Thomas Champness
Romans	113-27	Bill Weimer/Martha Reapsome/Carol Adeney
1 Corinthians	139-49	Jim Johnson rev. by Suellen Skinner
2 Corinthians	153-60	Reg Bradley
Galatians	100-05	Charles Hummel, rev. by Paul Byer
Ephesians	252-57	Paul Byer
Philippians	346-49	Don Fields
Colossians	355-58	Carol Adeney
1 Thessalonians	92-94	Elizabeth Thompson
2 Thessalonians	94-95	JoAnne Butts
1 Timothy	162-65	George Ensworth, rev. by Burton Harding
2 Timothy	166-68	George Ensworth, rev. by Burton Harding
Titus	165-66	George Ensworth, rev. by Burton Harding
Philemon	358	George Ensworth, rev. by Reg Bradley
Hebrews	176-87	William McConnell
James	446-48	Margaret Howlett
1 Peter	235-39	Charlotte Williams/ Bill Weimer
2 Peter	486-88	Bill Weimer
1 John	332-35	Margaret Barnes
2 John	335	Margaret Barnes
3 John	336	Margaret Barnes
Jude	488	Marion Snyder
Revelation	497-510	Ron Ehresman

Before You Start

The Bible is the book about God and his relationship to people. That the infinite God of the universe desires to relate to people is probably the most awesome fact of history. The Bible records the thoughts and experiences of rulers, poets, wives, husbands, doctors, prophets, carpenters, students, business people . . . as they lived and learned to understand God's relationship to them.

But the Bible is not only about other people; it is about you too. You will find your own mental, emotional, social struggles in its pages. As you read the Bible, God's words will focus on your contemporary situation. They will show you how and why God wants to relate to you. The Bible can change your life.

About This Morning with God

What?
This Morning with God is a guide to help you discover what the Bible says and means to you. By following this plan, you can study the entire

Bible in just over four years. Each book of the Bible is divided into a number of daily studies which cover several paragraphs of the book.

Each daily study contains several get-at-the-meaning questions. You will find that the questions are of three basic types: to help you observe (What does the text say?), interpret (What does it mean?) and apply (What does it mean *to you?*). These different questions are balanced to help keep your study from becoming *only* subjective. They have been chosen to focus on the main ideas in your daily reading.

The questions are based on the Revised Standard Version of the Bible because of its paragraph divisions and its up-to-date language. Supplementary comparison with other translations can often explain and simplify difficult passages.

Who?

This Morning with God is for anyone who wants to know how the Bible affects and transforms life. It assumes that you are serious about the Bible's content, not *only* interested in its historical or literary merits.

If you have never read the Bible before, *This Morning with God* can help you grasp the main ideas. If you know a lot *about* the Bible but have little firsthand discovery, *This Morning with God* can guide you as you dig out the truth for yourself. If you have never stuck to a plan of Bible reading before, *This Morning with God* can stimulate you to digest bite-sized readings with down-to-earth questions. If you want a fresh guide to spark and vitalize your Bible reading, *This Morning with God* can be that shot in the arm. Students, business people, wives, husbands, Sunday-school teachers, secretaries, farmers, nurses . . *This Morning with God* is for you.

Why?

This Morning with God is a guide for *inductive* study of the Bible. It asks questions to help you discover what the passages mean. It does not contain outlines, historical notes, opinions, commentary, inspirational thoughts. *This Morning with God* focuses on the text of the Bible —to let the Bible speak for itself.

This inductive method does not predetermine nor prejudice your investigation; it enables you to come to your own conclusions. It does not spoon feed you; it allows you the joy of independent discovery. It does not give you ready-made answers; it acquaints you with primary source material to test the validity of answers. It is not the ultimate; it aims to help you establish good inductive study methods.

Because *This Morning with God* is not a study by themes, but book-by-book, it contains few topical cross-references. It respects the author's time of writing and source material. Books which directly relate to one another are grouped for your own comparison. For example, because Moses did not refer to Hebrews since it was not written then, the study of Moses' books does not contain cross-references to Hebrews. But because the author of Hebrews had access to Moses' writings, appropriate cross-references are included in Hebrews. Also, Moses' books and Hebrews are grouped so that the background books are studied first.

The study order aims for variety among the long and short books, Old and New Testaments, and various book types. Since many people have written and revised the questions on a book, you will find different styles and emphases.

When?

This Morning with God is designed especially for use during your quiet time. The daily studies, which require about twenty minutes, are grouped in thirty-day sequences so that you may start the plan at the beginning of any month. Use the extra days in thirty-one-day months for review and evaluation.

You will probably find that forming a time-habit will help you keep at it. But your schedule of a definite twenty-minute uninterrupted period every day may need to be flexible enough for unexpected events. You may also want to allow extra time during the week for catching up or for further study

Where?

This Morning with God is for you to use anywhere—student union, kitchen, library, commuter train. Wherever you can concentrate well is an appropriate place for *This Morning with God* and you.

How?

This Morning with God is only a means to an end. The end is knowing and enjoying God and his relationship with you. A specific means cannot guarantee an end, but these suggestions may help make your study time more effective.

1. *Expect to Learn Something Definite.* You have, no doubt, found that your attitude at the beginning of any reading or study is very important. When you expect to learn nothing, your preparation and reading tend to be haphazard. But when you expect to learn something,

you prepare and read *actively*. You don't sit back and hope for some magic osmosis; you become involved with what you are reading.

Active preparation should include concentration and prayer. Ask the Holy Spirit to guide as you pray, read, interpret and apply. Ask him to overcome any blocks due to your mood, attitude or distractions, and to show you what you should learn in your present situation.

Active reading should include alertness and a method of study. Watch for important clues to the context, content, meaning and purpose of the book; use a dictionary; organize what you find in whatever way most benefits you. The daily questions are meant to help organize your observation, interpretation and application. You may also want to jot down questions and notes of your own.

2. *Write Down What You Learn.* Writing is an important part of understanding. It helps clarify and organize your thinking. Write down specific ideas, principles, applications, resolutions. Summary sentences, outlines, charts, poetry and paraphrases may be useful. You may also want to list questions and problems for further study.

3. *Act Out What You Learn.* You can test your understanding of what you learn by examining the results in your life. When your thoughts, attitudes and actions remain the same, your understanding is superficial. You may want to write out specific resolutions, review them periodically and evaluate the results. Ask the Holy Spirit to make what you learn a part of your life in the classroom, office, kitchen, dorm, ballpark, cornfield, hospital, church and restaurant.

About Supplementary Helps

In addition to your Bible, *This Morning with God*, a dictionary and notebooks, you may also want to use some of these supplementary helps (but read the Bible first):

Oxford Concise Concordance (RSV)—an alphabetical list of biblical words with their parallel passages

The New Bible Commentary*—extensive comments and explanation of biblical passages, paragraph-by-paragraph

The New Bible Dictionary*—definitions and explanations of biblical names, places, objects, concepts, customs, language, categories

Search the Scriptures*—a three-year plan for studying the whole Bible using daily studies with questions and a few explanatory notes; can be used alternately with *This Morning with God* for variety

a Bible atlas—location and background of biblical places

*available from InterVarsity Press, Box F, Downers Grove, IL 60515

YEAR
ONE

Month 1

DAY *1* △ *Introduction to Luke*

Luke is an educated Gentile — physician, historian, and traveler — concerned with the logical and historical development of the gospel Jesus proclaims. He shows that the kingdom of God is not contained in the boundaries set by Jewish religious leaders. The good news of the gospel is also to poor, sick, outcasts, women, children, foreigners. *Luke 1:1-25* 1/ What does Luke's own introduction reveal about his reliability, source material, purpose, and distinction? 2/ Characterize Zechariah and Elizabeth (note their ancestry). What is Zechariah's occupation (cf. Ex. 30:7-8; 1 Chron. 24:1-10, 19)? 3/ Imagine their feelings toward Elizabeth's barrenness (if they have no children, they can't be ancestors of the coming Messiah). 4/ Describe the situation when the angel appears. 5/ What is Zechariah's immediate reaction? 6/ Characterize John as to *a*—reaction to his birth, *b*—his relationship to God, and *c*—his ministry. 7/ Imagine how Zechariah feels when these predictions are made about his future child. Why does he look for proof? What is the angel's reply? 8/ In what ways have you questioned God's message to you? When? How has God confirmed his message? 9/ Imagine the people's feelings. How do you respond to God's work in other people? 10/ What is Elizabeth's attitude toward this coming event?

DAY 2   △   *Luke 1:26-38*

1/ Compare and contrast God's announcements to Zechariah and Mary as to *a*–salutation, *b*–basis of selection, and *c*–reaction to the message. 2/ In what ways are Elizabeth's and Mary's situation similar and different? 3/ What does the angel reveal about the identity and destiny of Jesus? 4/ What makes this birth impossible? possible? unique? What illustration is given to Mary? 5/ Contrast Mary's immediate and secondary responses. 6/ Imagine her mixed emotions (cf. Deut. 22:13-21). 7/ In what situations have you chosen between the approval of others or submission to God with a resulting stigma? What choice have you made? Why?

DAY 3   △   *Luke 1:39-56*

1/ Imagine this meeting. 2/ Describe Elizabeth's reception of Mary. How does she know Mary's "secret"? What attitude does she have toward Mary? 3/ What does Mary say concerning *a*–the character of God, *b*–his actions and activity, and *c*–his attitude toward people? On what basis does he "show partiality" (vv. 48-50, 52)? 4/ What reason does Mary give for this mighty act? 5/ Characterize these two women. 6/ In what ways is Mary personally aware of God's attributes? 7/ For which of God's attributes can you praise him today? 8/ How can you view immediate problems in the perspective of past and future history as Mary does?

DAY 4   △   *Luke 1:57-80*

1/ What controversy arises after Elizabeth gives birth? How is it stopped? 2/ How is tradition sometimes a test to your obedience? 3/ At what point is Zechariah's speech restored? 4/ If you were unable to talk for nine months or more, what would be your first words? 5/ How do the people react? In light of Zechariah's occupation account for the spread of and interest in the news. 6/ Divide Zechariah's prophecy into general and specific information. To whom does the first part refer (cf. vv. 68-69 with v. 27)? 7/ What does he say about *a*—the coming and purpose of the Messiah, *b*—the purpose of his own son, and *c*—the character and actions of God? 8/ What is the purpose of deliverance (vv. 74-75)? Relate *salvation* (v. 77) to this purpose and further mission (v. 79). 9/ How have you experienced this full deliverance? 10/ Measure the purpose of your life with verses 73-75 and 79. 11/ What is significant about both Zechariah's and Mary's referring to the broad sweep of history? 12/ Describe John's youth.

DAY 5 △ *Luke 2:1-20*

1/ Imagine yourself in the place of these people. What are your feelings? 2/ Trace the trip of Joseph and Mary on a map. From the divine perspective why is the trip necessary (cf. Micah 5:2)? 3/ Imagine the hardship of the trip for Mary's physical condition. 4/ Describe the conditions surrounding the birth. 5/ How much hardship, frustration, and inconvenience are you willing to endure as God's instrument? 6/ To whom and under what circumstances is the first birth announcement made? What vital statistics are given about the baby? 7/ Imagine the shepherds' feelings as they tend to business. Visualize the night interruption. What is the shepherds' initial reaction? 8/ In what ways do you limit the time and place of God's message to you? Do you listen to him as you go about your daily work (cf. 2:8 with 1:8ff.)? 9/ What do the shepherds do after the concert? 10/ Compare the responses of *a*—the shepherds, *b*—those who hear the spreading news, and *c*—Mary. 11/ What are the three phases of the shepherds' response? In what ways does their response parallel your experience?

DAY 6 △ *Luke 2:21-39*

1/ How do Joseph and Mary comply with God's demands (cf. Gen. 17:9-13; Ex. 13:2, 13; Lev. 12)? 2/ What does verse 24 reveal about their economic situation (cf. Lev. 12:8)? 3/ In what ways does the birth, parentage, etc. of Jesus differ from your expectations of the birth of a king (cf. 1:32-33)? 4/ Characterize Simeon. What is he doing in the temple (v. 27)? 5/ How does he view the new baby? How does he have this insight? What does he prophesy about Jesus? What does he foresee for Mary? 6/ In what way does Simeon have revelation beyond that given to Zechariah (cf. vv. 31-32 with 1:77)? 7/ Imagine yourself in the place of Joseph and Mary, doing what is required after the birth of a child. What is your reaction to all of this? Compare or contrast Joseph and Mary's reaction with your imagined one. 8/ Characterize Anna. What is her evaluation and response to the child? 9/ In a society dominated by tradition under pagan government what is significant about the people described in these chapters? 10/ Compare this situation to church and national life today.   11/ Can you characterize yourself as *righteous and devout?* On what basis.

DAY 7   △   *Luke 2:40-52*

1/ What additional insight do verses 41-42 reveal about Jesus' home (cf. Ex. 13:3-10) and his parents' attitude toward God (cf. v. 39)? 2/ Depict the sitution on the way home. 3/ What has this twelve-year-old been doing for probably five days? What is so astonishing about this? What is the teachers' response? 4/ With what are you occupied when not involved in the daily routine of life? 5/ What are Jesus' views of *a*—his identity, *b*—his parents' anxiety? 6/ Have you ever felt that you are not fully understood by your parents or family? Imagine how Jesus feels in this situation.   7/ What is his relationship with Joseph and his attitude toward parental authority (vv. 49-51)? 8/ What is your attitude toward authority? 9/ Compare verse 51 with verses 19 and 33 to see how Mary handles information which she can't understand.   10/ From verses 40 and 52 describe Jesus' childhood. Are you growing in similar directions?

DAY 8   △   *Luke 3:1-20*

1/ Establish the religious and political setting as John begins his preaching. Locate on a map and identify the historical cross-references. 2/ How do these references support the trustworthiness of the record? 3/ What is John's purpose (messengers are customarily sent to warn and exhort people to get ready for a royal visit—relate John's purpose to the times)? his message? his authority? 4/ How does he approach the people? 5/ Characterize *vipers.* How is this metaphor apt? 6/ How is John's message a fulfillment of Isaiah's prophecy?   7/ Relate his message to road building (vv.

4-5), wood cutting (v. 9), and harvesting (v. 17).   8/ What is
a—God's and *b*—man's part in these actions?   9/ What are the practical outreaches of true repentance? What is the effect of obedience
personally? to others?   10/ In what ways do you bear *fruits of
repentance?* What effect does this have on others? What can you do
today?   11/ What misconception does John clear up? What is
John's self concept when compared to Christ?   12/ In what way
is his message *good news?* How are exhortations *good news?*   13/
Contrast the responses to his preaching.   14/ What is your reaction
when your sin and injustice is exposed? What is *good news* about
that?   15/ What stands out about John's character?

DAY 9   △   *Luke 3:21-38*
1/ Why is John baptizing (v. 3)?   2/ Contrast this with the reason Jesus is baptized (cf. Mt. 3:13-15). How does Jesus' baptism
show the extent he identifies with man?   3/ In what two ways is
Jesus' divine identity shown?   4/ What is said about his *a*—identity,
b—origin, and *c*—character?   5/ When does Jesus start his public
ministry?   6/ What preparation have you given to your "ministry"?
Do you often get impatient?   7/ Skim Jesus' genealogy of human
descent. What is his royal lineage (cf. v. 32 with 1:32, 69)? his
religious ancestry (cf. v. 34 with 1:55)?   8/ Why does Jesus as
both divine and human have significance for you?   9/ What is your
response to one with such an endorsement?

DAY 10   △   *Luke 4:1-15*
1/ Describe this wilderness experience of Jesus.   2/ In what ways
is he susceptible to Satan's attacks?   3/At what times are you most
susceptible to Satan's attacks?   4/ Compare the three tests Satan
puts to Jesus as to *a*—specific content, *b*—appeal **to wh**at aspect of
human nature, *c*—progression in intensity, and *d*—Jesus' reply.   5/
What is the real issue of the first temptation?   6/ How does the
second test clarify your understanding of the problem of evil and
world affairs (cf. vv. 6-7 with 1:32-33)?   7/ To whom does ultimate rule rightfully belong?   8/ Explain how Jesus' answer to the
third test is a fitting response to Satan's challenge.   9/ Do you
recognize temptation for what it is?   10/ Are the issues here still
temptations to the Christian church?   11/How are these temptations inconclusive?   12/ Of what value to you is knowing that

Jesus has been tempted in every way you are? 13/ Describe his return to Galilee. Imagine Satan's reaction to these facts.

DAY *11* △ *Luke 4:16-30*
1/ What habit does Jesus have? 2/ According to Isaiah's prophecy what is the commission and power of the messenger? Describe each of these as spiritual benefits. 3/ What does Jesus claim about himself? 4/ What is his attitude toward the scriptures? 5/ With what situations in Isaiah's prophecy do you identify? 6/ In what ways have you been *released?* been given 20—20 spiritual vision? found *liberty?* 7/ Why does Jesus refuse to perform miracles in Nazareth? 8/ What two illustrations does he use to prove his point? 9/ Contrast the reaction to his reading of scripture (vv. 20-22) and his application of it (vv. 28-30). 10/ When do you react similarly? 11/ Since Satan fails to defeat Christ (v. 13), trace throughout Luke how he attempts to destroy him and the potency of his message. 12/ How does this enlarge your understanding of Satan's tactics and your ability to cope with life?

DAY *12* △ *Luke 4:31-44*
1/ What impression does Jesus make on the people in the synagogue? 2/ What two things produce this impression? 3/ Where and under what circumstances does Luke's first recorded miracle occur? 4/ What duel identity does the demon-possessed man recognize? 5/ Contrast his expectation of Jesus's action with what Jesus does. 6/ How does this miracle support Jesus' teachings? 7/ To comprehend the next miracle consider the effect of severe illness with high fever on the human body and the need for recuperation. How complete is her healing? 8/ How does Jesus' day end? 9/ What is distinctive about the healing of demon-possessed people? 10/ Why does Jesus rebuke the demons? 11/ How does demon possession differ from common forms of insanity? 12/ How does Jesus' understanding of his purpose affect his activities and relationships? 13/ What is your purpose or goal? In what ways does this affect your activities and relationships?

DAY *13* △ *Luke 5:1-11*
1/ Visualize this beach scene. 2/ Why are the people here? 3/ What is the advantage of speaking from the boat? 4/ Imagine

your response to a stranger asking to borrow your equipment and
have you chauffeur him. 5/ What command does Jesus give? 6/
Describe Peter's response to interference with his fishing business.
7/ What crisis does obedience to Jesus bring? What does Peter
do about it? 8/ When faced with a responsibility beyond your
capabilities, what do you do? 9/ Imagine the scene as the boats
pull to shore. Mentally listen to the spectators' exclamations. 10/
What two alternatives seem to be possible for Peter? 11/ Imagine
yourself as Peter telling your wife what has happened and why
you are going to change your job. 12/ What is your response to
the mighty acts of God: *a*-to push him out because you feel un-
comfortable, *b*-to take him into business so you will be more successful, or *c*-to leave all and follow him?

DAY *14* △ *Luke 5:12-26*
1/ What social and psychological problems result from the physical
problem of leprosy (cf. Lev. 13:45-46)? 2/ Imagine how life
will be changed by Jesus' words and act. 3/ How does the leper
evidence faith? What does he doubt? How does Jesus dispel it? 4/
What is the first requirement of the law (cf. v. 14 with Lev. 14)?
What does this reveal about Jesus' attitude toward the law? 5/
What happens as a result? How does Jesus meet this? 6/ What
do you do when the pressures mount? 7/ What disturbance
arises in the house? 8/ What kind of controversy does Jesus
trigger? Of what is he accused? Why? 9/ How does he support
his claim to forgive sin? 10/ Give three evidences of Jesus' deity
from this miracle. 11/ What are three responses? 12/ On what
basis are the leper and paralyzed man healed? 13/ When have
you inconvenienced yourself to bring a helpless person to Christ?

DAY *15* △ *Luke 5:27—6:11*
1/ List three complaints which the Pharisees lodge against Jesus.
Give the setting for each and the incident which triggers each. 2/
How do Jesus' answers reveal the principles on which he acts? 3/
Are you as consistent in words and action? 4/ What is the point
of the two parables? 5/ To what kind of men can the *new* be
entrusted? 6/ Can the *new* be combined with the *old*? What will
be the reaction of those who are accustomed to the *old* when they
hear the *new*? 7/ What people or institutions that you know try

to adapt Christian principles to their own religious systems? What is the result? 8/ What "patches" have you tried to put on your life to disguise rips, cover holes, stop leaks? What has been the result? 9/ Distinguish originality and freshness from disrespect for heritage. 10/ What are you doing to develop a *taste for new wine?* 11/ What do the Pharisees object to in verses 1-2? 12/ What is Jesus' reply to this? 13/ Do you allow the Son of man to control your life or do you bind yourself and others by your tradition? 14/ How can you express understanding and mercy within the limits God has established? 15/ How does Jesus call the bluff of the Pharisees in the last incident? What reaction does this bring? 16/ Are you saving or destroying life—doing good or doing nothing? Be specific.

DAY *16* △ *Luke 6:12-38*
1/ How does Jesus reveal his sense of responsibility when he has to choose apostles to take future leadership? 2/ What principle can you learn from his actions to apply to electing officers for your Christian group? 3/ Describe Jesus' popularity and power. 4/ Describe the present condition of those a-who are *blessed* and b-who are lamentable. Why? Contrast the present and future condition of each. 5/ Imagine the disciples' feelings about such statements. 6/ Do you feel blessed when you weep and woeful when men speak well of you? 7/ What specific actions are commanded? What is the basic principle of these actions? 8/ What are the marked differences between sinners and believers? Distinguish their motives. 9/ How are these commandments related to God's motives and actions? 10/ How can you be kind to ungrateful and selfish people today? 11/ How will the a-negative and b-positive commands in verses 37-38 fulfill the previous commands? 12/ What in your present attitudes and daily living will you change as a result of what you have learned here?

DAY *17* △ *Luke 6:39-49*
1/ What is required in your life before you can help others? Do you have to be free from faults? 2/ How does Jesus illustrate the principles of verses 39-42? 3/ What is the cause and effect relationship in nature? in man? 4/ What do your actions reveal about

you? 5/ What is the essential difference between the two men
(and their metaphors)? 6/ With which do you identify now?
7/ Contrast their futures. 8/ Summarize Jesus' *a*-standards and *b*-
authority in this teaching. 9/ Imagine the response of the people.
What is your response?

DAY *18* △ *Luke 7:1-17*
1/ What does the centurion recognize in Jesus? How does he explain
this to Jesus? 2/ Contrast the centurion's estimate of himself with
a-his estimate of Jesus, *b*-the Jews' estimate of him, and *c*-Jesus'
estimate of him. 3/ Does his faith or Jesus' healing rest in the
worthiness attributed to him by others? 4/ How does your faith
in Jesus affect the lives of others dear to you? 5/ Imagine yourself
a member of the funeral procession. Visualize the happenings as
you meet the great procession Jesus is leading. 6/ What extraordinary power does Jesus display? 7/ What qualities of Jesus are
revealed by his actions toward the mother and son? 8/ How do
the people respond to his actions? Imagine the feelings of the mother, son, and mourners. 9/ Imagine yourself one of the people
who spread the report. What do you tell others? How do you answer
the inevitable question, *How did he do it?*

DAY *19* △ *Luke 7:18-35*
1/ Imagine John's perplexity (cf. his message in 3:7-20). 2/ How
does Jesus answer John's inquiry (cf. Isa. 35:5-6; 61:1)? 3/ What
is Jesus' attitude toward him? How does Jesus characterize John
(cf. Mal. 3:1)? 4/ What is Jesus' attitude toward the poor? Contrast this with the political, social, and religious opinion of the time.
5/ Contrast the response of *a*-the people and *b*-the Jewish leaders
to the preaching of John. 6/ Contrast the methods of John and
Jesus. 7/ How are the Jewish leaders like children in their reaction
to John and Jesus? 8/ Imagine how contemporary religious leaders
would have responded to John's and Jesus' preaching. 9/ What
does verse 30 reveal about the seriousness of rejecting a true message
because you don't like the method? 10/ How can you honor
(*justify*) real wisdom today?

DAY *20* △ *Luke 7:36-50*
1/ How does this scene reveal that Jesus' ministry is not one-sided?

2/ Visualize the scene. 3/ Describe the woman's frame of mind with at least four adjectives (people—but not usually notorious sinners—come uninvited into dining rooms and sit around the walls; for a Jewish woman to let down her hair in public is a disgrace; kissing the feet of a teacher is a sign of deep respect). 4/ What is Simon's attitude toward *a*-himself, *b*-Jesus, and *c*-the woman? With what criterion does Simon judge Jesus (v.39)? 5/ How does Jesus reveal his knowledge of Simon and the woman? 6/ What does he rebuke in Simon? 7/ In what three ways does Jesus compare Simon with the woman? 8/ Imagine *a*-Simon's, *b*-the woman's, and *c*-the others' feelings. 9/ How does Jesus commend her love but make clear that her love has not saved her? 10/ What is the extent of her forgiveness? What are its results to herself? to others? 11/ Compare or contrast Jesus' attitudes and actions in this incident with your attitudes and actions to sinners. How do you feel around social sinners? 12/ What is the basis for your love of Jesus? To what extent?

DAY *21* △ *Luke 8:1-21*

1/ Imagine you are a disciple who has left a lucrative fishing business to preach. How do you look on this means of support (vv. 1-3)? 2/ What is the purpose of a parable? 3/ Distinguish this type of teaching from Jesus' teaching of 6:17-49. 4/ Why, do you think, does Jesus use examples from the ordinary life of the people? Compare and contrast his methods with the methods of contemporary teachers, religious leaders, and philosophers. 5/ Distinguish the four places where seeds fall and their counterparts in man. 6/ How is the word of God like *seed*? 7/ Are you responsible for how you receive the *seed*? 8/ Contrast the results of the different ways of hearing Jesus' words. 9/ How could the disciples respond to their "secret knowledge"? How are they to respond? 10/ Since hearing the truth is not the key to spiritual understanding, what is? 11/ How can you have more insight into the truths of God's word? 12/ According to his teaching how are you related to Jesus?

DAY 22 △ *Luke 8:22-39*

1/ Over what realms does Jesus show authority (unexpected,

violent storms are common on Galilee)? Imagine Satan's feelings
as the storm intensifies.   2/ Relate Jesus' question to the disciples
with their attitudes *a*-before and *b*-after the miracle.   3/ Characterize the man before and after his encounter with Jesus.   4/ What
significant facts are revealed in *a*-the attitude of the demons toward
Jesus and *b*-their requests of him?   5/ How do Jesus and Satan
show the supreme value they place on one man?   6/ What about
their concern do the people reveal by their response to Jesus' healing?   7/ How does Jesus' command to this Gentile take into account his previous state of personality and his previous reputation?
8/ How can you *declare* at home what God is doing for you?   9/
How is your faith in Jesus eliminating fear of circumstances, others,
and Satan in practical ways? In what specific situations?

DAY *23*   △   *Luke 8:40-56*
1/ What is the attitude of this ruler of the Jews toward Jesus in
the beginning?   2/ Imagine Jairus' feelings at *a*-the interruption
and *b*-the further news.   3/ In what ways may the incident with
the woman have strengthened his faith in Jesus?   4/ Considering
her problem (cf. Lev. 15:23-30) imagine the woman's state of mind.
5/ How does Jesus make clear to her what has made her well
(contrast with her initial action)?   6/ How do you know that
Jesus' healing is not magic (cf. v. 46)?   7/ Is Jesus' healing power
dependent on man's faith?   How are his miracles and man's faith
related?   8/ What qualities of Jesus are revealed by his attitudes
and actions in this passage?   9/ How does Jesus' command to the
parents differ from his command to the man of the Gerasenes? Why,
do you think?   10/ How does the Lord's knowledge of situations
strengthen your faith in his specific commands to you? Can you be
trusted to be silent as well as to speak?

DAY *24*   △   *Luke 9:1-17*
1/ What is the twofold ministry of the twelve?   2/ What is the
source of their power and authority?   3/ How does this endowment
insure the continuance of Jesus' works after his death?   4/ Compare and contrast this power and continuance with later and contemporary movements.   5/ How are the twelve supported (pagan
priests carry *bags* for money they receive from begging)?   6/ What

attitudes are required to follow Jesus' instructions? 7/ Imagine
the people's feelings as the disciples act in accordance with verse 5.
8/ What impresses Herod? 9/ What situations of leadership
training does Jesus put the disciples through (vv. 1-2, 10, 13)?
10/ What leadership principles can you learn from this section?
11/ What part does man's physical need have in the ministry of
Jesus and his disciples? 12/ What is your attitude toward meeting people's physical needs? 13/ Work out the account of verses
12-17 in columns of *a*-demand and *b*-available supply. 14/ List
the areas in your life where the demands seem much greater than
your supply. What help do you find here?

DAY 25   △   *Luke 9:18-36*
1/ What are various opinions of Jesus' identity? 2/ How does
Peter's understanding differ from the other opinions? 3/ How have
Jesus' past teaching and actions contributed to the disciples' understanding of his identity? 4/ Why, do you think, does Jesus choose
this time to announce his future? What do the Jews expect about
the Messiah? 5/ List and explain the requirements of one who
wishes to follow *the Christ of God.* 6/ What additional meaning
does *follow me* have after verse 22? 7/ In what ways will you
deny yourself and *follow* Jesus today? 8/ What happens as Jesus
prays (cf. other situations in 3:21; 6:12; 9:18)? 9/ Describe Jesus'
appearance (cf. v. 26). Define *glory.* 10/ What is the meaning
of the transfiguration to Jesus? to Peter, John, and James? What is
the purpose of Moses and Elijah? of God's voice? 11/ What suggestion does Peter make? What does he misunderstand? 12/ How,
do you think, does he recognize Moses and Elijah? 13/ Imagine
the effect of this incident on the development of the three disciples'
understanding and character. 14/ In what ways has God recently
enlarged your understanding of him? How has this understanding
been revealed in your character?

DAY 26   △   *Luke 9:37-62*
1/ What do the disciples know about Jesus (v. 20)? 2/ What do
they expect from him after verse 27? 3/ What may they have
concluded from the experiences of verses 28-32 and 43? 4/ How
does the statement of Jesus in verse 44 contrast with their expectations? 5/ What is the result in their understanding? 6/ What

kind of attitude do the disciples have in verses 40, 46, 49-50, 54-56?
How does Jesus deal with their attitude?   7/ What do the disciples
misunderstand about the kingdom of God?   8/ Contrast *a*-the
disciples' (v. 46) and Jesus' concern (v. 44) and *b*-the disciples'
and Jesus' concept of greatness.   9/ Imagine the bitterness of the
Jewish-Samaritan feud (cf. Ezra 4:1-5; Neh. 2:20).   10/ What is
a-Jesus' and *b*-your attitude toward other Christian groups? Toward
people who are hostile toward him?   11/ In what practical ways
does individual and group pride distort what you and others know
of God?   12/ How does Jesus respond to the three people who
want to follow him?   13/ Do you use the same principles in your
witness?   14/ Briefly summarize what you have learned so far
from *Luke* about *a*-God, *b*-Jesus, *c*-Satan, *d*-the disciples, *e*-the
religious leaders, *f*-the masses, and *g*-you.

DAY 27   △   *Introduction to Genesis*
Genesis introduces every theme and problem discussed in scripture.
Genesis is the key to God's eternal plan and purpose in creation and
to man's fall and increasingly deeper estrangement from God, himself, and others. And it is above all a record of God's continuous
reconciling actions both in and through individuals and the Jewish
nation. *Genesis 1*   1/ Given a formless void, how would you have
created the universe differently (not that *create* does not mean *re-
fashion*)?   2/ How, do you think, are God's imagination and his
words related?   3/ How is man in God's image? How does he differ
in kind, not merely in degree, from other creatures?   4/ What
difference does this fact make in your daily life, especially in your
relations with others?   5/ What in the story of creation shows not
only God's greatness but also his goodness?   6/ How do you show
God's concern for nature in your treatment of wildlife and natural
resources?

DAY 28   △   *Genesis 2*
1/ What seems to be God's view of the "natural"? What are your
views?   2/ Describe man's setting. Why, do you think, does God
give man work to do before his fall?   3/ How are you approaching
today's manual and mental tasks?   4/ Does God create evil (*i.e.*,
the experiential knowledge of it)? Give reason for his allowing such
a possibility here.   5/ How do you know that God is interested in

your loneliness? What difference, practically, does knowing God make in this area?

DAY 29   △   *Genesis 3*

1/ Characterize the serpent.   2/ How does Eve fall? What is the progression?   3/ How do you respond or react to what God says? Why?   4/ What are Adam and Eve's responses to God's sound? How are their responses the normal reaction of all men?   5/ What difference does this knowledge make in how you witness?   6/ What are their responses to a discovered sin?   7/ What do you blame your sins and problems on?   8/ What is significant about God's words to the serpent, Adam, and Eve?   9/ How is the attitude toward work changed?   10/ What do you learn here about God's character for which to praise him?

DAY 30   △   *Genesis 4*

1/ How do you *know* God (the Jewish idea of *knowing* is not mere intellectual apprehension of a fact but experiential, intimate, active, existential knowledge)? To what extent?   2/ What is Cain's problem?   3/ In what ways does Cain disclaim responsibility for his actions? What are the results of his actions?   4/ Who is responsible for your actions?   5/ What happens to man and his environment to make him suddenly *call upon the name of the Lord?*   6/ Compare this and today's situation. Would these people call on God for anything different today?

Month 2

DAY 1   △   *Genesis 5*

1/ Suppose there were more than two sexes. What if God had left this matter to "natural selection"?   2/ Apart from difficulties in transmitting and translating Hebrew numbers, why, do you think, do people seem to live longer here?   3/ What does to *walk with God* mean? How are you *walking with God* today?

DAY 2   △   *Genesis 6*

1/ How are the moral and physical world related?   2/ In what ways is the *earth* corrupt? What does this show about God?   3/ How does this state of man, including those you expect to be godly, compare with man today?   4/ Do you think God is "sorry" that he has made you?   5/ In the long time of building the ark what reservations, fears, doubts, and problems may have beset Noah? 6/ How do you respond to "incredible, strange, and unpopular" instructions from God?

DAY *3*   △   *Genesis 7*
1/ Characterize Noah.   2/ What happens to him? to the earth? 3/ Imagine Noah's situation with all those animals.   4/ While you are protected by God, what job has he given you to do today?   5/ How do man's sins affect the natural environment? What are you doing to lessen these effects?

DAY *4*   △   *Genesis 8*
1/ Imagine Noah's feelings after such a catastrophy.   2/ What are your feelings when tragedy happens to those who reject God?   3/ How does Noah respond to God's deliverance?   4/ What has God done for you recently? How have you responded?   5/ What is God's view of man   6/ What makes man a sinner—what he does or what he is? How does this fact make a crucial difference in your attitude toward yourself and others?

DAY *5*   △   *Genesis 9*
1/ What is God's view of human life? What are his provisions for it?   2/ What is the change in man's diet? the stipulation?   3/ What makes Ham's actions so despicable?   4/ How does Noah react to Ham's actions (cursing the son of an offender reflects on the father)?   5/ How do you react to someone's sin against you?   6/ What do you think of someone who under the guise of "concern" spreads his conception of your weaknesses and sins? With God's help how can you be trusted to understand and take care of your fellow Christian's weaknesses?

DAY *6*   △   *Genesis 10*
1/ Why, do you think, does God give the names of so many "un-important" people? What do these name lists reveal about God?   2/ Project an historical record of you thousands of years hence. How would you like to be described?   3/ What phrase would accurately characterize your life thus far?   4/ In what area of your life today

is the fact that God knows you by name and has a place for you important? 5/ How are the nations delineated here related to each other?

DAY 7 △ *Genesis 11:1-26*
1/ In what ways does pride and rebellion against God inevitably lead to an inability to understand and be understood by other men? 2/ In what areas of your life has this result of pride been evident? 3/ How and when do you "build" similar structures? Why? 3/ What are a-you and b-your Christian group "building" now?

DAY 8 △ *Genesis 11:27–12:19*
1/ What is God's attitude toward the Jews? What is yours? 2/ How have some of God's promises regarding the Jews already been fulfilled? 3/ How are you an active *blessing* to the people of Abram's promised seed? 4/ Trace Abram's travels on a map (continue in subsequent days). 5/ What prompts Abram's journey? his plan concerning Sarai? How does he fare because of the agreement? 6/ How does his lack of trust in God affect others? 7/ In what difficult areas is God calling you to trust him? How is your response affecting others?

DAY 9 △ *Genesis 13*
1/ What is Abram and Lot's problem? 2/ How does Abram resolve the problem? What does his handling of the problem reveal about his character? 3/ How does the way you settle differences and arguments reveal your trust (or lack of it) in God? 4/ What does Lot's choice reveal about his character? 5/ In view of God's clear will expressed to Abram what is your attitude toward Israel? How do you actually express your attitude?

DAY 10 △ *Genesis 14*
1/ What happens to the "innocent bystander" Lot? 2/ What are the dangers of close association with ungodly people? 3/ Imagine Lot's feelings after his rescue. 4/ Who is Melchizedek? How does he, a stranger to the group, have God's revelation? 5/ How do these two strangers, Abram and Melchizedek, respond to each other? 6/ In what ways do you limit the ways, times, and places God can get through to people? How do you act toward fellow Christians? 7/ Why does Abram refuse the war spoils?

DAY *11* △ *Genesis 15*

1/ How does God encourage Abram?   2/ What is Abram's main concern?   3/ On what basis is Abraham declared righteous (i.e. right with God)?   4/ What land does God covenant to give the Jews? How large? What do they have today?   5/ What predictions and promises does God make while Abram is asleep (watch the future developments)?   6/ How do you show that you believe God's words to you?

DAY *12* △ *Genesis 16*

1/ How do Sarai and Abram try to "push" God? What is their basic problem? Imagine the household situation.   2/ What are the usual results of becoming impatient with God's timing and trying to rush things?   3/ Why do you tend to ignore results when you act impatiently?   4/ Why, do you think, does God not strike them down for procuring, adultery, and child-snatching respectively?   5/ How does God treat Hagar (the Ishmaelites are the Arabs)? What do his actions reveal about his character and purpose?   6/ In what ways do your actions affect future generations?

DAY *13* △ *Genesis 17*

1/ How does God identify himself here?   2/ Of what does the Abrahamic covenant consist?   3/ How are God's commands and promises related?   4/ How does Abraham respond to God's promises? to his commands? What do these responses reveal about Abraham?   5/ Imagine the feelings of Abraham and Sarah as they watch Ishmael grow up.   6/ What promises has God given you? How are you responding to them today?

DAY *14* △ *Genesis 18*

1/ How does God appear to Abraham?   2/ How does Abraham treat the three men? Why?   3/ How does Sarah react to God's promise?   4/ What is God's reaction to the general sinfulness of Sodom and Gomorrah? Abraham's response to God's threat?   5/ From the dialogue of God and Abraham what do you learn about God? about intercessory prayer?

DAY *15* △ *Genesis 19*

1/ Where is "innocent bystander" Lot?   2/ Characterize the men

of Sodom. What makes them so adamant concerning Lot and his
godly friends? 3/ Explain Lot's predicament. 4/ Why don't
Lot's relatives listen to him? Characterize his relatives as revealed
by their actions. 5/ Describe the effect of this display of God's
judgment on Lot. 6/ What are some of the immediate results of
Lot's close association with the "swingers" of Sodom? Do you think
his main motive has been to witness? 7/ Examine your influence
on and witness to others. Do they understand your beliefs and respect your words? Why?

DAY *16* △ *Genesis 20*
1/ What is Abraham's basic problem here (cf. 12:10-19)? 2/ In
what areas of your life do you have repeated downfalls? Why? 3/
How does God show his faithfulness to *a*-Abraham and *b*-Abi-
melech? 4/ Why, do you think, are unchristian people sometimes
more ethical than Christians? 5/ In what areas of your life are
your ethics questionable? 6/ In what ways is Abimelech an example to follow?

DAY *17* △ *Genesis 21*
1/ What "impossible" promise does God fulfill? 2/ What are
some promises you have claimed? How can you be sure of them?
3/ Imagine Hagar's feelings as she is sent away. What provision
does God make for her and Ishmael? 4/ How is Abraham including God more frequently in his relationships with others? What is
happening to him? 5/ Why, do you think, does Abimelech believe
that God is with Abraham—because of Abraham's conduct or God's
faithfulness? 6/ What attribute of God is revealed by his name in
verse 33?

DAY *18* △ *Genesis 22*
1/ What makes this test extremely difficult? Imagine Isaac's feelings. 2/ What is God teaching Abraham about himself and his
relationship to him? 3/ List some reasons God doesn't take Abraham's "sacrifice" after all. 4/ What does God really want from
you? How does he typically treat your treasures when you are willing
to offer them to him? 5/ What does this experience reveal about
God's character? 6/ How does an experience as this reveal your
concept of God?

DAY *19* △ *Genesis 23*

1/ How must Abraham have behaved to arouse this response from strangers? 2/ What here should you imitate? 3/ Why, do you think, does Abraham insist on paying? 4/ Compare this incident and the one in 14:21-24. What qualities of Abraham do these incidents reveal? 5/ What is the difference between humility and "inferiority complex"? between humble independence and the inability to accept a gift?

DAY *20* △ *Genesis 24*

1/ What makes Abraham so set against Isaac's intermarriage and even contact with the Canaanites? 2/ What does the servant believe about God in order to make the kind of prayer he makes? 3/ How does he show his faith by his subsequent actions? How does he know the will of God? 4/ How do Rebekah's relatives respond to the servant's request? Why doesn't Laban suspect the servant who wants to take his sister? 5/ How do you react to someone who tells you "God's will" concerning you? 6/ Characterize Rebekah and Isaac.

DAY *21* △ *Genesis 25*

1/ Summarize what you have learned about Abraham, about his relationship with God, and about God's covenant with him. 2/ What does God predict about Rebekah's sons (watch the future developments)? 3/ Characterize Esau and Jacob. What about their characters and concerns does the incident in verses 29-34 reveal? 4/ What are the valued things and priorities in your life? Why?

DAY *22* △ *Genesis 26*

1/ What does God promise Isaac? Why? 2/ What seems to be the attitude toward established personal relationships? 3/ What are some of Isaac's problems? 4/ How do you (or will you) influence your children to help them not repeat your sins? 5/ What kind of man is Abimelech turning out to be? What counterparts of his type are in today's world? 6/ Summarize what you have learned so far from *Genesis* about a-God, b-man, and c-yourself.

DAY *23* △ *Luke 10:1-24*

1/ Summarize what Jesus has done for the people of the first nine chapters. 2/ How does Jesus intensify his ministry (cf. 9:1-6)? 3/ Do you pray in accordance with verse 2? 4/ Describe this realistic missionary preparation under these headings: the purpose, method, message and activity, conduct, result, and hearers' responsibility. 5/ How do these principles apply to your witness 6/ What is a-God's and b-man's part in man's understanding of God's truths? 7/ How are hearing and receiving Christians like hearing and receiving Christ? 8/ How is the opportunity for hearing related to the severity of judgment? 9/ How is God's omniscience necessary for his judgment? 10/ What facts reveal that Satan has lost his exalted power? 11/ What is the supreme cause for *rejoicing?* What makes Jesus rejoice? 12/ How are the persons of the trinity related? 13/ How are the disciples privileged? How are you?

DAY *24* △ *Luke 10:25-42*

1/ What are the law's requirements for eternal life? Have you done these? In what way do you have eternal life? 2/ How does this parable bring out the difference between knowledge and action? 3/ How does Jesus point out the segregation of the lawyer? 4/ Contrast the seeing, feeling, and activity of the three characters. 5/ Who is your *neighbor?* How can you be a *neighbor* to them today? What will be your basic attitude toward them? 6/ In what ways do you try to maintain a balance between quiet worship and practical service? How can you know which is more appropriate in a given situation?

DAY *25* △ *Luke 11:1-13*

1/ On what basis can a-the disciples and b-you approach God? Contrast this with the salutation and content of Jewish prayers (cf. 1:67-68). 2/ List and explain the specific concerns of the prayer. 3/ Are you asking the Lord to teach you to pray? 4/ What qualities of God are revealed by these parables? 5/ What are the two relationships pictured in verses 5-13? 6/ Compare the friend's answer (with possible mixed motives) with God's answer. 7/ Contrast the son's requests with the conjectures of supply. Compare the father's actual supply with God's supply. 8/ Imagine as a disciple how this prayer and the parables enlarge your concept of God. 9/ Is there any reason for hesitating to go to God in time of need? Is time a barrier to God's answering? How certain is his answer?

DAY 26 △ *Luke 11:14-36*

1/ What are the responses to Jesus' miracle? 2/ How are *a*-Satan and *b*-God consistent in the way they work? 3/ What awkward double standard does Jesus reveal in the thinking of the Jews? 4/ Contrast the extent of *a*-Jesus' and *b*-the sons' power. 5/ What tremendous claims does Jesus make here? 6/ How does he show that neutrality in not an option? 7/ What is *a*-God's and *b*-your part in overcoming Satan and his devils? 8/ What is the outcome of mere renunciation of sins? 9/ Who, does Jesus say, is *blessed* (the woman's type of honoring expression is common—cf. 1:42)? 10/ What sign will be given to the people (the Ninevites regard Jonah as it were raised from the dead—cf. Jonah 1:11-17; 2:10)? 11/ How and why will *this generation* be judged (cf. 1 Kings 10: 1-14; Jonah 3)? 12/ How do verses 33-36 relate to the reason the Jews demand a sign? 13/ How does Jesus' use of the metaphor of *light* here differ from what he is illustrating in 8:16? 14/ What can you do to guard against the *light* in you becoming *darkness?*

DAY 27 △ *Luke 11:37-54*

1/ How is the attitude of this Pharisee toward Jesus different from most Pharisees? 2/ Following through with the illustration of the cup and platter (the cleansing is ceremonial) describe the inside and outside of the Pharisees. 3/ What will and will not make the Pharisees *clean?* 4/ What is Jesus' attitude to outward forms and ceremonies? 5/ How does the Pharisees' hypocrisy affect other people (Jews mark graves to prevent unconscious defilement—cf. Num. 29:16)? 6/ In what ways does your inner life differ from your projected image? How can a discrepancy have a detrimental effect on others? 7/ What does Jesus condemn in the lawyers (cf. 2 Chron. 24:20-22—Chronicles is the last book of the Jewish canon)? 8/ What is the result of their sin concerning themselves? concerning other people? 9/What are modern counterparts of the Pharisees' and lawyers' sins? 10/ Imagine the kind of pressure Jesus endures during his lifetime.

DAY 28 △ *Luke 12:1-12*

1/ In what ways is hypocrisy futile? 2/ What does Jesus tell his disciples that prepares them for the future? 3/ What *a*-encouragement and *b*-warning does he give them? 4/ Who will *a*-defend them, *b*-protect them, and *c*-guarantee their eternal destiny? 5/ Are *fear him* (v. 5) and *fear not* (v.7) contradictory? 6/ How do Jesus' words affect the content of your message to students, neighbors, associates, others? 7/ What is the awful result for people who refuse the witness of the Holy Spirit? 8/ How can this knowledge incite *a*-the disciples and *b*-you to a bold, persuasive witness?

DAY 29 △ *Luke 12:13-34*
1/ How does the man misunderstand Jesus' purpose? 2/ List what Jesus says about *a*-the attitudes apt to be produced by honest accumulation of earthly possessions (underline the pronouns in the parable), *b*-the right attitude toward possessions, *c*-God's estimate of the value of possessions (compare with the value of life), and *d*-what to do with possessions and why. 3/ How does a right view of possessions reflect a right view of God? 4/ How does Jesus reveal that God is concerned with the whole of man not just his soul? 5/ Why is *worrying* utterly worthless? 6/ In what ways are ravens, lilies, and grass (grass is used for fuel in Palestine) dependent on God? What principle do they illustrate? 7/ What does this passage teach about *a*-life and *b*-the kingdom of heaven? 8/ In what practical ways do you see God's concern for and value of you?

DAY 30 △ *Luke 12:35-59*
1/ How does the attitude toward the Lord's return reveal where a man's treasure (cf. v. 34) is? 2/ How can you be *ready* for the Lord's return? 3/ How are *a*-readiness and *b*-unreadiness manifest in the three parables in verses 35-48 (the typical long garments hinder activity)? 4/ What will be the result of *a*-readiness and *b*-unreadiness? 5/ How much more important is faithfulness than ability in measuring results? 6/ How are you using the abilities and opportunities God is giving you? 7/ In what ways does God's knowledge of your opportunities *a*-comfort and *b*-convict you? 8/ Characterize *fire*. What *baptism* is Jesus referring to? 9/ Contrast the peace the Jews expect to accompany the Messiah's coming with what Jesus brings. 10/ How are the people hypocrites in regard to interpreting signs? 11/ How are verses 58-59 an illustration of eternal destiny?

Month 3

DAY 1   △   *Luke 13:1-21*

1/ What is the basic question raised in verses 1-5? Who raises it? Why?   2/ Is this idea still prevalent today? What "superstitions" do you have about death?   3/ Contrast the reasons for *a*-present and *b*-final destruction.   4/ How do these verses relate to the parable of verses 6-9 (fig trees mature in three years)?   5/ What is the effect of freedom on the woman?   6/ In what ways are the Jews hypocrites regarding the law of the sabbath?   7/ List what the animals and the woman can claim as needs.   8/ What fact about the kingdom of God is Jesus illustrating with the metaphors of the *mustard seed* and *leaven?*   9/ What are the responsibilities of the *man* in verse 19 and the *woman* in verse 21?   10/ What are your responsibilities in relation to the kingdom of God?

DAY 2   △   *Luke 13:22-35*

1/ Compare 9:51 and 10:1 with verse 22.   2/ How does Jesus answer the academic question, How many will be saved?   3/ What is his main concern (*strive* refers to strenuous wholehearted determination)?   4/ What do the *workers of iniquity* misunderstand about entering the door? What are the consequences?   5/ How will the situation of verses 28-30 be amazingly dreadful for the Jews?   6/ On what do many today base the careless assumption that they are Christians?   7/ On what basis will you be admitted?   8/ Is Jesus absorbed with preoccupations and self pity as his death approaches (*the third day* is a poetic expression meaning at the time of completion)?   9/ Imagine how you would feel.   10/ What qualities of Jesus are revealed by his attitude here?   11/ In what ways are you conscious of your purpose in life? How do you express that purpose?

DAY 3   △   *Luke 14:1-24*

1/ What, do you think, motivates Jesus to accept this social invitation?   2/ Do you give prayerful planning and concern to your social and recreational life? How can you meet the need of others during these times?   3/ Who determines the placing of the guests?   4/ Contrast man's self concept with the judgment of God.   5/ What is the right attitude of hospitality?   6/ What are your motives in planning a dinner or party? What kind of people do you invite (the tense of *invite* in v. 12 refers to *continually*)? What about foreign students, the disliked, unattractive, and poorly dressed? 7/ What does one of the Pharisee's guests falsely assume (cf. v. 14)? 8/ In what ways is the invitation inclusive (cf. who finally comes)? 9/ In what ways are the excuses ridiculous? On what basis are the people excluded? 10/ What is the principle of this parable?

DAY 4 △ *Luke 14:25-35*

1/ What is significant in the Lord's addressing these words to the great multitude desirous of following him (cf. 9:57-62)? 2/ List and explain the demands of following Jesus (cf. each with v. 33). 3/ In what ways may your attitude toward Jesus *cost* yourself (the man bearing the cross expects to be crucified)? others (determine the meaning of *hate* in v. 26)? 4/ Compare or contrast the content of your attitude and message with Jesus' message here. 5/ How is the man who ignores the totality of Jesus' demands like salt-less salt?

DAY 5 △ *Luke 15:1-32*

1/ Contrast the attitude of *a*-the Pharisees and *b*-Jesus toward sinners. 2/ To whom does Jesus address these stories? Under what circumstances? 3/ What is the unifying theme of the three? 4/ What are their distinctive features? What do each emphasize about the search? 5/ What is the attitude at the completion of the search (vv. 5-7, 9, 23-24, 32)? 6/ How, do you think, do Jesus' announcements of what happens in heaven affect his listeners? What do these announcements reveal about Jesus? 7/ Contrast the attitude of the son before he leaves and after he returns. What causes him to return? What is the essential change in him? 8/ How can rebellion sometimes lead to worse subordination? 9/ What is the elder brother's self concept? Do you think he is necessarily good or just afraid to outwardly rebel? 10/ Compare the father's attitude toward both sons. 11/ What is *a*-God's and *b*-man's part in spiritual restoration? 12/ In what ways have you experienced the qualities of God revealed by Jesus in these stories?

DAY 6 △ *Luke 16:1-13*

1/ Who is addressed here? Who overhears (cf. v. 14)? 2/ Describe the steward's business practices and motives. In what ways does he protect himself against a legal suit if found out? 3/ Explain what the rich man commends in his steward. 4/ In what ways does a misunderstanding of the principles of 12:22-34 parallel the charges in verses 1 and 8? 5/ What is your attitude toward your possessions? 6/ In what ways do you use them to *make friends?* to repulse people? 7/ How do these verses reveal the fallacy of the concept: you can be ethical in major responsibilities but fudge in small details? 8/ What is the relation of character and principles in everyday affairs with character and principles in "spiritual" affairs? 9/ How is your use of your possessions related to eternity? 10/ Contrast the attitudes, motives, and actions of people who *serve a*-God and *b*-mammon. 11/ Which *master* do you *serve?* How is your service reflected in your daily living?

DAY 7   △   *Luke 16:14-31*

1/ Contrast the attitude of *a*-Jesus (cf. vv. 9-13) and *b*-the Pharisees (they regard riches as a reward for their law abiding). 2/ Explain what Jesus means by *violently* here. How have you entered the kingdom of God? 3/ Does the gospel void the law (cf. 10:25-28)? Contrast Jesus' statement in verse 18 with Jewish morality of the time. 4/ Compare the parable of the rich man and Lazarus with Jesus' statement in verse 15. 5/ Contrast the life and death of each. How are their positions reversed? 6/ How does this parable show the seriousness of your attitudes and actions during your life? 7/ What is the principle of the parable?

DAY 8   △   *Luke 17:1-19*

1/ What two truths does Jesus emphasize concerning sin and responsibility for sin? 2/ What is your attitude toward sin and sinning brothers? Do you practice the aspect of forgiveness taught in verses 1-4? 3/ What are you doing about the quality of your faith (cf. the characteristics of a mustard seed in 13:18-19)? 4/ What is the effect of this kind of faith (sycamine trees have powerfully gripping roots)? 5/ As a servant what is the right attitude to service and its rewards? 6/ What do you expect from and give to God? 7/ What two commendable qualities are found in all ten lepers? 8/ Why, do you think, doesn't Jesus give the leprosy back to the nine? 9/ How are thanks and *praise to God* related? 10/ How will you show your gratitude to God today?

DAY **9** △ *Luke 17:20-37*

1/ Imagine the Jewish interest in the Messiah's kingdom (relate this to their political situation). 2/ In what ways does the kingdom differ from their expectations? 3/ How does a realistic understanding of the kingdom of God prevent gullibility in regard to predictions? 4/ Describe the situation before and after the final revelation of the Son of man. 5/ What principle do Noah (cf. Gen. 6:11-22) and Lot (cf. Gen. 19:12-26) exemplify? 6/ How will the final revelation disregard human intimacy and ties? 7/ Relate the proverb in verse 37 with the inquiry about *where* the people will be left. 8/ Measure the purposes and consequence of your life with verse 33.

DAY **10** △ *Luke 18:1-8*

1/ How should *a*-the disciples and *b*-you act when the coming of the Lord seems delayed? 2/ What is the one lesson the story about this judge teaches about God? 3/ Contrast the motives of *a*-the judge and *b*-God in answering prayer. What are their different attitudes toward people who come to them? 4/ Describe the woman's actions. Do you think it is easy for her to keep coming to the judge? Why? 5/ From verses 7-8 what do you learn about God's timing? 6/ Describe the situation of the earth when the Son of man finally comes (cf. 17:26-30). 7/ In view of the earth's situation relate God's *delay* and *speed*. 8/ How do you reveal your perseverance? Can you maintain faith over the long haul?

DAY **11** △ *Luke 18:9-17*

1/ How is the Pharisee's view of himself and others related? different? 2/ What are the negative and positive (the law requires tithing of only certain kinds of income) aspects of his actions? 3/ Why, do you think, does God despise a haughty self concept so much (cf. v. 14 with 14:11; 16:15)? 4/ What are the attitude and actions of the tax collector? 5/ How can you *humble yourself* rightly? 6/ What do your public and private prayers reveal about your character? about your concept of others? 7/ Why, do you think, do intelligent adults have a hard time *trusting* as children? In what other ways can you *receive the kingdom of God* as a child?

DAY **12** △ *Luke 18:18-30*

1/ What point is Jesus making clear by questioning the ruler's use of *good* in his address? 2/ What does the ruler misunderstand about the true fulfillment of the law? 3/ If this man is willing to do so much for his eternal life, why, do you think, doesn't he *sell all?* 4/ Why, do you think, is it *hard* for the rich to enter the kingdom of God? How is it possible? 5/ Imagine the feelings which prompt the question in verse 26 (cf. the Jewish concept that riches-God's favor; poverty-God's punishment). 5/ Does giving up possessions guarantee eternal life? 6/ What are your motives in following Christ?

DAY *13* △ *Luke 18:31-43*

1/ What additional facts does Jesus now give the disciples about his future (cf. 9:22, 44)? Imagine why these words are so incredible to them. 2/ Imagine the life situation of the blind man. 3/ Why, do you think, do the people tell him to be quiet? 4/ In what ways can you be guilty of similar *rebuking?* 5/ Why, do you think, does Jesus ask such an obvious question? 6/ What qualities of Jesus are revealed by his actions in regard to the blind man? 7/ For what kind of happenings do you *give praise to God?*

DAY *14* △ *Luke 19:1-10*

1/ What is Zacchaeus' attitude toward Jesus? List specific phrases. 2/ What is the people's attitude toward the event (cf. 5:27-32; 7:39-42; 15:1-2)? 3/ What, do you think, about Jesus' life prompts Zacchaeus' great change? 4/ Imagine the effect of these actions on the people concerned. 5/ In what ways does your *salvation* have practical and restorative outreach? 6/ Do you expect sinners to be saved or do you really expect only religiously inclined people to be interested?

DAY *15* △ *Luke 19:11-28*

1/ Describe the situation which prompts this parable. 2/ Recall to whom Jesus is telling this parable. 3/ What will the lord's return mean to his servants? 4/ Relate the rewards to the nobleman's command. 5/ On what basis is a servant called *good* and another *wicked?* 6/ What kind of concept does the *wicked* servant have of the lord? 7/ What will the lord's return mean for his enemies (vv. 14, 27)? 8/ How does the Lord make clear in this parable that he will not set up his kingdom immediately? 9/ What do you learn here about the authority of the Lord? 10/ What do you anticipate at the Lord's return in light of verse 26? 11/ What is your concept of God as reflected in your obedience and service?

DAY *16*   △   *Luke 10:1–19:28*
1/ Summarize the ways in which Jesus is influencing a-his disciples, b-the multitudes and individuals, and c-the Jewish religious leaders. 2/ How is the split between Jesus and the Jewish leaders becoming more and more apparent? 3/ Group the parables according to a-whom addressed and b-topics. 4/ Summarize what you have learned about a-the kingdom of God, b-Jesus' purpose on earth, and c-the demands of following (serving) Jesus.

DAY *17*   △   *Genesis 27:1-45*
1/ Briefly summarize Isaac's life before this event. 2/ What kind of person is Jacob? Esau? Rebekah? 3/ How do the people regard oral blessings and promises? How binding is Isaac's original blessing? What problem results? 4/ How do you feel about breaking your word (especially when you have been tricked)? 5/ Contrast the content of the two blessings.

DAY *18*   △   *Genesis 27:46–28:22*
1/ How does Esau try to regain his lost favor with Isaac? 2/ What does God promise Jacob? How has some of it been fulfilled? 3/ What is Jacob's response to God's presence? Why? 4/ What is Jacob's concept of God as revealed by his vow at Bethel? 5/ When and why do you make similar "agreements" with God?

DAY *19*   △   *Genesis 29*
1/ Trace Jacob's travels on a map (continue in subsequent days.) 2/ In what ways is Laban a hypocrite? 3/ Where do you see God's concern for the underdogs in this passage? 4/ In what ways is God teaching Jacob? 5/ What counterparts does Jacob have today?

DAY *20*   △   *Genesis 30*
1/ In what ways do a-Jacob, b-Rachel, c-Leah, and d-Laban show an understanding of God's omnipotence and sovereignty? 2/ Describe the homelife and parental influences Jacob's twelve sons are coming under. 3/ Compare and contrast Jacob's pledge of honesty (v. 33) with his actions. What is the difference between shrewdness

and cheating?   4/ How are you relating now to someone who has wronged you?

DAY 21 △ *Genesis 31*
1/ How does Jacob know he should return to Canaan?   2/ Compare and contrast Jacob's report of the situation with the feelings of Laban and his sons.   3/ What is Rachel and Leah's opinion of their father?   4/ What is strange about Laban's talk of God and his gods (rights to the family inheritance)? How does this account for some of his behavior?   5/ What is the significance of the covenant at Mizpah (contrast with its popular use)?   6/ In God's dealings with Jacob, what do you learn about God's character? about his dealings with sinners? with you?

DAY 22 △ *Genesis 32*
1/ In what ways has God shown love and faithfulness to Jacob?   2/ In what way is Jacob trying to take care of the situation with Esau? What do these actions reveal about Jacob's character?   3/ What occurs during Jacob's struggle with the man? What does this incident reveal about God?   4/ What is Jacob learning about *a*-himself and *b*-God?

DAY 23 △ *Genesis 33*
1/ Contrast this meeting of the brothers with their previous life together.   2/ What has happened to Esau in the meantime? to Jacob?   3/ What can you learn here about resolving conflicts with others? What positive action can you do today to help resolve a conflict with someone?   4/ How does Jacob deceive Esau again?   5/ What is significant about the name of the altar (cf. 32:9)?

DAY 24 △ *Genesis 34*
1/ What is the temptation presented to Jacob? How does he meet it?   2/ Why do Jacob's sons react so strongly?   3/ Contrast the main concerns of *a*-Hamor, *b*-Shechem, *c*-Jacob's sons, and *d*-Jacob.   4/ Characterize each as revealed by their actions.   5/ How does God's attitude toward intermarriage of his followers and those who don't know him affect your dating and courtship patterns?

DAY 25 △ *Genesis 35*
1/ Basically what has happened to Jacob between his first encounter

with God at Bethel and his return? 2/ What has gone wrong?
Why? What has he finally learned? 3/ What else happens to affect Jacob during this crisis period? 4/ How are God's promises
being fulfilled in and through Jacob? What do you learn here about
God's character? 5/ What has happened since your first real encounter with God?

DAY 26 △ *Genesis 36*
1/ What marks the differences between the families, possessions,
and attitudes of Esau and Jacob? In what lands do they settle? 2/
What have you learned about the differences in their characters?
List specific qualities of each. 3/ In what ways are these qualities
passed on to their children? 4/ What difference does realizing that
your "small" evil actions today can have long-term, far-reaching
implications make in your living?

DAY 27 △ *Genesis 37*
1/ How is Joseph tactless in his relations with people? How do most
people, not only brothers, react to such a person? What kind of person is Joseph now? 2/ What are the problems of Jacob's other
sons? Who are responsible? 3/ To what extent are you responsible
for the effect in your life of other people's sins against you? 4/ In
what ways is Jacob at fault in the whole situation? What are the
consequences for him? for Joseph?

DAY 28 △ *Genesis 38*
1/ What is Onan's sin (this custom is levirate marriage)? 2/ What
kind of man is Judah? What "double standard" is evident here? 3/
What kind of person is usually severest in his treatment of a sinner?
What about your character do your attitudes to the sins of others
reveal? 4/ How is Tamar more righteous than Judah (when there
are no brother-in-laws to perform the levirate duty, the father-in-law
has the responsibility)?

DAY 29 △ *Genesis 39*
1/ What kind of man is Joseph becoming? In what areas of his life
is God *with him?* 2/ Describe his apparent work habits. What
opinion do your employers and teachers have of you? Why? 3/
How does Joseph overcome temptation? 4/ Does faithfully following God guarantee a trouble-free life? 5/ What do you do when

you are wrongly accused? What is your attitude toward people who believe the accusation?

DAY *30*   △   *Genesis 40*
1/ How does Joseph make use of his circumstances? Imagine yourself in the situation. What is your probable reaction?   2/ How does Joseph behave toward those who don't know God?   3/ What is Joseph's concept of God? How is he an example for you today?

Month 4

DAY *1*   △   *Genesis 41*
1/ What is the place of dreams in guidance? Why, do you think, does God give Pharoah advance warning in such a way?   2/ How does this event help Joseph?   3/ In what ways is Joseph concerned for the welfare of his enemies the Egyptians? How does Joseph's concern and ability to convey God's thought affect Pharaoh?   4/ In what ways does your witness to those around you affect the world?

DAY *2*   △   *Genesis 42*
1/ What circumstances bring about the meeting of Joseph and his brothers?   2/ What has happened to Joseph's brothers in the meantime? How do they feel about their past crime and God's activity? 3/ How is Joseph testing his brothers?   4/ What kind of person is Reuben (cf. 35:22; 37:21-30)?   5/ What do you learn here about God and his work through men to help you in your prayer life? in today's circumstances?

DAY *3*   △   *Genesis 43*
1/ How is God dealing with Jacob? How is he responsible for his sons' behavior and its present consequences?   2/ What is his attitude toward the loss of his children? What is yours?   3/ What kind of influence is Joseph having politically and personally in Egypt? in the surrounding lands?   4/ What shows that Joseph is not compromising his convictions about God in Egypt (cf. previous chaps.)? 5/ To what extent does he adopt the mores of Egypt? To what extent should you practice the mores of your culture?

DAY *4*   △   *Genesis 44*
1/ In what way are Joseph's dreams (chap. 37) fulfilled here?   2/

What is God teaching *a*-the brothers and *b*-Jacob through Joseph?
3/ Characterize Judah (cf. 37:26-27; chap. 38; 43:3-10). 4/
What is your attitude toward those questionable deeds of yours done
in the past that no one knows about? Do you wait in fear for God's
retribution or do you confess them? 5/ What should be a Christian's attitude toward sorrow? What is yours?

DAY 5 △ *Genesis 45*
1/ For what is God responsible? How far, *practically*, does God's
sovereignty extend? How are the brothers responsible? 2/ What is
your attitude right now to your particular circumstances? What is
Joseph's? 3/ Imagine the brothers' conversation on the way home.
What is Jacob's response to the news?

DAY 6 △ *Genesis 46*
1/ How does Jacob know, despite the promise regarding Canaan,
that he should settle his family in Egypt? 2/ Imagine the reunion
of father and son. In what ways has each changed over the years?
3/ How is Joseph, familiar with the Egyptian scene, trying to insure
Israel's separation? 4/ Distinguish separation from isolation.

DAY 7 △ *Genesis 47*
1/ How does Jacob sum up his life? 2/ Describe the extent of the
famine. 3/ How does Joseph show compassion to an alien people?
With what economic principles does he deal with the hungry and
under-privileged? What is their response to him? 4/ What qualities do you reveal in your vocation and everyday duties?

DAY 8 △ *Genesis 48*
1/ What do you learn about God here? 2/ How does Jacob sum
up his life here (contrast his summation in chap. 47)? 3/ In what
ways are the predictions for Ephraim and Manasseh similar to the
predictions and fulfillment for Jacob and Esau? (cf. 25:21-34; chap.
27)? 4/ What is Jacob's perspective in this situation? 5/ How
do you look at present circumstances—politically, socially, and personally—in the light of God's announced plans? To what extent do
you look for God's further deliverance?

DAY 9 △ *Genesis 49*
1/ On what basis does Jacob predict his sons' futures (follow their

careers in later Jewish history)? Compare his summation of their
characters with what you have learned about them. List and explain
the metaphors he uses to describe them.   2/ In what ways is Judah
singled out?   3/ What kind of future, especially spiritual, would
someone who knows you well predict for you?

DAY *10*   △   *Genesis 50*
1/ What are Joseph's relations with Pharaoh?   2/ How does Joseph
feel about defending himself or taking revenge?   3/ Summarize
Joseph's influence on *a*-the people of Egypt and the surrounding
lands and *b*-his family.   4/ In what ways are you influencing those
around you?   5/ Summarize how the Israelites come to be in Egypt.
What are Jacob's and Joseph's predictions for Israel (cf. vv. 24-25
with 48:21—follow the fulfillment in *Exodus*)?

DAY *11*   △   *Luke 19:29-48*
1/ Summarize the main thrusts of Jesus' teaching from the first nine-
teen chapters.   2/ Describe the entry into Jerusalem. What part
do each of the following have: Jesus, the disciples, the multitudes?
Imagine their feelings (recall their views of the kingdom of God).
3/ What is the significance of getting the colt (cf. Zech. 9:9)?   4/
Why, do you think, do the Pharisees want Jesus to rebuke his disciples (relate to their political situation)?   5/ What does Jesus'
answer reveal as to his consciousness of his identity?   6/ What do
the multitudes misunderstand about *peace* (cf. vv. 38, 42-44 with
the destruction of Jerusalem in A.D. 70)?   7/ What is Jesus' attitude
when he speaks judgment?   8/ In what ways does Jesus show
authority?   9/ What is your purpose in the world in relation to
history? In what ways does this knowledge of your purpose give
you courage in the face of opposition?

DAY *12*   △   *Luke 20:1-18*
1/ Imagine the Pharisees' reaction to Jesus' reform in the temple
(cf. 19:45-46).   2/ In what ways is there a conflict of authority
between the religious leaders and Jesus?   3/ How does the Pharisees' plan to reveal this conflict backfire?   4/ Think through their
motives for asking their question and not answering Jesus' question.
What do these motives reveal about their character?   5/ How does
Jesus reveal that he knows their motives?   6/ Relate the parable
to the past and future history of the Jewish nation (cf. Isa. 5:1-7;

Luke 11:46-52; 13:32-35; 9:22; 19:42-44).   7/ In what areas of your life do you recognize Jesus' authority?

DAY *13*   △   *Luke 20:19-26*
1/ Describe the leaders with at least three adjectives.   2/ What new methods do they employ to trap Jesus?   3/ In what ways will the spies' question not arouse the people's suspicion?   4/ Contrast the content of the spies' words with their motives for what they say.   5/ In what ways is Jesus' answer appropriate in view of *a*-the political and religious situation and *b*-his teaching?   6/ In what ways do state and church concerns seem to conflict today? What is your moral obligation in each case?

DAY *14*   △   *Luke 20:27-47*
1/ What is the basis for the Sadducees' question (cf. Deut. 25:5-10)?   2/ In what two ways have they completely misunderstood the resurrection (v. 35)?   3/ How does Jesus show that Moses (the Sadducees believe that Moses never teaches the resurrection) refers to the truth of the resurrection (cf. Ex. 3:6)?   4/ What is the basic error of the Jewish leaders regarding Jesus' identity (cf. 3:31)?   5/ On what do you base your answers to religious and practical issues?   6/ Characterize the scribes.   7/ List modern counterparts of their characteristics.   8/ In what ways do you make a *pretense* of piety?

DAY *15*   △   *Luke 21:1-19*
1/ In what ways does the widow give *more?*   2/ In what ways may you be tempted to cite injustices done to you (cf. 20:47) as an excuse for sacrificing (cf. 21:2-4)?   3/ Imagine the splendor of the temple and the effect of Jesus' words.   4/ What are the *a*-political, *b*-natural, *c*-religious, and *d*-personal *signs?* Relate verse 13 to these events.   5/ How does Jesus' refutation of his opponents strengthen the promise of verse 15?   6/ How does this discourse enlarge on 12:4-12?   7/ What quality must the disciples possess?   8/ How are you revealing this quality in your daily living?

DAY *16*   △   *Luke 21:20-38*
1/ What is the reason for the destruction of Jerusalem (cf. 11:50; 19:43-44)? Describe and imagine the desolation.   2/ In what way does Jesus enlarge the scope of his predictions?   3/ Contrast the purpose of what will happen to *a*-Jerusalem (v. 22) and *b*-the world

(v. 28). 4/ What attitudes and events can be clearly known and expected (cf. the parable from nature)? 5/ What specific commands are given to govern life in the meantime (cf. v. 36 with v. 19)? 6/ How certain are these predictions (cf. v. 8)? 7/ Contrast Jesus' birth and his return as to the effect on people (cf. v. 27 with 1:31-33; chap. 2). Compare the business as usual preceeding both events (esp. 12:40; 17:26-30). 8/ How seriously do you take these predictions? 9/ How does your faith in the Son of man overcome *fear* and *foreboding?* 10/ Distinguish a realistic expectation of future events from pessimism.

DAY *17* △ *Luke 22:1-20*

1/ What is *a*-Satan's and *b*-Judas' part in the betrayal of Jesus? 2/ Relate verses 5-6 and verse 2. 3/ In what ways are you aware of Satan's power in individuals today (cf. 17:1-3)? 4/ Imagine the suspense and intrigue of this last week in view of Jesus' knowledge of Judas' plan and his final teaching (cf. 21:37-38; v. 15). 5/ What precautions does Jesus make about the place for the passover (only women carry water jars)? 6/ Imagine what you say to your family and friends if it is your last meal together (but they don't realize it). 7/ What is the significance of the Lord's passover supper (cf. v. 7; Ex. 12:1-20)?

DAY *18* △ *Luke 22:21-38*

1/ Contrast the concerns of *a*-the disciples (v. 24) and *b*-Jesus (vv. 14-19). 2/ In what way is leadership among Christians different from the current concept of authority? Describe the qualities and attitudes of a Christian leader. 3/ In what ways does Jesus show his knowledge of *a*-Satan, *b*-Simon, *c*-the future, and *d*-meeting Satan's attacks? 4/ How can you strengthen others to meet temptation? 5/ What reception have the disciples gotten previously because of their connection with Jesus as an honored teacher (cf. chaps. 9-10)? In what ways will this reception change? 6/ What do the disciples misunderstand about Jesus' meaning of *sword?* 7/ What is your defense in the face of opposition?

DAY *19* △ *Luke 22:39-53*

1/ Describe the pressures on *a*-Jesus and *b*-his disciples. How does each deal with them? 2/ What is Jesus' main concern for *a*-himself and *b*-his disciples? 3/ What is the chief obstacle to the dis-

ciples' praying? 4/ What pressures do you have? How do you deal
with them? Why? 5/ Imagine the two companies meeting. What
shows that Jesus submits voluntarily to the powers of darkness?

DAY **20** △ *Luke 22:54-71*

1/ Imagine the disciples' feelings after the event on the Mount of
Olives. 2/ Imagine the gossip in the courtyard about the new
prisoner. How does Peter handle the awkward situation he is in?
3/ How do you act when you realize you have denied Christ in a
difficult situation? Why? 4/ How is Jesus treated psychologically
and physically (cf. 18:32)? 5/ What is the council trying to get
Jesus to "admit"? When they succeed, how do they act? 6/ Why,
do you think, does Jesus give a clear affirmative answer here (cf.
4:18-22; 5:20-26; 6:5; 9:18-22; 20:9-18, 41-44)?

DAY **21** △ *Luke 23:1-12*

1/ Although the Jewish council want to put Jesus to death because
he claims to be the Son of God (the charge—blasphemy), what
charges do they bring before Pilate? 2/ Imagine the Roman-Jewish
relations. What about the charges can make Pilate suspicious of their
validity? 3/ What about the accusations is false? 4/ Account for
the "politics" of Pilate after his statement of verse 4. 5/ What is
Herod's attitude toward Jesus (cf. 9:7-9)? 6/ In what ways do
you try to avoid making decisions? Why? Does it work?

DAY **22** △ *Luke 23:13-31*

1/ What about Jesus is repeatedly stressed in this passage? 2/
What makes Pilate back down on his original verdict (cf. v. 4—
chastising is a preliminary to a prisoner's crucifixion)? 3/ Imagine
the mob hysteria. 4/ What kind of man is Barabbas? 5/ In what
ways are your decisions a result of your convictions? of popular
opinion and demand? 6/ Imagine Jesus' physical condition from
the agony on the Mount of Olives, the all-night trial, and the chastise-
ment. 7/ What perspective does Jesus try to give the mourning
women? Imagine the effect of Jesus' words (cf. the Jewish feeling
toward barrenness—1:7, 24-25).

DAY **23** △ *Luke 23:32-43*

1/ Visualize the scene and the characters. What are the attitudes of
the people and soldiers toward Jesus? 2/ What does Jesus pray?

For what purpose? 3/ What is the significance of the inscription? 4/ Contrast the attitudes revealed by the requests of the two criminals. What kinds of deliverance are they seeking? 5/ What, do you think, about Jesus makes such an impression on one criminal? 6/ What kind of people do you usually regard as impenetrable to the gospel? 7/ Contrast the people's attitude toward the criminals with Jesus' attitude toward them.

DAY *24* △ *Luke 23:44-56*

1/ Describe the natural and religious phenomena that accompany Jesus' death. 2/ What are the various reactions of the people to these events? What is common among them? 3/ What is the significance of Jesus' death for you? What is your response? 4/ Characterize Joseph. What do he and the women do after Jesus' death? 5/ Contrast the actions of Joseph and the women with the attitudes and actions of the people in the first part of chapter 23. What makes the difference?

DAY *25* △ *Luke 24:1-12*

1/ Who are the first to discover the fact that Jesus is raised from the dead? 2/ Are you discovering daily the life of Christ because you seek him through acts of love? 3/ Imagine the women's confusion at the angels' question in verse 5. 4/ To what "proof" of Jesus' resurrection do the angels refer (cf. vv. 6-7 with 9:22, 18:31-33)? 5/ What is the natural response to such a discovery? 6/ Imagine yourself one of the women. What do you say to try to convince the despondent disciples of Jesus' resurrection? 7/ How do the disciples respond to the news (cf. 9:45, 18:34)? 8/ Who will you tell that Christ is alive today?

DAY *26* △ *Luke 24:13-35*

1/ Imagine the disciples' reaction at the intrusion of a "stranger" while they discuss such things. 2/ What about their attitude toward Jesus is revealed by what they tell the "stranger"? 3/ How does Jesus explain the events? 4/ What motive for Bible study does this give you? Do you know what is written about him by the prophets? 5/ List the factors which contribute to the disciples' recognition of Jesus. 6/ What is their response to their new knowledge? 7/ What is your basic way of gaining knowledge of Christ?

8/ What marks the turn of events in this passage? Contrast the countenance and attitudes of the disciples before and after.

DAY 27 △ *Luke 24:36-53*
1/ What is the psychological state of the disciples when Jesus appears to them?   2/ With what kinds of evidence of his resurrection is Jesus concerned?   3/ What is the disciples' part in the evidence? How will they be able to fulfill their part?   4/ Trace the progression in the disciples' understanding and response.   5/ What is Christ's command to you today in your immediate situation? How will you be able to fulfill it?   6/ Are you asking God about his will for you in terms of *all nations?*   7/ Imagine you are a disciple. How does this event change your life?   8/ How does the fact of the resurrection affect your daily living?

DAY 28 △ *Luke 1–24*
1/ In what ways does Luke keep his audience in mind throughout his book (cf. main Greek concerns)?   2/ In what ways does he portray Jesus' *a*-humanity and *b*-deity?   3/ Summarize the ministry and methods of Jesus.   4/ What is the purpose of Jesus' death and resurrection?   5/ In what ways does Luke convince you of *a*-the historic reality of Jesus' life and *b*-the truth of his teachings?

DAY 29 △ *Introduction to the Psalms*
The *Psalms* are personal and public poems of worship used as hymns. They represent a range of emotional tones, subjects, and authors. Read the psalms aloud and imagine the experiences and feelings which prompt their writing. *Psalm 1*   1/ Contrast the righteous and the wicked.   2/ How are delight and meditation connected? Do you daily study and obey the word of God?   3/ What characteristics of the evergreen tree are given? How do these characteristics relate to the righteous man?   4/ How do you compare to the righteous man? What *fruit* is God producing in your life to nourish others?   5/ What presently in your life can be classified as *chaff?*   6/ Title this psalm as to content.

DAY 30 △ *Psalm 2*
1/ Compare this and the first psalm.   2/ What are the actions and destiny of evil nations?   3/ How effective are the plots? What is

God's response to them? 4/ What is the author David's answer to the opposition against him as God's representative? 5/ How do you relate national and international crises to God? Is God sovereign? 6/ Contrast the activities of the nations with the purposes of God. 7/ What advice does the psalmist give the kings? Why? 8/ What is your relationship to the last statement in this psalm? 9/ Title this psalm as to content.

Month 5

DAY *1* △ *Psalm 3*

1/ Compare 2 Samuel 15 (esp. vv. 12-13). 2/ Trace the concept of *deliverance* through this psalm. 3/ What is the significance of *but* in verse 3? 4/ To what extent are verses 5-6 true in your life? Why? 5/ Does the first half of verse 7 contradict verses 5-6? Give your reasons. 6/ List the problems confronting David in this psalm. List the solutions. 7/ How do these problems and solutions relate to your experience? 8/ Title this psalm as to content.

DAY *2* △ *Psalm 4*

1/ In the midst of this uprising to whom does David appeal? 2/ What charges does David make against the people? 3/ What exhortations does he give them? 4/ How does David speak of his relationship to God? How do you define your relationship to him? 5/ Explain the positive tone of verses 7-8. How does verse 8 relate to verse 5? 6/How can you *offer right sacrifices* today? 7/ Title this psalm as to content.

DAY *3* △ *Psalm 5*

1/ At what time of day is this prayer made? 2/ What evidence does this psalm give of the personal relationship between David and God? 3/ What is the significance of *watch* in verse 3? 4/ What answers do you expect from your prayers as you watch for them? 5/ On what basis is David's confidence as he makes request for his deliverance and his enemies' destruction (vv. 4-8)? 6/ Characterize evil-doers. Are any of these characteristics present in your life? 7/ What men have cause to anticipate the judgment of God? to rejoice? 8/ In the light of this psalm what is your present attitude? Why? 9/ Title this psalm as to content.

DAY *4* △ *Psalm 6*
1/ Read this psalm aloud (Sheminith probably means an octave
lower). 2/ What is its mood through verse 7? What happens in
verses 8-10? 3/How do you know this is a *personal* psalm? 4/
What characteristics of distress do you find? of rejoicing? 5/Do you
ever feel this way? Why? 6/ Compare verse 4 with verses 8-10.
How can David speak with such assurance? 7/ How can you have
assurance about your prayers? 8/Title this psalm as to content.

DAY *5* △ *Psalm 7*
1/ How do verses 1-2 set the tone of this psalm? 2/ What is David
doing in verses 3-5? What is he willing to have done to him if he is
guilty? 3/ How does David picture God? 4/ What does he ask
God to do? 5/ Characterize the wicked man (cf. vv. 1-2). 6/
How does verse 17 relate to the rest of the psalm? 7/ At what
points can you identify with this psalm? Why? 8/ Title this psalm
as to content.

DAY *6* △ *Psalm 8*
1/ Compare verse 1 with verse 9. What purpose do these two verses
have in the psalm? 2/ Can you include yourself in the use of *our*?
Why? 3/ What things are said about God? about man? Compare
and contrast God and man. 4/ What is the significance of the
questions in verse 4? How does verse 4 relate to verse 3? 5/ How
does verse 2 fit in with the remainder of this psalm? 6/ How would
you describe and title this psalm? Why?

DAY *7* △ *Psalm 9*
1/ In the opening verses what does David say he will do? 2/
Which of these are presently a part of your life? 3/ What is the
experience of the enemies? Why? 4/ What is said about God?
5/ What reasons are given for praising God? Compare the use of
praise in verses 2, 11, 14. 6/ Compare the *nations* and *wicked*.
7/ Contrast the enemy (vv. 15-17) and the Lord (vv. 7-12). 8/
Compare verse 18 with verses 15-17. What differences are given?
9/ In verses 19-20 whom is David calling God to judge? 10/ Considering the world situation to what extent can you make this **your**
prayer? 11/ Title this psalm as to content.

DAY *8* △ *Psalm 10*

1/ What problem is expressed here? Compare this and the ninth psalm.   2/ What is said about the attitude of the wicked? his actions? his relationship to God? How do his attitude and actions illustrate his belief of verses 4, 11?   3/ What does the psalmist ask God to do? On what basis does he appeal to God?   4/ List the characteristics of God's rule.   5/ Explain the last half of verse 18. What is significant about what it says?   6/ Contrast the present and final situations of man.   7/ Is verse 4 or 17 more appropriate to your life?   8/ Title this psalm as to content.

DAY *9* △ *Psalm 11*

1/ In verse 1 what two sources of refuge are mentioned? Which does David choose?   2/ What is the target of the wicked? What do they hope to do (cf. 1 Sam. 18:10-11; 19:9-10)?   3/ Explain verse 3. How does this relate to what is said of the Lord in verses 4-7?   4/ What is the difference in God's dealing with the righteous and the wicked?   5/ How is God dealing with you now? Do you know why?   6/ Compare the three references to righteous and uprightness in verse 7. How is each related to God?   7/ Can a man see God? How have you seen him recently?   8/ Title this psalm as to content.

DAY *10* △ *Psalm 12*

1/ What sin is expressed in verse 1?   2/ In verses 2-4 what is discussed? How many different sins are mentioned?   3/ Which of these weaknesses are present in your life? in society?   4/ Whom does God assist?   5/ What is the difficulty in verse 5? What does God say he will do?   6/ Contrast the words of God with the words of men.   7/ How does this difference encourage you to trust God?   8/ What is verse 8 saying? What evidences of this do you see today?   9/ Title this psalm as to content.

DAY *11* △ *Introduction to Acts*

Luke continues his orderly account of the extension of Christianity through the apostles and the Holy Spirit. *Acts 1:1-12*   1/ How does Jesus spend his time on earth after he rises from the dead?   2/ What are his plans for the disciples? What concerns them (cf. their concern throughout *Luke*)? How does Jesus answer their questions?   3/ What do Jesus' disciples *see* and *hear* in verses 9-11?   4/ What does this passage reveal about God's plan for your life during the time between Christ's ascension and return? 5/ What divine resource has God provided for you? 6/ Are you aware of any specific way the Holy Spirit has empowered you recently to witness of Christ?

DAY *12* △ *Acts 1:12-26*

1/ How do Jesus' disciples spend their time after Jesus leaves them? 2/ On what grounds does Peter declare that another apostle will be chosen? To what will the new apostle witness? 3/ How do scripture, prayer, and providence (the lots) have a part in the new selection? 4/ With which of these three things do the disciples begin when they want to discern God's will? 5/ On what basis will you make today's decisions?

DAY *13* △ *Acts 2:1-13*

1/ In what ways is Jesus' promise (1:5, 8) fulfilled in this passage? 2/ Describe the physical manifestations of the Spirit's coming. 3/ How does the Holy Spirit empower these men to be witnesses to the whole world (locate the countries on a map) at this time? 4/ Describe the reactions of the crowd. 5/ What is the disciples' message? 6/ What message do you share as you witness to others? 7/ How can you find power to be an effective witness for Christ?

DAY *14* △ *Acts 2:12-36*

1/ How does Peter answer the charge that the disciples are drunk? 2/ When people misunderstand your Christian life and witness, what should you do? 3/ Which aspects of God's plan concerning Jesus of Nazareth does God accomplish through men and which without men (vv. 22-24)? 4/ Paraphrase Peter's argument of verses 24-36 (cf. Ps. 16:8-11). What does he try to prove? 5/ In verses 32-36, what does Jesus do now that he has been made *both Lord and Christ*? 6/ What difference does the risen, ascended, active Christ make in your daily living?

DAY *15* △ *Acts 2:37-47*

1/ How do people respond to Peter's address? Have you ever responded in this way? When? For what reason? 2/ What action does Peter urge? 3/ What evidence is in this passage that God is concerned to save entire families? Have you claimed the promises of

God for the other members of your family?   4/ List the aspects or manifestations of the new life of those who receive Peter's word. Which of these aspects characterize you?

DAY *16* △   *Acts 3:1-10*
1/ How do Peter and John show their love to God and to men on this day?   2/ Contrast what the lame man expects with what he receives.   3/ How do the people involved in this miracle—Peter and John, lame man, spectators—give glory to God?   4/ What has God given you that you can share today with people in need?

DAY *17* △   *Acts 3:11-26*
1/ What does Peter say about Jesus? Of what does Peter accuse the crowd?   2/ Summarize how each verse of this passage is appropriate to the Jewish audience Peter is addressing.   3/ As you witness of Christ, how can you make the message appropriate and meaningful to your audience?   4/ What does Peter say will be the result of repentance?   5/ What kind of response does God expect to the words of Jesus?   6/ In verse 25 what does Peter say about the extent of God's gracious purposes? In what ways have you experienced these *blessings?*

DAY *18* △   *Acts 4:1-12*
1/ Why do the priests and Sadducees arrest Peter and John?   2/ what question do the Jewish leaders ask them? How does Peter answer it?   3/ List five things that Peter says about Jesus Christ. Why does saying each to this audience require a Spirit-given boldness?   4/ When has God put you in a difficult situation and filled you with his Spirit to testify of Christ? What has happened?

DAY *19* △   *Acts 4:13-31*
1/ Why do the men of the council say nothing publicly in opposition to Peter and John? Why are they concerned about them?   2/ Imagine yourself in the situation. How do you answer the warning given? Compare your answer with the answer of Peter and John. 3/ List the different parts of the disciples' prayer. What is significant about its order?   4/ Describe the God in whom the disciples believe as revealed by their prayer.   4/ In what way does faith in such a God make their witness bold?   5/ How does God answer

their prayer?   6/ Do you usually pray for deliverance from trying circumstances or for boldness in them?

DAY *20*   △   *Acts 1:1–4:31*
1/ Describe the early church's concerns, activities, and growth. 2/ What is its effect on people?   3/ Compare or contrast these characteristics of the early church with your church's fellowship and outreach. What needs changing? How?   4/ What place does the Old Testament have in the thought and action of the early church? 5/ Summarize the main thoughts in Peter's sermons.   6/ What place does the Bible have in your thought and actions?   7/ What causes the beginning of persecution? From whom?

DAY *21*   △   *Acts 4:32-37*
1/ How do you feel about your possessions?   2/ In what ways is the filling of the Holy Spirit (v. 31) manifest in today's passage? 3/ Describe the apostles' testimony. Is this an accurate description of your testimony?   4/ Why are those who believe in no need?   5/ Describe the profound change in the disciples' mode of living.   6/ What is different about your life because you belong to the church?

DAY *22*   △   *Acts 5:1-12*
1/ Precisely what is the lie that Ananias and Sapphira agree to tell the apostles?   2/ What do verses 3-4 teach about the identity of the Holy Spirit? Do you think of the Holy Spirit in this way?   3/ What is God's reaction to sin in the church? What happens to Ananias and Sapphira?   4/ What does this incident teach you about God?   5/ In what ways are you holding back from God?   6/ Have you been completely honest with other people during the last week? 7/ In what ways are you dishonest with God? Do you pray that he will help you to be honest?

DAY *23*   △   *Acts 5:12-42*
1/ What happens after the church is filled with fear?   2/ Why do the Sadducees oppose what God is doing through the apostles? Have you ever opposed what God is doing through others for this reason?   3/ How are the disciples let out of prison? For what reason? When do they start to obey the angel's command?   4/ What is significant about the place where they teach?   5/ Contrast the fear of the temple officers with the boldness of Peter and the

other apostles.   6/ What in Peter's bold words enrages the Jewish council?   7/ Why does Gamaliel advise caution about the treatment of the apostles? Are your plans and activities of God or of men?   8/ How do the apostles respond to their beating? How do you respond to trying times in your Christian life?

DAY 24 △ Acts 6
1/ What growing pains does the early church experience?   2/ List the qualifications demanded of the seven who are chosen to serve tables. Would you require such qualifications for men with this duty? Why or why not?   3/ How does your Christian group select leaders?   4/ What is your attitude toward routine service?   5/ Describe the attitude of the twelve toward priorities in their lives.   6/ To what does God want you to give priority in your life?   7/ Can some responsibility you are now carrying in your Christian group be assigned to someone else?   8/ What are the practical results in Jerusalem after the church makes a division of labor?   9/ After the problem within the church is settled, what problem does the church now face from outside? Describe the methods employed by the church's enemies.   10/ What evidences God's presence with Stephen?   11/ Have you ever been in a situation similar to Stephen's? What have you done?

DAY 25 △ Acts 7–8:1
1/ How does Stephen identify with the council?   2/ Is this an appropriate time for a history lesson? How well-acquainted are you with the way God has guided the people of Israel?   3/ List what Stephen says God has done.   4/ Summarize the interplay of God's speech and actions. Are the actions alone sufficient?   5/ How does history repeat itself in this chapter? In what situations are you resisting God's purposes for you?   6/ Contrast the council's reaction to Stephen's defense with Stephen's response to the council's rage. What makes the difference?

DAY 26 △ Acts 8:2-25
1/ What causes the church to spread out to other regions? How do you regard such a happening to your Christian group?   2/ What do those who are scattered do?   3/ Contrast Philip (cf. 6:5) and Simon considering their reputation, results of their activity, and attitude toward the Holy Spirit.   4/ Why do you want the power

of God in your life? 5/ How concerned are you about what the other Christians in your group think of you? What are your motives for being "spiritual"?

DAY 27 △ *Acts 8:26-40*
1/ What instructions does Philip receive from the angel? 2/ How has God already prepared the eunuch to hear the message of Christ? In what ways has God prepared you for the gospel? 3/ How does Philip initiate the conversation? When does he start talking about the good news of Christ? 4/ What evidence does the eunuch give of believing the message? 5/ What is the last impression you have of him? Compare this with the last impression of Simon in yesterday's reading. 6/ Summarize what God does for the eunuch and for Philip. How does this encourage you to talk with someone today about Jesus?

DAY 28 △ *Acts 4:32–8:40*
1/ What is the result of persecution for the church's outreach? 2/ List the various problems the church faces. How is each handled? 3/ What are the evidences of the Holy Spirit's work in the early church? 4/ Compare or contrast the results of the Holy Spirit's presence in the early church with the results of his presence in your church. 5/ Describe the people in these chapters (excluding those cited in sermons) as to a-personal characteristics, b-response to God, and c-service to others.

DAY 29 △ *Acts 9:1-31*
1/ Visualize the change in Saul (cf. 7:58–8:3). 2/ List his before and after characteristics. 3/ Under what circumstances has Jesus confronted you? How have you responded? 4/ Why is Ananias hesitant about God's command? How does God answer him? How are you acting now about something God wants you to do for him? 5/ How do the events of verses 17-30 confirm and illustrate what God says to Ananias (vv. 15-16)? 6/ How has your commitment to Christ involved you in suffering? 7/ To what extent does your Christian group experience what the early church experiences in verse 31?

DAY 30 △ *Acts 9:32-43*
1/ Who heals the paralyzed man? What is the result? 2/ What

are some of the good works and acts of love of Tabitha? What good works and acts of love will you do today? 3/ What evidences that Peter raises Tabitha to life by the power of God? What is the result? 4/ Has anyone ever believed in the Lord after seeing the power of God in your life?

Month 6

DAY *1* △ *Acts 10:1-33a*
1/ Characterize Cornelius. To what extent does he believe the revelation that God has given in the Old Testament? 2/ How, do you think, has Cornelius learned about the true God? Why does God send an angel to him (v. 4)? 3/ How does God prepare Peter for his encounter with this gentile army officer? 4/ Put yourself in Peter's place. Imagine some animal you hate to touch, much less eat. What are your thoughts, emotions, and reactions as a result of such a vision? 5/ How do the events in this chapter further Christ's purpose as expressed in 1:8? 6/ What feelings do you have toward a group on race that prevent you from entering whole-heartedly into Christ's purpose for the world?

DAY *2* △ *Acts 10:1-48*
1/ What difference does the vision of the unclean animals make in Peter's personal contact with Cornelius? 2/ How does Peter's sermon (vv. 34-43) differ from his other sermons in this book (e.g. 2:14-36)? 3/ List the facts that Peter wants Cornelius to know about Jesus Christ. 4/ What must you do to receive forgiveness of sins? 5/ How does God show his pleasure with the preaching of Peter and the faith of Cornelius? What additional command does Peter give?

DAY *3* △ *Acts 11:1-18*
1/ Who objects to Peter's contact with the Gentiles? What does Peter do when confronted with criticism? What do you do? 2/ How does the circumcision party respond to Peter's patient explanation of what has happened? 3/ What gift does God give the Gentiles as well as the Jews? Have you received this gift? How do you know? 4/ Who motivates men to repent? How does this affect your prayers? What is the outcome of repentance? 5/ How does your Christian group handle matters of contention? Can you discover

from today's passage a way to handle contention which can result in glorifying God?

DAY *4*   △   *Acts 11:19-30*
1/ Categorize specifically what *a*-God and *b*-men do to spread the gospel. What is the result? To whom is the result attributed?   2/ Describe the relationship between the churches at Antioch and Jerusalem. How do they mutually aid one another?   3/ How is your Christian group related to other Christian groups? In what ways does your group show love and concern for Christians in other places?   4/ List what is said about Barnabas. What specific things does Barnabas do and say to help these new Christians?   5/ What principles of Christian giving can you discover from today's passage?

DAY *5*   △   *Acts 12:1-19*
1/ What does Herod do to James and Peter? How does the church respond?   2/ What instructions does the angel give Peter? When does Peter know that the events are not a dream?   3/ Imagine you are here. How do you respond to Rhoda's news and the sight of Peter? Is Rhoda's reaction different from that of the others? When has an answer to prayer surprised you?   4/ Compare your view of angels with what is said here.   5/ Contrast the outcome of Herod's persecution in the lives of *a*-James and *b*-Peter. Is death or deliverance equally acceptable to you?

DAY *6*   △   *Acts 12:20-25*
1/ What kind of man is Herod (cf. vv. 1-19)? What does God have to do to him? Why?   2/ How does this passage add to what you learned yesterday about angels?   3/ When you are in a position of leadership, how can you *give God the glory?* How important does God consider this?   4/ Describe the activity of God in the life of this unChristian ruler. Even though God permits him to do much that is harmful, what is the final outcome concerning the word of God?   5/ Does God still rule the lives of authorities? How does this affect your prayers?   6/ Summarize the growth of the early church geographically and ethnically in spite of religious opposition.

DAY *7*   △   *Introduction to Exodus*
God has made a covenant with Abraham (review Gen. 12:1-3, 7;

13:14-17; 15:13-16; 17:1-21), reiterated to Abraham's son and grandson (review Gen. 26:24; 28:13-15). According to God's prediction Abraham's descendants have become exiles in Egypt (skim Gen. 45-48). Moses now records their deliverance as a nation. *Exodus 1* 1/ How has the political climate changed since Joseph's death? What is the new Pharaoh's view of the situation? 2/ In what three ways does Pharaoh try to stem the population explosion? Account for his lack of success and need for more drastic measures. 3/ What is the Egyptian view of human life? 4/ Compare and contrast the attitude of *a*-the king, *b*-the Egyptians, and *c*-the Hebrew midwives toward the Israelites. 5/ How does the midwives' attitude toward God affect their attitude toward people? the king's edict? What is the effect of the midwives' obedience on themselves? the Israelites? Pharaoh? 6/ When in tension between fear of God and fear of people and human authority to whom do you give allegiance? When and in what ways has your obedience to God affected others?

DAY 8 △ *Exodus 2*
1/ How does one couple circumvent Pharaoh's edict? Imagine how you would have acted. Why? 2/ How do the two environments of home and palace contribute to Moses' education, training, and preparation for leadership? 3/ Recount your experiences which have contributed to your present work or future plans. What experiences do you sometimes regard as wasted? Evaluate your attitude toward these considering this passage. 4/ What circumstances lead to Moses' losing identity as a prince and becoming an exile? 5/ How has God used even your sins to accomplish his purpose for you? 6/ Describe the condition of the Israelite minority when the king dies. Where is God in this (underline and explain the verbs of vv. 24-25)? 7/ Have you felt as if life is too much? When? What have you done? What facts here can strengthen your confidence and faith in God and his plan when you face similar situations in the future?

DAY 9 △ *Exodus 3*
1/ Imaginatively contrast Moses as a prince with Moses as an exile. Describe the circumstances that bring him to the mountain of God. How does the Lord get his attention here? 3/ What does Moses learn of God's character and identity? What is significant about God's

66

name (cf. his previous titles: Gen. 17:1; 28:3; 35:11)?   4/ Relate
God's knowledge of the situation to his command to Moses.   5/ In
what ways is the Lord revealing to you the desperation of people?
What are you doing about it?   6/ List *a*—the two objections Moses
raises in this passage and *b*—God's answer to each. Test the reason-
ableness of each objection in the light of God's answers.   7/ Summarize the job God is giving Moses (as God previews it): his message to the elders and to Pharaoh; the responses. On what does the
success of the project rest?

DAY *10*   △   *Exodus 4*

1/ List two more objections Moses raises. What is God's reply to
each?   2/ What objections do you raise when God gives you a job?
How reasonable are they in view of his call and equipping?   3/
What is the purpose of the signs? What do these signs reveal about
God's attitude toward people who doubt his word or messengers?
4/ What is the basic objection with Moses (v. 13)?   5/ In what
recent situation have you given God reason to be angry with you?
Why?   6/ How does God counter Moses' refusal to be his spokesman?   7/ What is Moses' first step in obedience? Find the additional facts God gives him.   8/ How has God confirmed his call to
you after your initial obedience in a given situation?   9/ Account
for God's harsh dealing with Moses considering Genesis 17:9-14.
10/ What disobedience (by default or deliberate) in your life must
be dealt with before you can carry out God's orders?   11/ Which
objections that Moses has raised are voided in verses 27-31?

DAY *11*   △   *Exodus 5–6:1*

1/ In their first skirmish with Pharaoh what do Moses and Aaron
ask (the Israelites cannot sacrifice within Egyptian limits because
animals, esp. cows, are sacred to Egyptians—cf. 8:26)?   2/ What is
Pharaoh's attitude toward the God of the Hebrews (each god has
his own jurisdiction and circumscribed power)?   3/ What new demands does Pharaoh place on the people as a result?   4/ Reconstruct the dialogue between the foremen and Pharaoh. How have
the foremen viewed the new problem? What is Pharaoh's interpretation?   5/ What are the reactions of the people to increased forced
labor? of Moses to their criticism?   6/ How do you react to the
pressure of multiplied problems and criticism?   7/ Relate the suit-
ability of God's answer (6:1) to the problem.

DAY *12* △ *Exodus 6:2-25*

1/ What new aspect of his being does God reveal through his name (cf. vv. 2-3 with 3:14-16)? 2/ List the seven aspects of God's deliverance for Israel. Compare these with what he has done and will do for you. 3/ What difference does *a*—knowing that God is actively involved in history and *b*—knowing something of his overall plan make in your attitude toward life? 4/ Contrast the attitude of the Israelites now (v. 9) with their initial reaction to Moses and Aaron (4:31). Account for the difference. 5/ How are your convictions affected by circumstances? 6/ How is this request (vv. 10-13) to Pharaoh different from the previous one? 7/ In view of the hopeless situation in verse 12 why don't they quit? 8/ When confronted with a hopeless situation is your tendency to quit or to look for a solution? 9/ Determine the meaning of *uncircumcised* in this context. 10/ What is significant about the three life spans specifically recorded here (cf. Gen. 6:3)?

DAY *13* △ *Exodus 6:26—7:24*

1/ How does God answer Moses' despairing plea? Who will really move Pharaoh? 2/ What effect will these actions ultimately have on the Egyptians? 3/ In what ways have non-Christians known God's identity through your actions? 4/ Contrast the power by which Aaron and the magicians perform their signs. 5/ What is the underlying reason for the plagues? 6/ Imagine how this first plague would affect your own senses and needs. Imagine how the plagues would affect the attitude of the Israelites. 7/ How is Pharaoh affected by the plague (the Nile god is a main object of worship)? by his people's needs? 8/ Relate Pharaoh's disobedience with *a*—his ignorance of God's identity (cf. v. 17 with 5:2) and *b*—his evaluation of himself. 9/ How is your obedience or disobedience contingent on your view of God? How can you have a more clear and accurate understanding of him?

DAY *14* △ *Exodus 7:25—8:32*

1/ Begin an outline or chart of the plagues, noting their characteristics, physical effects, changes in intensity over previous ones, the realm over which God displays power, reaction of Pharaoh, etc. 2/ Though the magicians imitate Moses and Aaron, where does Pharaoh turn for relief? 2/ Why doesn't Moses seek immediate relief since Pharaoh is willing to bargain with God (v. 10)? 3/ Contrast Moses and Pharaoh in their responsibilities to the agreement and their responses. 4/ In the plague of the gnats what indirect counsel does Pharaoh receive from his advisors? How do they recognize the power of God? 5/ Recall situations in which you have had a choice of listening to advisors and God or of becoming hardened to the voice of God. What has been your reaction in the situation? 6/ What is the new distinction in the plague of flies? Imagine the Israelites' feelings. 7/ How far does Pharaoh go in his bargaining now? Why doesn't Moses agree to the first concession? What further concession does Pharaoh make? What is Moses' warning to him?

DAY *15* △ *Exodus 9*
1/ Distinguish the twofold purpose of God in sending these catastrophes. 2/ On what basis is the plague of hail "selective"? 3/ What is Pharaoh's reaction this time? What does he admit? Do you think he is genuinely sorry for sin or remorseful because of the consequences? 4/ For what reasons is the plague stopped? 5/ What is the danger to you in not listening to God? 6/ What qualities of *a*—Pharaoh, *b*—Moses, and *c*—God are revealed by their actions here?

DAY *16* △ *Exodus 10*
1/ What additional insight does God give for all these signs? 2/To what extent do God's purposes take into account the Egyptians' attitude toward him? 3/ What is *a*—God's and *b*—Pharaoh's part in Pharaoh's hardened heart? 4/ How can you encourage others by telling what God has done? 5/ Imagine the pressure placed on Pharaoh by God and by Pharaoh's servants. What are the two points of view? 6/ How does the ninth plague affront the Egyptian sun god Ra? 7/ As events build toward the final battle, with Egypt a disaster area, for what truce terms does Pharaoh hold out (vv. 8-11, 24)? 8/ How has Pharaoh sinned against *a*—God and *b*—Moses and Aaron? 9/ Contrast the ultimate implications if Moses agrees to Pharaoh's terms or holds out for unconditional surrender (cf. 6:5-8). 10/ How many opportunities has God given Pharaoh to repent? Considering this what is different about the last catastrophe?

DAY *17* △ *Exodus 11–12:20*
1/ Account for the attitude of the Egyptians and Pharaoh's servants toward Moses and Israelites. What is one practical consequence of this attitude? 2/ Summarize God's description of his next strategic

move against Pharaoh (death of the sacred animals is a major religious catastrophe). 3/ Single out the requirements of the lamb and how it is to be prepared and used for the initial celebration. 4/ What is the criterion for safety from this plague? 5/ What are additional instructions for the annual memorial? the consequences of disobedience? 6/ In what ways do you observe or remember what the Lord has done for you? How meaningful is this to you? Why?

DAY 18 △ *Exodus 12:21–13:16*

1/ Add to your previous list of requirements for the passover celebration the additional instructions Moses gives the elders. What is the response of the people? 2/ Imagine the terror and anguish spreading from house to house. 3/ Contrast Pharoah's response now to his previous reactions. How do the Egyptians punctuate his command? 4/ Describe and imagine Egypt before and after God's acts of judgment. 5/ Summarize the contrasting responses of Moses and Pharaoh to God in these encounters. What is the basic issue that differentiates them? 6/ How do you respond to God's commandments? Why? 7/ Who and what constitute this emigration? Consider the effect of these facts on their speed in travel. 8/ Compare 12:40-42 and 13:3-10 with Genesis 15:13-16. List the specific fulfillments of God's promise (note in vv. 9, 16—phylacteries are rolled parchments inscribed with passages from the law, placed into small boxes and attached to Jewish males' wrist and put on the forehead during prayer). 9/ Who is unable to celebrate the annual passover feast. On what basis is this altered? 10/ What does the Lord demand regarding the firstborn? What provision does he make for the life of a firstborn son? 11/ In what specific ways can you put God first in considering possessions and family?

DAY 19 △ *Exodus 13:17–14:31*

1/ Why doesn't God lead the people through a short cut? 2/ How are they to know their way through the desert without a road map? 3/ Follow their journey on a map (continue in subsequent days). 4/ With Egypt a disaster area and its labor force gone consider the logic and strategy in Pharaoh's next move. 5/ Describe your feelings were you an Israelite in this situation: surrounded by sea, desert, mountains, and an armed enemy. 6/ Contrast the reactions of *a*–the people and *b*–Moses. 7/ Trace the steps as God delivers Israel again. 8/ Describe and imagine the weather conditions as Israel crosses. Why is instant obedience essential? 9/ Contrast the reaction of *a*—the Egyptians and *b*—the Israelites to God's actions. 10/ What tough situations have you been in recently? Can you see God's design in these? What specifically have you learned today that can help you face hopeless situations?   11/ Contrast the Egyptians' end with the previous Pharaoh's intentions of 1:9-10.

DAY 20   △   *Exodus 15:1-21*

1/ Divide this folk song into appropriate stanzas and refrains. Summarize the thought of each.   2/ Describe God as to his character and his work as portrayed in the song.   3/ How is Moses' confidence for the future built on *a*—his knowledge of the character of God and *b*—his past experience?   4/ On what do you base your hope and plans for the future?   5/ How do you usually praise God freely?   6/ Write a song or verse praising God for what you have learned about him.

DAY 21   △   *Exodus 15:22—16:36*

1/ Imagine that you are one of this human mass. Recall the events of the previous days. How do you react in the face of the present situation?   2/ Differentiate the attitudes of *a*—the people and *b*—Moses at Marah. What is God's answer?   3/ What are the conditions of the promise God makes with the people? What right has he to ask so much?   4/ What is Israel's plight in the wilderness of Sin? Whom do they blame? Whom are they really griping against?   5/ When you complain about difficult circumstances, whom are you complaining against?   6/ What instructions accompany God's provision?   7/ Contrast the effects of obedience and disobedience to the detailed instructions.   8/ In what ways have you experienced the Lord's provision? What has been your response?

DAY 22   △   *Exodus 17*

1/ Compare this plight with those of 15:22-25 and 16:1-8 (type of test, reaction of Israel, reaction of the leaders, the answer). Is any progress evidenced?   2/ What point does Moses make clear in verse 2? What is his part in meeting the need?   3/ Describe Israel's first battle with an organized army.   4/ What part do each of the following have in the battle and victory: Joshua and the army? Moses? Aaron and Hur?   5/ What is the significance of God's new revelation to them?   6/ Account for the difference of character of *a*—Israel and *b*—Moses. With whom would you have to identify now?

71

7/ What are you learning from this study that can orient you in developing a right character and attitude toward God?

DAY *23* △ *Exodus 18*
1/ What is the leader Moses' attitude toward his father-in-law? 2/ List the areas of concern Moses covers in his report (v. 8). 3/ When and how have you recently given a spiritual progress report? Do you usually include both hardships and victory honestly? 4/ What is Jethro's response? What does he learn about God from this account? 5/ How have you been convinced of God's greatness? 6/ Imagine the disputes which arise among 600,000 men with their wives and families, uprooted from home traveling through the desert. How are these settled? 7/ What advice does Jethro give? 8/ What kind of men is Moses to choose? 9/ Differentiate the part of *a*—the assistants and *b*—Moses. 10/ Would you meet Jethro's qualifications? 11/ Why would you like men of similar quality over you? 12/ What responsibilities of yours have you delegated to others? Have you been gracious as Moses?

DAY *24* △ *Exodus 19*
1/ Contrast Israel's past status with God's future for them (the eagle flies beneath fledglings to support them if necessary). 2/ What is Israel's part in this agreement? 3/ How does God's goal for Israel relate to his statement *all the earth is mine?* 4/ What has God done for you? 5/ How do the people respond (v. 8)? 6/ What is God's next step? What is Moses' role in this? 7/ List the actions and precautions the people are to take when God speaks with Moses. 8/ Describe the scene the third day (note the positions of *a*—the people and *b*—Moses in relation to God). Imagine their feelings. 9/ What attributes of God's character are demonstrated in this chapter? 10/ Summarize God's activity in this chapter as to *a*— contact with people, *b*—the way he reveals himself, and *c*—the limitations he sets.

DAY *25* △ *Exodus 20*
1/ What right does God have to demand Israel's primary allegiance? 2/ List the next three commandments and God's reason for asking obedience to each (vv. 4-11). What aspect of God's being does each protect? 3/ How do you keep the sabbath day *holy?* 4/ With what relationship do verses 12-17 deal? Which ones concern person-

ality? physical body? possessions?   5/ In what ways have you been thoughtless of the total well-being of parents and other people this week?   6/ How do the people react to this event?   7/ What reason does Moses give for God's action?   8/ What evidence do you see in your life that God is more eager to keep you from sin than you are to avoid it?   9/ Summarize what Israel learns of God's character and nature from this confrontation.   10/ How does this encounter enlarge or change your concept of God?   11 What additional demands does he make concerning worship?   12/ Contrast the content of these commandments with the practices of the surrounding nations.   13/ Briefly summarize the content and principles of *Exodus* so far.

DAY 26 △ *Acts 13:1-3*
1/ Summarize the effects of church growth and the power of the Holy Spirit as related in the first twelve chapters.   2/ Describe the church at Antioch. How similar to this church is your Christian group? What do you do when you get together? What results?   3/ Distinguish the part of God and the part of the church in sending out missionaries. What principles regarding a missionary call do you derive from this?   4/ Is your ministry from the Holy Spirit or one you have thought up?

DAY 27 △ *Acts 13:4-12*
1/ Trace the travels of these men on a map (continue on subsequent days).   2/ How do Paul and his company make their initial contacts in each town?   3/ What do you do with obvious opportunities God gives you? What is your attitude toward telling others about Jesus?   4/ Find at least four evidences that the Holy Spirit is active in the incident with Sergius Paulus and Elymas (cf. the events of vv. 1-3).   5/ When have you been bold for God in a difficult situation? What has happened? How can you have more boldness?

DAY 28 △ *Acts 13:13-41*
1/ Visualize this situation. To whom is Paul speaking? How does his audience affect what he says and how he says it?   2/ Do you keep in mind your listeners' background when speaking of the gospel?   3/ List what this message teaches you about God (underline the verbs in vv. 17-23).   4/ What is the main point of Paul's

sermon? List what facts he gives about Jesus.   5/ What does Paul
mean by *the good news* (v. 32)? Is your message to those about you
good news to them?   6/ What is the content of your message: a
living person or ethics, rules, and religious convictions?   7/ What
place does God's word have in Paul's message? in yours?

DAY 29   △   *Acts 13:42-52*
1/ What are the initial results of Paul's witness in the synagogue
at Antioch? What is the reaction to Paul's message a week later?
Why?   2/ How do Paul and Barnabas answer those who are op-
posing them?   3/ When your gospel witness is reviled, are you
justified in similar actions?   4/ Who decides who will believe the
gospel message (v. 48)? How can this fact encourage you in your
witness today?   5/ What different emotions does the gospel stir up
in Antioch? In what ways are you prepared for these varying responses to your Christian witness?

DAY 30   △   *Acts 14:1-7*
1/ How is Paul's reception at Iconium similar to his reception at
Antioch? What circumstances lead Paul to decide to remain a long
time here?   2/ What is the source of the opposition?   3/ Summarize Paul's message (cf. v. 3—the word of God's grace) as presented in chapter 13.   4/ What specific help does God give Paul
and Barnabas at Iconium? In what ways does the Lord *bear witness*
to your message?   5/ How do the people of the city respond to
the miraculous?   6/ At what point do Paul and Barnabas decide
to leave Iconium? Where do they go? What do they do?

Month 7

DAY 1   △   *Acts 14:8-28*
1/ How does Paul's approach at Lystra differ from his approach at
Antioch and Iconium?   2/ Describe the religion of the people of
Lystra. What do they learn about the one true God this day?   3/
What ideas of God are held by those around you?   4/ Contrast
the attitudes of the people toward the apostles in *a*-verse 18 and *b*-
verse 19. What does this reveal about the psychology of these people?   5/ How important is follow up to Paul? How does he counsel
new Christians (v. 22)? To whom can you give this counsel today?

74

6/ How do Paul and Barnabas provide for the future needs of the believers in Lystra, Iconium, and Antioch (v. 23)? 7/ What is Paul's relation to the Antioch church which has sent them out (cf. 13:1-3)? What principles can you derive from this relationship as to how you and your Christian work should be related to a local church?

DAY 2 △ *Acts 15:1-21*
1/ What is the issue that occasions this conference? Why is this such an important and controversial matter (esp. vv. 1, 5, 10-11)? 2/ Have you ever had a disagreement with anyone over what men must do to be saved? What position have you taken? 3/ How do the apostles and elders arrive at their conclusion? What can you learn from this about handling controversies among believers? 4/ To whom should a local church appeal when it cannot resolve its controversies? To whom does the church at Antioch appeal? 5/ What do the apostles and elders finally decide? 6/ When someone from a background very different from yours becomes a Christian, what do you expect of him? 7/ What do you consider essential to being a Christian? to Christian life and growth? What is the basis for your opinions?

DAY 3 △ *Acts 15:22-35*
1/ How do the apostles and elders carry out their solution to the problem confronting Gentile believers (cf. v. 5)? How well do you implement your decisions? 2/ What kind of men are chosen to take the letter to Antioch? 3/ Does Jesus Christ mean more to you than your life? How do you know? 4/ How is the news received in Antioch? 5/ What are some "burdens" you lay on yourself and other Christians? In what ways have you drifted into a legalism that demands what God has not demanded? 6/ How can the kind of relationship between the churches at Antioch and Jerusalem be fostered in church relations today?

DAY 4 △ *Acts 15:36—16:5*
1/ What causes sharp contention between Paul and Barnabas (cf. 13:13)? What happens? How does God overrule this argument for good? 2/ Why, do you think, do Paul and Barnabas choose to work with someone else rather than alone? Do you have a friend

with whom you work, pray, and share God's workings? If not, can you ask God to give you such a person?   3/ How can you reconcile Paul's action regarding Timothy with the decision of the apostles and elders in chapter 15?

DAY 5   △   *Acts 16:6-10*

1/ What indicates that Luke probably joins Paul at this time?   2/ How is Paul guided to cross over from Asia into Europe with the gospel?   3/ In what ways does God guide you into the right places? Where does he want you today?   4/ What persons of the trinity are mentioned in these verses? What is said about each?   5/ What terms does Luke use in this passage to describe Paul's evangelistic work? Can your Christian testimony truthfully be described by these terms?

DAY 6   △   *Acts 16:11-24*

1/ What kind of place is Philippi? What light does this give to Paul's missionary strategy here?   2/ Contrast the various people the apostle encounters in this city.   3/ Why does Lydia believe Paul's message?   4/ Why do the owners of the slave girl oppose Paul? What charge do they bring against Paul and Silas (cf. with the events of vv. 16-18)?   5/ Contrast Paul's treatment in Philippi with the vision in verse 9. Does doing the will of God necessarily exclude trouble?

DAY 7   △   *Acts 16:25-40*

1/ How do Paul and Silas respond to the discouraging circumstances of verse 22-24? When you think God clearly leads you into a situation, and then everything goes wrong, how do you feel?   2/ Imagine the events of verse 26 taking place at your state penitentiary. What is the result?   3/ Contrast the outcome of Paul and Silas' remaining at the prison with the probable outcome of their escape (cf. esp. v. 28).   4/ How important, do you think, is their conduct in the jailer's conversion?   5/ What do these circumstances and results teach you about the ways of God?   6/ When has God worked in your life similarly to his work in Paul and Silas' experience? How can God advance the gospel through your troubles today?   7/ What encouragement can you find in today's passage (cf. v. 15; 2:39) concerning God's purposes for the unsaved members of your family? Are you praying regularly for those in your family who as yet are not Christians?   8/ What do verses 35-40 teach about a right concern for public reputation?

DAY 8   △   *Acts 17:1-15*

1/ Contrast the attitudes of the Jews in Thessalonica and Beroea toward Paul's teaching. What is his method of teaching? What is the result in both places (follow his correspondence in *1* and *2 Thessalonians*)?   2/ How will the example of the Jews in Beroea affect the frequency and method of your personal Bible study?   3/ What is the basis of your witness to non-Christians?   4/ Who incites opposition? Why?

DAY 9   △   *Acts 17:16-34*

1/What different kinds of people does Paul meet in Athens? What are their interests and beliefs (contrast the Epicurean and Stoic philosophies)?   2/ How does Paul begin his missionary work in this city?   3/ In his sermon at the Areopagus how does Paul move step by step from the Athenian idols to Jesus Christ? What does Paul tell the Athenians that God wants them to do?   4/ At what point and in what ways does Paul's message conflict with Epicurean and Stoic beliefs?   5/ What are common philosophies of life around you? In what ways does the Christian message differ from these?   6/ How much stress do you place on repentance and future judgment in your Christian witness?   7/ What is the result of the message of Christ in Athens?

DAY 10   △   *Acts 18:1-11*

1/ How does God lead Paul in Corinth with regard to housing, activity, and length of stay? What does this teach you about God? about Paul? Do you seek God's guidance in these areas?   2/ What significant change in strategy does Paul make when the Jews of the synagogue oppose his message? What do you do when you meet with continual opposition to the gospel from certain groups?   3/ What does God's counsel to Paul (vv. 9-10) indicate about Paul's feelings toward remaining in Corinth (follow his correspondence in *1* and *2 Corinthians*)   4/ In what ways have you experienced God's protection from opposition? What kind of situation are you in now: much response or little response? How do you know?

DAY *11* △ *Acts 18:12-28*

1/ Of what do the Jews accuse Paul? What is Gallio's response? 2/
Describe Gallio's attitudes and actions as a civil ruler in this instance.
Do you think that government officials today should try to decide
religious controversies? 3/ How much ground does Paul cover
here (keep checking Paul's travels on a map)? 4/ What conditions does Paul place on his promise to return to Ephesus? What
does this reveal about Paul's concept of God? What about your
concept of God do your plans and promises reveal? 5/ What gifts
does Apollos have? How is he using them? What is missing in his
knowledge of the Christian message? 6/ What ministry do Priscilla
and Aquila have to Apollos? What does this interaction reveal about
the early Christians (compare or contrast with your interactions
with other Christians today)? 7/ In what situations are you open
and teachable from the Lord? from other Christians? 8/ What
does Apollos do with his new knowledge? What do you do with the
enlarged understanding you receive about God?

DAY *12* △ *Acts 19:1-10*

1/ Compare the situation of the twelve disciples at Ephesus with
Apollos' situation in 18:24-26. How does Paul explain the true
significance of John's baptism (cf. Luke 3:3-17)? How do these
men show their faith in Jesus? 2/ What evidence is in your life
that you have been *baptized* by the Holy Spirit? 3/ What is Paul's
reaction to stubbornness, disbelief, and slander? 4/ What is the
time span involved? 5/ What steps are you taking now to bring
about a situation in your community similar to verse 10?

DAY *13* △ *Acts 19:11-22*

1/ What extraordinary results does God produce in Ephesus? Why,
do you think, does he work in this way (cf. the superstition, magical
practices, and worship of the moon goddess Diana in Ephesus)? 2/
Of what significance is the incident of verses 14-17 to *a*-the exorcists
and *b*-the people? What does this incident reveal about *a*-Satan and
b-God? 3/ What are some modern counterparts of the Ephesian
superstition and magic? 4/ What difference does being a Christian
make in your practices? In what ways can God use you to rout basic
evils in the culture in which he places you? 5/ What long-range
planning does Paul make in verses 21-22 (follow the unusual circumstances and delays he encounters in the rest of Acts)? What inter-

mediate steps does he take?   6/ What long-range plans do you have for your Christian service? What steps will you need to take to fulfill those plans?

DAY *14*   △   *Acts 19:23-41*
1/ What causes the new wave of opposition? What brings it to an end?   2/ Describe the crowd as to their *a*-zeal for the moon goddess Diana (Artemis), *b*-confusion, *c*-impulsiveness, and *d*-prejudice. Are they different from people you know?   3/ What does this incident reveal about the results of the gospel in society? What observable changes have resulted from the gospel where you have been?

DAY *15*   △   *Acts 20:1-12*
1/ Imagine the fellowship of these Christians traveling together. Where do they go? What do they talk about? pray about? share of fears and joys?   2/ Describe the attitude of the church at Troas toward learning more about the Lord.   3/ In what ways does the occupation of Luke bear on the *a*-veracity and *b*-inclusion of the incident concerning Eutychus?   4/ Imagine the physical strain of Paul's ministry (cf. previous chaps.).   5/ In what ways do you take advantage of the opportunities God gives you for spiritual growth (even when it causes you personal inconvenience)?

DAY *16*   △   *Acts 20:13-38*
1/ Try to capture the vivid picture Paul gives here of his service for Jesus Christ. What does this service involve in terms of his *a*-motivation, *b*-message, *c*-methods, *d*-self image, *e*-trials, and *f*-relationships with people? To what degree is this an accurate description of your service for the Lord?   2/ What can you learn from this passage about the government of a local church?   3/ To what dangers is a local church exposed? What safeguards does Paul present? What are the responsibilities of the elders?   4/How is Paul supported in Ephesus (cf. 18:3; 28:30)? What is his reason?   5/ What is the elders' response to Paul?

DAY *17*   △   *Acts 21:1-6*
1/ What initiative does Paul take at Tyre?   2/ In what ways and for what reasons do you actively seek out other Christians at the place where you work? in your neighborhood? on your campus?   3/ Compare this beach incident with 20:36-37. What qualities of

79

fellowship are revealed? Characterize your relationship with other Christians.

DAY *18* △ *Acts 21:7-16*
1/ How do Paul's friends feel about his going to Jerusalem? Why? 2/ What is Paul's conviction? Why (cf. 19:21; 20:22-24)? 3/ When the advice of Christian friends conflicts with your own conviction, what do you do? 4/ What differing views of suffering and trouble are reflected in this passage? When and in what kind of situations do you usually take the easy way out to bypass unpleasantness?

DAY *19* △ *Acts 21:17-39*
1/ Imagine the growth of the Jerusalem church during the intervening years. What conflict still exists (cf. 15:4-35)? 2/ What results when Paul relates God's workings to the brethren in Jerusalem? What kind of happenings do you share with Christian friends? 3/ What problem do the elders anticipate by Paul's presence in Jerusalem? What counsel do they give (cf. Num. 6:13-21)? What is Paul's response? 4/ Without compromising principle how do you accommodate yourself to the attitudes and convictions of other Christians? 5/ What danger befalls Paul when he takes the advice of the elders (cf. the charge against Stephen in 6:8-15)? What means does God use to save Paul's life?

DAY *20* △ *Acts 21:40—22:29*
1/ Imagine the scene and tension (cf. 21:27-39). Why, do you think, does Paul want to address this crowd instead of accepting the safety of the barracks? 2/ What is the *a*-content and *b*-basis of Paul's defense? What can you learn from this defense about giving a testimony? 3/ How does the crowd respond to Paul's speech? What about their attitudes does the crowd's response reveal? 4/ What are modern counterparts of this situation? 5/ In what situations do you *a*-relate the whole truth of God's message and *b*-leave out unpopular truths in the face of antagonistic opinion? What are the consequences in each situation?

DAY *21* △ *Acts 22:30—23:11*
1/ How does Paul show his willingness to submit to the scriptures? 2/ When do you judge your conduct by the Word of God (even

when those around you are flagrantly violating it)? 3/ How do the Pharisees and Sadducees differ theologically? What is Paul's strategy in raising the question of the resurrection of the dead? 4/ Imagine the uproar of the council. 5/ What special encouragement does God give Paul at this time? In what times of need have you been encouraged by God?

DAY 22 △ *Acts 23:12-35*
1/ How does God rescue Paul from the guerrilla attempt to kill him? 2/ Characterize Paul's nephew. Imagine the family concern for Paul. 3/ What does this incident reveal about a-Paul's reputation, b-the Roman government, and c-God's work in the world? 4/ What is the basis of your confidence amidst turmoil and unrest?

DAY 23 △ *Acts 24:1-27*
1/ List the specific accusations against Paul (cf. v. 5 with v. 2)? 2/ What is Paul's defense? How does he answer each charge? 3/ What is the core of the problem according to Paul? 4/ What concept of Christianity do those around you have from what you a-tell them and b-indicate by your attitude and conduct? 5/ Characterize Felix. What are his responses? his motives?

DAY 24 △ *Acts 25:1-22*
1/ What kind of person is Festus? What fault do Felix and Festus have in common? 2/ What kind of influence is Paul having on the authorities (cf. 9:15-16)? 3/ What are Paul's views of justice? What are yours? 4/ What is the movement toward Rome here? How does Festus present Paul's case to Agrippa? 5/ Imagine you are Paul. What are your feelings now?

DAY 25 △ *Acts 25:23–26:32*
1/ Imagine the contents of Festus' letter to Caesar. 2/ Picture this situation. What is the source of Paul's courage (cf. 23:11)? 2/ Characterize Paul's early life. To what does he ascribe the revolutionary change in his life? 3/ According to Paul what is the real issue of his defense? 4/ What has been your response to your knowledge of God? 5/ Compare the responses of Festus and Agrippa. 6/ In what ways has your knowing God been worth what it has *cost* you?

DAY 26 △ *Acts 27:1-44*

1/ With whom does Paul sail (follow the trip on a map)? 2/ Imagine the weather conditions and frantic measures to keep afloat. 3/ Contrast the reactions of *a*-Paul and *b*-those on board throughout this chapter. What do their reactions show about them? 4/ What kind of influence does Paul have on the ship? Why, do you think? 5/ What do these events reveal about God (esp. vv. 23-24)? 6/ What do your reactions in times of stress and difficulty reveal about your faith in God's control of every situation? How do your reactions affect others?

DAY 27 △ *Acts 28:1-10*

1/ How does God continue to manifest his sovereignty? 2/ Describe Paul's action and character here. In what ways do you try to be observant and helpful in your immediate situations? 3/ Through what means does God provide opportunities for service in Malta? How does Paul serve others here? Imagine Paul's feelings. 4/ What *a*-everyday or occasional contacts and *b*-time do you consider useless or lacking in potential for service opportunities? In what ways can you change this attitude today?

DAY 28 △ *Acts 28:11-22*

1/ Imagine yourself in Paul's situation. What are your feelings as you dock (cf. 19:21)? 2/ What does Paul do when he arrives? 3/ How does Paul's arrival in Rome demonstrate God's faithfulness (cf. 23:11)? Do you really believe that God keeps his promises? What promises are especially relevant to your needs today? 4/ What kind of response does Paul receive from the Jews in Rome? Characterize these Jews.

DAY 29 △ *Acts 28:23-31*

1/ What is Paul's message to the Jews in Rome? What is his authority as he preaches? 2/ In what ways is their response typical? 3/ What does the passage quoted from Isaiah teach about the nature of man? Why don't people understand God's message? 4/ What should you do when your friends and neighbors don't understand? 5/ What does Paul do now that he is living in Rome?

DAY 30 △ *Acts 13—28*

1/ Summarize what Paul accomplishes on each of his missionary

journeys.   2/ What types of *a*-people and *b*-problems does he encounter? What is his influence on the people? How does he deal
with the problems?   3/ Summarize the Jewish-Gentile controversy.
What are Paul's views (follow his arguments in *Galatians*)?   4/
Describe Paul's method of teaching and policy of follow up.   5/
Describe Christianity as presented here. Compare or contrast your
belief and experience.

Month 8

DAY *1* △ *Introduction to Amos*
Amos is from Judah (the southern kingdom) but prophesies to Israel
(the northern kingdom) during the reign of Jeroboam II. Israel is
very prosperous but morally decadent. *Amos 1:1–2:5* 1/ Pinpoint
on a map the seven nations (or their capitals) to which God speaks
words of judgment.   2/ List the sins evoking God's judgment.
What do they have in common?   3/ Imagine the people's feelings
when they hear the doom of the surrounding nations.   4/ What is
Judah's sin? How is it different from that of the other nations?   5/
At what point are you rejecting God's law for your life? Are you
building your life on lies?   6/ How can you see yourself in God's
perspective?

DAY *2* △ *Amos 2:6-16*
1/ How does God's judgment now become personal? Why will God
punish Israel (cf. v. 8 with Ex. 22:26)? Categorize their sins.   2/
How does Israel's sin profane God's name? How does yours?   3/
What are three specific things God has done for Israel?   4/ How
has Israel welcomed God's men (Nazarites) sent to them? How do
you respond to God's messengers today (even if their message ex-
poses your sin)?   5/ What inevitable consequences follow when
a person or group turn away from God?

DAY *3* △ *Amos 3*
1/ What relationship does God have with Israel?   2/ How does
Amos justify his prophesying?   3/ What does God do before he
acts in judgment?   4/ How do you feel when your sin is exposed
in front of people you want to impress?   5/ How will God bring
judgment? Describe its extent.   6/ What do the closing verses

suggest about the affluence and materialism of Israel (cf. 6:4-7)?
7/ What will happen to *a*-Israel's and *b*-your material possessions?

DAY *4* △ *Amos 4*
1/ In addition to the destruction of their cities and homes what
will happen to the people of Israel because of their sin? 2/ To
whom does *cows of Bashan* refer? Imagine your reaction to this description. 3/ What is ironical about the people's actions and God's
attitude toward them in verses 4-5? What are you trying to accomplish through your religious activities? 4/ How has God warned
Israel before its final destruction? What does this reveal about God's
attitude toward his people? 5/ If they refuse the early warnings,
what must they face? 6/ What are God's feelings about punishment and judgment? 7/ What qualities of God's character are
evident from this passage? 8/ How are his character and acts
related?

DAY *5* △ *Amos 5–6*
1/ What two manifestations of God's nature are seen in 5:1-15?
How are they related? 2/ List and explain Israel's sins. What will
be the consequences (esp. 5:16, 27; 6:7)? 3/ Contrast Israel's
feelings of safety and confidence with these consequences. 4/
what makes God hate the religious activities of his people? 5/
What does he want in their lives? How can you show these qualities
in your life today?

DAY *6* △ *Amos 7*
1/ What three visions are given to Amos in verses 1-9? Distinguish
their types of destruction. 2/ How does God respond to Amos'
pleas for mercy? What do these actions reveal about *a*-Amos' and
b-God's character? 3/ What charge does Amaziah the priest bring
against Amos? How does Amos answer the charge? Contrast *a*-
Amaziah's and *b*-God's instructions to Amos. 4/ Imagine the
priest's reaction to Amos' prophecy regarding him. 5/ Why is
God's messenger and message not always cordially welcome in
society (even among religious leaders)? Whom do you usually
heed—God's message and messenger or accepted (but doctrinally
questionable) religious leaders? Why?

DAY 7 △ *Amos 8*
1/What does the vision of summer fruit (which is over-ripe, spoiling) illustrate? What will change? 2/ What motives prompt the sins of verses 4-6? 3/ What kind of famine is predicted in verses 11-12? Is the word of God daily food to your life? What difference would a similar famine today make in your life? 4/ How have you been nourished by the study of *Amos?*

DAY 8 △ *Amos 9*
1/ What is Amos' final vision? What does this vision reveal about the judgment of God? 2/ What will happen after the forthcoming judgment (vv. 11-15)? 3/ What is your hope beyond the destructions of this life? How does your conduct show that you have a hope? 4/ What is revealed in this book about the character of God? 5/ Briefly characterize Amos. Summarize his message. What metaphors does he use to convey his message? 6/ Briefly summarize the moral, socio-economic, and political situation of Israel here.

DAY 9 △ *Introduction to Hosea*
Hosea prophesies from the end of Jeroboam II's rule (741) to 701. The kingdoms of Israel and Judah are divided. He speaks primarily to Israel. The book mirrors the political, social, and religious condition of Israel at the time. *Hosea 1* 1/ List the ways in which Hosea's domestic life portrays the life of the nation of Israel. 2/ How are the children's names significant (cf. 2 Kings 10)? What progression is sketched by the meaning of these names? 3/ What image is portrayed by the last paragraph? What relation do verses 10-11 have to verses 4-8? How can these contrasting images come from the same person?

DAY 10 △ *Hosea 2:1-13*
1/ Make two columns (Hosea—Gomer and God—Israel) to compare Hosea's married life with the life of Israel under God. 2/ Imagine Hosea's (God's) feelings about the developments in his marriage. Why doesn't he plead with Gomer (Israel) directly? 3/ What is his version of the reasons she leaves him? 4/ What action does he plan to take? 5/ In what ways are you like Gomer? 6/ How has God made you realize that life's good things are from him?

DAY *11* △ *Hosea 2:14-23*
1/ How is this section connected with verses 1-13? 2/ List God's
acts of restoration. What is his objective in this restoration? 3/
List the characteristics of God's betrothal. 4/ In what way has
God "courted" you? What are the characteristics of your betrothal
relationship? How do you handle other suitors?

DAY *12* △ *Hosea 3-4*
1/ What has happened to Gomer? What is involved before Hosea
can live with her again? 2/ How does this reunion depict God's
relationship with Israel? with you? 3/ What indictment does God
make about Israel (Ephraim means Israel here)? What is the ex-
tended effect of sin? 4/ How does God diagnose the cause of this
plight? 5/ How are the people's sins related to the priests' sins?
6/ Define *knowledge*. What are you doing to acquire this knowledge?

DAY *13* △ *Hosea 5-6*
1/ List the charges God brings against Israel? What imagery does
he use? 2/ What responsibility do the leaders have for the spiritual
decline? 3/ List the consequences of their sins. 4/ How is God's
judgment rehabilitative? 5/ How does Ephraim react to God's
judgment? 6/ How are you like Ephraim? What can you learn
from their mistakes? 7/ What does this passage reveal about God?
8/ How can you guard against superficial response to God?

DAY *14* △ *Hosea 7-8*
1/ List the metaphors describing Israel. What do they reveal? 2/
What is God's attitude toward Israel? 3/ Why hasn't Israel turned
to him for forgiveness? Account for their blindness. 4/ How do
you guard against blindness to sin?

DAY *15* △ *Hosea 9*
1/ What forms will God's judgment take? How will the people be
affected? 2/ Why does God do this? 3/ How are God's love and
his judgment related? 4/ What do you learn about the seriousness
of sin? What is your attitude toward sin?

DAY *16* △ *Hosea 10*
1/ Describe the reaction of Israel to each of the following national

conditions: prosperity, loss of their king, destruction of their idols, military might.   2/ Why do affluence and military prowess pose threats for the people of God?   3/ How much of your life is aimed at achieving security?   4/ Can God trust you with affluence?

DAY *17* △ *Hosea 11-12*
1/ List the actions of God toward the people. How do they respond? 2/ Describe God's feelings toward them. What confidence does this knowledge of God give to you?   3/ Describe God as judge. Why is his judgment vindictive?   4/ How should this knowledge of God affect your acts of confession of sin?

DAY *18* △ *Hosea 13*
1/ How is Israel described?   2/ Trace the spiritual decline.   3/ Why do they defect?   4/ Why doesn't God offer them another chance?   5/ What are the warnings for you through Israel's example? What are the errors to avoid?

DAY *19* △ *Hosea 14*
1/ What have you expected to read in the last chapter of this book? 2/ What are some characteristics of the repentance to which Hosea calls Israel?   3/ Why does repentance involve specifics as in verse 3?   4/ What is the cause and effect relationship in repentance? Why do men hesitate to return to God in repentance? Why do you? 5/ Resketch the manner in which Hosea's life with Gomer is a reflection of God's relationship with Israel. How do the children's names (and new names) portray the content of the entire book?

DAY *20* △ *Psalm 13*
1/ How many times are first person pronouns used in this psalm? What does this reveal?   2/ What seems to be the psalmist's problem?   3/ For what reasons is he sorrowful?   4/ What does he ask God to do? Why?   5/ Contrast verses 1-2 with verses 5-6. What is the difference in the mood of the psalmist?   6/ What three things characterize David in these two closing verses? What three things characterize God? To what extent can you identify with verses 5-6? 7/ Title this psalm as to content.

DAY *21* △ *Psalm 14*
1/ What kind of person says "There is no God"? How does God re-

gard such a person? 2/ What effects are produced in daily living
by this kind of attitude toward God? 3/ What moral standards is
God looking for? What does he find? 4/ Define *refuge*. For whom
is God a *refuge*? 5/ What does *no knowledge of God* produce?
How has your knowledge of God deepened recently? 6/ What is
the effect of the injustice and corruption on David? What is his hope?
7/ How much of the fool's unauthoritative principle of living in this
psalm fits your experience? 8/ Title this psalm as to content.

DAY 22 △ *Psalm 15*

1/ What relationship is pictured in verse 1? 2/ List and explain
the qualifications for the person who wants to live in fellowship with
God? How can these be real in your life? 3/ What areas of human
experience are included in this list? 4/ What is the godly man's
goal? What is his attitude toward himself? toward others? 5/ By
what single standard does the man who pleases God judge others?
6/ How do you score on this check-list? Where are your problem
areas? What are you going to do about them? when? 7/ Title this
psalm as to content.

DAY 23 △ *Psalm 16*

1/ What is the opening petition? Why is David hopeful? 2/ With
whom does David identify? Why? 3/ What attitudes does he express toward fellow believers? toward the ungodly? 4/ List and
meditate on what he says God does for or means to him. How many
of these do you find real in your life? 5/ What kind of God does
David know and trust? What expressions of assurance grow out of
this knowledge? 6/ On what note does this psalm close? Why?
7/ What threefold progression of mood and thought is revealed in
the psalm? 8/ How does trusting God like this affect you? 9/
Title this psalm as to content.

DAY 24 △ *Psalm 17*

1/ In this prayer distinguish and title David's petitions (vv. 1-5,
6-12, 13-15). What is the basis of each petition? 2/ How does
David describe himself to the Lord? How does he describe God?
the wicked? 3/ What are the contrasting goals of himself and his
enemies? 4/ What does David ask God to do (vv. 13-14)? 5/
Contrast this petition with verse 15. What does this reveal about

David?   6/ How much of verses 1-5 can you make your prayer?
How does your assurance compare with David's in verse 15?   7/
Title this psalm as to content.

DAY 25   △   *Psalm 18:1-24*

1/ What is David's trial (cf. vv. 1-6 with 2 Samuel 22:1-51)?   2/
What things are said of God? To what extent have you found these
descriptions true in your experience?   3/ What chief characteristic
of God is set forth in verses 7-15? Explain the imagery. How do you
describe the characteristic? in your viewpoint is it positive or negative? Why?   4/ In what ways has your experience paralleled the
description of God in verses 16-19?   5/ As a rewarder how does
God act? For what reasons does God deliver David? In what ways
can you identify with David here?

DAY 26   △   *Psalm 18:25-50*

1/ How is the justness of God shown in verses 25-30? What is your
part in the way God acts toward you?   2/ What qualities does God
honor in the man who prays?   3/ List the ways in which God is
described as an enabler in verses 31-45. Which thought in this section is most important to you personally? Why?   4/ What physical
advantages does David have? What does he credit as the source of
these advantages?   5/ What does David emphasize in verses 46-50?
How much of this are you prepared to claim as your experience today? in the days ahead?   6/ Title this psalm as to content (cf. vv.
1-24).

DAY 27   △   *Psalm 19*

1/ What are two sources by which man can receive the knowledge
of God?   2/ What aspects of creation are mentioned in verses 1-6?
What is David attempting to point out here?   3/ How many things
of the Lord are listed in verses 7-10? Where are they all found?
Summarize their purpose.   4/ What is more important than wealth
or luxuries?   5/ In verses 11-13 what is David's chief concern?   6/
What three types of sins are mentioned in these verses? Which of
these do you currently practice? What can you do today to change
that situation?   7/ What are the two aspects of the prayer in verse
14? How can you make it your prayer now?   8/ Title this psalm as
to content.

DAY *28* △ *Psalms 20–21*

1/ What type of situation prompts these psalms? 2/ List the words which show God's positive relationship with the people and king. 3/ What things does David desire? How does he express this desire (cf. 20:4 with 21:2)? 4/ In what ways does God *bless* the king (20:1-7)? 5/ Contrast David's and his enemies' confidence. What is the outcome of each? 6/ How does God deal with his enemies? 7/ In Psalm 21 how does verse 13 relate to verse 1? What is the significance of this relationship? 8/ What do you do when surrounded by trouble? Who is at the center of your plans? 9/ How do you go about getting *victory* in various situations? How does this compare with David's way? What is your response to *victory*? 10/ Title these psalms as to content.

DAY *29* △ *Psalm 22*

1/ What emotional and physical experience prompt the expression of verses 1-2? 2/ What moods of the psalmist are evident? 3/ What is the basis for his belief in God? 4/ Is this psalm primarily negative or positive? Why? 5/ Contrast the beginning and ending. What makes the difference? 6/ What evidences do you find that this psalm has more than only immediate implications? 7/ At what points does this psalm depict your experiences? How? 8/ Title this psalm as to content.

DAY *30* △ *Psalm 23*

1/ Characterize God as a shepherd and host. What areas of life's need are cared for by the shepherd? 2/ What phrases reveal David's attitudes toward God? 3/ What is significant about the use of pronouns? 4/ What is happening in verse 4 when David shifts to direct address? 5/ What time elements are present? What is their significance? 6/ Contrast the *a*-rest and activity, *b*-fear and comfort, *c*-danger and security, and *d*-want and provision. What do these contrasts reveal about God and man? How do they apply in your life? 7/ In what ways is the Lord your shepherd? 8/ Title this psalm as to content.

Month 9

DAY *1* △ *Psalm 24*

1/ To what extent is God sovereign? Why? 2/ What is the essen-

tial question in verse 3 (relate to the characteristics of God in vv.
1-2)?   3/ What standards are included in answer to that question?
4/ What is the historic and spiritual significance of verses 7-10?   5/
What is the major thrust of this psalm? Title the psalm.   6/ Where
does this psalm affect you most penetratingly? Why?   7/ Who is
the *King of glory?* How do you know?

DAY 2 △ *Psalm 25*
1/ List the references which show David's dependence on God.
How does his dependence relate to God's guidance?   2/ To what
qualities of God's character does David appeal?   3/ What does
God do for the humble? for the obedient? Why?   4/ In which category does David place himself? On what basis does he ask for par-
don?   5/ In verses 11-15 what do you learn about the man who
fears God?   6/ Summarize the thought in verses 12-14 and contrast with David's picture of his own need in verses 16-21.   7/
Which of David's words are familiar to your experience?   8/ What
requests does David make of God in the closing verses? Which of
these do you consider most important? Why?   9/ Title this psalm
as to content.

DAY 3 △ *Psalm 26*
1/ What is the dominant theme of this psalm? List the phrases that
relate specifically to this theme.   2/ What picture of David is revealed here? What areas of his life does he include in his defense?
What indicates his recognition of sin and guilt?   3/ How does
David describe the wicked?   4/ What actions and attitudes should
characterize a man of God? In how many of these can you honestly
insert your name?   5/ How can you maintain *integrity* in an evil
society?   6/ Title this psalm as to content.

DAY 4 △ *Psalm 27*
1/ What do you learn about fear from this psalm?   2/ In what
ways is the Lord your *a-light,* *b-salvation,* and *c-stronghold?*   3/
What is the singular desire of David? What do you want more than
anything else this year?   4/ Why does David say he will *sing and
make melody to the Lord?*   5/ Relate verses 7-10 with verse 4.
What is the relationship of verses 11-12 with verses 1-3?   6/ Explain David's optimism in verse 13. What is the relationship between
seeing and *believing* in the Christian life?   7/ What is David's *a-*

admonition and *b*-hope? What do these reveal about his view of God and man?   8/ What have you experienced to verify this relationship?   9/ Title this psalm as to content.

DAY 5   △   *Psalm 28*
1/ What problem does David bring before God?   2/ Why is he so fervent in presenting this problem to God? When do you feel that God is silent—neither listening nor responding to you?   3/ Compare your problems to those David describes. How does David indicate his prayer has been answered?   4/ How has God *heard your voice?* Can you make verses 6-7 your own prayer?   5/ In what ways is the Lord your *a-strength, b-refuge,* and *c-shepherd?*   6/ Title this psalm as to content.

DAY 6   △   *Psalm 29*
1/ Rephrase verses 1-2 so that they constitute a definition of worship. 2/ Trace the course of the storm (vv. 3-9). What qualities of God are revealed in the storm and its aftermath?   3/ Recreate imaginatively the whole picture presented in this psalm.   4/ How does the psalm help you *ascribe to the Lord glory and strength?*   5/ Title this psalm as to content.

DAY 7   △   *Introduction to 1 Thessalonians*
Paul has sent Timothy to bring him reports about the new Christians he has abruptly left (cf. Acts 17:1-9) in Thessalonica. In response to Timothy's news Paul writes this letter to encourage the converts and complete his teaching of Christ's return. *1 Thessalonians 1*   1/ What are the evidences that God has worked in the lives of the Thessalonians? What similar evidences (or lack of them) are in your life?   2/ What specific areas of your relationship with people and with God are you able to describe with *work of faith, labor of love,* and *steadfastness of hope?*   3/ Describe Paul's presentation of the gospel and follow up.   4/ How do the Thessalonians and other people in the area hear about Jesus Christ (compare or contrast with the way people on your campus and in your neighborhood hear about him)?

DAY 8   △   *1 Thessalonians 2:1-16*
1/ List the charges brought against Paul, Silas, and Timothy. How does Paul defend himself and his companions?   2/ What is their

attitude toward preaching the gospel? What is yours?   3/ Characterize the persecuting Jews?   4/ How can Paul and the others preach with joy and perseverance in the face of this persecution (v. 4)? How can you?   5/ What characteristics do Paul and the others show as they work with these new Christians?   6/ What characteristics of your life tend to prevent you from helping young Christians in such a way?

DAY 9   △   *1 Thessalonians 2:17–3:12*

1/ For what reasons is Timothy sent to visit the Thessalonian Christians?   2/ How have the Thessalonians responded to affliction? How have you?   3/ What indications of Paul's concern for them do they receive in this chapter?   4/ What ideas do you see in this chapter about how you can encourage other Christians (esp. those who are away from you)?   5/ What requests does Paul make of God for the Thessalonians?   6/Who are two Christians you can begin to pray for in this way?

DAY 10   △   *1 Thessalonians 4*

1/ What specific instructions does Paul give about God's will? What areas of life are involved?   2/ Which happenings in your life right now (and planned for the future) are in accordance with God's will? Which are not?   3/ How are the Thessalonians to express dynamically their love for others?   4/ How have you experienced God's teaching you to love other Christians recently?   5/ How are *holiness* and *love* related?   6/ What two reasons does Paul give for clarifying the second coming of Christ (vv. 13, 18)? 7/ What will happen to Christians who have died (*fallen asleep*) before Christ returns? those who are alive at the time?   8/ How does Paul substantiate these statements?   9/ Why are these facts an encouragement to you?

DAY 11   △   *1 Thessalonians 5*

1/ How is Christ's return unexpected? imminent?   2/ How are *a*-the Thessalonians and *b*-you to live in the meantime?   3/ Characterize and contrast people of *a-light* and *b-darkness*.   4/ Differentiate the three meanings of *sleep* in verses 1-10.   5/ List Paul's specific directions about responsibility to *a*-others and *b*-God.   6/ How does he remind them of the way in which a Christian becomes holy (vv. 23-24)?   7/ In what instances can you see this taking place in your life?

DAY *12* △ *Introduction to 2 Thessalonians*
In the face of additional misunderstanding Paul clarifies further his teaching about the second coming of Christ. *2 Thessalonians 1*   1/ Why does Paul thank God for the Thessalonians? What in their lives causes Paul to boast about them?   2/ Can anyone observe these things in your life?   3/ To what end does Paul always pray for the Thessalonians? What connection does this prayer have with Christ's return?   4/ Which concerns you most: your growth in Christ or Christ's return to judge the unbeliever? Why? How does this concern affect the way you live?   5/ Contrast the *a*-present and *b*-future final situation of those who *a*-know and *b*-do not know God.   6/ Compare and contrast *a*-Paul's style of writing and *b*-the content of this chapter with the first of *1 Thessalonians*.

DAY *13* △ *2 Thessalonians 2:1-12*
1/ What warning does Paul give the Thessalonians regarding Christ's return? In what ways can you be similarly deceived?   2/ What happenings and attitudes will preceed Christ's return?   3/ Which of these seem to be fulfilled in the Roman Empire? Which seem to be fulfilled today?   4/ How will Jesus' coming *destroy* the *man of lawlessness?*   5/ On what basis will people be condemned?   6/ How will you express the truth today?

DAY *14* △ *2 Thessalonians 2:13–3:5*
1/ Who are responsible for the Thessalonians' belief? In what ways? List what each has done and will do for the Thessalonians.   2/ What direction does Paul want the Thessalonians to take in their faith? On what basis?   3/ On what do you base your faith and belief?

DAY *15* △ *2 Thessalonians 3:6-17*
1/ What problem is discussed here?   2/ What part does jumping to conclusions about Christ's return have in this problem?   3/ What kind of example are you for others?   4/ How does Paul recommend treating a disobedient Christian?   5/ How does the Lord's peace help you in the Christian community?   6/ Summarize

94

what you have learned from 1 and 2 Thessalonians about *a*-Christ's return and *b*-life in the meantime.

DAY *16* △ *Introduction to Joshua*
God chooses Joshua to assume the responsibility which has been Moses'—to lead the Israelites into the promised land of Canaan (cf. Gen. 35:9-12; Deut. 3:23-28; 34:1-9). *Joshua 1* 1/ What promises does God give to Joshua concerning himself? concerning the people of Israel? 2/ What commands does God give Joshua? What does God stress about his law? 3/ What do you learn here about the relationship between obedience and success? about the importance of learning scripture? 4/ Contrast the contemporary view of success with the kind of success promised here. 5/ How does Joshua respond to God's commission? On what basis does he deal with the two and a half tribes (cf. Num. 32:1-32)? 6/ On what condition do the people pledge obedience to Joshua? What fact about Moses is stressed here and throughout the chapter? 7/ How does God's promise to Joshua in verses 5 and 9 apply in your life today? In what situations?

DAY *17* △ *Joshua 2*
1/ Why, do you think, does Joshua send the spies to Jericho? What does this show about Joshua? 2/ What risk does Rahab take in hiding the spies? On what facts does she base her actions? 3/ How does this chapter demonstrate that she acts in faith (esp. v. 11)? 4/ How are facts and faith related in your life? 5/ How does Rahab's faith affect the spies? 6/ How do you expect to see God going before you as he has for Israel?

DAY *18* △ *Joshua 3*
1/ Imagine the thoughts and conversations of the Israelites during the three days encampment by the Jordan River. Imagine you are one of them. How do you feel in this situation? 2/ When does God tell Joshua how the people will cross the river? 3/ What do you learn here about acting and trusting God? 4/ What three things will the people learn from this miracle? What phrase describes the Lord? How is it significant here? 5/ What do you learn about God's promises from this chapter?

DAY *19* △ *Joshua 4*

1/ What is the importance of the stone memorials?   2/ When faced
with difficulty do you remember what God has done for you in past
situations?   3/ How are the day's events significant for Joshua (cf.
1:5; 3:7)?   4/ How do the people go across the river (cf. v. 10)?
Imagine the procession.   5/ What is the significance of the presence
of the ark of the covenant?   6/ What does the timing in verse 18
indicate about the crossing (cf. v. 23)?

DAY *20* △ *Joshua 5*

1/ How does the news of God's actions (chap. 4) affect the surrounding peoples?   2/ For what reason does God command the
renewal of circumcision (cf. Gen. 17:1-4; Ex. 12:48)?   3/ In what
ways does this temporary disablement seem foolish? How has God
prepared the way for it? What do you learn from Joshua at this point?
4/ What about your character is revealed by your response to all of
God's commands?   5/ What does the celebration of the passover,
the celebration of the feast of unleavened bread, and the cessation of
manna mean to Israel at this time?   6/ How is the man (v. 13)
related to the Israelites? How does Joshua respond to him?

DAY *21* △ *Joshua 6*

1/ What is God's promise to Joshua concerning Jericho? Locate this
(and subsequent cities) on a map.   2/ Imagine yourself as *a*-Joshua,
b-a watching soldier on the walls of Jericho, and *c*-a marching Israelite. How do you respond to what is happening? Why?   3/ How is
this battle to be won?   4/ What is the meaning of Jericho being
devoted to the Lord for destruction?   5/ Imagine the effect of deliverance on Rahab and her family. What happens to them?   6/
Compare verse 26 with 1 Kings 16:34.   7/ What do you learn here
about God's word to and through men?

DAY *22* △ *Joshua 7*

1/ What does Joshua do in the face of failure? What are his concerns?   2/ How do you respond to unexpected and demoralizing
failure?   3/ What is the reason for Israel's defeat?   4/ How does
God view one man's sin (cf. v. 11)? What is God's remedy for the
situation? Why is the penalty so severe (cf. 6:18-19; 7:11-12; Ex.
20:17)?   5/ How does Achan's sin affect his family and possessions?

6/ What does this chapter reveal about God's attitude toward sin? What is your attitude toward your sin?

DAY 23 △ *Joshua 8*

1/ What is the plan in this second attack on Ai? Where does Joshua get his strategy? 2/ What is the reason for Israel's victory? 3/ Why does Israel destroy all the people of Ai? 4/ Why does Joshua stop the campaign and build an altar? Compare the events of verses 30-35 with Deuteronomy 11:26-32 and 27:2-26. 5/ What is the place of the law of God in the life of this people? in your life?

DAY 24 △ *Joshua 9*

1/ Why do the Gibeonites devise their plan of deception? Why are the leaders of Israel fooled by them? 2/ What results among the people due to this failure? 3/ When you are a leader, what can you do to avoid this type of mistake? 4/ Why aren't the Gibeonites destroyed as the people of Jericho and Ai have been (cf. vv. 19-20, 24)? What does Joshua do to them? 5/ How do you feel about breaking your word (especially in a similarly deceptive situation)? 6/ Compare or contrast your position before God with the Gibeonites before Joshua. What do you learn from their attitude? 7/ Do you think the Gibeonites' sentence is a curse or a blessing? Why?

DAY 25 △ *Joshua 10*

1/ How is the Ammonites' reaction to the invading Israelites different from the Gibeonites'? Why, do you think, don't the Ammonites attack the Israelites directly? 2/ What does Joshua do when he hears of the attack on Gibeon? 3/ What is your responsibility to other Christians under attack? 4/ Describe the apparent physical condition of the Israelites (cf. v. 9 with 9:17). Where is their confidence placed? 5/ List all that the Lord does for Israel and Gibeon in this battle. Imagine the effect of the victory on the *a*-Gibeonites and *b*-Israelites. 6/ How does Joshua use this situation as a basis for engendering future trust in God? In what ways is God's presence and power in your life today related to your future situations? 7/ Why does Joshua completely destroy the Ammonite kings and people?

DAY 26 △ *Joshua 11-12*

1/ How is Israel's conquest of the north similar to its southern cam-

paign in chapter 10 (locate the lands on a map)?   2/ What underlies God's repeated command to his people, Do not be afraid (cf.
1:9; 8:1; 10:8; 11:6)? How can you be fearless in the face of the
aggression of nations today?   3/ Summarize the victories of Israel
so far.   4/ What is *a*-God's and *b*-the kings' part in coming to battle
with Israel? What is *a*-God's and *b*-the Israelites' part in overcoming
the lands (cf. previous chaps.; Deut. 9:4-5)? What does this indicate about God's relation to the movement of history?

DAY 27   △   *Joshua 13*
1/ What does God point out to Joshua at the beginning of this
chapter?   2/ In what ways do you evaluate your present activities
in view of your goal in life? What do you discover?   3/ What does
God command Joshua to do now? How much of the land is not yet
conquered?   4/ Where is the land allotted to the two and a half
tribes?   5/ Why does God call this land an *inheritance* for Israel
(cf. Gen. 15:12-21; 17:7-8)? What has been the basis for their possession of it all along?   6/ What is the inheritance of Levi (cf.
Num. 18:19-24)?

DAY 28   △   *Joshua 14–15*
1/ By what method is the land divided (cf. 14:2 with Num. 33:54)?
Who is making the decisions?   2/ What is the special request of
Caleb? Why does God give him the request (cf. Num. 14:24)?   3/
What about Caleb's character is revealed by his request? by his subsequent conquest?   4/ Of what tribe is Caleb a member? What
tribe's inheritance, by lot, is his land in?   5/ What do you learn
from these chapters about the promises and providence of God?

DAY 29   △   *Joshua 16–19*
1/ Contrast the attitude of the tribe of Joseph with the attitude of
Caleb (cf. 14:12). How does Joshua answer Ephraim and Manasseh?
2/ What problem does Joshua point out in 18:3 (cf. 15:63; 16:10;
17:12-13; Num. 33:54-56)? What is the people's part to experience
full possession of their inheritance?   3/ What can you learn from
this principle?   4/ What principle underlies the Israelites' acceptance of inheritance by lot?   5/ Of what significance is God's sovereignty in your present situation? in your future?

DAY *30* △ *Joshua 20–21*

1/ Analyze the pattern in 20:1-2, 7-8 and 21:2-3. What is God continually requiring from his people? What does this mean to you? 2/ What is the purpose of the cities of refuge (locate them on a map)? What does the command to establish them show about the nature of God? 3/ From where do the Levites receive their cities and pasture lands? How does this principle apply today? 4/ How many of the cities of refuge are inhabited by Levites? What, do you think, is the reason for this (cf. 18:7a)? 5/ What is the major thought of the writer in looking back over the partition of the land? 6/ In what *a*-past and *b*-recent situations have you experienced God's faithfulness?

Month 10

DAY *1* △ *Joshua 22*

1/ What is Joshua's primary concern for the Israelites who will be living on the other side of the Jordan? With what else is he concerned? 2/ What is the scope of your concern for other Christians? 3/ Why do the eastern tribes build an altar by the Jordan? 4/ To what motive do the other tribes attribute their action? What do the other tribes misunderstand? 5/ What can you learn from this event about your consideration for the actions of others? about your attitude toward those who have misunderstood your actions? 6/ Describe and imagine the religious life of Israel.

DAY *2* △ *Joshua 23*

1/ What is Joshua's first reminder to the leaders of Israel? What fact about God does he again point out to them? 2/ What is God's promise to them? What are the conditions of the promise? Relate these conditions to the previous commands about their method of conquest (cf. 3:5; 6:17-18; chap. 7; 11:12-15). 3/ What attribute of God does Joshua praise in verse 14? How does this attitude of God relate to his promise of judgment? 4/ When you are a leader, what can you do to help insure purity of character in those for whom you are responsible?

DAY *3* △ *Joshua 24*

1/ What does Joshua emphasize in his review of Israel's history in the presence of all the people (cf. Ex. 3:23-33)? 2/ What is the acceptable response he urges on Israel? Underline the verb (used sixteen times). What does this thought indicate about *a*-the Israelites and *b*-your relationship with God? 3/ Why does Joshua refuse to accept the quick response of the people? 4/ What attributes of God does he stress? Summarize the qualities of God and their expression in this book. 5/ How are you affected by these aspects of God's nature? 6/ What does Joshua tell the people about making a covenant with God (cf. 23:15-16)? 7/ Summarize *a*-the quality of Joshua's leadership and *b*-the response of the people in this book.

DAY 4 △ *Introduction to Galatians*

These Gentile Christians (possibly in Derbe, Lystra, Iconium, and Pisidian Antioch in Southern Galatia) have been converted from heathenism during Paul's first missionary journey. Some Jewish Christians are trying to impose the Jewish ritual and moral law on them. Paul is now compelled to write them this vigorous letter (probably A.D. 48-49). 1/ Read through the book at one sitting. 2/ What is Paul's tone in writing? 3/ List briefly the contrasts found throughout the letter between the *gospel of Christ* and the *perverted gospel.* 4/ Which of these qualities in the lists characterize your life? 5/ What is the origin of the gospel Paul preaches?

DAY 5 △ *Galatians 1:1-10*

1/ How does Paul introduce himself? Who is the source of his authority? 2/ What is the relationship of *grace* and *peace* to the things Christ has done for them and you? 3/ To what extent does Paul have confidence in the gospel he preaches? 4/ How can you have a similar certainty in what you believe? 5/ Distinguish what would please *a*-God and *b*-men in this controversy. 6/ Whom do you want to please today?

DAY 6 △ *Galatians 1:11-24*

1/ How has Paul received the gospel (cf. Acts 9:1-19)? 2/ Characterize Paul's life before and after his conversion. 3/ How do the facts of his life substantiate the source of the gospel he now preaches? 4/ For what purpose has God saved Paul? 5/What is God's purpose in saving you and placing you in your present circumstances? 6/ Whom do you know that can be characterized by the statement of verse 24? 7/ How can other people *glorify* God because of you?

DAY 7 △ *Galatians 2:1-10*
1/ How does Paul's account of his contact with the Jerusalem leaders strengthen the case for his independent apostleship? On what grounds do they accept him (cf. 1:1)? 2/ What is the content of the gospel to the circumcised? of the gospel to the uncircumcised? 3/ How would adding circumcision to the gospel make Paul *run in vain* and bring the Gentile Christians into bondage? 4/ Does the gospel you give to others lead them into freedom or bondage? 5/ What additional sphere of service does Peter request Paul to remember? 6/ How can you be concerned with the poor around you?

DAY 8 △ *Galatians 2:11–3:1*
1/ What different ways of thinking do Peter (Cephas) and Paul represent? 2/ What makes Peter change his mind about eating with Gentile Christians (cf. Acts 10:28, 11:1-18)? 3/ How do Peter's actions affect the others? 4/ Why do Paul oppose Peter's change in thinking? 5/ List the two ways of being justified (although Paul condemns the one even as he states it). 6/ In each case on whose action does justification depend? 7/ Which way actually nullifies God's grace and makes Christ's death of no purpose? 8/ Why can't this way ever again be possible to Paul in view of verse 20? 9/ How does this fact explain Paul's action toward Peter and his vigorous judgment of those who present a "different" gospel (cf. 1:6-9)? 10/ Which gospel does your life portray?

DAY 9 △ *Galatians 3:2-9*
1/ On what basis does a person *receive the Spirit*? 2/ When does this happen? Who gives the Spirit? 3/ How does these additions to the gospel contradict the way the Galatians have received the Spirit? 4/ How have you recently tried to perfect your life in Christ (which has begun supernaturally) by some natural means? How is this action foolish? 5/ How had Abraham become righteous? Did he have the law of Moses? 6/ In what way are you a son of Abraham? How is this fact important? 7/ What had Abraham

believed (cf. Gen. 15:1-6)?   8/ What specific promise or commandment is God asking you to believe (act on) today?

DAY *10* △ *Galatians 3:10-14*

1/ Contrast *men of faith* with *all who rely on works of the law.* Which do *a*-the "circumcision party" and *b*-you belong to?   2/ Have you ever broken one of God's laws? What is God's right judgment on you?   3/ Can you erase past guilt by trying harder to obey the law in the present? Whom do you know trying to do this? What is the result?   4/ Does the law justly punish two men for a single act of lawlessness? Who is the guilty party?   5/ Who has brought you out of the curse (punishment) of the law? How? Why?   6/ According to Paul what is the fulfillment of God's promise to Abraham?

DAY *11* △ *Galatians 3:15-18*

1/ Is any condition laid on Abraham to receive the promise (cf. Gen. 15:1-21)? Are any conditions laid on the people (cf. Ex. 19: 3-9)?   2/ Compare and contrast these two events.   3/ How does Paul refute the objection that the law of Moses annuls the promise to Abraham and show the priority of faith?   4/ How do you receive the *inheritance* of salvation?

DAY *12* △ *Galatians 3:19-29*

1/ Underline the references to *a-promise, b-law* (scripture), and *c-faith.*   2/ List what the *law a*-does and *b*-cannot do.   3/ How does Paul answer, *Why then the law?*   4/ Since the *law* does not invalidate *promise,* why is the *law* not antagonistic to *promise?*   5/ List what *faith* does. Compare what *faith* does with what the *law* cannot do.   6/ To whom are all the *promises* of God to Abraham given (v. 16)?   7/How then are these *promises* rightly made available to others, including yourself (v. 27)? (For the meaning of *baptism* as used here cf. Rom. 6:3-11.)   8/ Since the only possible way to become a *son* is through identification with Christ by *faith,* is any social, political, racial, etc. difference among believers able to divide their unity?   9/ How can you display this oneness with other believers in Christ today?

DAY *13* △ *Galatians 4:1-11*

1/ How does Paul illustrate the condition of men before Christ?

Are men still so enslaved today? 2/ List the blessings and privileges which are yours through God's Son being born in this world. 3/ Contrast the former condition of the Galatians with the spiritual wealth they now have in Christ. 4/ In what ways do they act as in their former predicament? 5/ Have you been approached by groups which claim to lead you into new "truth" and new "ways" to gain Christ's benefits? How can you be true to the gospel in the face of this kind of error?

DAY *14* △ *Galatians 4:12-20*
1/ What does this section reveal about the motivation of others who have developed an interest in the Galatians? 2/ What motivates Paul? 3/ Contrast the former and present relations of Paul and the Galatians. What makes the difference? 4/ How does this explain the intensity of Paul's argument in this letter? 5/ What are the tests which Paul uses to check a relationship to determine if it is sound? 6/ Who is concerned about you? How do you respond to them? 7/ Whom are you similarly concerned about? How can you express this concern for them today?

DAY *15* △ *Galatians 4:21—5:1*
1/ How does Paul argue from his opponents' own terms? 2/ Contrast Abraham's two sons and what they represent (cf. Gen. 16:1-3, 15; 17:15-21; 21:1-2, 8-12). 3/ Whom are you like? Why? 4/ To whom does Paul liken the propagators of a different gospel? Why? 5/ List in two columns the contrasting ideas in the allegory. 6/ In what ways does the scripture cited in verse 30 make possible Paul's attitude toward the *false brethren* (cf. 1:7-9)? 7/ What are the responsibilities of being made free in Christ? How will you exercise them today?

DAY *16* △ *Galatians 5:2-12*
1/ What is significant about Paul's reemphasis of who is speaking (cf. 1:1, 11-24)? 2/ Where is the authoritative gospel of the apostles found today? Are you constantly checking the gospel you live by and present to others against this authoritative source? 3/ What are the consequences if someone who has professed justification by faith in Christ now begins to also trust in his own activity to give him acceptance with God? 4/ What contemporary beliefs attempt to add other things to the gospel (cf. 4:8-10) Which do

you find in your life? 5/ Being justified, what is your hope as a believer? How does this fact affect your attitude toward *a*-yourself, *b*-others (esp. non-Christians) and *c*-God? 6/ Contrast the bondage of outward observance with the freedom in Christ Jesus.

DAY *17* △ *Galatians 5:13-24*
1/ What is the freedom to which you have been *called* (cf. 5:1)? 2/ What are the practical limits and responsibilities of this freedom? 3/ Characterize the antithetical ways of living (*flesh* here means the whole personality of man organized for its own ends). 4/ Determine the meaning of each word in both lists. Distinguish which are *a*-Godward, *b*-manward, and *c*-selfward. 5/ How does each list relate to the law? 6/ In what specific areas of your life are you keenly aware of the desires of the flesh? How does your identification with Christ (cf. 2:20; 3:27) relate to these problems? 7/ Distinguish a realistic expectation of human nature from pessimism. 8/ In what particular situation today will you *serve* someone *through love?* How? 9/ How can you *walk* by the Spirit today? in the future?

DAY *18* △ *Galatians 5:25–6:10*
1/ What are the attitudes you must develop toward *a*-yourself and *b*-others if you are to walk by the Spirit (cf. 5:14)? 2/ What is the *law of Christ?* 3/ Explain from their context why verses 2 and 5 are not contradictory. 4/ How can you share *good things* with those who teach you the Bible? 5/ What is the cause and effect relationship of life for man (vv. 7-9)? 6/ Contrast *corruption* with *eternal life* (note the increased yield in both cases). 7/ What will hinder the reaping? 8/ In today's schedule how will you *do good* to some specific individuals?

DAY *19* △ *Galatians 6:11-18*
1/ What are the motives of the false teachers? How are they inconsistent? What do these motives reveal about them? 2/ What motivates Paul? 3/ Instead of circumcision what *marks* does Paul bear? 4/ How has Paul become a new creation (cf. 2:20)? Have you made Paul's statement your own? 5/ Summarize briefly *a*-the important issue at stake here, *b*-the two alternatives, and *c*-Paul's assertions about the issue. 6/ Summarize the marks of a false gospel (cf. 2:21; 3:12; 4:3, 10; 5:4) and the marks of the gospel

of Christ (cf. 1:11-12; 2:20; 3:14, 22, 27-28; 4:6; 5:24). What does the law accomplish in each gospel? How is a person made righteous in each case? 7/ Imagine you are a Galatian in this situation. How do Paul's personal, historical, exegetical, and moral arguments convince you of your error? 8/ How is the gospel of Christ changing your daily life?

DAY 20 △ *Exodus 21*

1/What is the situation in which these laws are given? How have the Israelites gotten here? 2/ Contrast the master–slave relationships here with what you know of the Israelites' position in Egypt. On what basis is the slavery permanent? 3/ List the crimes and misdemeanors in verses 12-35. Which of the commandments in chapter 20 are elaborated here? Which call for capital punishment? for punishment of another nature? Account for the distinction. 4/ Compare verses 15 and 17 with 20:12. Evaluate your attitude toward your parents in view of this standard. Imagine you are an Israelite. Do you expect long life or stand under the death penalty? How can you show *honor* to your parents today? 5/ What is to be the attitude toward the person and possessions of others? 6/ What belonging of someone should you replace because of your misuse or carelessness (cf. vv. 33-34)? 7/ How does knowing God make a difference in your relationships with others? 8/ By what scale of justice do you measure your life?

DAY 21 △ *Exodus 22:1-15*

1/ What penalty is laid out for deliberate theft? 2/ How suitable is this sliding scale? 3/ List the careless acts which are under the law and the penalty for each. How does the penalty differ from that for deliberate theft? 4/ In which is the borrower not held responsible? On what basis? 5/ How can a person prove his innocence? 6/ Is your conduct and attitude toward God such that your word, before God, can establish your innocence? 7/ In this elaboration of the eighth commandment what about the justice of God is reflected in his instruction for the attitude toward that which belongs to others? 8/ Do you have a concern for others that extends to their possessions? In what ways do you fall short of this standard?

DAY 22 △ *Exodus 22:16-31*

1/ Explain the relationship between sexual perversion and spiritual perversion. 2/ In view of pagan fertility rites and sacrifices relate verse 20 specifically to the acts of perversion described in verses 16-19. 3/ How does the attitude toward those in need illustrate the mercy and compassion of God? 4/ What characteristics of God does the penalty for disobedience to these principles illustrate? 5/ Is it possible to love and serve God and be indifferent to the physical needs of others? What can you do about this today? 6/ Measure your attitude toward specific authority against the command in verse 28. 7/ To what areas does the principle developed in verses 29-31 extend for the Israelites? 8/ What object lesson does God use to remind Israel that he is to be absolutely first? 9/ List the things you give to God. How do they relate to your priorities? How are you going to give him first place in the future? 10/ Summarize the quality of life to characterize God's people. How can this quality become a reality in your life?

DAY 23 △ *Exodus 23:1-19*

1/ Summarize the content of each of the specific commands in verses 1-8. 2/ What quality of life is God seeking to develop in his people here? What does this reflect of his own nature? 3/ What characteristics of his nature is God seeking to be evident in his people in verse 9 (cf. 22:21-27)? 4/ What needs do the commands of verses 10-13 meet? 5/ What changes can you make so that a day of rest is a time of renewal instead of frantic activity for you and others? 6/ Recall the original command given to Israel concerning the passover and the purpose of the memorial feast. What other two occasions are they to celebrate? 7/ When and how do you express gratitude to God? 8/ How does verse 19ᵇ relate to harvesting (this is a Canaanite magical technique to produce early rains)? 9/ What do you give God in expenditure of the honest results of your work (cf. his command to Israel here)?

DAY 24 △ *Exodus 23:20-33*

1/ What are the provisional conditions and promises God makes? 2/ What is the reason for the seriousness of God's demand for obedience? 3/ Account for the necessity of driving the pagan tribes out of the land. Why doesn't God get rid of all of them at once and thus eliminate temptation? 4/ What compromises that you have **made** are now a *snare* to you in your full obedience and worship to the Lord? How can you disengage yourself from any of

those which are temporary or non-covenant? 5/ Summarize the
areas in which God will bless Israel if they serve him. 6/ Do you
have any real needs God has not fully met? Relate these to the
extent of your commitment and obedience to him. Have you failed to
meet God's standard or has he reneged on his word?

DAY **25** △ *Exodus 24*
1/ How do the people respond when Moses relays God's message
to them? 2/ How and where is this agreement ratified? 3/ Describe God as seen by the seventy-four leaders. What kind of men
are the leaders (cf. 18:21)? 4/ What is the significance of verse
11 (cf. 19:12-13, 21-22)? 5/ What privilege does God allow
Moses? 6/ How does God's glory appear to the people below? 7/
Contrast the three groups of people mentioned in this chapter as to
a-number, *b*-privilege given, *c*-intimacy with God, and *d*-view of
God from each perspective. Account, if possible, for the difference
between each grouping. 8/ What is your goal as to knowing God?
Compare or contrast your goal with what the three groups in this
chapter know of God. 9/ What areas of your life need to be
brought into obedience to God today to have deepened knowledge
of God?

DAY **26** △ *Exodus 25:1-22*
1/ What command does God give Moses? Who is to participate?
2/ What are the gifts' *a*-variety and *b*-value (cf. 11:2-3; 12:35-36)?
3/ What is the use of these gifts now? 4/ What is the purpose of
the sanctuary? Who is to draw up the blueprint? 5/ Draw a
mental picture of each sanctuary item (continue in subsequent
chapters). Imagine the materials and workmanship. 6/ What is
to be put in the *ark*? What is on top? 7/ What is the purpose and
significance of the ark? 8/ Recount how God has taken the initiative in meeting and speaking with you. Do you seek opportunities
to meet him and to listen to his orders?

DAY **27** △ *Exodus 25:23-40*
1/ Imagine the craftsmanship and delicate detail work in each
piece. 2/ What skills can you use in worship and service to the
Lord? 3/ Determine the significance of *a*-incense, *b*-libation, and
c-bread of the Presence in connection with the *table*. 4/ What
is the source of your nourishment? 5/ What means does God

ordain to illuminate the interior? 6/ What command does God repeat (cf. v. 9)? 7/ To what extent does God govern the specific details of your life?

DAY 28 △ *Exodus 26*
1/ Imagine the workmanship of the *linen curtains*. What are the dimensions? the unifying factors? 2/ What is the relationship of the linen curtains, the goats' hair curtains, and the leather tent? 3/ Contrast the appearance of the tabernacle from the outside (with natural light) to the inside. 4/ What is the balance between beauty and function? Which is most obvious? 5/ How much time do you give to cultivating internal beauty in proportion to external attractiveness? 6/ In observing the physical world what is the balance between beauty and function? In what ways do you reveal an appreciation for God's encompassing protection and the expression of himself in beauty? 7/ Where is the *veil* to be hung? What is its purpose? 8/ Where is the ark located in relation to the veil? to the other furnishings mentioned so far?

DAY 29 △ *Exodus 27*
1/ What is the function of the *altar*? 2/ How often is the command *as it has been shown you on the mountain* repeated in the instructions for the tabernacle? 3/ Compare or contrast this emphasis on obedience to your attitude toward obedience. 4/ Compare the construction of the outer court in size and materials with that of the inner (or holy) places. 5/ What insurance is made for the lamp? Account for the need of continual lighting in the context of the tabernacle construction. 6/ What about the character of God is reflected in the construction and furnishing of the tabernacle?

DAY 30 △ *Exodus 28*
1/ Who are to serve God as priests? Why are they to be dressed differently? 2/ Who is to make this clothing? What is the source of their ability? 3/ Contrast this recorded fact with contemporary opinion about wisdom and ability. 4/ List and describe each garment as to *a*-particular features, *b*-specific reasons or purposes, and *c*-where the garment or special features are worn. From this determine the responsibility given to Aaron. 5/ What is the relation of art and religion? 6/ What are the prerequisites of service as a priest? 7/ What are the consequences of failure to comply

to the details of the instructions? 8/ Is God more lenient in asking for your obedience and allegiance? Are your motives for obeying based on his command or on your feelings at the moment?

Month 11

DAY *1* △ *Exodus 29:1-37*
1/ List each step in the consecration of verses 1-9. 2/ Distinguish the offerings to be made. What is the significance of their order? 3/ Project and imagine the feelings of Aaron and his sons concerning their clothing, the ceremony, and the instructions about the offerings. 4/ Compare the different ways in which Aaron and his sons identify with each offering. Determine the significance of each means of identification in view of the offering. 5/ How have you identified with Christ as your sin offering? 6/ What three parts of Aaron's and his sons' bodies are consecrated with the blood of the second ram? In what order? Why, do you think? 7/ What is to happen to the flesh of the ram of ordination? 8/ How long is the ceremony of atonement and consecration to last? 9/ What special "precaution" is taken with regard to the altar?

DAY *2* △ *Exodus 29:38–30:38*
1/ Describe the *burnt offering* as to *a*-nature of offering, *b*-frequency, and *c*-termination. 2/ What is the purpose of the *tent of meeting*? How is it sanctified? 3/ What is God's promise to Israel and their anticipated response? 4/ On what basis do you know the Lord is your God? In what way does he *dwell* with you? 5/ How often is the *altar of incense* used? When is atonement for it to be made? How? 6/ Describe the census tax. For what is it to be used? 7/ What is the function of the *laver*? What is its significance? What is the penalty for disregarding its function? 8/ Contrast the uses of the *anointing oil* and the *incense*. Determine the significance of each. 9/ What is the penalty for counterfeiting? 10/ How do these objects, functions, and penalties reflect the character of God (cf. v. 10)?

DAY *3* △ *Exodus 31*
1/ Summarize verse 1-11 as to *a*-whom God chooses to do his work, *b*-what "equipment" he gives them, and *c*-what they are to do. 2/ What is the Spirit of God's relation to *artistic design*? What effect

does this have on your evaluation of yourself? of others? 3/ What is your attitude toward physical work? toward those whom God has equipped to work with material things? 4/ What added significance is given to the sabbath (cf. 20:8-11)? 5/ Identify the characteristics in your life which a-reflect God's creative activity and b-uniquely distinguish you as one set apart by the Lord. 6/ What are the two significant factors about the stone tablets? 7/ Imagine you are in Moses' sandals. How highly do you value these tablets for what they represent? 8/ How highly do you view the Bible as the word of God?

DAY 4 △ *Exodus 32:1-14*

1/ How long is Moses away? 2/ Whom do the people look to for leadership? 3/ Contrast their request with God's commands and their commitment six weeks before (cf. 20:3-4; 19:8). 4/ What specific commitments have to be made to God? How long do you remember and practice these solemn promises? 5/ Contrast Aaron's privileged experience six weeks before (24:9-11) with his actions now. How does he try to appease the people? 6/ How do the people respond to his creation? In what further ways does Aaron encourage their sin? What is the significance of verse 5? 7/ How do you respond when God's actions seem delayed? 8/ What are the implications of taking matters into your own hands in your role as a leader or example to others? 9/ What is the Lord's analysis and judgment of this situation? 10/ List the reasons Moses uses in interceding for Israel. What is the basis for his plea? 11/ Analyze Moses' attitude in view of verse 10b. What effect does he have? 12/ Determine the meaning of *repent* and *evil* as used in verse 14. Reconcile this with what you have learned of God's holiness and righteousness. What is the essential meaning of verse 14?

DAY 5 △ *Exodus 32:15-35*

1/ Reconstruct the events when Moses comes down the mountain. 2/ Contrast the attitudes and actions of Moses, Aaron, and the Levites. How does Moses' attitude differ from when the Lord first tells him about the idolatry? 3/ Whom does Moses hold accountable? 4/ What is Aaron's reply? In what ways does his answer differ from the record in verses 1-6? 5/ When called for an account, do you give all the facts (even when they expose your sin)?

6/ What qualities of leadership do you observe in Moses? 7/ In what ways do the Levites prove themselves fit for the service of the Lord? 8/ Having dealt in judgment with the sin, what is Moses' next step? Describe his attitude. 9/ What is God's answer for the people? for Moses? for the future? 10/ What is your attitude toward your sin and its consequences? 11/ Can you intercede with fervency after administering discipline? 12/ Compare the qualities of justice and mercy shown by Moses to illustrate characteristics of God.

DAY *6* △ *Exodus 33*

1/ List the promises in this chapter to *a*-Israel and *b*-Moses. What is the basis or reason for each? 2/ What culminating event finally results in Israel's repentance? 3/ What indicates that they will not soon forget this (vv. 5-6)? Contrast this to the use of ornaments in chapter 32. 4/ What is Moses' regular habit? Who goes with him? 5/ What evidences that he actually meets God there? What kind of relationship exists? 6/ Analyze Moses' conversation with God as to *a*-his requests, *b*-the basis for the requests, and *c*-God's response. 7/ What evidences that Israel is different from other nations and tribes? How is this related to God's sovereignty? 8/ What instructions does the Lord give in answer to Moses' last bold request? Why can't Moses see God's *face*? 9/ Characterize your relationship with God. Are you more concerned with knowing him or receiving from him? What are the effects of your attitude in your life? 10/What steps will you take today toward an intimate friendship?

DAY *7* △ *Exodus 34*

1/ What further preparations is Moses to make for this summit conference? 2/ To determine the meaning of *the Lord . . . proclaimed the name of the Lord* (v. 5) enumerate the characteristics which he describes. 3/ Distinguish the meaning of each. 4/ What is Moses' immediate reaction? Contrast his prayer of verse 9 with his previous demands (33:12-18). Account for his changed attitude. 5/ Compare verses 9-10 to determine Moses' request and the Lord's response. Which of the Lord's attributes (vv. 6-7) do these illustrate? 6/ What are the terms of the covenant (vv. 10-11)? 7/ Though God forgives sin, does this imply lowered or altered standards? 8/ List the essence of each command in verses 11-26. 9/ What priority is to be given to God in worship? in work? in rest? 10/ What

111

is the effect of this summit conference as far as *a*-God, *b*-Moses, and *c*-the people are concerned?   11/ In what ways do people around you know you have been with God?   12/ List the specific differences you have experienced in your life because of knowing God intimately.

DAY 8 △ *Exodus 35*

1/ Compare this emphasis on the sabbath with 20:8; 23:12; 31:12-17; and 34:21. What are the reasons given? Describe the relationship to the context for each.   2/ In view of this command in the context of the building of the tabernacle (even work dedicated to the Lord is stopped—lighting fires) what emphasis, do you think, should you place on a day of rest?   3/ List the items for which Moses requests materials. Does he omit anything concerning the Lord's command (cf. 25:2-7)?   4/ In verses 20-29 list the indications of motivation for giving.   5/ What motivates you to give: legalism? rivalry with others? pressure? tax advantages? needs of others? the Spirit of the Lord?   6/ What do you give?   7/ What is the important difference in verses 30-35 from 31:1-11?   8/ How does this affect the scope of your work? all work?

DAY 9 △ *Exodus 36:1–39:31*

1/ What command does Moses give? Why?   2/ Begin a sketch of the tabernacle as it is built. List the order of construction.   3/ What is the significance of the purposes of the furniture and priestly garb to the tabernacle?   4/ Imagine the weight and size of the completed structure. What features are built into it for mobility (e.g. 36:8-9, 20-22; 37:1-5)? for solidarity (cf. 38:27-31)?   5/ Underline every evidence of obedience to the blueprint and patterns.   6/ How does this reflect Moses' ability to communicate?   7/ Do you give God haphazard service or full obedience in details?

DAY 10 △ *Exodus 39:42–40:38*

1/ Underline all references to obedience.   2/ What evidences that Moses approves of the finished construction (39:43)?   3/ What is the time lapse between the erection of the tabernacle and the beginning of worship in it (40:1, 17)?   4/ Distinguish the logical order of erecting and furnishing the tabernacle (cf. 40:1-8, 18-33).   5/ Is your life characterized by disorder and impatience or by orderliness and the ability to wait?   6/ Cite the evidence of God's approval. 7/ How is the center of worship related to further guidance? Compare 40:36-38 with 33:14 to determine the fulfillment of promise. 8/ Who do you look to for guidance?

DAY *11* △ *Exodus 1–40*
1/ Trace Moses' development as a leader. 2/ What characteristics that you have observed in him will you incorporate in your life? 3/ What aspects of God's promises in 6:5-8 have been fulfilled? What are yet unfulfilled? 5/ Contrast the status of Israel prior to 19:1-6 with their identity and development as a nation thereafter. 6/ What is the place of the law? of worship? Account for the activity of God in this development from slaves to a holy nation. 7/ What are the main emphases of this book concerning the character of God? 8/ In what ways has your view of God been altered or enlarged? What effect does this have on your view of the kind of person you should and want to be? 9/ What principles or applications have you incorporated into your life? What additional steps of obedience do you need to take?

DAY *12* △ *Introduction to Romans*
Paul writes this letter to the church at Rome (which he has never as yet visited) while in Corinth on his third missionary journey. He introduces himself and gives a detailed explanation of the gospel. His desire to visit the center of the empire is fulfilled three years later when he arrives as a prisoner (cf. Acts 28:16-31). *Romans 1:1-7*
1/ In what way does Paul introduce himself? What does this description reveal about his view of himself? 2/ Characterize the recipients of the letter. Imagine how they (as a despised minority) respond to the fact that they are *called* and *beloved.* 3/ How do you respond to these facts? 4/ Describe the gospel as to its *a*-origin, *b*-content, *c*-power, *d*-proclamation, and *e*-destination. 5/ How should these facts affect your attitude toward the Old Testament? toward missions? 6/ What periods in Christ's life does Paul emphasize? How does each show that Christ is the *a*-center of the gospel and *b*-stimulus for proclaiming it?

DAY *13* △ *Romans 1:8-15*
1/ Describe Paul's attitude toward the Roman Christians. 2/ For what reasons does he want to visit them? 3/ What is the content of his prayers about them? 4/ What Christian can you pray for in

this way?   5/ What claims does Paul make? Why should this educated, cultured man consider himself *under obligation* to all men?
6/ Contrast or compare his attitude with your present attitude. What
types of people do you exclude from these categories?

DAY *14*   △   *Romans 1:16-17*

1/ List the facts about the gospel (cf. vv. 1-6, 15).   2/ What is
the significance of *for* in verses 16—17?   3/ Relate the first phrase
of verse 16 with the situation in Rome.   4/ Why is the gospel powerful? How is its power released?   5/ How is *faith* related to *salvation* and the *righteousness of God*?   6/ What is different about living by *faith* rather than by *a*-sight, *b*-works, or *c*-feelings?

DAY *15*   △   *Romans 1:18-23*

1/ How are God's *righteousness* (v. 17) and his *wrath* (v. 18) related?   2/ What actions of man prompt God's wrath?   3/ Characterize man's sin from *a*-what he chooses not to do and *b*-what he
does instead.   4/ How do these actions affect man's intellectual and
spiritual life? In what ways are the actions *foolish*?   5/ Why is every
man (even those in primitive societies) *without excuse*?   6/ To
what extent are you honoring God as God and being thankful?   7/
What form does idolatry take for you today?

DAY *16*   △   *Romans 1:24-32*

1/ How is God's repeated action (vv. 24, 26, 28) related to the
expression of wrath in verse 18?   2/ How is being allowed to have
your own way a punishment?   3/ How does man react to being
given up?   4/ Group the sins in verses 29-31 under *a*-*base mind*
and *b*-*improper conduct*. In what ways does this list differ from what
today's society considers sins?   5/ Why, do you think, are no de-
grees of sin given?   6/ From what do all these sins stem (cf. vv.
21, 25, 28, 32)?   7/ How does Paul show that these sins are *a*-cal-
culated and *b*-propagated?

DAY *17*   △   *Romans 2:1-11*

1/ Of what does Paul accuse the Jews who have the revelation of
God's law?   2/ What is Paul trying to clarify by his three questions
in verses 3—4?   3/ What should be the response to God's kindness
and patience?   4/ Contrast the *riches* (v. 4) with what is *stored up*
(v. 5).   5/ Describe God's judgment.   6/ Upon what will men be

judged? What changes do you need to make in your life in view of
the basis of judgment?

DAY *18* △ *Romans 2:12-16*
1/ On what basis will God judge the Jews who have the law? 2/
How will he judge the Gentiles who have no written law? Where is
their *law*? 3/ Further describe God's judgment (cf. vv. 1-11).
4/ Contrast God's judgment with man's judgment (v. 1). 5/ What
is your prayer today to this judge?

DAY *19* △ *Romans 2:17-29*
1/ For what reasons do the Jews compliment themselves? 2/ Of
what does Paul accuse them? 3/ How have they *blasphemed* God's
name? How have you? 4/ In what ways does the accusation of
verses 17-24 fit you and your Christian group? 5/ What is required
of the Jews if their outward religious symbol (circumcision) is to
have meaning? 6/ What will give meaning to your outward religious performance? 7/ Whose praise do you seek?

DAY *20* △ *Romans 3:1-18*
1/ What objections to his condemnation of Jewish "righteousness"
(in chap. 2) does Paul anticipate (vv. 1, 3, 5, 7-8)? 2/ How does
Paul answer each objection briefly? 3/ What attributes of God
remain unchanged? 4/ To what kind of people do you feel superior due to your specific advantages? 5/ By using Old Testament
quotations how does Paul verify his contention about all men in verse
9? 6/ From the quotations characterize man as to his *a*-attitudes,
b-direction, *c*-speech, and *d*-pursuits. 7/ Where do you fit into this
characterization? 8/ Compare these quotations with the picture
of man in 1:18-32.

DAY *21* △ *Romans 3:19-20*
1/ All of the above brings Paul to what conclusions about the purpose of the law? 2/ Who is included in those held accountable
before God? 3/ Determine the meaning of *justification*. 4/ What
way of justification is blocked in verse 20? 5/ What function does
the law have? 6/ Why is it impossible for you to be justified before God by your own efforts?

DAY 22 △ *Romans 3:21-31*
1/ Since legal obedience cannot make man acceptable to God, what will? 2/ How has 1:18–3:18 prepared you to consider God's way of righteousness? 3/ List and explain what is involved in God's way of righteousness. 4/ Who takes the initiative in providing a way to be justified? 5/ On what conditions is a person justified? 6/ In view of God's way of righteousness what happens to your pride and boasting? Why?

DAY 23 △ *Romans 4:1-12*
1/ What possible reaction to chapter 3 does Paul anticipate from his Jewish readers? 2/ How does Abraham receive right standing with God (cf. Paul's arguments in Gal. 3:6-18; 4:21-31)? 3/ Why can't Abraham boast before God or *claim his due*? 4/ When is he reckoned righteous (cf. Gen. 15; 17)? By whom? On what basis? 5/ What is the significance of circumcision in his life? 6/ Who are the children of Abraham? 7/ How does this way of righteousness affect your attitude toward God? toward good works?

DAY 24 △ *Romans 4:13-25*
1/ To whom is the *promise* (cf. Gen. 12:1-3, 7) made? On what does it depend? Why? 2/ From verses 18-25 list the five ways Abraham reacts to God's promise (cf. Gen. 15; 17). 3/ What circumstances are "incredible"? 4/ In what ways and situations do you *believe* in spite of circumstances? 5/ What is the result of Abraham's faith in an "incredible" promise? 6/ Compare what *a*-Abraham (v. 17b) and *b*-you (v. 24) have to believe about God to be righteous. 7/ What is the purpose of Jesus' death and resurrection? 8/ What about Abraham's faith needs to be true of your faith?

DAY 25 △ *Romans 5:1-11*
1/ List the consequences of justification by faith (by Christ's blood, death, and life). Which concern God's legal requirements? your life on earth? 2/ In what three things are you to rejoice? What has caused you to rejoice recently? What have been the results? 3/ Trace the progression and results of suffering. 4/ Contrast the Christian's past (vv. 6, 8, 10) with his present and future (vv. 9-11). 5/ How is God's love related to each needed change? 6/ How is

the security of a Christian related to *much more* in verses 9-10?   7/
How can you worship God for his love to you today?

DAY *26* △ *Romans 5:12-21*
1/ What do you learn here about sin and death? Which comes first?
With what effects?   2/ List the contrasts between Adam and Christ
as representatives of the human race.   3/ What is the *free gift?*
4/ What are the results of Adam's trespass and Christ's free gift?
5/ Summarize the effect of the law on sin (cf. vv. 13, 20 with 3:19-
20).   6/ How is God's grace *much more* than a match for sin?
7/ How can you move from the *reign of sin and death* to the *reign
of life?*

DAY *27* △ *Romans 6:1-11*
1/ What is the theme of this section?   2/ What experiences have
all Christians shared with Christ? With what results?   3/ In what
ways do you exploit God's grace? Why?   4/ What does the Christian *know* in verses 9-11?   5/ What is he to do in view of this
knowledge?   6/ What difference does this fact make in your attitude and action toward sin and temptation in your life?

DAY *28* △ *Romans 6:12-23*
1/ In order to live consistent with his position in Christ what must
a Christian do? not do?   2/ What role does your will have in de-
ciding what has dominion over you?   3/ In what ways will you
yield your members (physical and mental) today? How will this act
affect you? others?   4/ Contrast the two possible *masters* a person
can choose. What are the consequences of each slavery?   5/ How
does *yielding* relate to the fact of *belonging* (as in the master—slave
relationship)?   6/ Describe the past, present, and future of the
Christian.   7/ How is *sanctification* obtained (vv. 17, 19, 22-23)?
8/ How does verse 23 show that sanctification does not earn eternal
life?

DAY *29* △ *Romans 7:1-6*
1/ What analogy does Paul use to show the Christian's relationship
to the law?   2/ How does a person get free from the demands of
the law?   3/ Summarize the point of the illustration in verses 2-3.
4/ What application does Paul make in verse 4?   5/ What new
relationship is established?   6/ Contrast the *fruit* of the past and

117

present.   7/ Compare or contrast the fruit you *bear* with 6:10, 13, 17, and 19.

DAY *30*   △   *Romans 7:7-13*
1/ How does Paul show that the law and sin are not identical? How are they related?   2/ What is the purpose of the law?   3/ What does the law reveal to *a*-Paul and *b*-you?   4/ How do you react to prohibitions?   5/ How is sin personified?   6/ What effects does sin produce in *a*-Paul's and *b*-your life?   7/ Paraphrase the conclusion about sin in verse 13.   8/ How does this passage show that you do not attain holy living by trying to keep rules?

Month 12

DAY *1*   △   *Romans 7:14-25*
1/ What paradox does Paul experience (cf. Gal. 5:17)? Which force does he find stronger in his life?   2/ List what Paul *a*-can and *b*-cannot do. Relate verse 24 to this predicament.   3/ When do you experience this personal paradox? Why?   4/ Distinguish the two types of *law* here.   5/ What *a*-explanations and *b*-answer does Paul find to his struggle to please God by keeping the law of God?   6/ To what extent are you responsible for your actions?   7/ By what means are you trying to live pleasing to God? With what results?

DAY *2*   △   *Romans 8:1-11*
1/ How does Paul summarize his letter so far? On what relationship is this based?   2/ What reasons does Paul give in verses 2-4 for his confidence in verse 1?   3/ How can you be delivered from the struggle summarized in 7:14-25?   4/ List the contrasts between the two kinds of living in verses 4b-8.   5/ In verses 9-11 which of the two groups are addressed?   6/ What facts about them are true now? in the future?   7/ On what condition can these promises be yours?   8/ What do your actions reveal to people around you about your identification with one of the groups?

DAY *3*   △   *Romans 8:12-17*
1/ From verses 12-17 add to yesterday's list of facts about the two kind of living.   2/ Relate *put to death* (v. 13) to *set the mind* (vv. 4b-7) and *consider* and *yield* (6:11-13).   3/ Who empowers the Christian to live a holy life? to realize his relationship with God?

4/ Relate your relationship with God to the Roman custom of adoption (cf. Gal. 4:1-7).   5/ Contrast the two *spirits* in verse 15.   6/ List what each Christian has in common with Jesus Christ.   7/ To what extent are you enjoying these *a*-responsibilities and *b*-privileges of the Christian life?

DAY 4   △   *Romans 8:18-25*

1/ How do these verses compliment 5:2-5?   2/ How are *suffering* and *glory* related (cf. v. 17)?   3/ What is the glory to be revealed? 4/ What conditions of *a*-creation and *b*-Christians are described here? What is each awaiting?   5/ How are the outcomes in verses 21 and 23 related?   6/ How is the presence of the Holy Spirit in your life related to the coming glory?   7/ In what ways is *hope* as much a part of the Christian life as faith?   8/ For what reasons do you have hope regardless of circumstances?

DAY 5   △   *Romans 8:26-30*

1/ What else does the Spirit do for Christians (cf. v. 23)?   2/ What are the characteristics of the Spirit's prayers?   3/ How can they strengthen your prayer life?   4/ What additional assurance can you have in the face of suffering? What is *a*-God's and *b*-your part in that assurance?   5/ To what extent is God's goodness at work in the lives and circumstances of his people?   6/ Trace the progression of God's dealing with every Christian.   7/ What is his purpose in calling you? Relate this purpose to 5:2 and 8:18.   8/ How are you responding to God's high purposes for you?

DAY 6   △   *Romans 8:31-39*

1/ How does this section give perspective to Paul's previous development of God's grace and man's suffering?   2/ What are specific evidences of God's love?   3/ What does verse 34 reveal about the person and work of Jesus Christ?   4/ Over what kinds of situations can the Christian be victorious? How may he *conquer?*   5/ How does the list of powers in verses 38-39 begin similar to but far exceed the list in verses 35-36?   6/ List the problems and obstacles that cause you to despair and suffer. What is the basis of your confidence for victory over these and circumstances of any kind? How dependable are your resources?

DAY 7 △ *Romans 1–8*

1/ Summarize the ways man is estranged from God.   2/ Summarize the reasons *a*-pagans (1:18-32), *b*-moralists (2:1-16), *c*-Jews (2:17—3:8), and *d*-you are inexcusable in rejecting God.   3/ Summarize how *a*-Old Testament patriarchs, *b*-Jews, *c*-Gentiles, and *d*-you can have right standing with God.   4/ List the before and after characteristics in your life.   5/ In what ways are you free from *a*-sin, *b*-the law, and *c*-death? How do these facts affect your daily living?

DAY 8 △ *Romans 9:1-5*

1/ In what ways does Paul establish his veracity? How does this relate to a possible misunderstanding as to Paul's attitude toward Jews (cf. previous chaps.)?   2/ What is the extent of Paul's concern for the Jews (cf. the meaning of *accursed* in Gal. 1:8-9; Josh. 6:17)?   3/ What concern do you have for the truthfulness of what you say? for those around you who have a mistaken idea about their relationship with God?   4/ What heritage belongs to the Jews (cf. Ex. 4:22, 19:16—21:1; 40:34-38)?   5/ How is Christ related to the Jews? supracultural?

DAY 9 △ *Romans 9:6-13*

1/ Why is the faithfulness of God's word not affected by Israel's unbelief?   2/ Who are the true descendants of Abraham (cf. 4:18-24; Gal. 3:29)?   3/ Who are the children of God? How do they become God's children?   4/ To whom are the promises given (cf. 4:12-13)?   5/ What principle is illustrated by Jacob and Esau?   6/ What is God's attitude toward you? What is your response to him?   7/ In what ways is God's *hate* different from man's hate?

DAY 10 △ *Romans 9:14-24*

1/ What objections does Paul anticipate to his statements in *a*-verses 6-13 and *b*-verse 18?   2/ How does he answer them?   3/ Does God exist for man's purposes or vice versa? How does this relate to ultimate authority and God's will?   4/ How is God's *mercy* based on his sovereignty?   5/ What are God's sovereign rights over men as sinners? To what purpose does God use them and their acts?   6/ How does Paul illustrate God's rights over all men?   7/ What is the significance to you to know you can't "make" God be merciful to you?   8/ In what ways do you respond to God's *a*-mercy and *b*-authority?

DAY *11* △ *Romans 9:25-33*

1/ In what way does Paul apply Hosea's words to the Gentiles (cf. Hos. 1:2-11; 2:23)? How do they relate to the attributes of God as revealed in verses 6-24? 2/ How does Paul apply Isaiah's words to the previous statements about Israel (esp. v. 6)? 3/ What is the relation of human responsibility to the sovereignty of God? 4/ What is the ironical situation concerning Jews and Gentiles? Why? 5/ What are two responses to the *rock?* With which do you identify now? With what results?

DAY *12* △ *Romans 10:1-10*

1/ Recall Paul's attitude for his *brethren* in chapter 9 (vv. 1-3). What is his action here? 2/ Determine what will *enlighten* the Jews' zeal. 3/ What people that you know have a similar ignorance of the way to attain righteousness? What can you do about it? 4/ Contrast the judgment of ignorance here with the contemporary popular opinion concerning responsibility when ignorant. 5/ Distinguish the two types of *righteousness* here. 6/ Where is true righteousness found? Contrast this with the extremes of verses 6-7. 7/ In what way do these questions (vv. 6-7) reflect unbelief? 8/ What must a person do to be *saved?* 9/ In what ways does the *a*-confession and *b*-belief relate to the unbelief in verses 6-7? 10/ How are confession and belief related in your life?

DAY *13* △ *Romans 10:11-17*

1/ What is the reason God justifies Jews and Gentiles in the same way (cf. 3:29-30)? 2/ How does Paul confirm this principle from the Old Testament (cf. Gen. 12:8; 21:33; 26:25)? 3/ What is involved in to *call upon the name of the Lord?* Can belief exist in a vacuum? 4/ What is the content of what must be preached? Is this the content of your message? Why? 5/ What is your attitude toward those who do not *heed* the gospel (cf. Paul's concern in v. 1; 9:1-3)?

DAY *14* △ *Romans 10:18-21*

1/ How does Paul show that hearing does not produce faith? 2/ How are faith and hearing related in your life (cf. v. 17)? 3/ To what extent is the gospel *heard* (cf. 1:19-20; Ps. 19)? 4/ What happens to Israel because of the extent of the gospel (v. 19)? To what extent does Israel *know* this is going to happen? 5/ Contrast

God's attitude toward the *a*-Gentiles (cf. 9:30) and *b*-Jews with Israel's attitude toward God (cf. 10:2). 6/ What is your attitude toward God? Why? 7/ What qualities of God are revealed by Isaiah's quotes? 8/ Summarize Paul's method in showing that Israel is inexcusable.

DAY 15 △ *Romans 11:1-6*
1/ What is a mistaken conclusion to the theme of chapter 10? 2/ In what ways does *a*-Paul's identity as a Jew, *b*-God's *foreknowledge* (cf. 9:6-13), and *c*-Elijah's experience (cf. 1 Kings 19:10, 14, 17-18) show that this conclusion is mistaken? 3/ What is God's action on the part of the *remnant* (cf. 9:27) of seven thousand men? 4/ Characterize God's *grace*. How is it antithetical to works (cf. 9:11)? 5/ What is your response to this God of grace?

DAY 16 △ *Romans 11:7-16*
1/ All of the above brings Paul to what summary? 2/ To which group do you belong? How do you know? 3/ How do the Old Testament quotations support verse 7? 4/ What are the normal and right functions and intent of *eyes, ears,* and *feasts* (cf. Ps. 69:22-23)? 5/ How are these functions and intents reversed? For whom? 6/ Compare this characterization of Israel with the attitudes and activities of the Jews Paul encounters during his travels in *Acts.* 7/ What are God's purposes through the stumbling (v. 11) and rejection (v. 15) of Israel? 8/ How does the Jews' *full inclusion* relate to their *trespass* and *failure*? 9/ Why does Paul want to make the Jews *jealous?* 10/ Who are the *first fruits* and *root* (cf. v. 28)? What is their effect on Israel? 11/ Is God's rejection of Israel total? final? 12/ What qualities of God are revealed here?

DAY 17 △ *Romans 11:17-24*
1/ How does Paul illustrate his statements about Israel? 2/ Who are the *root* and *natural branches?* What has happened to some of the branches? Why? 3/ Who are the *wild shoots?* What is done to them? Why? 4/ What is the correct attitude of those identified by the wild shoots? Why? 5/ In what ways can the original process in Paul's analogy be reversed? 6/ How are God's *kindness, severity,* and *power* related? 7/ What is your attitude toward your part in God's plan? Why?

DAY *18* △ *Romans 11:25-36*

1/ What is God's *mystery* concerning Jews and Gentiles? 2/ Determine the meaning of *all* in verse 26 (cf. vv. 12, 15, 23-24). 3/ What is the status of the Gentiles before God's mercy? 4/ What is the status of the Jews as Paul writes? in the future? 5/ How does Paul use Isaiah's (59:20-21) and Jeremiah's (31:33-34) words to support the truth of the future status of Israel? 6/ What is your attitude toward Old Testament scripture (cf. Paul's attitude here and in previous chaps.)? 7/ How can the Jews be both *enemies* and *beloved* at the same time? 8/ What is the relation of the disobedience of Israel to God's mercy to the Gentiles? of the disobedience of the Gentiles to God's mercy to the Jews? 9/ What is the only context in which *mercy* can have meaning? 10/ In what ways are verses 33-36 a fitting summary of the facts about Jews and Gentiles in chapters 9-11? 11/ In what ways will you share your knowledge of God's *mystery* with others today? in the future?

DAY *19* △ *Romans 12:1-8*

1/ How does Paul's appeal relate to the new status you have in Christ (cf. 6:1–7:6)? 2/ What commands relate to the body? to the mind? What is the standard? 3/ What disciplines are you exercising to renew your body and mind? 4/ How is this in contrast to the pattern of the world? 5/ What are the areas of diversity among Christians? 6/ Describe the kind of attitude Paul asks for among Christians in view of these diversities. 7/ In what way is an underestimate of abilities as critical as an overestimate? 8/ List and explain the different gifts mentioned here. 9/ What function and gifts do you have? 10/ How can you show today that you are a member of *a*-the body of Christ and *b*-one another?

DAY *20* △ *Romans 12:9-21*

1/ Categorize and explain these exhortations. What main ideas are expressed and emphasized? 2/ How are these exhortations a logical outgrowth of verses 1-2? 3/ Compare or contrast these exhortations with your present ethics. 4/ Imagine the effect of obeying them. What would be the specific results in your life? in your group? with other people? 5/ How will you obey them today?

DAY *21* △ *Romans 13:1-7*

1/ What are your obligations to civil authorities (relate to 12:2)?

2/ Determine the meaning of *subject*. Why must a person be subject? 3/ Determine the meaning of *governing*. How does this relate to revolutions? 4/ In what ways are authorities an extension of God's authority in relation to men? 5/ When does a person have reason to fear rulers? 6/ In what specific ways do you try to "get around" your obligations? Why? What effects do these actions have on your conscience toward God? 7/ What is the basis of criminal retribution? Contrast this with contemporary popular opinion about the priority of the criminal's welfare. 8/ Imagine you are in the place of authority. As a result of understanding these principles what is your attitude toward *a*-God, *b*-your authority, *c*-those who are *subject* to you? 9/ What attitude, do you think, should a Christian have if he is being punished when he believes he is right?

DAY 22 △ *Romans 13:8-14*
1/ How is love related to justice (cf. vv. 1-7)? to the law? 2/ In what ways does love enable you to fulfill obligations to others? 3/ Characterize this kind of *love*. If man truly loved like this, would any commandment ever be broken? Why, do you think? 4/ How will you *love your neighbor as yourself* today? In what specific ways? 5/ What is another reason for fulfilling your obligations to others? In what way does Paul picture your realization of this fact? 6/ Characterize the attitudes and actions belonging to *a-darkness* and *night* and *b-light* and *day* (cf. 6:1-10). 7/ Categorize your present ethics and behavior under these headings. 8/ What is Paul's command concerning these attitudes and actions? What is your response to that command?

DAY 23 △ *Romans 14:1-12*
1/ Relate the necessity of Paul's words here to the cosmopolitan nature of Rome. 2/ To whom are Paul's words addressed? 3/ List the distinctions between the *strong* and the *weak* as to their opinions. 4/ How is each conscious of his indebtedness to God (cf. 12:1-2)? 4/ What are the likely attitudes of the *strong* toward the *weak*? the *weak* toward the *strong*? Why is each of these attitudes condemned? 5/ What is your attitude toward Christians with whom you differ in conviction and practice? Why? 6/ In what ways does judging others on these matters ignore *a*-the power of Christ and *b*-the final authority and place of judgment? 7/ In what

ways do you recognize the lordship of Christ in your opinions, actions, and life?

DAY *24* △ *Romans 14:13-23*
1/ What substitute for *judging* does Paul command? 2/ What is the basic fallacy of the *weak's* conviction concerning abstinence (cf. vv. 1-12)? In what ways is it based on a false view of *a*-God and *b*-human responsibility? 4/ How then are the actions of a person who believes he can "eat" but abstains because of possible injury to someone who believes he can't "eat" related to love? to Christ's death? 5/ In what ways can the *good* (liberty) of the *strong* become *evil*? 6/ When questions of food and drink are a Christian's main concern, what does this reveal about his perspective as to the kingdom of God? 7/ How does Paul define *a-right* and *wrong* and *b*-sin here? Apply these to your situation. 8/ With whom must you ultimately keep your faith and life? 9/ How can you *serve* Christ and *act in faith* in similar situations today? in the future?

DAY *25* △ *Romans 15:1-13*
1/ What is to characterize Christians' relationships with each other? 2/ What are the *strong's* obligation to the *weak*? 3/ To what ends are you to *please* and *welcome* your neighbor (cf. 14:15-16)? Why? 4/ What restraints and qualifications do you place on your acceptance of other Christians? In what ways do these actions ignore Christ's example? 5/ What are the two specific things Christ's example has accomplished? 6/ What is the purpose of Old Testament scripture? 7/ What is the main emphasis of the quotations concerning the Gentiles? 8/ How are *steadfastness, encouragement,* and *hope* related to the Scriptures? to God? Can hope exist in a vacuum? 9/ What is the source of your *joy* and *peace*?

DAY *26* △ *Romans 15:14-33*
1/ What is Paul's assessment of the virtues of the Roman Christians? 2/ How does Paul picture his relationship to them (cf. 1:5; 11:13; 12:3)? 3/ Why is Paul *proud* of his work? Contrast this kind of pride with the boasting in 2:17-23 and 3:27-28. 4/ Distinguish the references to the persons of the trinity. 5/ In what ways does Christ act through the apostle? What are the results? 6/ Describe the policy of Paul's ministry as to its *a*-scope and *b*-limitation. How

does he support his policy from *Isaiah*?   7/ What is the motive and purpose of the contribution of Macedonia and Achaia?   8/ In what ways do you contribute materially to those who have given you *spiritual blessings*?   9/ Describe the kind of prayer Paul requests. 10/ What is the content of your prayers for missionaries?   11/ In what situations does the God of peace give you peace?

DAY 27   △   *Romans 16:1-16*
1/ How does Paul show personal concern for the Romans?   2/ What is the place of letters and greetings in your life?   3/ List and explain the characteristics of the people Paul mentions.   4/ Imagine you are a Roman Christian. What phrase honestly characterizes you?   5/ How, do you think, does Paul know about the Christians when he has not been to Rome yet?   6/ In what ways does Paul reveal his consciousness of his connection to the church (cf. 12:4-5)? What is your relation to the church in the world? How can you express this relationship?

DAY 28   △   *Romans 16:17-27*
1/ Characterize the people Paul warns against. Why?   2/ In what ways can you be *wise* and *guileless* today?   3/ Relate God's *peace* (cf. 15:33) to *a*-Satan's defeat and *b*-Christ's *grace*.   4/ Compare this doxology (vv. 25-27) with Paul's salutation and introduction (1:1-17).   5/ How is *strength* related to the gospel?   6/ Describe the mystery of God as to *a*-purpose, *b*-authority, *c*-agent of disclosure, and *d*-scope of application.   7/ Relate God's *wisdom* to *a*-the mystery and *b*-verses 17-20.   8/ In what ways will you glorify God today?

DAY 29   △   *Romans 9—16*
1/ Summarize Paul's teaching about God's sovereignty and man's responsibility. How does this apply to Israel? to the Gentiles?   2/ Summarize how a Christian is to act toward *a*-God, *b*-the state, *c*-other Christians, and *d*-all men.   3/ How are love and obligation related?   4/ Distinguish *weakness* (chap. 14) in the contemporary world. Why can't it be gluttony or drunkenness?   5/ Summarize what is included in the *doctrine which you have been taught* (16: 17).   6/ What is your doctrine? In what ways is it a part of your daily living?

DAY *30* △ *Romans 1—16*

1/ Summarize Paul's teaching of *a*-sin and righteousness, *b*-law and grace, *c*-works and faith, *d*-death and life, and *e*-flesh and spirit. 2/ What analogies and illustrations does Paul use to explain his teaching? In what ways are they appropriate? 3/ Compare or contrast your *a*-attitude toward and *b*-knowledge of the Old Testament scripture with Paul's. 4/ How have the truths of *Romans* affected your *a*-understanding of the relationship of Jews and Gentiles; *b*-understanding of God, Jesus Christ, and the Holy Spirit; *c*-understanding of yourself; and *d*-relationship with others?

YEAR TWO

Month 13

day 1 △ *Introduction to Proverbs*
This collection of proverbs urges conduct that expresses a person's relationship with God in everyday situations. Keep a list of the metaphors (especially for the wise and foolish men). Keep a list of the themes (relate to wisdom and foolishness). *Proverbs 1* 1/What is Solomon's purpose in writing? Distinguish his audience. 2/What is the basis of wisdom? 3/Why is parental instruction important? 4/Describe the *sinners'* method of enticement (cf. with your situation today). Why does Solomon warn against them? 5/How have you been enticed to share in *wanton* deals? What have you done? Explain verse 17. 6/What is paradoxical about the principle in verses 18-19 (cf. vv. 11-14)? 7/Where does personified Wisdom cry? What three classes of people pay no attention? Characterize and distinguish these people throughout *Proverbs.* 8/What are the consequences of ignoring wisdom? What destroys fools? 9/What are the results of heeding wisdom? 10/How are *knowledge* and

the *fear of the Lord* related (cf. vv. 29, 7)?   11/Why do you panic? How can you be *secure*?   12/List the specific wisdom and instruction you need to know for today's situations. How can you have this wisdom?

day 2 Δ Proverbs 2
1/What is *a*-God's and *b*-your part in your understanding of wisdom?   2/Relate wisdom and *silver*.   3/Who is the source of wisdom? What does he do for his saints?   4/How do righteousness, justice, and equity (cf. 1:3) relate to wisdom?   5/Contrast saints and evil men. What are their ends?   6/What are the benefits of possessing wisdom?   7/Describe the prostitute and her house. Whom does the prostitute doubly wrong?   8/What is your attitude toward wisdom?   9/Why do you need wisdom today?

day 3 Δ Proverbs 3
1/List the imperatives.   2/What results for those who keep wisdom's commands?   3/How is wisdom related to daily living?   4/List the personal and public manifestations of wisdom.   5/What are the effects of wisdom and discretion in your life? In what ways do they *heal* and *refresh* you?   6/How do you respond to the Lord's discipline to make you wise (relate to the father-son picture)?   7/In what way is the Lord's wisdom revealed?   8/What is the Lord's attitude toward the types of people in verses 32-35?   9/How can you fulfill verse 27 today?   10/How can you be *in the Lord's confidence?*

day 4 Δ Proverbs 4
1/How does this autobiographical insertion reinforce the previous statements about wisdom?   2/Circle and explain the metaphors.   3/What do you want most from life? Why?   4/How do the Old Testament writers regard longevity of life (cf. v. 10 with 3:2, 16; Ex. 20:12)? Why, do you think?   5/Contrast the righteous and the wicked. How can you avoid evil?   6/In what ways does wisdom give you freedom?   7/List the commands of verses 20-27.   8/What

parts of the body are involved? 9/Why must your *heart* (in Hebrew, the intellectual, moral, and emotional faculties) be disciplined by wisdom?

day 5   △   Proverbs 5–6:19

1/Describe the adulteress. 2/Why should you keep away from her? 3/List the personal and public results for the adulterer. 4/What does 5:15-21 reveal about God's plan for sex and love? 5/How can you be *wise* in your relationships with the other sex? 6/Relate *discipline* to wisdom concerning sex. 7/Compare 6:1-5 with Exodus 22:25-27. In what modern situations are similar personal commitments a problem for you? 8/Characterize the ant. 9/In what ways are the man who has become surety, the sluggard, and the wicked man *foolish*? 10/Relate the description of the wicked man with 6:16-19. 11/What things in you does the Lord *hate*? What can you do today to get rid of them in your life?

day 6   △   Proverbs 6:20–7:27

1/Relate God's commandments to *a*-wisdom, *b*-light, and *c*-life. 2/What are the consequences for the man who commits adultery? 3/What progression can you see in 6:25-35? 4/How is a man who commits adultery like a thief? unlike a thief (relate to the wronged husband)? 5/Describe the relationship you are to have with wisdom (cf. your present relationship). 6/What experience does wisdom relate? 7/Characterize the young man and the harlot (explain the metaphors). 8/Which of these characteristics are a part of your life? What can you do today to become *wise* in these areas? 9/Upon what pretense does the harlot invite the young man (cf. Lev. 7:11-18)? 10/Contrast the ends of wisdom and the harlot (cf. vv. 1-2, 26-27).

day 7   △   Proverbs 8

1/To whom does wisdom appeal? 2/Contrast the harlot (cf. 3:16-19; 5:3-14; 6:24-26; 7:6-27) and wisdom concerning their *a*-relationship and approach to men, *b*-place and time, *c*-what they offer, *d*-words, and *e*-character. 3/What is involved in the *fear of the Lord?* 4/What are wisdom's *a*-identity and *b*-authority in the world? in creation? 5/List different attitudes toward wisdom. What results from each attitude? 6/In what areas do you need to *keep wisdom's ways* today? Why?

day 8 △ Proverbs 9

1/Contrast the banquets of Wisdom and Folly. Whom do each call? What do they offer? with what results? 2/Distinguish the responses of the scoffer and wise man. 3/How does this picture summarize the teachings of chapters 1–8? 4/What is your attitude toward reproof and instruction? Why? 5/To what extent do you have wisdom and insight according to the definitions of verse 10?

day 9 △ Proverbs 10

1/Keep a list of the *a*-qualities and *b*-benefits of wisdom, righteousness, etc. and their counterparts. 2/What is the style and structure of these proverbs? What connections do you see among them? 3/What parts of the body are included in the comments? 4/Circle and explain the metaphors. 5/List the themes in the passage. 6/In what ways is your speech a *fountain of life?* 7/How are wisdom and righteousness related to your life? 8/Choose and memorize a proverb from this passage. Explain its relation to your daily living.

day 10 △ Proverbs 11

1/How are *a*-wickedness and *b*-righteousness manifested in everyday *a*-personal and *b*-social life? 2/What are God's attitudes toward the *a*-wicked and *b*-righteous man? 3/To what extent are *a*-straightness and righteousness and *b*-crookedness and wickedness related here (cf. 2:15; 3:6; 4:24-27; 6:12; 8:8-9)? Why, do you think? 4/Compare verse 15 with 6:1-5. 5/What do your actions reveal about the basic qualities of your life? 6/Circle and explain the metaphors. 7/List the themes. Memorize a proverb. Explain its relation to your daily living.

day 11 △ Proverbs 12

1/Contrast the *a*-intentions and *b*-ends of the *a*-wicked and *b*-righteous man. 2/In what areas of life are these contrasts evident? 3/How do *a*-fools and *b*-wise men relate to others? 4/Circle and explain the metaphors. 5/List the themes. 6/How do you react to insults? Why? 7/What kind of speech is most associated with you? Why? 8/Contrast diligence and sloth (cf. 6:6-17; 10:4, 26). 9/Memorize a proverb.

day 12 △ Proverbs 13

1/What is the *wise* attitude toward *a*-parental and *b*-God-given instruction (cf. 1:8-9; 3:11-12; 4:1-9; 6:20-23; 12:1)? 2/Relate wisdom and discipline. 3/In what areas of your life do you want to be more disciplined? 4/What are the principles here about riches and poverty? 5/Compare verse 14 with 10:11. 6/Circle and explain the metaphors. 7/List the themes. 8/How can you develop wisdom? 9/Memorize a proverb.

day 13 △ Proverbs 14

1/Contrast the attitudes toward God in this chapter. 2/What is significant about the emotions revealed here? 3/What are the rewards for the upright? consequences for wickedness? 4/List the *a*-mental and *b*-physical characteristics of the wise and the foolish man. 5/What is the author's attitude toward the *poor*? 5/Compare verse 27 with 13:14 and 10:11. 6/How do verses 34-35 relate to Solomon's interests? 7/List the themes. 8/Memorize a proverb.

day 14 △ Proverbs 15

1/What are the characteristics of the speech of a wise and a foolish man? 2/To what extent are you *wise* in your speech? 3/Relate *good* and *evil* with the *wise* and *fools*. 4/What attributes of God are revealed here? 5/Account for the different attitudes of the Lord toward the various types of people in this chapter. 6/What emotional stability do righteous men have in the face of changing circumstances? 7/Circle and explain the metaphors. 8/List the themes. 9/Memorize a proverb.

day 15 Δ *Proverbs 16*

1/What part do *a*-you and *b*-God have in your plans (relate to God's sovereignty)? 2/Summarize the teaching here (cf. previous proverbs) about *a*-pride, *b*-a good king, *c*-justice (cf. v. 11 with 11:1; Deut. 25:13-16), and *d*-self-control. 3/Explain verse 6 (cf. 10:12). 4/Compare verse 22 with 14:27; 13:14; and 10:11. 5/Characterize perverse men (underline and explain the verbs in verses 27-30). 6/To what extent are you *getting wisdom* as a result of studying *Proverbs*? Why? 7/To what extent have you been able to relate the proverbs to your daily living? Why? 8/Circle and explain the metaphors. 9/Memorize a proverb.

day 16 Δ *Proverbs 17*

1/What should be your attitude toward your ethics considering verse 3? 2/Where is the source of wickedness? Account for its connection with the parts of a body as in verses 4 and 20 (cf. 6:16-18; 12:19). 3/List the relationships in this chapter. What principles do you see for interaction in these relationships (cf. v. 5 with 14:31; vv. 8, 18, 23 with 6:1-5)? 4/In what ways do these principles relate to your interaction with *a*-God, *b*-your family, *c*-your friends, and *d*-your neighbors? 5/Compare verses 14, 20, 27-28. 6/List the themes. 7/Circle and explain the metaphors. 8/Memorize a proverb.

day 17 Δ *Proverbs 18*

1/Observe the types of people in this chapter. What happens to them? Why? 2/To what extent does your conversation reflect the *a*-negative and *b*-positive comments about speech here? 3/Circle and explain the metaphors. 4/In what specific ways is the *name of the Lord* your *strong tower*? 5/List the themes. 6/Memorize a proverb.

day 18 △ *Proverbs 19*
1/Contrast the rich and the poor as to their *a*-popularity and
b-ultimate success. 2/What is your attitude toward *a*-the rich and
b-the poor? 3/Is poverty necessarily related to sloth?
Why? 4/How can you be *kind* to the poor today? 5/To what
extent does a fool evade his responsibility? 6/What positive
qualities from this chapter need to be a part of your life today?
What negative qualities need to be rooted out of your life? 7/List
the themes. 8/Circle and explain the metaphors. 9/Memorize a
proverb.

day 19 △ *Proverbs 20*
1/Categorize these proverbs as to *a*-observation, *b*-interpretation,
and *c*-application. 2/In what ways does each category reveal
wisdom? 3/Write three proverbs on a theme in each category. 4/Imagine the feelings of the authors of the proverbs in this
chapter. 5/What is distinctive about the *a*-message and *b*-style of a
proverb? 6/Determine the meaning of *winnows* in verses 8,
26. 7/Circle and explain the metaphors. 8/Memorize a proverb.

day 20 △ *Proverbs 21*
1/List the themes of these proverbs. 2/What is your response to
the law of God in the particular areas of these proverbs? Why? In
which area do you need to change today? 3/Relate *crookedness*
and *guilt* in your life. 4/Contrast the futures of righteous and
wicked men. 5/Circle and explain the metaphors. 6/Memorize a
proverb.

day 21 △ *Proverbs 22:1-16*
1/List the themes here. 2/Summarize the principles concerning
a-speech, *b*-the rich and poor, *c*-sloth, *d*-justice, *e*-relationships
(negative and positive), and *f*-God's sovereignty in chapters
10–22. 3/Summarize the characteristics of *a*-the righteous and
wise man and *b*-the wicked and foolish man. 4/Review the
proverbs you have memorized. 5/Recall situations in which the
proverbs have been a source of wisdom in your daily living.

day 22 Δ *Proverbs 22:17–24:2*

1/List the attitudes and actions that a wise man must *a*-avoid and *b*-apply himself to. Why? 2/How does wisdom affect others? 3/Relate the *fear of the Lord* with *a*-wisdom and *b*-hope. 4/Contrast the metaphors of *a*-the harlot and *b*-wine with modern feelings in these areas. 5/To what extent do you *envy* evil? Why?

day 23 Δ *Proverbs 24:3-34*

1/Compare verses 3-4 with verse 27. 2/Relate *wisdom* and *strength*. 3/To what extent is your social concern accompanied by action (cf. vv. 11-12)? 4/Contrast the ends of the *a*-righteous and *b*-wicked men. How does this fact affect your daily living? 5/Relate verses 10 and 16. 6/What is your responsibility to *a*-God and *b*-national leaders? 7/Compare verses 17 and 29. 8/Compare the parable in verses 30-34 with 6:6-11. 9/How do you know when your sleep is necessary and when it is merely escape?

day 24 Δ *Proverbs 25*

1/Compare and contrast the purposes of *a*-God and *b*-a king (review Luke 14:8-10 for Jesus' use of vv. 6-7). 2/Investigate the beautiful meanings of the metaphors. Try to imagine Solomon's feelings as he uses the metaphors. Why, do you think, does he choose metaphors to express these truths? 3/What should be your attitudes and actions toward your *a*-neighbor and *b*-enemy (review Rom. 12:20 for Paul's use of vv. 21-22)? 4/Memorize a metaphor proverb. Write at least three more metaphors for the same proverb. 5/To what extent are verses 19 and 26 a part of your experience? Why? 6/How can you experience *self-control* in the difficult areas of your life today?

day 25 Δ *Proverbs 26*

1/Characterize a *fool*. 2/What should be your response to a fool? 3/How can you distinguish fools and wise men (cf. previous chaps.)? 4/Compare and contrast a conceited person and a

fool. 5/Account for the apparent contradiction of verses
4-5. 6/Characterize *a*-the sluggard (cf. v. 13 with 22:13; v. 15 with
19:24), *b*-the quarrelsome person, *c*-the practical joker, *d*-the
gossip, and *e*-the hypocrite. 7/In what ways are the metaphors
apt? 8/Which traits do you need to remove from your life?

day 26 Δ Proverbs 27
1/What relationships are cited here? List the *a*-positive and
b-negative manifestations. 2/To whom are you *a*-positively and
b-negatively related now? Why? 3/What can you do today to have
right relationships with others? 4/Relate verses 2 and 21. 5/Re-
late the comments of verses 23-27 with Israel's situation during
Solomon's time. Why, do you think, are these remarks necessary?

day 27 Δ Proverbs 28
1/How do a nation's sins affect its rulers? vice versa? 2/Relate
verses 2-3 to Hezekiah's time. 3/What qualities of character and
action are commended? condemned? 4/What is the prerequisite
for knowledge? for mercy? 5/In which of these proverbs do you
see divine justice revealed? 6/Which part of verse 13 generally
describes your reaction to your sin? Why? 7/Circle and explain
the metaphors. 8/Memorize a proverb.

day 28 Δ Proverbs 29
1/Contrast the righteous and wicked as to their *a*-temperament and
b-ultimate end. 2/Summarize the observations about a king (cf.
previous chaps.). 3/Explain verse 18 (relate to the current cry for
"law and order"). How does verse 18 relate to the section on
discipline (vv. 15-19)? 4/What negative qualities observed here do
you need to especially get rid of in your life? 5/What is the
paradox in verse 23 (relate to other paradoxes you have noted in
Proverbs)?

day 29 Δ Proverbs 30
1/Try to imagine Agur's emotions as he writes here. 2/What is his

tone in verses 1-4? 3/What is the purpose of the hypothetical man
and son's ventures in verse 4? What kind of knowledge would
result? 4/What are Agur's attitudes toward God's *a*-Word, *b*-suste-
nance, and *c*-creation? 5/Describe the types of people cited
here. 6/Memorize one of the series of *four* descriptions. Why, do
you think, does Agur choose these particular descriptions? 7/In
what areas of life have you been *foolish*? How can you become
wise in these areas?

day 30 △ Proverbs 31
1/What does Lemuel's mother warn against? urge? 2/Characterize
a *good wife* (cf. 12:4; 18:22; 19:14). 3/Contrast the good wife
with the harlot (Folly) of previous chapters. Compare her with
Wisdom. 4/What can you as a woman do to develop these *good*
qualities in your life? 5/How has the study of *Proverbs* helped
you experience *wisdom* in your daily living? To what extent has
your conduct been affected? Why? In what specific areas? 6/Write
a sentence summary on each theme you have discovered in
Proverbs.

Month 14

day 1 △ Introduction to 1 Corinthians
Paul writes this letter in response to questions the Christians at
Corinth have asked and to the news he has received about their
problems (divisions in the church, moral faults, etc.). Investigate
the historical background setting of Corinth. Skim your notes on 1
and 2 Thessalonians and Acts 18. *1 Corinthians 1:1-17* 1/With
what authority does Paul write to the Corinthian church? 2/What
authority do you claim for the positions you hold in church,
school or work, and community? 3/Describe the spiritual character and resources of this church which lead Paul to give thanks to
God. What characteristics does Paul attribute to God? 4/In

contrast what situation among the Corinthians makes Paul's appeal for unity necessary? 5/What personal interests are producing similar results in your Christian group or community? 6/What is the basis of Paul's plea for unity? How does this basis affect his ministry? 7/What steps do you need to take to promote unity among Christians in your school, business, community, and church?

day 2 ∆ 1 Corinthians 1:18-31
1/Contrast the two viewpoints which the message produces. 2/How has the wisdom of this world been made *foolish*? 3/Contrast the *a*-Jewish and *b*-Greek approach to wisdom. 4/What is true wisdom? its goal? its relation to the cross? its endurance? 5/How are God's people described here? Why has God chosen such people to represent him? 6/What does to have Christ as your *wisdom, righteousness, sanctification, and redemption* in all your daily affairs mean to you? 7/How does Paul's message attack the problem in the Corinthian church (cf. 1:1-17)?

day 3 ∆ 1 Corinthians 2
1/What is the content of Paul's message? 2/How is it an example of his explanation of true wisdom (cf. 1:18-31)? 3/Describe Paul's presentation of the gospel. 4/What is his *a*-purpose and *b*-resource in "evangelism"? 5/In what ways can Paul's purpose and resource influence your own message? 6/Characterize and describe God's wisdom (source, purpose, recipients). 7/What do you learn here about the work of the Holy Spirit? 8/What is the condition of your *a*-spiritual discernment and *b*-ability to make right judgments? Why? In what ways do these make you an enigma to non-Christians? Why? 9/How does what the Holy Spirit teaches you affect your understanding of God and Jesus Christ? Scripture? other people? your purpose in life?

day 4 ∆ 1 Corinthians 3
1/What figures of speech does Paul use to characterize the

Corinthian church? 2/What do you as a teacher learn here about adapting your message to the capacity of your listeners? 3/What indicates the Corinthians' lack of progress? Why? 4/To whom does Paul give credit for what has happened in Corinth (vv. 5-9)? 5/Who receives praise for the work in your group or community? Why? 6/Identify and describe the building (builders, materials, etc.). 7/What is your responsibility in building on the foundation? 8/Which is your emphasis in building: quantity or quality? Which is God's? 9/In what way do verses 16-17 reveal the seriousness of the Corinthian divisions? 10/How can you have a realistic self-view? 11/Is God against academic excellence? Distinguish the kind of *wisdom* to which Paul is referring (cf. 1:18-31). 12/In what sense is verse 21 a logical conclusion to verses 18-19? How does verse 21 relate to the thought which follows?

day 5 Δ *1 Corinthians 4*
1/How does Paul describe the apostles? 2/Define and distinguish *servants* and *stewards*. 3/What truth about God does Paul introduce (vv. 2-5)? 4/What scriptural principles should you apply when you would judge *a*-yourself or *b*-another person? 5/What is the source of your gifts? How should the realization of this source affect your attitude toward *a*-yourself and *b*-others? 6/How does Paul contrast the position of the apostles and the Corinthian church? With which group do you identify? Why? 7/Imagine Paul's feelings as he writes verses 8-13. 8/What is the Greek attitude toward such people as described in verses 11-13? 9/What result does Paul hope for in the Corinthians? 10/How does Paul describe the kingdom of God? 11/In what ways does your life manifest *power*?

day 6 Δ *1 Corinthians 5*
1/Compare the first-century Greek attitude and modern attitudes toward sexual morality. 2/What is the attitude of the Corinthian church to the problem? How does Paul instruct them to act? 3/In what way would the immoral man's presence in the church be like

yeast? 4/What should you do with any corrupting influence in your life? in your fellowship group? Why? 5/Specify those with whom the church is not to associate. How far does their practical excommunication go? 6/With whom can you associate (or not) if you follow the instructions Paul gives?

day 7 △ 1 Corinthians 6:1-11

1/What in the Corinthians' legal practice upsets Paul? 2/What reasons does Paul give to confirm the principles he suggests? Relate these reasons to Paul's explanation of wisdom (1:18–2:16). 3/What attitude does Paul commend to the aggrieved party? 4/Imagine Paul's reaction to your group's divisions and their airings. 5/Compare or contrast your *a*-ethics among fellow Christians and *b*-love for Christians with that of the Corinthians. In what ways can you work toward right ethics and love today? 6/What determines whether a person will *inherit* the kingdom of God? 7/Explain how you have been *washed, sanctified,* and *justified.* How are these happenings obvious in your life today?

day 8 △ 1 Corinthians 6:12-20

1/What misapplication of Christian freedom does Paul attack? On what grounds? 2/How can you guard against the indulgence and enslavement of your freedom? 3/Is feasting in itself wrong? fornication? Why? 4/Which misuses of the body does Paul specify? 5/In what ways do you misuse your body? Why? 6/What is the purpose of man's body? 7/How does the truth of verses 19-20 govern your eating and sleeping habits? the exercise of your body? your sexual life? 8/What should be a Christian's attitude toward his body? 9/Summarize Paul's teaching about the moral laxity in the church.

day 9 △ 1 Corinthians 7:1-24

1/What responsibilities do a husband and wife have to each other? 2/Do married people necessarily lack self-con-

trol? 3/Compare or contrast your feelings concerning marriage
with Paul's. 4/Under what conditions is marriage advisable? 5/For what reasons does Paul encourage a Christian to
remain with an unbelieving partner? 6/Determine the meaning of
consecrated, unclean, and *holy* in verses 14-16. 7/What principle
regarding external change does Paul enunciate for new Christians?
What relationship supersedes status and external conditions? 8/What personal encouragement do you find in these
verses?

   day 10   Δ   1 Corinthians 7:25-40
1/List and explain the reasons Paul counsels *a*-to remain single and
b-to marry. 2/Relate verses 26-28, 40 with verses 17-24. 3/What
basic attitudes toward earthly values and relationships does Paul
urge? Why? Compare or contrast your attitudes. 4/To what extent
are you willing to forego good legitimate things in order to *secure
your undivided devotion to the Lord?* 5/What are the realistic (relate to your *gifts*–v. 7) advantages and disadvantages of marriage
for you? of singleness? 6/To what extent are you *a*-living con-
structively (v. 17) and *b*-devoted to the Lord in your present state?

   day 11   Δ   1 Corinthians 8
1/What is the problem here (relate to the Corinthians' circumstances)? 2/What knowledge do some Corinthian Christians
possess that others do not? 3/How are they failing to show *love* to
the others? 4/What may result if "stronger" Christians flaunt their
knowledge and liberty? 5/What principle does Paul suggest the
Corinthians with knowledge consider when making a decision as to
whether to participate in certain activities? 6/What responsibility
do you have to another person's conscience? 7/In what ways are
you building up a Christian brother by not flaunting your
knowledge to his detriment?

   day 12   Δ   1 Corinthians 9:1-18
1/Compare and contrast Paul's situation with other apostles' as to

a-claim to apostleship and *b*-maintenance at the church's expense. 2/How do the illustrations from *a*-life and *b*-the law substantiate his rights? 3/Relate Paul's example to his teaching about *rights* in previous chapters. 4/What causes Paul to forego his rights? What is his attitude? 5/What rights might you forego in order to *proclaim the gospel*? What is your attitude? 6/What is the extent of Paul's responsibility to God's *commission*? What is yours? 7/What is the irony of Paul's *reward*?

day 13 △ *1 Corinthians 9:19-27*
1/What is Paul's *a*-attitude and *b*-purpose in personal relationships? 2/What would it mean for you to be a slave to *a*-social misfits, *b*-legalists, *c*-pagans, *d*-cultured intelligentsia, and *e*-nonconformists? 3/How is Paul free to be like all men without becoming carried away with this freedom? 4/What are you doing to keep in shape spiritually? What prize do you seek? 5/Compare or contrast your present condition with that of a competitive athlete.

day 14 △ *1 Corinthians 10:1-14*
1/Contrast the benefits of Israel (vv. 1-4) with their response to God (vv. 5-10). How has Christ been related to the Israelites? 2/How do these Old Testament activities add force to Paul's argument? 3/How does verse 13 relate to 9:24–10:22? 4/Compare the *a*-Israelites', *b*-Corinthians', and *c*-your situations. 5/How do you deal with temptation in your life? How does the faithfulness of God relate to your situation?

day 15 △ *1 Corinthians 10:14–11:1*
1/What basis of Christian unity is in the Lord's supper? 2/Why does participation in the Lord's supper exclude participation in idol feasts? vice versa? 3/What are Paul's major considerations in exercising Christian liberty (cf. 9:22)? 4/List reasons for restricting your liberty (cf. 8:13). 5/What about Christian liberty have you questioned recently? What principles from this passage will

you apply to your specific problems? 6/Summarize Paul's teaching on the problem of meat sacrificed to idols.

day 16 Δ 1 Corinthians 11:2-16
1/State the relationship between *a*-God and man and *b*-man and woman. 2/In what ways does your relationship to God govern your behavior when you meet other Christians? 3/What is the proper attitude of a woman toward a man? a man toward a woman? 4/Compare or contrast the attitude of *a*-women toward men and *b*-men toward women in your church or Christian fellowship. 5/What reasons are given for the rules about covering heads (cf. the Jewish custom of everyone's head covered and the Greek custom of no one's head covered)? 6/To what extent does Paul adapt these principles from the general practice of the day?

day 17 Δ 1 Corinthians 11:17-34
1/Describe and imagine what Paul has heard about the Corinthians' gatherings. 2/What is Paul's reaction to what he has heard? 3/Compare or contrast the Corinthian and your gatherings for communion. 4/What explanation does Paul give the church about the communion meal? Of what two events does communion speak? 5/What is the significance of *therefore* in verse 27? 6/Explain what Paul means by *an unworthy manner*. What results from eating and drinking in an unworthy manner? 7/How should a person approach the communion meal with others? 8/What is the relation between wrong spiritual attitudes and physical ills? 9/What does communion mean to you? What attitudes or practices do you need to change?

day 18 Δ 1 Corinthians 12:1-13
1/What does Paul want the Corinthians to understand about spiritual gifts? 2/What are your gifts? 3/What is the unity among the diverse gifts? List the areas in which the Holy Spirit is manifest. 4/What is the purpose of the gifts? 5/How are a person's specific gifts determined? How does this fact relate to

your attitude toward your gifts? 6/What distinction does Paul
make between the *a*-emotional ecstacy and *b*-content of utter-
ances? 7/Relate *baptized* and *drink* in verse 13. 8/How does the
Holy Spirit's work relate to the unity of Christians? 9/Is the truth
of verse 13 apparent in your group? In what ways?

day 19 △ *1 Corinthians 12:12-31*

1/How does Paul compare a physical body with the body of
Christ? Explain how diversity is the essence of each. 2/How does
Paul reconcile *unity* and *diversity* among Christians? 3/How are
the activities of the body coordinated? 4/What is the right
attitude of a person with a less spectacular gift to a person with a
more spectacular gift? vice versa? 5/To what degree do you accept
your place in Christ's body? 6/How important is each member to
the church? What does this say to "lone wolf" Christians? 7/How
do verses 23-26 describe God's plan for Christian relationships?
What hinders fulfillment of God's plan in your Christian group?

day 20 △ *1 Corinthians 12:27–13:13*

1/What spiritual gifts are mentioned in 13:1-3? 2/What are the
higher gifts (12:31)? What relation does love have to these gifts?
3/Describe love by paraphrasing 13:4-7 in relation to your specific
situation today. 4/List what you need to change about your attitudes and actions toward your *a*-roommate, *b*-husband or wife,
c-employer, *d*-fellow workers, etc. to conform to this description
of love. Refer to your paraphrase and list throughout the day.
5/What is the *a*-purpose and *b*-future of spiritual gifts? How are
faith, hope, and *love* superior? 6/How do the illustrations of
a-Paul's growing up process and *b*-Corinthian mirrors relate to the
future of spiritual gifts?

day 21 △ *1 Corinthians 14:1-19*

1/Describe the gifts of *a*-prophecy and *b*-tongues. Compare and
contrast these gifts as to their *a*-purposes, *b*-benefits and those
benefited, and *c*-Paul's attitude toward each. 2/For what reasons

does Paul encourage the Corinthians to desire the gift of prophecy over tongues (relate his illustrations of instruments and a bugle)? 3/In what ways can you make Paul's advice in verse 12 the standard of behavior and desire in your group? Do you desire tongues? prophecy? Why? 4/How does Paul substantiate his statements to the Corinthians?

day 22   Δ   *1 Corinthians 14:20-40*

1/How does Paul's illustration of children (cf. 13:11) relate to the desire for tongues? 2/What is the anticipated attitude and response of unbelievers toward *a*-prophecy and *b*-tongues? What effect does your group's behavior have on outsiders? 3/What are the parts of a Corinthian meeting? 4/List the rules Paul gives concerning conduct in the church. What principles underlie the rules? 5/In what ways are tongues and prophecy controllable? How does this control relate to the nature of God? 6/Relate verse 36 to Christian groups today who ignore the Christian heritage. How can you keep a balance between *a*-respect for Christian heritage and *b*-innovations relating to the contemporary generation? 7/Relate Paul's directions as to the place of women in the church to *a*-the Greek culture and *b*-the struggle of the Corinthian church to maintain respectability. Compare or contrast today's situation.

day 23   Δ   *1 Corinthians 15:1-11*

1/What is the *gospel* Paul summarizes? List the facts. For what reasons does Paul include these particular facts? 2/What facts in your message are most significant to your hearers? 3/How does Paul substantiate Christ's resurrection? 4/List Paul's references to himself. What do these reveal about his self-attitude? Compare or contrast your self-attitude. 5/How is God's *grace* shown in your life?

day 24   Δ   *1 Corinthians 15:12-34*

1/What logical conclusions follow if there is no resurrection of the dead? 2/Investigate the meaning of *first fruits* in relation to Christ's resurrection (cf. Lev. 23:10 ff.). 3/What kind of attitude and behavior would result in those who believe in resurrection? 4/What kind of attitude and behavior is evident in your life because Jesus Christ has risen from the dead? 5/How does the defeat of death fit into God's overall plan? How does Jesus Christ fit into this plan? 6/Explain Christ's subjection *a*-to death and *b*-to God.   7/Relate Paul's attitude toward death to his risks and peril. 8/How are you fitting into God's overall plan? 9/Relate verse 29 to the possibility of Corinthian vicarious baptism. 10/How does Paul relate doctrine and conduct? 11/To whom does *bad company* apply?

day 25 △ *1 Corinthians 15:35-58*
1/How does Paul use parallels in nature to help the Corinthians grasp truths of the resurrection? 2/What is the relation between your present body and the one Christ will give you at the resurrection of the dead? 3/Describe the resurrected body. 4/Compare and contrast the first man Adam and the last Adam (cf. vv. 21-22; Rom. 5). 5/How does the Adam illustration fit in with the point Paul is making in this section? 6/Create imaginatively the moment of resurrection. 7/How will death be defeated ultimately? 8/Contrast the alternative attitudes toward death and resurrection (cf. v. 32 with v. 58). Which describes your attitude? Why? 9/In what ways do you and will you demonstrate the defeat of *a*-death and *b*-the sting of sin?

day 26 △ *1 Corinthians 16*
1/Rephrase Paul's directions and reasons for giving. 2/In what ways do you fulfill your responsibility to others and God in this area of your life? 3/About what things in other people is Paul concerned? 4/Review his letter to the Corinthians. Summarize what he notices and advises them. 5/What does Paul desire to see accomplished in other Christians as he works for and with them? 6/In what specific ways has studying *1 Corinthians* changed your *a*-doctrinal beliefs, *b*-ethical principles, and *c*-con-

duct? What still needs to change? Why? When? 7/List several themes or specific ideas you want to study further.

day 27 △ *Introduction to Psalms 30–41*
The *Psalms* are personal and public poems of worship used as hymns. They represent a range of emotional tones, subjects, and authors. Read the psalms aloud and imagine the experiences and feelings which prompt their writing. Keep a list of the metaphors. Relate their aesthetic and spiritual values. *Psalm 30* 1/What has been David's experience of security? What is the apparent source of the feeling of security he mentions in verse 6? 2/What happens to shake his confidence? 3/What is the source of a more solid sense of security? 4/Compare and contrast David's despair (vv. 8-10) with the final release from despair (vv. 11-12). 5/Honestly, what is the basis of your sense of security? 6/Title this psalm as to content.

day 28 △ *Psalm 31*
1/List David's requests for help (vv. 1-8). 2/Describe and categorize his problems (vv. 9-13). With which do you identify? Why? 3/What characteristics does David attribute to God? 4/What problems can you turn over to God? Why? 5/How can David's comfort in God be helpful to you? 6/How does David close the psalm? How can you follow the command of verses 23-24 today? 7/What is your response to God for your experiences of rescue from anxiety, uncertainty, and suspicion of others? 8/Title this psalm as to content.

day 29 △ *Psalm 32*
1/How does verse 1 capture the main idea of the psalm? 2/Trace the psychological and spiritual progress of the psalmist as sinner— unrepentant, repentant, and forgiven. What insight do you gain into the psychological implications of repressed and confessed sin? 3/Who appears to be speaking in verses 8-9? What is the command? 4/How have you been *like a horse or a mule* recently? 5/What sin in your life needs to be acknowledged to enable you to *rejoice*? 6/Give this psalm a title.

day 30 Δ *Psalm 33*
1/Compare and contrast this psalm and Psalm 32. What indicates that this psalm is designed for corporate worship? 2/What reasons does the psalmist give for praising God? 3/How does the psalmist picture God as creator? What part does God's *word* have? 4/How does God treat the plans of *nations*? 5/What, do you think, is God's attitude toward your nation's political, cultural, socio-economic, and military plans? toward yours? 6/What attributes of God are revealed in this psalm? 7/Upon what does the principle of God's deliverance and sustenance depend (cf. vv. 4-5)? What does God require of you? 8/Can you make the personal closing words your prayer? 9/Title this psalm as to content.

Month 15

day 1 Δ *Psalm 34*
1/Compare 1 Samuel 21:1–22:5 (the psalm is addressed to David's followers—1 Sam. 22:2). 2/For what does David praise God? 3/Relate the general remarks in the psalm to the specific details in 1 Samuel. 4/How do the remarks reflect your experiences? 5/What is David's counsel in verses 11-14? 6/What confidence does he show in verses 15-22? How can you have similar confidence? 7/What is your response to God for your deliverance from recent trouble? For what will you *praise* him today? 8/Summarize this psalm in one sentence.

day 2 Δ *Psalm 35*
1/What is the psalmist's tone as he calls on God to help him? 2/How can he be so confident of his own righteousness (cf. v. 24)? Are you similarly confident? Should you be? Why? 3/What do you need to do today to bring your life to David's standard? 4/Compare 1 Samuel 24 (possible situation for the psalm). How does this passage help to explain David's

tone?   5/How do you react in similar situations? Why?   6/In what
situations today will you expect God's deliverance and claim the
expressions of praise in verses 9-10, 18, and 28?   7/Title this psalm
as to content.

day 3 △ Psalm 36

1/How is the wicked person described?   2/What are his goals? his
views of a-God, b-himself, and c-truth?   3/What actually has
become the wicked man's god?   4/How can he be so fearless in
doing evil?   5/To what end does the wicked come (v. 12)?   6/How
is God contrasted to the wicked?   7/What quality of God's
righteousness does David stress?   8/What is David's prayer in view
of God's greatness?   9/What in verse 10 indicates his confidence of
his position before God? Has David always been so confident (cf.
Ps. 32)?   10/Why are you confident of God's love to
you?   11/What sin (as in vv. 1-4) do you need to confess?   12/For
what will you praise God now?   13/Summarize this psalm in a
title.

day 4 △ Psalm 37

1/What contrasts does David make between the righteous and the
wicked?   2/What commands are given in this psalm? What results
from obedience?   3/Which of these commands is most relevant to
your present relation to God?   4/What is your attitude toward the
prosperity and power of wicked people?   5/What is the security of
the righteous in the face of material loss (contrast the plight of the
wicked)?   6/What is the basis for the ultimate destruction of the
wicked?   7/Why does God deliver the righteous?   8/How will the
certainty of your future affect your living today?   9/Title this
psalm as to content.

day 5 △ Psalm 38

1/What is the psalmist's external and internal condition?   2/What
causes his anguish (cf. the different viewpoints of vv. 1-2, 4-5,
8)?   3/When have you known similar sorrow and helpless-

ness? 4/To what extent are your moral and physical problems related? 5/From whom does the psalmist expect relief (cf. vv. 11-12 with 15, 21-22)? 6/What part does the psalmist have in making his relief possible? 7/What pattern of life emerges from this psalm? 8/What can you do today to find relief from the guilt of sin? 9/Give the psalm a title.

day 6 Δ *Psalm 39*
1/Compare Psalms 32 and 38 with this psalm. 2/How deeply does this affliction strike David? 3/What is the consequence of his silence? 4/What are the causes of his sorrow? 5/To whom does David turn? 6/How does David appear to value his life? 7/In what ways does David base his plea for deliverance on his relationship to God? 8/Account for the difference in tones of the first and last parts of this psalm. 9/When have you experienced prolonged afflictions? What have you done? 10/Title this psalm to suggest both its content and attitude.

day 7 Δ *Psalm 40*
1/How does the experience described in verses 1-5 seem to fulfill David's requests in the two previous psalms? 2/To what extent does David's patience in waiting for deliverance (v. 1) describe your attitude under stress? 3/What are David's attitudes toward *a*-himself, *b*-his enemies, and *c*-God? Why? 4/What does God require of a man? 5/Contrast the tone of the opening (vv. 1-5) and the conclusion (vv. 11-17) of the psalm. What human experience does such an order of affairs suggest? 6/What attitudes to your life (its sin, failure, and triumph) does the psalm suggest as appropriate? 7/Summarize this psalm in a title.

day 8 Δ *Psalm 41*
1/List David's problems. How does he feel physically? mentally? spiritually? 2/What are his enemies' desires for him (cf. a possible experience for this psalm in 2 Sam. 15–16)? 3/Who upholds David? Why (cf. vv. 11-12 to the principles in vv. 1-3)? 4/Have

you ever experienced such deceit, gossip, and betrayal? How have you *held up*? Why? 5/How is the doxology of verse 13 (to mark the end of the first section of *Psalms*) appropriate to this psalm? 6/Title this psalm.

day 9   Δ   *Introduction to 2 Corinthians*
Paul writes this second letter to the Corinthians after he receives reassuring news from Titus about the Corinthian church and its problems. *2 Corinthians 1:1-11* 1/List what Paul states concerning the *a*-nature and *b*-activities of God. 2/How does *comfort* relate to the nature and activity of God (cf. each context of *comfort* in vv. 3-7)? 3/How does Paul understand his afflictions in relation to the comfort of God? 4/How do you react in times of difficulty and stress? Why? 5/Why does God allow disturbing circumstances to enter Paul's life? 6/If you are confident that God is actively involved in your life and circumstances, how should your confidence affect your attitude today (relate to *setting your hope*)? 7/Relate verses 8-11 to Paul's discussion of resurrection in 1 Corinthians 15. 8/If Paul is sure he will be released from prison, why, do you think, does he request prayer from the Corinthians?

day 10   Δ   *2 Corinthians 1:12-23*
1/What factors, does Paul claim, govern his conduct in relation to both Christians and non-Christians? 2/How would you defend Paul from the charges of *a*-insincerity and *b*-fickleness and indecision from this passage? 3/Characterize Paul's positive relation to the Corinthians. 4/In what ways would your life have to change to be able to similarly characterize your relationships? 5/What do verses 18-20 reveal about the nature and promises of God? 6/What evidence here demonstrates that God is faithful in keeping his promises? 7/How does Jesus Christ fulfill every promise of God? 8/What do you possess in and because of Christ? Determine the meaning of *guarantee*.

day 11   Δ   *2 Corinthians 1:23–2:11*
1/What reasons does Paul give for not visiting the Corinthian

church as he had formerly planned? 2/Imagine the type of rude conduct by the offender (v. 5). 3/How would you react under similar circumstances? Why? 4/What does Paul recommend that the Corinthians do to the offender? For what reasons? 5/What principles of church discipline and forgiveness does Paul teach from this incident? 6/What kind of conduct is expected of you in relation to the church? to the Christian fellowship where you live, work, or study? 7/Expand the characteristics of Paul's attitude and relationship to the Corinthians.

day 12   Δ   2 Corinthians 2:12–3:6
1/How is Paul's ministry influenced by fellow Christians? 2/Explain the significance of *always* in verse 14. 3/How are *a*-the knowledge of God, *b*-fragrance, *c*-life and death, and *d*-you related? 4/What has God done through you recently? What shows that the knowledge of God is spread through your character? 5/What facts *sufficiently* qualify Paul to be a minister of God's Word? 6/In what way are these facts the basis for his *confidence?* 7/How do the Corinthians *recommend* Paul? In what ways are they *letters?* 8/In what ways will you be a *letter from Christ* today? What will be your "content"?

day 13   Δ   2 Corinthians 3:7-18
1/Divide a sheet of paper and contrast the two dispensations or administrations introduced in verses 7-8 (cf. Ex. 34:29-35). 2/Which surpasses the other? In what ways? 3/How do the actions of *a*-Moses and *b*-Paul reflect the dispensations in which they participate? 4/What should characterize your attitude if you are personally involved in the dispensation of the Spirit (cf. Paul's claim to confidence in v. 4)? 5/Determine the meaning of *veil* in relation to *a*-Moses, *b*-Jewish people, and *c*-non-Christians. 6/How is the veil lifted? When? Why? 7/To what extent are you *being changed* daily? Why? How? What is the significance of the verb forms?

day 14 △ *2 Corinthians 4:1-15*

1/Describe the ministry Paul has been given. How has he received it? 2/What is involved in the *gospel* (relate to *light*)? 3/What do verses 1-7 teach you about the way the gospel should be presented? 4/Contrast the message of the gospel with the messengers who present it (relate to the metaphors Paul uses). 5/Why does God choose this way to reveal himself? 6/Relate Paul's experiences to the *a*-death and *b*-life of Jesus. 7/What does to be *given up to death for Jesus' sake* in your experiences at school, work, and among your family and friends mean for you, specifically? 8/What is Paul's basis for his *a*-hope and *b*-witness to Christ (cf. Ps. 116:10) even in tribulation? 9/What is the effect of *a*-affliction and *b*-the prospect of death on your hope and witness? Why? 10/How does Paul view thanksgiving in verse 15 (cf. 1:11)?

day 15 △ *2 Corinthians 4:16–5:10*

1/List each comparison Paul makes between the outer and the inner nature. 2/Describe how what is rooted in time affects what is eternal. 3/What objective or truth about life has completely grasped Paul and molded his attitudes and actions (relate to the metaphors he uses)? 4/List your attitudes and reactions to the difficulties you face in your studies and relationships at school, work, and home. Compare or contrast Paul's responses with yours. 5/What will you do to be *of good courage* today?

day 16 △ *2 Corinthians 5:11-19*

1/How does the fact of being known by God substantiate Paul's boldness? 2/Describe *a*-what Jesus Christ has done and *b*-who he is in relation to both God and man. 3/What has caused Paul to change the way he regards *a*-people and *b*-Christ (cf. the Jewish expectations of the Messiah)? 4/How does Paul regard people now that he is associated with Jesus? 5/What is the new creation? 6/List some of the ways your understanding of Christ has shaped your character and actions. 7/Can you list at least three new attitudes or types of activities that will reflect what you know of the new creation?

day 17 △ *2 Corinthians 5:20–6:10*
1/Describe Paul's actions which commend him as *a*-an ambassador
and *b*-a servant of God. 2/Why can he act with *a*-urgency and
b-confidence? 3/How does one become *the righteousness of God*?
Explain the paradox involved. 4/Determine the meaning of *to
accept the grace of God in vain*. Can you cite specific examples? 5/Categorize and explain *a*-the trials Paul has experienced
and *b*-the qualities he has exhibited. 6/What trials have you
experienced recently? To what extent have you *endured*?

day 18 △ *2 Corinthians 6:11–7:4*
1/What is Paul's desire for the Corinthian Christians? What does
he expect of them? 2/Explain why Paul warns against permanent
relationships with unbelievers (cf. the picture in Lev.
19:19). 3/What does this principle reveal about the character of
God? of a Christian (relate to the two pictures of relationships
here)? 4/Why is it difficult to please God while united improperly
to an unbeliever? 5/In what ways and in what areas should you be
separate? 6/Distinguish separation, identification, and isolation. 7/What is the purpose of a Christian's *separation*? 8/List
the principles suggested by this passage to help you live worthy of
a holy God who claims you as his own.

day 19 △ *2 Corinthians 7:5-16*
1/Imagine Paul's strain *without* and *within* (cf. 2:13). 2/Compare
and contrast *comfort* and *suffering* (cf. 1:1-11). 3/To what extent
does your *grief* about yourself and your sin make you *repent*? 4/Distinguish *godly* and *worldly* grief. 5/What should be
your attitude in suffering and grief to experience profitable
character building? 6/List at least two ways Titus witnesses to the
facts that *a*-God comforts and *b*-God's comfort is realized in
relationships. 7/How has God specifically comforted you through
another person? 8/How can you specifically comfort others in
your relationships this week at school, work, or home? 9/To what
extent and for what purposes does Paul *a*-criticize and *b*-commend
the Corinthians?

day 20 Δ 2 Corinthians 8:1-15
1/How have Paul's remarks in chapter 7 set the tone for the matter here? 2/Number each remark Paul gives the Corinthians as a guide and rationale for their giving. 3/Investigate the historical circumstances of Macedonia at this time (relate to their giving). 4/What is the motivation for giving? Why should commands to give be unnecessary? 5/What principles do you use as a guide for godly giving? 6/To what extent do you carry out your plans for giving? Why? 7/How has your giving *supplied* others? How has someone's giving to you *supplied* you? 8/What principles could improve your approach to giving?

day 21 Δ 2 Corinthians 8:16-24
1/What is Paul's major concern in administering such a large fund? 2/What are the qualifications of the three delegates Paul sends to the Corinthians for the task of collection? Why does he send more than one? 3/Why does Paul take such precautions to appear blameless? 4/What standards for honesty and giving full accounts of the use of money do you see in this section? 5/To what extent are you blameless in your personal accounts (budget, income tax, etc.)? others' accounts (as treasurer, paying help, etc.)? 6/What do you see in the relationship between Paul and Titus throughout this letter that you desire in your relations with Christians in your group (cf. 2:13; 7:6; 8:6, 16, 23)?

day 22 Δ 2 Corinthians 9
1/Compare verse 1 with 1 Corinthians 16:1-4. 2/Find the principles of giving in this section and paraphrase them. 3/In what ways are these principles presently a reality in your daily experience? 4/What does this section teach you about God's character and role in the area of giving? 5/What initiates thanksgiving to God (cf. 1:11; 4:15)? 6/How will the completion of the Corinthians' giving testify to the character of *a*-Paul, *b*-the gospel, and *c*-the Corinthians? 7/What do you learn about relating to others on the basis of what Paul assumes in his relationship with the Corinthians?

day 23 Δ 2 Corinthians 10:1-6
1/Determine the people Paul addresses now. What is their opinion
of him? 2/Describe *a*-the war Paul fights and *b*-the weapons he
uses. 3/What or who is the enemy? 4/What or who is Paul
defending? 5/What weapons do you use? Why? 6/In what ways
could your life be changed by *taking every thought captive to obey
Christ?* How can you do this today?

day 24 Δ 2 Corinthians 10:7-18
1/Write a character description of the men who oppose Paul at
Corinth based on what Paul says and implies about them in this
passage. 2/How does Paul defend himself in response to their
attack on his authority and consistency? 3/What is your opinion
of Paul's letters after studying *1, 2 Thessalonians, Romans,* and *1,
2 Corinthians*? 4/To what extent are your words and actions
related? 5/Compare or contrast the standards of self-measurement
of *a*-Paul, *b*-the renegade Corinthians (cf. 3:1; 5:12), and
c-you. 6/In what ways have you *built up* others this past week?

day 25 Δ 2 Corinthians 11:1-15
1/Add to your characterization of Paul's opponents. 2/List the
reasons Paul claims he can *boast* (cf. 1:12). 3/How does he use
irony in this passage? Imagine his feelings here. 4/Describe Paul's
concern for the Corinthians. Imagine the Corinthians' response. 5/In what ways can you share God's *jealousy* for your
friends, neighbors and family? 6/How have you been deceived by
Satan recently? What can you do to guard against his deception
today?

day 26 Δ 2 Corinthians 11:16-33
1/Summarize the kind of people who have been *boasting* to the
Corinthians. Of what have they boasted? 2/How have some of the
Corinthians responded to this boasting? 3/Summarize how their
response has made Paul speak *as a fool*. 4/What is ironical about
Paul's weakness? 5/Categorize the qualifications and experiences

from which Paul can claim to be a *better servant*. 6/Relate Paul's physical and mental suffering. In what similar ways are you identified with the church? 7/Imagine the response of the Corinthians to Paul's "boasting." What is your response? 8/Of what do you *boast* (cf. v. 30 with 1:12)? What can you claim to qualify you as a servant of Christ?

day 27 Δ *2 Corinthians 12:1-10*
1/Relate *boast, fool,* and *truth* in the vision Paul cites. 2/To what extent do you expose yourself to others? Why? 3/In one statement explain why Paul can be *content* with personal weaknesses, insults, hardship, etc. 4/How does Paul describe the meaning of strength? How and when can weakness be strength? 5/How can you be *content* with your weaknesses? Determine the meaning of *content* in this context (relate to your specific circumstances).

day 28 Δ *2 Corinthians 12:11-21*
1/Why has Paul spent so much time acting the ironic fool? 2/To whom has Paul's defense been directed? 3/For what reasons will Paul continue his former policy concerning support while at Corinth? 4/Summarize Paul's relationship with the Corinthians. 5/Can you think through possible relationships with friends and family when you could *gladly spend* for their benefit? 6/What are the reasons for Paul's apprehension regarding his forthcoming visit to the Corinthians?

day 29 Δ *2 Corinthians 13*
1/How will Paul act toward the Corinthians when he comes? Why? 2/Summarize the way Paul further develops the concepts of weakness and strength (power) in this passage. 3/What is Paul's concern in challenging the Corinthians to examine themselves? 4/How can Paul prove he has not failed? What is Paul more concerned about than proving he has succeeded? 5/How can you conduct your life so that you can claim to do nothing against *the*

truth? 6/How do you use your authority (cf. Paul's use of his authority throughout the letter)? 7/What must you do so that the *God of love and peace* will be with you (relate both nouns to the Corinthians' need for them)?

day 30 △ Introduction to Micah

Micah lives in a rural community (about twenty miles southwest of Jerusalem) during the general era of Isaiah, Amos, and Hosea. *Micah 1* 1/Visualize verses 2-7. Characterize God as portrayed here. 2/What will happen to *a*-nature and *b*-the capitals of the northern and southern kingdoms? Why? 3/Imagine the everyday life in Samaria and Jerusalem. Imagine the people's reactions to such judgment. 4/What authority does the prophet have to give his message? 5/How does the prophet personally feel about the situation? 6/What is your attitude toward people and nations involved in obvious sin? 7/Locate on a map the towns (each phrase connected with a town is a word-play on the Hebrew names of the towns) involved in destruction by the Assyrian army (cf. v. 15 with 1 Sam. 21:10–22:2). 8/What is Micah's appeal (shaving the head is a sign of mourning)?

Month 16

day 1 △ Micah 2

1/Characterize the wicked classes of people. 2/Relate the religious and economic evils. 3/Compare and contrast the two devisers of evil (vv. 1-2, 3-5) as to the *a*-kind of schemes devised, *b*-reasons, and *c*-sufferers. 4/To what extent do you speak out against *a*-religious and *b*-socio-economic injustices? Why? 5/What is the response of the people to the prophet's message? 6/What does their response reveal about their attitude toward God? 7/What is Micah's appeal here (cf. 1:16)? 8/What promises does the Lord make to Israel (vv. 12-13 are not part of Micah's denunciation here)?

day 2 △ Micah 3

1/Compare and contrast the characteristics of the leadership (rulers, prophets, priests) of Israel at this time. 2/How will God's judgment be shown to each group? 3/What qualifications does Micah have for his responsibility of warning the leadership of Israel? 4/To what extent would you be willing to have a ministry of warning? Why? 5/Compare the dilemma of these leaders with the hazards of present Christian leadership. 6/How can you avoid being *disgraced* by God?

day 3 △ Micah 4–5:1

1/Describe God's plans for the *latter days*. What do these plans reveal about God? 2/Contrast Micah's message in this chapter with the previous three chapters. 3/Compare the future of the people (culminating in their exile in Babylon) with a woman in travail. What indignities do they suffer? 4/In what ways are the people of God different from the *many nations*? 5/Compare the nations that besiege Jerusalem with *sheaves*. 6/To what extent is your nation trying to pattern its progress according to verses 3-4? To what extent, do you think, will it succeed? Why?

day 4 △ Micah 5:2-15

1/Compare 2:12-13 with this passage. 2/What type of leadership is promised Israel (contrast with the present leadership—esp. chap. 3)? 3/What needs of yours could be met by such leadership? 4/What will happen when Assyria invades the land? How will this news encourage the people (cf. their present situation)? 5/Read the poem of verses 7-9 aloud. What are the two different images portraying the remnant? 6/In what do the people now trust for their strength? How will God assert his strength? 7/What is the basis of your confidence about yourself and life?

day 5 △ Micah 6

1/Distinguish in which verses *a*-God and *b*-the people are speaking.

Summarize each side of the *controversy*. 2/What does God desire of you? 3/What do you learn of God's character from his comments regarding Israel's social and economic practices (cf. 1 Kings 16:21-34)? 4/What seems to be the central cause of Israel's separation from God? 5/Try to identify where your life is directed by the standards of your campus or job or community rather than by God.

day 6   Δ   *Micah 7*
1/Describe the spiritual character of Judah and Jerusalem. 2/Explain the metaphors Micah uses. 3/What has happened to human relationships? 4/What is Micah's attitude toward God while in a sinful society? Compare or contrast your attitude toward God while in your society. 5/Summarize Micah's view of God. What is Micah's tone here? 6/What is your response to a God possessing these characteristics and actions?

day 7   Δ   *Introduction to 1 Timothy*
The apostle Paul writes this letter to encourage young Timothy in the face of difficult responsibilities. 1/Establish the probable time of writing. 2/Read the entire letter as though you personally have received it. 3/What seems to be the underlying problem? Paul's remedy? 4/Keep a list of the qualifications and instructions for Christian leaders.

day 8   Δ   *1 Timothy 1:1-17*
1/What is the relationship between Paul and Timothy? Why has Paul left him at Ephesus? 2/What is the *a*-content and *b*-result of the *different doctrine*? Characterize the people who teach this doctrine. 3/What is the aim of true teaching? 4/What is the threefold origin of love? Determine the meaning of the adjectives here. 5/What is the purpose of the law? 6/How do you *use the law lawfully*? 7/Categorize the kind of people for which the law is *laid down*. 8/Determine the meaning of *blessed* in relation to God. 9/In what ways are verses 12-17 related to the previous

verses? 10/How is Paul's experience as a Christian an example to you of the *perfect patience* of Jesus Christ?

day 9 Δ *1 Timothy 1:18–2:7*

1/Relate *faith* and a *good conscience* (cf. 1:5). To what extent are they related in your life? How do they contribute toward your waging a *good warfare*? 2/What forms of prayer (what does each mean?) are urged? For whom? Why? 3/To what extent do you pray for *all men*? Why? 4/How is approach to God possible? 5/What does God desire for *all* men (cf. 2:4, 6 with 2:1)? How should this fact affect your attitude toward those you meet today?

day 10 Δ *1 Timothy 2:8-15*

1/Characterize the *a*-actions and *b*-attitudes of acceptable prayer (*hands* here stands for the whole of a person's life). 2/What, does Paul say, should *adorn* a woman? 3/List and explain the adverbs and adjectives. 4/In what way can lack of style and appropriateness in a woman's attire be a misunderstanding of this passage? 5/What should be the woman's place in the teaching ministry of the church in relation to men? Why? 6/Determine the meaning of verse 15. 7/Is this principle of a woman's status peculiar to Paul's time or generally applicable today?

day 11 Δ *1 Timothy 3:1-13*

1/List and explain the qualifications for *a*-bishops and *b*-deacons. 2/Account for the difference in the lists (relate to the differences in types of ministry). 3/What negative characteristics should you eliminate in your life? What positive ones should you cultivate? 4/What are the dangers of leadership by young Christians? 5/Relate verse 9 to 1:5, 18-19.

day 12 Δ *1 Timothy 3:14–4:5*

1/Why is Paul writing to Timothy? Do you take time to write to your younger Christian friends for similar reasons? 2/How does Paul relate the practical arrangements of the church to the meaning and purpose of the church (e.g., cf. v. 15 with vv. 4, 12)? 3/What is the core or *great mystery of our religion* as expressed in perhaps one of the first hymn-creeds of the church (v. 16)? 4/Relate the conditions of *a*-faith and *b*-conscience in 4:1-3 (cf. 1:5, 18-19; 3:9). 5/Contrast the two attitudes in 4:1-5. 6/What is the basic problem with the attitude in 4:1-3? 7/How can you guard against being led astray by false teaching?

day 13   Δ   1 Timothy 4:6-16
1/What will be Timothy's defense against false teaching? 2/With what results in his life? in the lives of those around him? 3/What should be your attitude toward wild religious ideas? 4/What should be the aim and result of your Bible study and living today? 5/List the clear commands Paul gives Timothy. 6/In what ways will your life be an *example* to others today? 7/What *gifts* do you have? 8/How can you *practice these duties* today?

day 14   Δ   1 Timothy 5:1-16
1/What practical advice does Paul give for relationships with other Christians? 2/What problem faces the church at Ephesus (*honor* implies financial aid)?   3/Who does Paul consider to be a *real* widow? 4/What three basic principles does Paul use to meet this problem? 5/What are the responsibilities of *a*-children and *b*-widows? 6/What kind of widows have no claim to the church's care? 7/What reasons does Paul give for these instructions (cf. vv. 7, 12, 14, 16)? 8/Explain the progression of categories of a widow's good deeds in verse 10. 9/What kind of special church duties, do you think, would the aged widows be suited for? 10/How do you treat widows you know? What can you do today to assist a widow?

day 15   Δ   1 Timothy 5:17–6:2
1/In what way is the principle of adequate payment for elders

backed by biblical teaching (cf. Deut. 25:4; Lk. 10:7)? 2/What would happen to gossip in your Christian group if you really heeded verse 19? 3/What four dangers is Timothy urged to guard against in verses 19-22 (*laying on of hands* may refer to ordination or restoration of an elder)? 4/Is *purity* necessarily abstention? 5/Relate the observations in verses 24-25 to 5:22 and 3:6, 10. 6/Considering 6:1-2 what should be your attitude toward your employer? What special danger must you guard against if he is a Christian?

day 16   Δ   1 Timothy 6:3-21

1/What are the characteristics of false teachers? their ruling motive? the results of their teaching? What has religion become to them? 2/How does the Christian *a*-aim and *b*-motive differ from theirs? 3/What are the results of sound teaching? 4/How are God and Jesus related? How does Paul characterize and praise each? 5/How can you *keep the commandment unstained* today? 6/What is the counsel for those who have become rich honestly? 7/Considering this letter how important is your daily study of Scripture to know sound doctrine? 8/How can you be certain that you have true teaching (cf. 1:5; 4:7-8; 6:3, 11-12)? 9/How can you guard that true teaching?

day 17   Δ   Introduction to Titus

Paul writes this letter to Titus, left in Crete to establish the churches. *Titus 1* 1/What two titles does Paul give himself? To what end is his ministry directed? 2/To what extent is your service influenced by *hope*? by present circumstances? 3/Outline the qualities of a Christian leader in relation to *a*-himself, *b*-others, and *c*-God (cf. 1 Tim. 3:1-13). 4/Could you be chosen as a leader under these qualifications? 5/Characterize the false teachers of Crete as to *a*-their conduct, *b*-their teaching, and *c*-the results of their teaching. 6/What is the Christian leader's responsibility to such people? 7/As a leader, how do you exercise this command of verse 13? 8/Determine the meaning of verse 15. 9/Relate your professed knowledge of God with your actions.

day 18 Δ *Titus 2*

1/List and explain Paul's imperatives to the various groups in verses 1-6. 2/Evaluate yourself in relation to the appropriate group. 3/To what extent do you want this pattern for your life? 4/How are you developing these qualities? 5/As a man/ woman, in what ways do your relationships with women/men encourage these qualities? 6/Which of the qualities Paul urges for your group need your special attention today? 7/To what extent are your example and teaching related? 8/How do you *put an opponent to shame* (cf. v. 8)? 9/Contrast the concepts of slavery and freedom in Christ. 10/Relate the principles of verses 9-10 to both concepts (cf. 1 Tim. 6:1-2). 11/To what extent does Paul work within the system of slavery without condoning it? 12/How do verses 9-10 apply to the relationship with your employer? 13/Relate the doctrine of verses 11-14 with the ethics of verses 1-10. 14/What is the effect of the *grace* of God in your life now?

day 19 Δ *Titus 3*

1/What should be a Christian's attitude and behavior in his society? 2/Contrast the expected present conduct with previous conduct. 3/In what specific ways have you been changed by the grace of God? 4/What about the three persons of the Trinity is revealed here? 5/On what basis is a person justified before God? 6/What should be your attitude toward *a*-false teaching and *b*-controversy in your Christian group? 7/What is your responsibility toward a factious person? 8/In what ways can you help a Christian friend in need today? 9/Summarize the teachings and commands of Paul to Titus. Imagine Titus' response. What is yours?

day 20 Δ *Introduction to 2 Timothy*

Paul writes his last letter in his prison cell shortly before his death. 1/Read the entire letter at one sitting. 2/What is important to Paul as he faces impending death? 3/Does his attitude come from his circumstances? 4/In what is his *hope* and *joy*?

day 21 Δ *2 Timothy 1:1-14*
1/What is Paul's relationship to Timothy? 2/What is the relation between your morality and your worship (cf. 1 Tim. 1:5, 18-19)? 3/To what extent has your environment influenced your faith? 4/Determine the meaning of *rekindle* and the nouns in verse 7. 5/For what reasons shouldn't Timothy be *ashamed*? 6/When are you *ashamed* of *a*-witness (cf. vv. 7-8, 12, 16) and *b*-suffering? Why? 7/From this passage what is the content of the gospel? 8/What imperatives does Paul give Timothy? 9/Considering this passage what is your responsibility today with the gospel (truth)?

day 22 Δ *2 Timothy 1:15–2:13*
1/Contrast *a*-Phygelus and Hermogenes and *b*-Onesiphorus. 2/How can you *refresh* another Christian today? 3/Imagine Paul's concern for the transmission of the gospel's truth as he faces death. 4/Describe the three metaphors of a Christian (2:1-7). 5/Relate these metaphors with Paul's concern. 6/Evaluate *a*-Paul's (cf. 2:8-10) and *b*-your life (on campus, in the neighborhood, on your job) in reference to these metaphors. 7/What motivates Paul to endure suffering (cf. 1:8-12)? 8/What is Paul's basis of security (cf. 1:8-12)?

day 23 Δ *2 Timothy 2:14-26*
1/What problem in the church concerns Paul (cf. 1 Tim.; Titus)? 2/What is the basis for *shame* in verse 15 (cf. 1:8, 12, 16)? 3/How can you be sure your doctrine is true? 4/What results from *godless chatter*? What should be your *a*-conduct and *b*-certainty in such situations? 5/What two truths does Paul draw from his illustration about the vessels (relate v. 20a and v. 20b to v. 19)? 6/Characterize a noble *vessel*. 7/List the negative and the positive aspects of the exhortations. 8/What should be your attitude toward those who oppose the gospel?

day 24 Δ *2 Timothy 3*
1/What is the effect of heresy on society? 2/Which characteristics

of verses 1-9 are present in your generation? in your life? Why? 3/Contrast Paul's life with lives of counterfeit faith. 4/How would Paul's life encourage Timothy in the face of the *stress* of the *last days*? 5/What should you expect if you live a godly life (cf. 2:12)? 6/Relate verses 9 and 13. 7/How does Scripture affect the life of Timothy (cf. 1:12-13; 2:1-2)? 8/What is the goal of your Bible study (cf. vv. 16-17)?

day 25   Δ   2 Timothy 4
1/List and categorize Paul's final imperatives to Timothy. 2/Relate these imperatives to *a*-Timothy's and *b*-modern situations. 3/What reasons does Paul give for urgency in the ministry? 4/What can you do today to experience Paul's claim of verses 6-8? 5/What do verses 9-22 reveal of Paul's *a*-concerns, *b*-needs, *c*-memories, and *d*-strength? 6/What can you learn from the people mentioned here? 7/Imagine Paul's feelings as he seals this letter. 8/Imagine the kind of letter you would write in a situation similar to Paul's. Compare or contrast the content of Paul's letter.

day 26   Δ   Introduction to Leviticus
God demands the highest standard of holiness from his nation Israel. Thus he gives to Moses while at Sinai specific laws and principles for the priests and people. Distinguish the ceremonial and moral laws of *Leviticus* and discover their purposes. *Leviticus 1* 1/Determine what is to be done with the *a*-blood, *b*-fat, and *c*-remaining parts of each of the three types of animals used for burnt offerings. 2/How would you answer someone who feels that the slaughter of an animal sacrifice is offensive? 3/Using both statement and symbolism from the text explain the relation between the animal and the person bringing it for an offering. 4/List the results of the offering regarding *a*-man and *b*-God. 5/Investigate ways in which the burnt offering may be a picture of a normal Christian life (review Rom. 12:1-2). 6/What kind of life does God expect of you?

day 27 ∆ *Leviticus 2 and 6:14-18*
1/What are the ingredients of a cereal offering? How are they to be prepared? 2/Determine its meaning (the Hebrew word for this offering—*michah*—is used in Gen. 32:13-21; 43:11, 25-26). 3/Whom is the cereal offering to feed? 4/Determine the meaning of *covenant* and *memorial* as related to the cereal offering (cf. their meaning in Ex.). 5/What feature of the description of this offering is common to that of the burnt offering?

day 28 ∆ *Leviticus 3 and 7:11-21*
1/What elements of the peace offering are reserved for the Lord? 2/What acts does the bringer of the offering perform? 3/What is the purpose of a peace offering (cf. Gen. 26:26-31)? 4/What indicates that God enjoys the occasion of this offering? 5/Can you do anything today to bring God pleasure? 6/Are you at peace with God? How do you know?

day 29 ∆ *Leviticus 4*
1/Compare and contrast this offering with the three previous offerings. 2/List the references in this chapter to atonement (cf. chap. 1). Distinguish what needs atonement in chapters 1 and 4. 3/Try to arrive at a definition for *sin* (the Hebrew root word for *sin* and *sin offering* are the same). 4/What is done with the *a*-blood and *b*-fat of the offering? 5/What indicates that *a*-the gravity of sin increases with positions of leadership and responsibility, *b*-no one is exempt from responsibility, and *c*-ignorance or inadvertence is no excuse? 6/How do you handle sin in your life? Can you plead ignorance? 7/What (in statement and symbolism) gives assurance of complete and final forgiveness for the beneficiary of the sacrifice?

day 30 ∆ *Leviticus 5:1–6:7*
1/List the uses of *guilt* and *guilt offering* (identical in the Hebrew text). 2/What is God's attitude toward a witness who hides his knowledge of a crime? 3/Contrast this attitude with contempo-

rary efforts to remain uninvolved. 4/List the *a*-acts and *b*-persons
guilt involves or relates to. 5/What two acts, beside the bringing of
the offering, are required of the wrongdoer? 6/What provisions
are made for the offerings of the poor? 7/In what ways is
violation of the rights of a neighbor a violation against
God? 8/Trace the significance of *fat, blood,* and *atonement*
through this section. 9/In what areas of your life have you
committed a *breach of faith*? What have you done about it? What
will you do today?

Month 17

day 1 ∆ *Leviticus 6:8-13, 19-30*
1/Trace the references to the altar fire in verses 8-13. How does
this fit in with the symbolism of the burnt offering? 2/What is the
continuity of your relationship with God? Why? 3/What is the
penalty for disobedience? 4/Examine the idea of holiness as
expressed in verses 19-30. Summarize its meaning. 5/How can you
be *holy* in your living?

day 2 ∆ *Leviticus 7:1-10, 22-38*
1/What portion of the offerings is due to the priests? For what
purpose? 2/In what respects are fat and blood to be treated
differently from other parts of the sacrifice (cf. 3:16-17)? 3/What
are the priest's duties? 4/Why should the fat be God's portion (cf.
the use of the word in Gen. 45:18)? 5/Does God receive the best
part of your life? Why? 6/Contrast what is done with the cereal
offerings of the *a*-people and *b*-priests. Account for the difference. 7/Where is the sin offering killed (cf. 1:11)?

day 3 ∆ *Leviticus 8*
1/What two words in this chapter indicate the purpose of the ritual
here described? 2/Who witnesses the ceremony? 3/What fluids

are used in the ceremonies? 4/Can you attach any meaning to their use? 5/What parts of the body are washed? What parts are anointed? What is the significance? 6/Can a sinner serve as a priest? Under what conditions? 7/Do you consider yourself as a priest in any sense? Why? 8/What qualities are expected of a priest? Why?

day 4 Δ Leviticus 9
1/Imagine the feelings of Aaron and his sons at their inaugura-tion. 2/Pick out words or phrases which characterize and empha-size their obedience. 3/What benefits do the people receive from the priests' ministry as recorded here? 4/Have any similar benefits come through you this week? Why? 5/What purposes are served by the appearance of God's glory? 6/What natural order is found in the priests' actions in this chapter?

day 5 Δ Leviticus 10
1/What is wrong about the act of Nadab and Abihu (cf. their previous privileges—Ex. 24:1, 9-10)? Try to imagine what may have prompted their action. 2/What is God's explanation of his reprisal? 3/What conflict between sacred and family obligations occurs here? Which has precedence here? 4/What similar conflicts of interest are in your life? in the lives of people you know? In any given case which way should the conflict be resolved? 5/What is the purpose of the priests' abstinence from wine? 6/Find another infraction of the ritual in this chapter. What is Aaron's explana-tion? Moses' response?

day 6 Δ Leviticus 11
1/State the general rule describing *a*-animals and *b*-fish allowed for food. 2/What characteristic is common to at least some of the forbidden birds? 3/Find a statement giving reasons for these dietary rules. What question seems to be left unanswered? 4/Find the positive imperative of this chapter. To what degree is this imperative still in force for God's people? for you?

171

day 7 △ *Leviticus 12*

1/Find some specific rules of hygiene embodied in these instructions. 2/Do these also apply to miscarriage? 3/What is the meaning of circumcision (cf. Gen. 17:9-14)? 4/What, do you think, is the significance of the two offerings in relation to childbirth (review Luke 2:24 to see how Mary fulfills her obligations)? 5/What commentary does this section offer to the assertion that "my private life is my own concern only"?

day 8 △ *Leviticus 13*

1/Summarize the hygienic rules of this section under the headings: *a*-diagnosis, *b*-quarantine, and *c*-prevention and control. 2/Who is the examiner? 3/List the different situations which may develop into leprosy in *a*-people and *b*-garments. 4/What is the plight of the leper (contrast 10:6—the actions commanded are signs of mourning)? 5/Attach to leprosy a symbolic meaning which seems valid to you.

day 9 △ *Leviticus 14*

1/Describe the ritual for restoration of the cleansed leper to the community. 2/What parts of this ritual are similar to that for installation of the priests (cf. chap. 8)? What is the significance of the similarity? 3/Are any obligations laid on you as a forgiven sinner? 4/What is distinctive about the leprosy of houses (esp. v. 34)?

day 10 △ *Leviticus 15*

1/Do these chapters imply that the physiology of sex and the normal relations of married people are inherently unclean? Try to support your answer from the text (cf. Lev. 11). 2/Why, do you think, is *atonement* necessary? 3/In what way would the unclean man and woman *defile* God's tabernacle? What does this reveal about God's standards for purity?

day 11 △ *Leviticus 16*

1/How does God appear in the tabernacle? What is the purpose of the incense? 2/What is the purpose of the yearly day of atonement? What are the restrictions? 3/In what ways do you sin even in worshipping God? Why? 4/What is the function of the goats *a*-for the Lord and *b*-for Azazel? Assign to each function a symbolic religious meaning which seems valid to you. 5/To what extent have your sins been banished? 6/What is the natural order in this chapter? 7/What is your response to this God who demands intense purity?

day 12 △ *Leviticus 17*

1/Who are the additional recipients of God's communication in this chapter? 2/Summarize the laws concerning the killing of animals for *a*-food and *b*-sacrifice. What are their purposes? 3/Which law is repealed when they enter Canaan (cf. Deut. 12:13-15)? Why (relate to its purpose)? 4/Relate the purpose of *blood* in sacrifice to the prohibition about it. 5/What about the relationship of God and man is revealed in this chapter? 6/To what extent do you manifest your relationship to God in your daily activities? Why?

day 13 △ *Leviticus 18*

1/What basic area of life is affected by these commands? 2/What should be your attitudes and actions in this area? 3/What is the result of obedience for *a*-the person himself and *b*-those to whom he is related? 4/Why must *a*-Israel and *b*-you obey the commands of God? 5/Relate defilement and adultery (cf. v. 24). Contrast this concept with the popular attitude toward such actions today. 6/What is the relationship between verses 20 and 21? 7/In what ways do you *profane* God's name? 8/What is *a*-God's and *b*-the land's reaction to such perversion?

day 14 △ *Leviticus 19*

1/What is the reason underlying all the commands here? 2/Why do you obey God? 3/Categorize these commands as they relate to *a*-God, *b*-man, and *c*-practical extensions. 4/What attitudes toward God and man are insured by these commands? 5/What *a*-penalties and *b*-remedies are given for disobedience here? 6/Compare verse 19 with 18:22-23. 7/Can you distinguish which of these commands have universal application? Which are only for Israel at this time?

day 15 Δ *Leviticus 20*

1/What are some penalties for the sins enumerated in the previous chapters? Which call for capital punishment? 2/Determine the meaning of *set my face against* in relation to God's judgment on disobedience. 3/Determine the meaning of *separate* in relation to the people of Israel. In what ways is their separation to be preserved? 4/Imagine the effect of Israel's practices on the surrounding nations. 5/Project the possible deterioration of the separateness and its reasons and meaning. 6/As a Christian in what ways should you be *separate*? Does this mean that you are "better" than non-Christians?

day 16 Δ *Leviticus 21*

1/In what ways are the laws of purity for priests more strict than for the congregation? Why? 2/In what ways are the priests' natural emotions and practices subservient to their duties to God? 3/When do your daily activities conflict with what God demands of you to be holy? How do you resolve the conflict? Why? 4/What part do the people have in insuring the priest's holiness? 5/Relate verses 16-24 with verse 5. 6/What physical characteristics disqualify Aaron's descendants for serving at the altar? Why, do you think? How do they still take part in the offerings?

day 17 Δ *Leviticus 22*

1/Distinguish the *holy things* and the priests' due (cf. previous chaps.). 2/In what way does the punishment for the disobedience of a priest differ from that of an Israelite (cf. v. 3 with 7:21, 25,

27; 19:8)? 3/What types of uncleanness (cf. chaps. 11–15) disqualify a normally qualified priest for serving at the altar? 4/What types of thoughts and actions prevent you from coming into God's presence? How can you be *clean*? 5/What disqualifications which apply to the priests (cf. 21:16-24) also apply to the sacrifices?

day 18 Δ Leviticus 23
1/Chart the annual feasts to be observed by the Israelites. Establish their *a*-chronological order, *b*-duration, *c*-place of celebration, and *d*-purpose (relate to the agricultural and national significance). 2/What *a*-offerings and *b*-activities are involved in their celebrations? What is prohibited? 3/What attitudes toward God underlie the feast celebrations? 4/Relate the private and public celebrations of the feasts. 5/In what ways do you remember and celebrate God's care for you?

day 19 Δ Leviticus 24
1/What are the daily rituals of Aaron? 2/What is the significance of each? 3/What is the meaning of *continually*? 4/What is the sin of Shelomith's son? What about his status makes the case unusual? 5/Contrast the penalty for a sojourner's curse of *a*-his God and *b*-the Name. Account for the difference. 6/What do you learn about God's justice from the general law he gives in verses 18-21? 7/Distinguish justice and revenge. 8/Do you ever have any right to avenge yourself?

day 20 Δ Leviticus 25
1/Summarize the attitudes which the Israelites are to show toward *a*-their neighbors and *b*-the land of Canaan. 2/In what ways are they a reflection of God's attitude? 3/What should be your attitude toward your personal property? the poor? Why? 4/Trace the concepts of rest, liberty, and redemption in this chapter. In what ways do the concepts relate to the *a*-sabbath and *b*-jubilee years?

day 21 Δ *Leviticus 26*

1/In what ways will an Israelite in the condition described in 25:17-35 be guarded against idolatry if he keeps the command of verse 2? 2/Review the *statutes* set forth in *Leviticus*. 3/What will be the *a*-religious, *b*-political, and *c*-socio-economic benefits which will accrue if the Israelites obey? 4/What is the cause of disobedience? 5/Why do you disobey God's commands for you? 6/What is the progression of the calamities which will result if the Israelites disobey? 7/What is the ultimate purpose of the calamities? 8/Imagine what the *a*-blessings and *b*-calamities will mean for Israel and her reputation among the nations.

day 22 Δ *Leviticus 27*

1/List the things a man can dedicate to the Lord by a vow. 2/What belongs to the Lord outright? 3/How are the vows to be evaluated? For what purpose? 4/How is the concept of redemption related to the vows? 5/What is your responsibility if you make a vow to the Lord? 6/Summarize how these vows and the laws of the previous chapters are meant to maintain Israel's holiness.

day 23 Δ *Introduction to Hebrews*

The teaching of *Hebrews* is for those who think they don't need it. The letter is written to a community of Jewish Christians who have made a good start in the Christian life, but who then mistake laziness and cowardice for maturity. They are about to slip back into their old beliefs without realizing the significance of their loss. Periodically review *Exodus* and *Leviticus* for background. *Hebrews 1:1-4* 1/Through whom has God communicated? Compare and contrast the extent of God's revelation in them. 2/In what ways does the Son demonstrate his deity? 3/How does the Son's nature reveal the Father to you? What should be your attitude toward the Son? 4/What has the Son accomplished in his incarnation (cf. the priests' duties in Lev.)?

day 24 ∆ *Hebrews 1:5-14*
1/From the Old Testament quotations (cf. v. 5 with Ps. 2:7, 2 Sam.
7:14; v. 6 with Deut. 32:43; v. 7 with Ps. 104:4; vv. 8-9 with Ps.
45:6-7; vv. 10-12 with Ps. 102:25-27; v. 13 with Ps. 110:1) contrast angels and the Son in regard to *a*-relation to God, *b*-sover-
eignty, and *c*-eternality.   2/What areas of your life still need to be
subjected to Christ?   3/What is the purpose of angels (cf.
2:2)?   4/How does this passage convince you of Christ's supremacy?   5/Determine the Jewish regard for angels. How does the
author of *Hebrews* show that the Son is superior to angels? In what
ways is this important for the readers' understanding?

day 25 ∆ *Hebrews 2:1-4*
1/How does *therefore* relate these four verses to the previous chapter?   2/To what extent are you *drifting away* or *neglecting* the
truths of the gospel? With what result?   3/How can you protect
against this plight? Why should you?   4/What indicates that the
recipients of this letter have heard the message of salvation?   5/Ex-
plain the activity of each person of the Godhead in salvation.

day 26 ∆ *Hebrews 2:5-13*
1/For what high destiny does God create man?   2/To what extent
has man succeeded in ruling the earth and himself?   3/What is the
purpose of Jesus' becoming a man?   4/To what extent has he identified with man?   5/How does this passage answer the anticipated
objection, "Being a mere man, Jesus is inferior to angels"?   6/What
is your new relationship to Christ (cf. v. 12 with Ps. 22:22; v. 13
with Is. 8:17-18)?   7/How will this relationship affect your destiny
to rule the world to come?   8/How does it affect your daily living?

day 27 ∆ *Hebrews 2:14-18*
1/What reasons are given here for Christ's *a*-becoming man,
b-death, and *c*-suffering?   2/To what extent are you free from
a-bondage and *b*-fear of death?   3/What is the work of Christ as
your *high priest*?   4/Relate the necessity of Christ's becoming man

177

with the necessity of his supremacy (cf. chaps. 1—2). 5/Compare
the kind and intensity of the temptations Christ has withstood
with those you face. 6/How does Christ's common lot with man
in suffering and temptation *help* you?

day 28 △ *Hebrews 3:1-6*
1/How does this passage build on what the readers know of Judaism? 2/Compare and contrast Jesus and Moses as to *a*-title, *b*-char-
acteristics, and *c*-relationship to the *house*. 3/Which characteristic
of Christ as high priest is most prominently set out in these
verses? 4/How is Moses a good example of this characteristic? 5/How is Moses' ministry different from Jesus'? 6/In what
way does the Hebrews' relationship with Christ supersede their
relationship with Moses? 7/In what areas of your life do your
actions reveal a low view of Jesus? What specific steps can you take
today to right these actions?

day 29 △ *Hebrews 3:7-12*
1/Determine the meaning of God's *rest* for the children of Israel
(cf. Ex.; Num. 14). 2/What is the reason for God's statement in
verse 11 (cf. Ps. 95:7-11)? 3/What about the nature of God is
revealed here? 4/What causes *hardness of heart*? 5/What can you
do to prevent such hardness in your heart? 6/What is God's feeling toward you now? Why? 7/List parallels between the situations
of *a*-the Israelites and *b*-the Hebrews (cf. vv. 1-6). 8/In what ways
is a return to Judaism a *falling away* from the *living God*?

day 30 △ *Hebrews 3:12-19*
1/Distinguish the three questions and answers in verses
16-18. 2/In what ways have you been aware recently of the *de-
ceitfulness* of sin? 3/List characteristics of the Israelites who did
not enter the land of rest. 4/Which of these characteristics describe your experience? Why? Contrast these with the thought in
verse 14. 5/What is the author's warning for *a*-the Hebrews and

b-you? 6/Whom should you *exhort* (v. 13) today? 7/How do you respond to *exhortation* from others? Why?

Month 18

day 1 Δ *Hebrews 4:1-10*
1/Compare or contrast the responses of *a*-the Israelites, *b*-the Hebrews, and *c*-you to the *good news*. 2/Upon what basis is the author convinced that believers now can enter God's *rest*? 3/What is the purpose of the illustration of creation in the discussion of *rest*? 4/**Expand** the meaning of God's *rest* (cf. 3:7-19; Joshua). 5/**What** is the qualification for entering that rest? 6/What are two **events** which allow a person to *enter God's rest*? Which is most likely meant here (cf. 2:8-9, 14-15)? 7/In what ways is your weekly *sabbath* representative of God's rest?

day 2 Δ *Hebrews 4:11-13*
1/Explain the *sort* of disobedience evidenced by the Israelites in the wilderness (cf. Ex. and 3:7-19). 2/What does *strive* mean? 3/What excuses do you use to hide spiritual laziness? Why? 4/Characterize the *word of God*. Compare or contrast your view of Scripture. 5/Why can't you fool God about your attitude toward him? 6/How does God's Word prevent you from pleading ignorance concerning your true attitude?

day 3 Δ *Hebrews 4:14–5:4*
1/Compare and contrast Aaron and Jesus as *high priest* (cf. Ex.). 2/What are the qualifications for a priest? What is his purpose? 3/Contrast the basis for *a*-a high priest's (e.g., Aaron) and *b*-Jesus' sympathy with human frailty. 4/Answer the misconception, "It is impossible for Jesus to sin, therefore temptation is meaningless to him" (cf. 2:17-18). 5/How do the qualifications of

Jesus as high priest enable you to act in accord with verse 16? 6/Honestly, what is your attitude toward *a*-the ignorant and *b*-the wayward? Why? 7/Determine the meaning of *deal gently.*

day 4 △ Hebrews 5:4-10

1/Although Jesus is not a descendant of Aaron (the family designated for priests), how is he able to be called a high priest (cf. Gen. 14:17-20; Ps. 110:4; chap. 7)? 2/In what ways does Jesus' life *a*-qualify him to be a high priest, *b*-demonstrate his priestly function, and *c*-become the *source* of man's salvation? 3/In what way (cf. 2:10; 4:15) has Jesus been made *perfect* (complete, mature)? 4/How is obedience related to suffering in *a*-Jesus' and *b*-your life? 5/What does this passage reveal about the relationship of God and Jesus?

day 5 △ Hebrews 5:11-14

1/What is the basic problem of the Hebrews? 2/To what extent is this your problem? What can you do today to change? 3/What distinguishes *a*-the child and *b*-the mature (relate to Judaism and Christianity)? 4/What is the standard for determining righteousness? 5/To what extent do you have trouble distinguishing *good* and *evil*? Why? How can you have accurate judgment? 6/How high in your priorities is knowledge of God's Word?

day 6 △ Hebrews 6:1-8

1/What is the significance of *therefore* in verse 1? 2/Define and categorize the six elementary truths which are the foundation of both Judaism and Christianity. 3/What is *a*-God's and *b*-your part in your maturing? 4/Explain the characteristics of the *enlightened*. 5/What is the reason for the "impossibility" (v. 4) in the author's hypothetical case? How does the illustration from nature (cf. Gen. 1:11-12; 3:17-18) substantiate the "impossibility"? 6/What, do you think, is the purpose of this warning at this place in the Hebrews' letter? 7/What is its meaning to you?

day 7 △ Hebrews 6:9-20
1/What is the significance of *beloved* in verse 9 (cf. 5:11–6:8)? 2/What qualities of God are revealed in this passage? 3/What characteristics of the Old Testament leaders are the Hebrews urged to imitate? Why (cf. v. 11)? 4/What is God's promise to Abraham (cf. Gen. 22:15-18)? 5/Describe how God assures Abraham of its fulfillment. 6/Relate the two metaphors (vv. 18-19) to Christian *hope*. 7/To what extent do *a*-God's actions here and *b*-the ideas of the metaphors encourage you? 8/Compare *hope* and *rest* (cf. chaps. 3–4). 9/What is the *a*-present and *b*-future of the Christian hope? 10/How does the position of Jesus Christ (cf. Lev. 16) demonstrate the reality of that hope?

day 8 △ Hebrews 7:1-10
1/List and explain the facts about Melchizedek (cf. Gen. 14:17-20). 2/In what ways is he an excellent representation of Christ? 3/In what ways is Melchizedek superior to Abraham? to Levi and his descendants (cf. Lev.)? 4/Summarize how Christ is superior to *a*-angels (chaps. 1–2), *b*-man (chap. 2), *c*-Moses (chap. 3), and *d*-Abraham. 5/Imagine the effect of these arguments on the Hebrews. 6/How do these truths affect you? What is your response?

day 9 △ Hebrews 7:11-17
1/Contrast the *a*-Levitical and *b*-*perfect* priesthood. 2/Explain the relationship between the *priesthood* and the *law* in Judaism (cf. Ex.; Lev.). 3/So what happens to the *law* when the *priesthood* is superseded? 4/To what tribe does Jesus belong? How does this disqualify him from serving as a priest at the altar? 5/To what does *this* in verse 15 refer? 6/What is Jesus' qualification to be a priest? 7/How does this qualification supersede the *law*? 8/Imagine you are a Hebrew listening to this letter. What would be your response here? Why?

day 10 △ Hebrews 7:18-28
1/Contrast the Levitical and Christ's *a*-authority and *b*-perma-

nence. 2/In what way is the *a*-hope and *b*-covenant through Christ *better* than the *a*-hope and *b*-covenant through the law? 3/Determine the meaning of *surety* and *covenant*. Explain verse 22 (cf. v. 25). 4/Summarize the characteristics of Jesus as high priest (cf. chaps. 1–7). 5/Summarize how he is superior to the Levitical priests (cf. Ex.; Lev.). 6/What is the impact of these truths in your thinking? in your daily living?

day 11 Δ *Hebrews 8:1-6*

1/What is the duty of a priest (cf. 5:1 with Ex.; Lev.)? 2/Where and how is Christ fulfilling his priestly duty? 3/In what ways is his heavenly ministry *a*-different from and *b*-an extension of his earthly ministry? 4/How is the earthly sanctuary a model for Christ's ministry? 5/Compare and contrast the earthly sanctuary with the heavenly sanctuary (cf. Ex. 25–27; 30; 35–38). 6/How is the earthly sanctuary an expression of the mind of God? 7/Determine the meaning of *shadow* and *pattern* in verse 5. 8/How is the setting of Christ's ministry as high priest superior to the setting of the ministry of earthly priests? 9/Imagine you are an Israelite living by the *old* ministry and covenant. 10/Now imagine the changes in your life and thinking as the *new* ministry and covenant are enacted.

day 12 Δ *Hebrews 8:7-13*

1/List in parallel columns the characteristics of the *old* and *new* covenants (cf. Ex.). 2/Among whom are the covenants made? 3/List two reasons the *old* covenant is inadequate for bringing salvation. 4/In what ways does God overcome this difficulty? What is the result? 5/What happens to the *old* covenant when God initiates the *new*? 6/How does God's attitude toward your sin (by the *new* covenant) affect your attitude toward *a*-your sin and *b*-God? 7/Explain how the *new* covenant is superior to the *old* as to *a*-security of relationship and *b*-depth of fellowship with God (cf. Gen.; Ex.; Lev.).

day 13 Δ *Hebrews 9:1-14*

1/Review Exodus 25–40 and Leviticus 1–9, 16, and

23–24:9. 2/Describe or draw the sanctuary (cf. Num. 17:1-11). 3/Where do the priests perform their duties? 4/Distinguish the daily services of the priests and the annual service of the high priest. 5/What is the significance of *a*-the curtain dividing the Holy Place from the Holy of Holies, *b*-the blood taken into the Holy of Holies, and *c*-the sacrifices and regulations of the *old* covenant? 6/Explain the *time of reformation* (cf. 8:6). 7/Compare and contrast the high priest's and Christ's functions. 8/List reasons that Christ's blood has unique significance. 9/To what extent is your *conscience* changed because of Christ's blood? 10/How does Christ's sacrifice release you from *dead works*?

day 14 Δ Hebrews 9:15-22

1/Explain the development of thought from verse 14 to verse 15. 2/Determine the meaning of *mediator* (cf. 8:6). 3/In what ways does a will illustrate the covenant of God (cf. Ex. 24, 40)? 4/How are *blood* and *death* related to *a*-the covenants and *b*-forgiveness of sins? 5/What does the death of Christ accomplish in regard to *a*-Old Testament believers, *b*-the symbolic ratification of the first covenant, and *c*-ratification of the new covenant? 6/How, then, is the death of Christ necessary? 7/How does Christ's death affect you? What is your response?

day 15 Δ Hebrews 9:23-28

1/What is Christ's purpose *a*-in the past on earth, *b*-in heaven now, and *c*-in the future on earth and in heaven? Try to determine the meaning of verse 23. 2/Contrast the priests' and Christ's sacrifices as to *a*-what is involved in the sacrifice, *b*-the results, and *c*-the sufficiency. 3/Summarize the similarities and differences of the earthly and heavenly sanctuaries (cf. 8–9:14). 4/What does the illustration of man's life history substantiate?

day 16 Δ Hebrews 10:1-10

1/What characteristics of the Old Testament sacrifices indicate that they are only preparatory? 2/Relate *shadow* and *reality* to the covenants. 3/Why, do you think, can't animals' blood take away sins (cf. Ps. 40:6-8)? 4/How would you answer the charge that God's system of sacrifices and offerings is sadistic (cruelty to animals, murder, etc.)? 5/What is revealed here about Jesus' relationship to God and God's will (relate to both his birth and death)? 6/How does Christ's obedience supersede sacrifices and offerings? 7/How does it qualify him as a *sacrifice*? 8/How do you know that Christ's death is no tragic mistake or accident? 9/In what ways do you try to substitute *sacrifices* for the obedience of your life? Why? 10/What is the result of Christ's sacrifice for you? What is your response?

day 17 Δ *Hebrews 10:11-25*

1/Summarize the similarities and differences of *a*-the human priests and their sacrifices and *b*-Christ and his sacrifice (cf. chaps. 1–10). 2/Relate the sanctuary *curtain* with Christ's *flesh*. 3/What will happen to Christ's enemies? Imagine their reaction. 4/What is the unique promise of the new covenant? How does this promise affect your attitude toward *a*-God, *b*-Jesus, *c*-your sin, and *d*-others' sins? 5/How does *therefore* connect verses 11-18 with verses 19-25? 6/How does the author urge the Hebrews to approach God (cf. 4:14-16)? On what basis? 7/Through what creative ways can you make *love and good works* a part of *a*-your life and *b*-others' lives? 8/What practical changes have you seen in your life as a result of realizing the theology of chapters 5–10? What else needs to change?

day 18 Δ *Hebrews 10:26-39*

1/What is the purpose of *for* in verse 26 (relate to vv. 19-25)? 2/What is the prospect for those who spurn the atoning sacrifice, Jesus Christ? 3/What attributes of God are revealed here (cf. Deut. 32:35-36)? 4/Describe the good beginning of these Hebrew Christians. 5/What is their great need? Why (cf. 2:1; 3:6-15; 10:22-25)? 6/What is the purpose of the quote in verses 37-38 (cf. Hab. 2:3-4)? 7/What is the plight of the Hebrews if they *shrink back* (cf. previous chaps.)? 8/What is your plight if you *throw away your confidence* in Jesus Christ? How can you prevent that plight?

day 19   △   Hebrews 11:1-12

1/Relate *faith* and *hope* (cf. 3:14). 2/Relate *faith* and reality. 3/What are the effects of faith as to *a*-man's understanding of God and creation (cf. v. 6) and *b*-God's attitude toward man? 4/List the Old Testament people in this section (cf. Gen. 4–6; 9–12; 17–18; 21). Describe *a*-the circumstances in which they exemplify faith, *b*-their attitude toward and understanding of their situations, *c*-the activity of God with each person, and *d*-the results. 5/From these examples what do you learn about the nature of God? 6/Relate *faith* and God's revealed Word. 7/Relate this passage with 10:39. 8/In what areas and circumstances is God now asking for your faith? With what results?

day 20   △   Hebrews 11:13-26

1/What are the attitudes of the people to whom God made promises to *a*-the promises and *b*-their life on earth (compare or contrast your attitudes)? 2/What is God's attitude toward these people? 3/Where will God ultimately fulfill his promises? 4/How do the men in this passage participate in the fulfillment of God's promises (cf. Gen.–esp. 15:13-18; Ex.)? 5/Try to determine the author's meaning of Moses' *abuse suffered for the Christ.* 6/How will your *a*-identification with Christ and *b*-faith in God's promises affect the choices you face today? in the future?

day 21   △   Hebrews 11:27-40

1/Relate *faith* and action. 2/Account for *a*-the Israelites' safety and *b*-the Egyptians' drowning in doing the same thing (cf. Ex. 14:21-31 with v. 29). 3/Contrast the results of faith in verses 32-35a with those in verses 35b-38. 4/Will your faith be affected by the results which come to you? Why? 5/Why haven't any of these as yet "received" God's ultimate promise? 6/How does the author interpret history in this chapter? 7/What unity do you have with Old Testament believers? 8/How does this unity affect your daily living (cf. 12:1)?

day 22 △ Hebrews 12:1-13

1/Describe the *race* you run. 2/In what ways are the Old Testament believers examples to you? 3/What specific sins *cling closely* to you? What can you do today to get rid of them? 4/In what ways does *considering* Jesus help you *endure*? 5/Compare the discipline of a father and God (cf. Prov. 3:11-12) as to *a*-necessity and *b*-purpose. 6/List reasons discipline is beneficial to you. What is the result of your enduring such training? 7/How do you know *a*-when and *b*-in what way God is disciplining you? 8/What is your attitude toward God during the training process? Why? 9/What attitudes show that you are accepting the challenge of God's discipline? 10/Relate the metaphors of verses 12-13 with the Hebrews' basic problem.

day 23 △ Hebrews 12:14-24

1/List the commands the author gives and the reasons for each. 2/How does your relationship to God affect your attitude toward others? 3/Under what circumstances have people in the past approached God (cf. Ex. 19—20)? What have been their reactions? 4/Where do people meet God now? 5/What is your response? 6/List the inhabitants of the city of God. 7/What is the purpose of this section of the letter?

day 24 △ Hebrews 12:25—13:8

1/Who are *they* in this section? 2/How is God's dealing with *them* a warning to the Hebrews? 3/How does the author show the superiority of the *new* revelation here (cf. Ex. 19; Haggai 2:6)? 4/What characteristics of the *new* kingdom are given here? 5/What attitudes toward God should result from an understanding of the privileges of the *new covenant*? 6/List the actions and qualities which the author urges. Give reasons for each. 7/With which do you have problems? Why? 8/How does the understanding of God in 12:25-29 lead to these actions and qualities? 9/How are you implementing these qualities?

day 25 Δ *Hebrews 13:9-16*

1/Relate verse 8 to verse 9. 2/What truths, does the author claim, are opposed to the *strange teachings*? 3/Who are *those who serve the tent*? In what ways are they concerned with externals? 4/Determine the meaning of *outside the camp*. Imagine what this will mean to the Hebrews. 5/To what extent do you identify with Christ? Why? 6/What is your response to abuse and intellectual opposition? 7/What are the suitable *sacrifices and offerings* to God? In what ways will you "make" them today?

day 26 Δ *Hebrews 13:17-24*

1/What is your responsibility to those in "spiritual" authority? Why? 2/How does the author regard intercessory prayer? 3/How does the benediction summarize the teaching of the letter concerning what God *a*-has done for the Hebrews and *b*-will do in them? 4/Rephrase verse 21 as God's personal promise to you. 5/Imagine the thoughts and feelings of the Hebrews at the end of this letter. Imagine their responses to its issues and exhortations. 6/What is your response?

day 27 Δ *Introduction to Numbers*

Numbers describes the way God leads the people of Israel from Sinai (Ex. 20–40; Lev.) to the plains of Moab and prepares them to cross over into the land of Canaan. 1/Briefly skim the first three books of Moses for background. 2/Keep a list of the instances of *a*-the Israelites' rebellion and *b*-God's response to their rebellion throughout the book. *Numbers 1–2* 1/What does God command Moses to do? Who is to assist Moses? 2/What are the *a*-criteria and *b*-purpose in being numbered? 3/How does the numbering show the Lord's concern for individuals? 4/What are the Levites' tasks? Why aren't they numbered (relate to the purpose of the census)? 5/What stipulation does God include to insure strict observance of his command? 6/Is the same kind of obedience still necessary in God's sight? To what extent do you obey God in this way? Why? 7/What plan of the camp does God command? Visualize the mass of people. 8/Where are the Levites situated in the plan? 9/To what extent is organization important to God? How can you have a similar type of organization in your group's activities?

day 28 Δ Numbers 3
1/What are the two main functions of the Levites? 2/How are the Levites and the priests related? 3/How are the priests chosen (cf. Ex. 28–29; Lev. 8–9)? 4/Why must the Levites take the place of the first-born? 5/How is the imbalance between the number of Levites and first-born taken care of? Why does this need to be done? 6/List the duties of the Levite families. 7/To what extent are you as careful in defining and attending to your spiritual responsibilities as Moses and Aaron are in this chapter?

day 29 Δ Numbers 4
1/Distinguish the duties assigned to each division of the Levites. 2/Which task is most important? 3/How is such working together demonstrated in your group or church fellowship? 4/How is each vessel in the sanctuary cared for when the camp moves? 5/What are the stipulations? 6/Why, do you think, is such attention given to the tent of meeting and its contents? 7/Try to imagine the Levites' response to these instructions. Do you think they understand why the instructions are so explicit? 8/What part, do you think, does the word of Moses and Aaron have in getting the Levites to follow the instructions? Why? 9/How do you handle directions given by those in authority over you?

day 30 Δ Numbers 5
1/How are uncleanness and defilement dealt with in this chapter? 2/What does the presence of God in the camp have to do

with defilement in verse 3? 3/List reasons God's presence and defilement cannot co-exist. What specific defilements in your life are excluding God's presence? 4/What is the nature of the sin (cf. Lev. 6:1-7) committed in verses 5-10? 5/What is the command in regard to this sin? To what extent do you follow this command in your life? 6/How do physical effects reveal sin in this chapter? 7/When truth is the standard as in verses 23-28, what are the results? 8/Imagine the feelings and reactions of the husband and the wife in this situation. 9/Why, do you think, is this type of defilement so carefully attended to (relate to the Israelites' circumstances)?

Month 19

day 1 △ Numbers 6:1-21

1/What are the three main instructions for the person who wants to make the Nazarite vow? 2/From what and to what or whom is he separated? Who decides to separate him? Why? 3/When have you chosen to be separate in this way for particular reasons? 4/What is the remedy for involuntary breaking of the oath? 5/Why, do you think, are these requirements so strict? 6/Are you so strict in keeping your vows to God? Why? 7/What is the procedure when the time of the Nazarite's separation is complete?

day 2 △ Numbers 6:22–7:89

1/What promises are given in the blessing of verses 24-26? What is revealed of God's love here? 2/What is the significance of the happenings in chapter 7? 3/How are the oxen and wagons divided? 4/Why aren't the sons of Kohath given any? Imagine their feelings. 5/When are you called to bear particular burdens alone? What is your response? 6/Would you have condensed this chapter if you were writing it? Why? 7/What does the detail of verses 12-88 show of God's concern for worship and offerings to him? 8/In what specific ways are you learning to walk in obedience to God day by day?

day 3 △ Numbers 8
1/Compare verses 1-4 with Exodus 25. 2/What does God do in verses 5-19? 3/What do his people do in verses 20-22? 4/Relate the physical and ceremonial cleansing. Of what significance is this relation? 5/What directions are given for Levites in verses 23-26? 6/Is one age more important than another? 7/In what ways are both age groups needed here? in your group?

day 4 △ Numbers 9
1/What particular words or phrases are repeated in this chapter? 2/What does this reveal about God and his concern for these people? 3/How does the command of God affect you in your situation? 4/What are the requirements of the passover (cf. Ex. 12)? 5/What conflicting laws pose a problem? 6/What is the attitude of the men that come to Moses? 7/What provisions are made for unique situations? 8/How does God guide his people here? How does he guide you?

day 5 △ Numbers 10
1/How are the trumpets to be used? What is their lasting significance? How are they related to God's guidance (cf. 9:15-23)? 2/What is the starting point and the destination of the first move (follow these moves on a map)? 3/Visualize the order (cf. chaps. 1—4). Contrast the exodus from Egypt. 4/How do the Israelites know where to go? 5/What does God give to them for direction? What other means of help is given in this chapter? 6/What is the significance of Moses' sayings in verses 35-36? 7/Do you usually demand exact details of each move you make? To what extent are you willing to trust God when you can't see ahead?

day 6 Δ *Numbers 11*

1/List *a*-the Israelites' and *b*-Moses' complaints and questions. 2/Imagine the kind of atmosphere in the group now. 3/When have you participated in such a spirit of pessimism in a group? Why? 4/In what way does this spirit hinder the work of God? 5/What is done about each complaint or question? 6/What have the Israelites forgotten about Egypt? about the Lord? 7/What characteristics of God are revealed in this chapter? 8/Account for *a*-Joshua's and *b*-Moses' response to Eldad and Medad's prophesying.

day 7 Δ *Numbers 12*

1/Define *meek*. How does this definition apply to Moses? 2/In what ways is Moses' relationship to God unique? How does God describe his relationship with Moses? 3/For what reasons have you reacted *a*-privately or *b*-publicly to someone's spiritual leadership in this way? What has been God's response? 4/To whom does Aaron address his plea? 5/What do Aaron and Miriam learn about God in this chapter? 6/Why, do you think, doesn't God comment on Miriam and Aaron's marital charge against Moses? 7/Imagine Moses' response to all of these happenings.

day 8 Δ *Numbers 13*

1/Follow the spies' travels on a map. 2/For what are the spies to look as they go into Canaan? 3/With what report do they return? What is their additional information? 4/How do the people respond to the news? 5/What have the ten spies forgotten about *a*-their purpose and *b*-the power of God? 6/To what extent do you question God's direction when you can't see how he will accomplish what he has commanded you? Why? 7/Ask God to help you obey him unconditionally today.

day 9 Δ *Numbers 14*

1/Imagine the atmosphere of the group now. 2/What position do *a*-the people and *b*-Joshua and Caleb take? When have you been in similar positions? 3/What does God want to do to the people? What is Moses' response? 4/By their actions what are the Israelites saying about God? 5/How does their perception of God affect their actions? 6/What do you learn of God's character in this chapter? 7/What are the basic differences between Caleb and Joshua and the rest of the Israelites? 8/Do these characteristics distinguish you from others around you? 9/What are the *a*-immediate and *b*-long-range results of the Israelites' disobedience to God (cf. v. 2 with vv. 28-29, 32, 35; v. 3 with vv. 31, 33, 44-45)? 10/Imagine the Israelites' reaction to their unsuccessful repentance.

day 10 Δ Numbers 15

1/What does God anticipate for the people in verses 1-2? 2/How would this encourage them after the events of the past two chapters? 3/What three occasions call for a burnt offering to the Lord? 4/Contrast the different types of sinning. How are they to be dealt with? 5/How can you avoid both extremes—*a*-sinning willfully and *b*-sinning ignorantly? 6/Relate the meaning of *sin* with the verbs in verses 30-31. 7/To what extent do you identify your sin so strictly? 8/Imagine you are with the Israelites stoning the man (vv. 32-36). What are your feelings toward *a*-the man and *b*-God? Why? 9/How does the Lord give the people a reassurance of his love and guidance in verses 37-41? 10/How are you reminded today of the commandments of God?

day 11 Δ Numbers 16

1/Distinguish the two groups demonstrating against Moses and Aaron. Who are involved? For what reasons? What are their charges? 2/How do the actions of the rebels affect the entire congregation? 3/What happens to the rebel groups? Why? 4/In what way does God show the congregation the authority of Moses and Aaron? 5/How do you respond to the authority of *a*-leaders and *b*-God? Why? 6/How is *atonement* made in verses 41-50? 7/Imagine the people's feelings in the aftermath of the events of this chapter.

day 12 △ *Numbers 17*

1/What is God's purpose in having Aaron's rod sprout and bear almonds (relate to the charges of *a*-Korah and *b*-Dathan and Abiram)? 2/Why do the people need this evidence now? 3/What is the people's reaction when they see what has happened? 4/How have the Israelites lost a perspective about the actions of God? 5/How is their attitude in verses 12-13 different from their attitude in chapter 16? 6/How can you avoid both extremes—*a*-refusing God's authority and *b*-thinking you have no hope at all?

day 13 △ *Numbers 18*

1/For what are *a*-Aaron and his sons and *b*-the Levites responsible? 2/What are *a*-Aaron and his sons and *b*-the Levites to receive from the people? 3/Why are they given special gifts? 4/What is their *inheritance* (contrast with the other tribes)? 5/To what extent do you accept your responsibilities as well as your rights in various situations? 6/How will God's clarification of duties in this chapter remove the people's fear concerning the tabernacle (cf. 17:12-13)?

day 14 △ *Numbers 19*

1/What is the purpose of the procedure in verses 1-10 (relate to 5:1; 16:49)? 2/Why, do you think, is such detail given? 3/What are the characteristics of the heifer? 4/How does the rest of the chapter make use of the first section? 5/Project the kind of incidents in which the people will have to make use of this offering (cf. 13:27-30). 6/What is the penalty for remaining unclean? Is any excuse acceptable? Why? 7/In what way are you *unclean* today? How can you become *cleansed*?

day 15 △ *Numbers 20*

1/What do the Israelites complain about this time? 2/Against whom are they really contending (cf. v. 3 with v. 13)? 3/What incurs God's judgment on Moses and Aaron? 4/Why, do you think, is God's judgment so harsh? Imagine their response. 5/How does the king of Edom respond to Moses' request? 6/Establish the ancestry of the Edomites. 7/How do you act when your rational requests are denied? Why? 8/What do you learn in this chapter about God's attitude toward disobedience?

day 16 ∆ Numbers 21

1/What enemies are encountered in this chapter? 2/What happens to each? 3/Follow Israel's progress on a map. 4/Why are the serpents sent among the people? 5/How does God answer their request of verse 7? 6/List the ways in which God acts on behalf of his people here. 7/Summarize what the Israelites have complained about all along (cf. 11:1, 4-5; 14:1-3; 16:3, 13-14, 41; 22:2-5). 8/Contrast God's responses to their complaints (cf. 11:1-2, 31-34; 14:22-23, 31-35; 16:32, 35, 47; 17:10; 20:8).

day 17 ∆ Numbers 22:1-40

1/Why does Balak send for Balaam? What does he expect Balaam to do? 2/What *a*-consistency and *b*-inconsistency do you find in Balaam's relationship to God? 3/Where does Balaam go wrong? 4/Account for the apparent contradiction of verses 20 and 22 (cf. v. 12). 5/How does Balaam recognize his mistake? What does he do about it? 6/Do you usually expect God to perform some miracle to extricate you from your mistakes? What do you do when you become aware of your mistakes? 7/Contrast the levels of Balak and Balaam's first conversation. 8/What do you learn about God from this chapter? 9/To what extent do you listen to God and obey him day by day?

day 18 ∆ Numbers 22:41–23:30

1/Imagine Balaam's feelings as he returns from the *bare height*. 2/How much encouragement does Balaam give to Balak? 3/How truthful is Balaam? 4/To what extent are you consistently truthful even though your statements are opposed to what others want to hear? 5/Imagine the feelings of Balak and the princes of Moab. 6/Distinguish Balaam's discourses (continue tomorrow) as to *a*-the offerings, *b*-the places, *c*-Balak's requests, *d*-the content of Balaam's answers, and *e*-the progression of God's Word through Balaam.

day 19 Δ Numbers 24
1/What seems to close the case and make Balaam come right out and bless Israel? 2/How does Balaam identify himself in the last two discourses? 3/How does Balaam describe Israel in verses 5-9 (list the metaphors)? 4/What is peculiar about Balak's angry statement to Balaam in verses 10-11? 5/How does Balak relate cursing, his *honor* (cf. 22:37), and the Lord's *honor*? 6/How often do you succumb to similar logic? Why? 7/With what is the final discourse of Balaam concerned? 8/What is the future of Balak's Moab? 9/List the references to the other nations here. Locate them on a map. 10/What is the future of each nation? Watch for the fulfillment in later books (e.g., cf. v. 21 with Num. 10:29-32; Judges 4:11; 1 Sam. 15:6).

day 20 Δ Numbers 25
1/Why is the Lord's anger so greatly *kindled* (Baal is the god of fertility worshipped on Mount Peor with immoral rites)? 2/How does God deal with Israel's sin? 3/On what basis does Phinehas act so harshly on this occasion? 4/What is the result of his action? 5/What does God's response to Phinehas reveal about God's justice? 6/How strictly do you obey the law of God? 7/Determine the Jewish meaning of *peace (shalom)*. 8/Relate God's *covenant of peace* (v. 12) with God's actions (vv. 4, 9) and Phinehas' actions (vv. 7-8).

day 21 Δ Numbers 26
1/In the second census which tribes have lost the most men (cf. chaps. 1–3)? Which have gained in number? 2/How has the number been lessened? 3/What is the significance of the small notes of history tucked in the numbering process (vv. 9-11, 60-62, 64-65)? 4/What instruction is given about dividing the

land? 5/How has God fulfilled his promise to the people? 6/What is your conception of the *fear* of the Lord and his justice (relate to what you have learned from *Numbers*)?

day 22 Δ Numbers 27

1/What is God's provision for the inheritance of a man who has died leaving no sons? 2/What causes God's decree in this matter at this particular time? 3/What is Moses' response to the Lord when he is told he will die soon (cf. 20:2-13)? 4/To what extent are you concerned and preparing for the future leadership of your group? 5/How is Joshua commissioned? What authority is he given? 6/What is his main qualification (cf. 11:27-29; 14:4-10, 30)? 7/To what extent are you this kind of person on your campus, on your job, or in your neighborhood?

day 23 Δ Numbers 28–29

1/Review the significance of the types of offerings (cf. Ex.; Lev.). 2/What special days require offerings? 3/What are the prescribed offerings of each day? 4/Determine the meaning of *pleasing odor* (cf. Ex. 29:38-42). 5/What are the characteristics of the lamb? 6/To what extent are you honest and open about your sin so God can forgive you and make you worthy to worship him? 7/Why, do you think, is there such detail about offerings? 8/What are the purposes of individual offerings (esp. 29:39)? 9/What can you *offer* to the Lord today?

day 24 Δ Numbers 30

1/What privileges does the woman have in making vows? 2/Where is the limit of these privileges? 3/What types of women are involved here? 4/To what extent is the man given authority over the woman? 5/Why, do you think, does he have this authority? 6/What responsibility accompanies his authority? 7/From this chapter what is revealed about the Israelites'concept of *a*-vows and *b*-women? 8/Compare or contrast your concepts.

day 25 △ *Numbers 31*

1/Why are the people of Israel to avenge the Midianites (cf. chap. 25)? 2/To what extent is there to be vengeance and victory? 3/Why is Moses angry with the army officers? Imagine their mixed emotions. 4/What are Moses' instructions to them? 5/Why are several cleansing agents used (cf. chap. 19)? 6/How is the spoil divided? 7/How are Eleazer and the Levites cared for? 8/To what extent do you continually *purify* the area in your life which snares you most often?

day 26 △ *Numbers 32*

1/What is the proposition put to Moses and Eleazer by the sons of Reuben and Gad? 2/Why does Moses hesitate? 3/How do the two tribes meet Moses' objections? 4/What is their promise to Moses (cf. Joshua 22:1-6)? 5/Locate the lands of Gad, Reuben, and Manasseh on a map. 6/How do the men care for their families? 7/How are they committed to the whole nation of Israel? 8/How are you committed to your church and fellowship group? 9/Speculate about the kinds of dangers these tribes could meet on this side of the Jordan (cf. Joshua 22:10-34).

day 27 △ *Numbers 33–34*

1/What summary is given in chapter 33 (cf. Ex. 12–17; Num. 10–21)? 2/Retrace the travels of these people on a map. 3/Summarize the actions of *a*-God, *b*-Moses and Aaron, and *c*-the people throughout the journey. 4/Summarize what the people have learned about God. 5/Summarize what you have learned about God from *Numbers*. 6/What instructions are given to Moses for the people as they pass over the Jordan into Canaan? What is the punishment for disobedience? 8/What are the boundaries in the land of Canaan? 9/Contrast the list of tribal leaders in verses 16-29 with the list in chapter 1.

day 28 △ *Numbers 35–36*

1/Describe the cities to be given to the Levites in the promised land. 2/How does God provide for justice to a manslayer? Relate this provision to *pollution* and *defilement*. 3/What problem comes up in chapter 36? How does Moses solve it? 4/Summarize the truths the children of Israel have been taught about God here. How do they respond? 5/What truths have you learned about God? 6/What specific actions have you taken because of what you have learned from *Numbers?*

day 29 △ *Introduction to Mark*

Mark leaves the Roman Christians a written document of what Peter has been preaching to them. Mark writes tersely and loads his narrative with facts and action (note the uses of *immediately*). Watch Jesus act with authority. Keep a list of the miracles he performs and for what reasons. Watch the personal reactions (note the verbs and adjectives). Distinguish the groups which are offended and angered by Jesus' teaching and actions. **Mark 1:1-13** 1/What does this book concern? 2/According to Isaiah, what is the function of a messenger? 3/How does the purpose of John's baptism agree with verse 2? Who comes to him? Why (consider the inconvenience as a measure of their seriousness)? 4/In what ways have you shown the seriousness of your commitment to God? 5/Describe John's *a*-appearance, *b*-attitude toward himself, and *c*-attitude toward the one to come after him. 6/What is your view of Jesus? your attitude toward yourself in comparison? 7/Contrast the two baptisms. 8/Describe the unusual events surrounding Jesus' baptism. At what point do these occur? 9/What is said about the Spirit? 10/Identify the voice and support your answer. What does it say concerning Jesus? 11/What is significant about this event? 12/Imagine the wilderness environment. 13/What are the roles of *a*-the Spirit, *b*-Satan, and *c*-the angels? How many weeks is Jesus subjected to this environment? 14/How does knowing that Jesus underwent this prolonged experience in utter loneliness help you? What is your resource when tempted?

day 30 △ *Mark 1:14-20*

1/When does Jesus begin preaching? What is the heart of his message? Compare his message with John's (v. 4). 2/What two commands does Jesus give? Determine the meaning of the verbs. How do these commands relate to the kingdom? 3/What evidences that you have obeyed these commands? 4/Compare the two sets of brothers as to their *a*-occupation or trade, *b*-activity as Jesus comes by, *c*-response to Jesus' call, and *d*-what each leaves behind. 5/Considering that Jesus is probably still a virtually unknown itinerant preacher, account for their immediate response to his call. Relate their response to his commands in verse 15. 6/What is the relationship between Jesus' call to Simon and Andrew and their occupation? 7/What promise does Jesus make to them? By what dynamic will they be changed? 8/How might Jesus relate his call to you in your present or future occupation? 9/By what means or power can you become a *fisher of men*? List the hindrances which you face.

Month 20

day 1   △   Mark 1:21-39

1/Investigate the identity of the scribes and the qualifications they have to be teachers. How does Jesus' teaching differ from theirs? 2/With what power is Jesus confronted in the synagogue? How does he identify Jesus? 3/Imagine the stir this scene probably creates in the synagogue. 4/How does Jesus meet this crisis? What are the *a*-immediate and *b*-long-range effects? 5/How does Jesus meet the next crisis? Considering the normal debilitating effects of fever, what evidences that the healing is complete? 6/How does the day end? How does the following day begin? 7/What observation does Simon's statement give as to the pressure on Jesus? 8/What effect, do you think, does Jesus' "quiet time" have in sorting out priorities and planning his moves? 9/After a busy day and evening, faced with more than you can do in a day, how do you begin a new day? Of what value to you is knowing that

Jesus deliberately talked with God at this point? 10/What immediate needs should you rearrange for the sake of major goals?

day 2 △ *Mark 1:40-45*

1/List all you know or can discover about leprosy as a disease with
social and religious implications at this time (cf. Lev. 13:45-46;
Num. 5:2-4). 2/What does the leper ask? How does he qualify his
question? 3/How does Jesus' action reflect his attitude toward the
outcast? What risk does he take (cf. Lev. 22:5-6)? 4/How have
your attitudes toward others determined your actions this
week? 5/State the negative and positive commands Jesus gives (cf.
Lev. 14:1-32 to discover what is required). 6/Why is the leper to
obey the law (v. 44)? 7/What does the healed man do? In view of
what has just happened, is this surprising? excusable?
Why? 8/What is the effect of the man's actions on Jesus' ministry? 9/Reflect on times you have obeyed your impulses. What
have been the consequences in terms of the gospel? 10/What has
happened when you have obeyed Jesus instead? Ask him to give
you power to obey today. 11/In what spheres is Jesus' activity
thus far consistent with his manner of teaching (cf. v. 22)?

day 3 △ *Mark 2:1-12*

1/Picture the Capernaum home. Imagine who may have been present (cf. 1:21-34). 2/Who else is here (2:6)? What is Jesus
doing? 3/What do the four friends expect as they bring the helpless paralytic to Jesus? 4/When they see the situation, what alternatives might they choose? with what effect on their
friend? 5/What is Jesus' first concern for the paralytic? What
urges his action? 6/Why are the scribes so upset? Examine their
thinking. Where is the fallacy? 7/Distinguish *power* and *authority*.
How are Jesus' power and authority interrelated? 8/Discover two
ways in which Jesus supports his words (relate to his identity). 9/What is the effect on the man? the crowd? Who gets the
credit? 10/In what ways can you compare yourself to *a*-the determined friends, *b*-the helpless paralytic, and *c*-the unbelieving
scribes? 11/What will you do to be a loving and helpful friend to
someone in need today?

day 4 △ *Mark 2:13-17*

1/Who is Levi? What effect does Jesus have on his life? 2/Whom
does Levi invite home for dinner? 3/Account for the storm of
protest. Who protests? What is the issue? With whom are the tax
collectors identified (in this nationalistic society, they are hated
because their office is associated with fraud and because they are
considered in collaboration with the hated pagan Roman government)? 4/What about this incident makes Jesus' social associations appear inconsistent with his words and actions? 5/Para-
phrase Jesus' statement (v. 17). How are his actions here consistent
with his purpose? 6/What is your purpose in life? With whom do
you identify in this: the sick or well? the sinner or righteous? the
critical scribes concerned about right associations or humble disciples risking reputation to be with Jesus? 7/What type of people
do you associate with? Why? 8/Find out about the beliefs and
observances of the Pharisees (continue in subsequent days). Who
are the scribes? What are their duties?

day 5 △ *Mark 2:18-3:6*

1/What is the issue raised in verse 18? 2/Relate Jesus' analogy
with his identity. What veiled reference does he make about the
future? 3/What general situations prompt fasting in the
Bible? 4/How do verses 21-22 relate to the question? 5/In what
ways are you bound by external religious observance? 6/What
fresh expression of Christianity needs to be a part of your life?
Why? 7/What next provokes criticism? 8/According to Jesus
what is the purpose of the sabbath (refer to the origin of and God's
command concerning the sabbath—Gen. 2:2; Ex. 20:8-11;
31:12-17)? 9/How have the legalists twisted this meaning? 10/What is the essence of Jesus' claim in verse 28? 11/How
do you use a *sabbath*: ignore it? rest and renewal in holiness? or
bound by it? Why? 12/Visualize the synagogue scene. Who is
here? Why the tension? What is the issue as Jesus states it? 13/Ac-
count for the response to Jesus' question. 14/How does Jesus
answer his own question? 15/Contrast the reaction of the critics
to Jesus with Jesus' reaction to them. 16/What two groups join to
begin a plot? Investigate how the two groups differ ideologically.

day 6 Δ *Mark 3:7-19a*

1/Check a map to determine the geographic origins of the multitude. 2/Considering the means of transportation and communication what does this reveal about Jesus' reputation? 3/How is Jesus identified? How does he handle this? 4/In what ways has your concept of Jesus grown or changed in the last week? Why? 5/On what basis does Jesus call some followers (v. 13)? What is their response? 6/For what three reasons does Jesus appoint twelve men? 7/Write down what you know about these twelve men from this and previous statements in *Mark*. What kind of men has Jesus chosen (continue to add information throughout *Mark* to characterize the men Jesus chooses to form the core team for the spread of the gospel)?

day 7 Δ *Mark 3:19b-35*

1/What two opinions are stated? Who holds each? 2/How does Jesus show that the scribes' conclusion is illogical? 3/In terms of the context (vv. 22-30) what sin is described? How serious is it? 4/How would you answer someone who says he thinks he has "committed the unpardonable sin"? 5/According to verses 31-35 what is the basis for family relationship with Jesus? 6/What is Jesus' place in your relationships? What does this reveal about your attitude toward the will of God? 7/Review chapters 1–3 to summarize *a*-Jesus' direct and indirect claims, and *b*-the evidences of his authority. In what spheres does he demonstrate authority? 8/How do these facts affect your attitude and response to him?

day 8 Δ *Mark 4:1-20*

1/Chart out *a*-the four kinds of soil, *b*-the situations of the seed, and *c*-the interpretation. 2/What is the *seed*? Account for the difference in yield. 3/Rephrase verse 9 in contemporary language. 4/When does Jesus explain the parable? To whom? Why does he speak in parables? 5/What is the general purpose of parables? In what way is the truth of this parable both *a*-hidden and *b*-revealed? 6/Can you discover a relationship between verses

11-12 and the four kinds of soil? 7/What is your responsibility to the Word? 8/As you consider the parable describe your most recent response to God's Word. 9/To what extent are a-you, b-Satan, and c-God responsible for your response? 10/How can you determine which type of response here describes you? 11/Can you determine which multiple of fruit you bear? Why? 12/What is your responsibility to what you have learned from this parable?

day 9 △ *Mark 4:21-25*

1/What is the purpose of light? of a lamp? 2/What happens to light from an oil lamp (common in Jesus' day) which is placed in a closed container? 3/Relate the purpose of light to the previous discussion about parables (vv. 10-13). What paradox is involved? 4/What spiritual principles is Jesus illustrating here? 5/What are you doing with what you have *heard* so far in this study of *Mark*? Why? 6/Measured against your attitude and obedience to God's Word, do you welcome the fact of verses 24-25 as a promise or fear it as a warning? Why? ➤

day 10 △ *Mark 4:26-34*

1/What is true of seed which is also true of the kingdom? 2/What are the stages of growth described here? How does growth occur? When does harvest come? 3/What is the responsibility of a farmer in a-planting, b-growing, and c-harvesting? 4/To what extent are you aware of a-your growth and b-the growth of the kingdom? Why? 5/In what way is the kingdom of God like a mustard plant (the Palestine variety of *mustard* is a large bush)? 6/To whom does Jesus direct the parables (cf. 4:1)? To whom does he explain them? 7/How does the understanding of these parables alter or enlarge your view of God's work a-in you and b-throughout history?

day 11 △ *Mark 4:35-41*

1/What command does Jesus give? 2/Imagine the situation which a-the disciples and b-the people in the other boats face (consider the knowledge of the sea which at least four disciples have—cf. 1:16-20). 3/How severe is the storm? What do the disciples do? 4/Imagine what the disciples expect of Jesus when they wake him. Compare or contrast what he does. 5/How does Jesus demonstrate his authority? Account for the extent of Jesus' authority. 6/Why is Jesus' rebuke to the disciples appropriate (cf. v. 35)? 7/When have you recently been afraid even though you knew you were obeying Jesus' commands to you? Why? 8/What is the disciples' reaction to everything? 9/Give evidence from this passage of Jesus' humanity and divinity.

day 12 △ Mark 5:1-20
1/Describe fully the man who meets Jesus as to his physical appearance and strength, self-control, and social status. 2/What is the man's reaction to Jesus? 3/What does the spirit beg Jesus to do? What are the results of Jesus' action for the spirits? the swineherds? the man? 4/What do you learn here about Jesus' authority? 5/Why does a crowd gather? What do they find? Can you account for their reaction? 6/Contrast the man's desire with Jesus' command. Where is he to go? What happens because he obeys? 7/How does the man's news differ from the swineherds' in a-content and b-result? 8/Contrast Jesus' command to the demoniac with those given the a-leper (1:44-45) and b-unclean spirits (3:12). What makes the difference? 9/Given the command of verse 19 what would you say? To whom would you have to speak?

day 13 △ Mark 5:21-34
1/What do you discover here about Jesus' view of individuals? Give at least three facts about Jairus. 2/Contrast Mark's (vv. 25-26) and Luke's (8:43) description of the woman's physical and material condition. Account for the difference. 3/What effect would her situation have on the woman's emotional outlook on life? 4/Imagine her feelings as she tells about her disease (cf. Lev. 15:25-31). 5/Cite evidence that she is healed. On what basis? 6/In what ways have you openly and honestly acknowledged your need and Jesus' power this week?

day 14 △ *Mark 5:21-43*
1/Compare and contrast the needs of *a*-Jairus and his wife, *b*-Jairus'
daughter, and *c*-the hemorrhaging woman. 2/What evidences that
Jesus has full knowledge of the needs and is in control of the
situations? 3/What is Jesus' response to each need?
When? 4/Whom does Jesus allow to go with him to Jairus' home?
into the house? Who is excluded? Can you give a reason for the
exclusion? 5/Account for the contrasting emotions of the mourners. 6/Over what spheres does Jesus show his authority? 7/List
Jesus' commands in this section. What is the response to
each? 8/How do you respond to interruptions and delays when
you feel you are in a desperate situation? 9/As you learn of Jesus'
control and authority, in what ways is your faith strengthened for
any situation?

day 15 △ *Mark 6:1-6*
1/List the forces over which Jesus has been victor so far in
Mark. 2/Compare and contrast the reception of Jesus' neighbors
and townspeople with the reception of the people in Capernaum
(cf. 1:23-28) to his teaching. 3/Why are the hometown people
skeptical? 4/How does their attitude affect Jesus' work
here? 5/In what instances are you limiting God's work because
you have prejudged another person on the basis of past association? 6/Compare Jesus' attitude toward the people with their attitude toward him. 7/What course of action does he follow?

day 16 △ *Mark 6:7-13*
1/Compare verse 7 with 3:14. How is this commission a fulfillment
of Jesus' original appointment? 2/What is the source of the disciples' authority? 3/What instructions does Jesus give the disciples
about luggage and food? 4/Compare the content of their preaching with 1:4, 14-15. 5/What are they to do if people refuse to
listen (relate to their authority)? 6/What is the content of your
message? 7/What do you do when someone refuses to listen: engage in logical argument? wilt? become angry? withdraw quietly
but firmly? or react in some other way? 7/How "successful" are

the disciples? Relate their results to the *a*-certainty of their call, *b*-specific mission, and *c*-authority given them. 8/What is your call and source of authority? 9/On this basis what can you expect God to do through you? 10/If (and when) some do not listen, how will their response affect your call?

day 17 Δ Mark 6:14-29

1/With whom is Jesus identified? 2/What does Herod's reaction to Jesus reveal about his psyche? 3/Contrast Herodias and Herod in their attitudes toward John. 4/On what issue could you take a stand for right and truth today? What are the risks you face? What qualities of character do you need? 5/Trace Herod's steps to the "political" murder of John. 6/In the final analysis is Herod any "better" than Herodias? Why? 7/Imagine the effect of this incident on Herodias' daughter. 8/Relating this section to the spiritual principles Jesus teaches, what kind of response does Herod illustrate (cf. v. 20 with 4:16-17)? 9/When have you acted hastily and later regretted your actions? What have been the consequences? How can you avoid future conflicts brought by similar action? 10/What is the touching finale to this parenthesis?

day 18 Δ Mark 6:30-44

1/Describe the pace of Jesus and his disciples. 2/From Jesus' suggestion how, do you think, would Jesus suggest you regulate your life? 3/What happens to disrupt the day off? 4/Describe Jesus' attitude and action as it relates to shepherdless *sheep*. 5/In the dialogue about food between the disciples and Jesus, whose solution seems more practical? 6/What is Jesus' part in feeding the crowd? 7/How does organization fit into the situation? 8/In what ways do you rely on organization instead of spiritual resources? neglect organization because it seems "unspiritual"? What should you do to bring the extremes into balance in your life and in your group? 9/Give two evidences that this miracle is adequate. 10/Have you faced, or are you facing, a humanly impossible situation? How does this incident strengthen your convictions that Jesus is able to meet your needs?

day 19 △ *Mark 6:45-56*
1/In dismissing the crowd how does Jesus meet the disciples'
needs? his own needs? 2/How does Jesus show his *a*-complete
mastery of nature and *b*-superiority over humans? 3/What are the
emotions of the men before and after Jesus gets into the boat?
Why are their reactions abnormal (v. 52)? 4/What evidences that
Jesus understands them though they don't understand him? 5/Re-
call at least one unusual thing God has done for you which has
a-strengthened your confidence to expect more or *b*-utterly as-
tounded you. How can such past experiences build your faith for
present and future needs? 6/How do the sick come into contact
with Jesus? Imagine Jesus' feelings as he heals so many people.

day 20 △ *Mark 7:1-13*
1/What insights do you gain concerning the Pharisees? 2/What is
their complaint? Against whom do they seem to direct their attack? Against whom is it really directed? 3/How does Jesus turn
the attack? What is the real basis of the problem? 4/What is one
example of Jesus' statement in verse 8? 5/What commandment
does it violate (cf. Ex. 20:12)? How? (*Corban* property couldn't be
given to anyone but could be used by its owner for his personal
gratification and delight.) 6/Examine the behavior patterns which
you associate with your being a Christian. Which have bases in the
commandment of God? Which in the *tradition of men*? 7/What
place does Scripture have in Jesus' reply? 8/What are you doing to
know and use Scripture effectively and wisely? 9/On what areas
do you stamp God's insignia but are really motivated from selfish
reasons? 10/Ask God to give you honesty as you examine your
thoughts and actions.

day 21 △ *Mark 7:14-30*
1/Relate the parable of verses 14-15 to the Pharisees' attack. 2/How does the parable attack the whole ritual law? 3/De-
fine *defilement* as Jesus means. 4/According to Jesus what are the
sources of defilement? 5/Why, do you think, doesn't Jesus separate thoughts and actions in his list? 6/What are you bringing into

207

your life which *defiles* you? What are you doing to curtail and get rid of this evil? Why?   7/What evidences that you are concerned with internal purity?   8/Locate the region of Tyre and Sidon.   9/What is the likely reason for Jesus to go there now?   10/Account for Jesus' response to the woman (Jews consider Gentiles underprivileged and refer to them as *dogs*).   11/How does Jesus respond to her faith?   12/What hints of future benefit to Gentiles?   13/What do you discover here about *a*-faith, *b*-persistence, and *c*-wisdom which you can apply to your relationship with Christ?   14/How are the Pharisees' view of defilement and their attitude toward the Gentile minority parallel? How are Jesus' teaching and action parallel?

day 22   △   Mark 7:31-37

1/Recall Jesus' previous visit in the Decapolis and his reason for leaving (cf. 5:1-20). Account for his ability to return now.   2/Contrast how the crowd expects Jesus to heal the man with how he actually does.   3/Account for Jesus' actions in healing (relate to the man's understanding).   4/In what ways does God deal with you *privately*? Why?   5/Contrast Jesus' command to this man and crowd with his command to Legion. Explain the difference.   6/Contrast the reaction of the people now with the previous reaction in chapter 5.   7/To what extent are you *astonished* at the perfection of God's creative acts?   8/What effect does your obedience to Jesus have on others?

day 23   △   Mark 8:1-10

1/For comparison and contrast list the specific details from Mark 6:30-44 and Mark 8:1-10 in columns.   2/What is Jesus' motive in his action here?   3/Who initiates the question of food?   4/What does the disciples' answer reveal of their understanding?   5/In what ways have you allowed previous hopeless experiences to stimulate your faith in God?   6/What potentially faith-stimulating experiences have you forgotten or ignored?   7/How is Jesus' attitude toward people and their needs an example for you?

day 24 △ *Mark 8:11-26*
1/Why, do you think, does Jesus refuse the Pharisees' request (relate to 4:21-25)? 2/What is *leaven* and its function? 3/What warning does Jesus give? Is he blaming the disciples for their forgetfulness? Explain his meaning. 4/With what level of life are the disciples concerned? 5/What are the disciples supposed to *understand* when Jesus reminds them of the leftovers? 6/When has your preoccupation with physical needs caused you to lose sight of long-range spiritual lessons? 7/What actions of Jesus here are particularly appropriate to the blind man and his needs? 8/Review the miracles of healing so far in *Mark*. In what ways is Jesus' act always appropriate to the need?

day 25 △ *Mark 8:27–9:1*
1/Distinguish the two questions Jesus asks and the answers given. From what knowledge or evidence are conclusions drawn? 2/Relate Peter's answer to the Jews' understanding of *the Christ* (Messiah). 3/What is the opinion of your contemporaries regarding the identity of Jesus? What is your opinion? On what do you base your conclusion? 4/What new teaching does Jesus introduce now? 5/Why do Peter and Jesus rebuke each other? What does Jesus' rebuke reveal about the origin of Peter's idea? 6/To whom does Jesus address his next remarks (vv. 34-38)? 7/List the paradoxes and conditions of discipleship. 8/Contrast the present and future of a person who avoids the issue. 9/What hindrances to discipleship do you face? What can you do to keep your perspective clear? 10/What promise does Jesus make? Relate this promise to the goals and hope of a disciple.

day 26 △ *Mark 9:2-13*
1/Why, do you think, does Jesus take these three disciples with him (cf. previous occasions)? 2/Define *transfigured*. 3/Imagine the appearance of Jesus. 4/What is significant about the color (dark colors are the most practical for daily work outfits; teachers wear a maize color)? 5/What part of Jewish history does Moses represent? Elijah? 6/Relate Peter's impulsive statements with Jew-

ish history. 7/Compare and contrast verse 7 with 1:11. What do
these statements underscore about Jesus' identity? 8/What activities of Jesus which you have studied support this view of his identity? 9/How does the "interview" end? 10/What caution does
Jesus give the disciples? When is the ban to be lifted? How do the
three react? 11/How does Jesus' identification and subsequent
command affect you personally? 12/How do *a*-the scribes and
b-Jesus interpret the prophecy of Malachi 4:5-6? 13/How does
the scribes' rejection of John the Baptist point to a similar rejection of the *Son of man?*

day 27 △ Mark 9:14-29

1/What are the disciples at the base of the mountain involved in
when Jesus returns? 2/Catch the emotion of the father. How have
his hopes thus far been crushed? 3/Imagine Jesus' feelings toward
a-his disciples, *b*-the scribes, *c*-the man, and *d*-the boy. 4/What
happens when they bring the boy to Jesus? What additional information does Jesus gather? 5/What is the criterion for healing? 6/Explain the seeming paradox of the father's answer. 7/Does God require perfect and complete belief from you
before he can act? Why? 8/Give evidence that this "case" is particularly difficult. 9/What insights have you gained from this case
history to help you *believe?*

day 28 △ Mark 9:30-41

1/Why the sudden secrecy as Jesus and his disciples travel (relate to
priorities and selection)? 2/Contrast this seclusion to their previous availability to people. 3/What is the response of the disciples
this time (cf. 8:31-33) as Jesus projects his future? Relate his
teaching here to 8:34-37. 4/What is Jesus' concept of greatness? 5/Summarize how he exemplifies the concept. 6/In what
ways have you tried to become *great?* Why? 7/What characteristics of a *servant* attitude do you need to absorb into your daily
living with your roommate, husband or wife, neighbor, employer,
employee, etc.? 8/Imagine what the disciples say to the man cast-
ing out demons. 9/How does Jesus view such a person in relation

to his work (relate to his name)? 10/When have you been critical of others because they aren't in your group or doing things your way? How does the principle Jesus states relate to determining the basis of *a*-their action and *b*-your attitude?

day 29 △ Mark 9:42-50
1/What does the suggested penalty show about the seriousness of influencing others to sin? 2/For each offense indicate the radical surgery Jesus prescribes. 3/What do these statements reveal about Jesus' attitude toward sin? 4/Contrast the present handicaps with the future torment (cf. Is. 66:24). 5/Compare verses 43-48 with 7:20-23. Relate the internal and external stimuli to sin. 6/What alternatives are possible for man? 7/What do you learn about hell from Jesus' statements? 8/Compare or contrast Jesus' and your attitudes toward sin. What sins of thought and action do you coddle and encourage? What will you do today to cut yourself off from these sins? 9/What are the functions of salt? 10/Relate and explain the two commands Jesus gives in verse 50. 11/List the highlights of Jesus' ministry in Galilee (chaps. 1–9). 12/What have been your impressions about *a*-Jesus, *b*-the disciples, *c*-opposition groups, and *d*-the public? 13/Summarize Jesus' authority as expressed in his *a*-radical teaching and *b*-actions. What are his credentials? 14/On this basis what steps will you take today to acknowledge his authority in your life?

day 30 △ Introduction to Deuteronomy
The literary structure of *Deuteronomy* is similar to that of the treaties imposed in the Near East by victors on vassal states in the second millenium B.C. The Lord (Yahweh) is Israel's sovereign. He has delivered her from Egyptian bondage. Thus he demands her undivided loyalty and service. He has entered into *covenant* with her at Sinai (cf. Ex. 20–24) and now renews and expands this covenant here as Israel stands on the threshold of a new land and a new life. Briefly skim the book to see the different kinds of materials included. Be prepared to see God in his fierce justice, jealousy, and marvelous mercy. *Deuteronomy 1–2* 1/Establish the setting of

Moses' speech (cf. chap. 1 with Num. 11–14; chap. 2 with Num. 20:14–21:32). 2/Who will have authority after Moses dies (1:9-18, 38)? 3/Characterize God's faithfulness. 4/Summarize the past responses of Israel to the Lord. 5/How does Israel's *a*-obedience and *b*-disobedience affect the surrounding nations? In what areas? 6/How would the information in chapter 2 give renewed confidence to the Israelites? 7/How do you view *a*-your parents' and *b*-your own past failures? 8/How has God used *a*-their and *b*-your experiences to build your confidence in him?

Month 21

day 1 △ Deuteronomy 3
1/Imagine the effect of this review of Israel's wilderness history on the people listening (cf. Num. 21:33-35; 27:12-23). 2/Summarize *a*-God's and *b*-Israel's part in the military victories. 3/Relate verse 20 to what you have learned about *rest* from *Hebrews*. 4/What can you learn about prayer from Moses' prayer? What do you think of the Lord's answer? 5/Imagine Moses' feelings as he sees the promised land. 6/What are Moses' final duties?

day 2 △ Deuteronomy 4
1/Relate this summary of the covenant to what you have learned about the *covenant* from *Hebrews*. 2/What important principles and themes are affirmed here? 3/Relate God's self-revelation to the Israelites with the prohibition of idolatry. 4/Compare and contrast Israel's *law* with the laws and practices of surrounding nations. 5/What are the consequences of Israel's *a*-obedience and *b*-disobedience to this covenant? 6/What can you learn here of *a*-Israel's place in God's plan and *b*-the uniqueness of Israel's self-understanding? 7/What about the character of God is revealed here (list and explain the metaphors)? 8/What is your response to this God?

day 3 △ *Deuteronomy 5*

1/Imagine Moses' feelings as he recounts the events here. 2/Account for the different responses of *a*-Moses and *b*-the people to the Horeb experience. 3/Imagine your response to such an experience. 4/What is the basis for God's appeal for *a*-the Israelites' and *b*-your allegiance and trust? 5/In what way do the ten commandments (cf. Ex. 20) place all of life under God's claim (relate v. 6 and the commandments). 6/Explain the significance of the ten commandments as a *covenant*, not simply a moral code. 7/Account for the added meaning given the commandment about the sabbath (cf. Ex. 21:11). 8/Account for the added areas in the commandment about coveting (cf. Ex. 20:17). 9/What is Moses' role in Israel's life? 10/To what extent do you *keep all* God's commandments?

day 4 △ *Deuteronomy 6*

1/What do you learn about the character of God from this material? 2/To what extent are longevity of physical life and obedience to God related (cf. 5:16)? 3/In what ways is God *a*-unique and *b*-exclusive? 4/Why can he demand such exclusive devotion from *a*-the Israelites and *b*-you? 5/How can you follow the commands of verses 4-9 today? Should you follow them *literally*? 6/What significance does Israel's redemption from Egypt have in this chapter? 7/Compare what God has done and will do (esp. vv. 10-11) for Israel. 8/How can you both *love* and *fear* God? 9/In what ways do you *a*-forget and *b*-test God? What can you do today to avoid these attitudes? 10/What do you see here about Moses' perspective?

day 5 △ *Deuteronomy 7*

1/Characterize the relationship between Israel and God. 2/What is the quality of allegiance that God demands? To what extent do you give God this allegiance in all areas of your life? 3/What is the purpose of Israel's conquests and extermination program? 4/What will God do for the Israelites? 5/To what areas does God's *blessing* of the Israelites extend? 6/Is sickness, barrenness, loss, etc.

necessarily due to sin in your life? How do you know? **7**/What is God's response to those who *a*-love and *b*-hate him? **8**/In what way is the Israelites' response to other people and nations to be a reflection of God's attitude toward them?

day 6 Δ *Deuteronomy 8*

1/What has been the significance of Israel's wilderness experience? What has the Lord taught them there? **2**/How will their wilderness experience relate to their relationship to God in the land of possession? **3**/In what ways are you dependent on God? **4**/How and why has the Lord *humbled* Israel? **5**/What experiences in your life has God used to *humble* you? What have been the results? **6**/Describe the land of Canaan. How are the Israelites to regard its natural resources? **7**/How is pride dealt with in this chapter? **8**/To what extent do you like to take sole credit for what God has enabled you to do? What will you do today to change?

day 7 Δ *Deuteronomy 9*

1/How is Israel's potential self-righteousness dealt with in this chapter? **2**/How is this attitude different from the attitude in 8:17? **3**/To what extent do you cite your morality or service as the basis of your "superiority" or "success"? What is wrong with this attitude? **4**/Describe Moses' relationship with God. **5**/What has been Moses' role during the times of Israel's rebellion (cf. Ex. 32)? **6**/Imagine you are an Israelite listening to Moses. What is the impact of his words on you?

day 8 Δ *Deuteronomy 10*

1/In what ways has God's *patience* and *forgiveness* been shown repeatedly to the Israelites (cf. previous chaps.)? **2**/Put 10:1-5; 9:18-21, 25-29 in chronological order (cf. Ex. 32, 34–35, 40). Why, do you think, isn't **Moses** concerned with chronology here? **3**/What is distinctive **about** the tribe of Levi (cf. Ex. 28–29)? **4**/Underline the **verbs** in verses 10-22. What is revealed here about the character of God (relate his attributes to Moses' commands of *fear* and *love*)? 5/In what way does verse 16 fulfill the *covenant* (cf. Gen. 17:9-14)? 6/What is the relationship between verses 18 and 19? How can this teaching affect your attitudes toward migrant workers, transients, and dispossessed people in your society? 7/In what way is God *your praise*?

day 9 Δ *Deuteronomy 11*

1/To what past signs of God does Moses refer here (cf. Ex. 14:21-31; Num. 16)? 2/List and categorize all the results promised Israel if they keep God's commandments. 3/How does Moses relate God and nature? Why (cf. 10:14)? 4/Investigate from Palestine geography the importance of the *early* and *later* rain. 5/What is the role of the parents in religious instruction (cf. 6:7, 20)? Why is this kind of perpetuation of the covenant so important at this time? 6/What is *a*-God's and *b*-Israel's part in the *blessing* or *curse* (cf. Joshua 8:31-35)? 7/In what practical ways do you acknowledge the sovereignty of God in your daily living? With what results?

day 10 Δ *Deuteronomy 12*

1/Contrast the Canaanite gods with the Lord God. How does this difference make the extermination of the gods *a*-possible and *b*-necessary? 2/What are the *a*-purpose and *b*-importance of a central place of worship for Israel? 3/When is the central place to be established? 4/What is the importance of the corporate sacrifices (vv. 7, 18)? How are they different from family feasts? 5/What is to be their attitude in worship? 6/To what extent are these factors important today for your worship? 7/What brings *rejoicing* into your worship? 8/In what ways are the Levites dependent on the kindness of the Israelites? 9/In what *a*-corporate and *b*-individual ways will you express your loyalty to God today? 10/Relate God's prohibitions regarding *blood* to the Canaanite ritual practices.

day 11 Δ *Deuteronomy 13*

1/What are the areas of enticement here? 2/Why is the penalty so severe (relate to the essence of the covenant)? 3/How does this material help you to understand the meaning of God's *jealousy* (cf. 5:9; 6:15)? 4/Underline and explain the significance of the verbs in this chapter. 5/In today's culture what and who entice you from God? What happens?

day 12 △ *Deuteronomy 14*

1/What is Israel's relationship to God? 2/In what ways are their practices to reflect their distinctiveness (cf. v. 1 with Lev. 19:28; vv. 3-21 with Lev. 11:2-23; Ex. 23:19)? 3/What, do you think, is the purpose of the dietary regulations (cf. 8:3)? 4/What is the purpose of the tithe? 5/What is the significance of the corporate participation in the tithe? 6/Compare or contrast the Israelites' tithing with modern concepts of tithing. 7/What is the active quality of your worship?

day 13 △ *Deuteronomy 15*

1/What are the ultimate values in the Hebrew law (compare or contrast with the law of your society)? 2/How would the values here affect *a*-the Israelites' and *b*-your relations with others? 3/What is the significance of the seventh-year *release*? 4/With what attitudes are the laws about debts and servants to be enacted? 5/Considering the seventh-year release how could *a*-the creditor and *b*-the debtor *sin*? 6/Relate verses 4 and 11. 7/Of what significance, do you think, is the fact that the rich *lend* rather than give to the poor?

day 14 △ *Deuteronomy 16:1-17*

1/What three annual events require meeting at the central place of worship (cf. Ex. 12; Lev. 23; Num. 28–29)? 2/What are the common elements of these feast times? 3/What is the basis of Hebrew worship? 4/Explain *bread of affliction*. 5/What is the significance of *a-remember* and *b-joy* in connection with these events? 6/What are you prepared to do to bring joy into worship? How important is its corporate expression?

day 15 Δ *Deuteronomy 16:18–17:20*

1/Why, do you think, are the provisions here to assure justice so important (cf. 10:17-18)? 2/Are these principles important for your nation? Why? 3/What makes idolatry wrong for the Hebrew nation (cf. 4:15-40)? 4/What do you do when you become aware of idolatry in your life? 5/What are the stipulations regarding a future *king* for Israel?

day 16 Δ *Deuteronomy 18–19*

1/Why do the Levites have a *due* (cf. Num. 8:14-19)? 2/What Canaanite practices are *abominable* to the Lord? 3/How will God reveal himself to the Israelites? 4/In what ways has Moses been *prophet* to the Israelites? 5/How will false prophets be exposed? 6/What provisions are included here to secure justice? 7/Relate the command of verse 14 to *a-inheritance* and *b*-false witness. 8/Why, do you think, are false witnesses dealt with so severely? Does this have any bearing on the integrity of your witness to Jesus Christ?

day 17 Δ *Deuteronomy 20*

1/What is the basis of Israel's trust in God during war? 2/In what way are the Israelites' military conquests a judgment of God on the conquered nations? 3/Contrast the function of the priest in war with the function of modern chaplains. Account for the difference. 4/What situations prompt legal exemption from military service? 5/Account for the difference in the conquest of *far* and near nations. 6/To what extent are God's commandments practical? 7/What can you do to become more aware of this dimension to life?

day 18 Δ *Deuteronomy 21–22*

1/In reading this collection of laws, what, do you think, are the important values stressed? 2/Who has the final authority in the cities? 3/Compare 21:8-9 with Numbers 35:33-34. 4/What are the *a*-rights and *b*-responsibilities of family members? 5/Why, do you think, are proper family relations so crucial? 6/What basic principles govern your life with your *a*-family and *b*-neighbors (cf. 22:1-4)? 7/In what way does treatment of *a*-neighbors and *b*-wife reflect a man's attitude toward God? 8/Relate these commands to the authority of *a*-the priests, *b*-man, and *c*-God.

day 19 Δ *Deuteronomy 23–24*
1/What basic religious and social values are affirmed in these laws? 2/Upon what basis are people excluded from the congregation? 3/Why, do you think, is purity in worship so important in Israel's faith? 4/Relate the sanctity of the congregation with the necessary sanctity of the Israelites' military camps. 5/To what extent is exploitation forbidden (relate to the sanctity of others)? 6/What about your basic values is revealed in your everyday actions toward *a*-non-Christians, *b*-Christians, *c*-your family, *d*-your neighbors, *e*-the poor and needy, and *f*-God?

day 20 Δ *Deuteronomy 25–26*
1/In what ways do these commands assure respect for God's *a*-image in his servants and *b*-covenant with them? 2/How does 25:1-3 relate with 25:4? 3/Compare 25:17-19 with Exodus 17:8-16. 4/In what ways are the *first fruit* and tithe an acknowledgement of God's *a*-past and *b*-continual care for the Israelites? 5/Summarize the values underlying the laws governing Israel's religious, social, political, and moral life (chaps. 12–26). 6/How do these values affect your attitudes toward the major issues facing your nation (e.g., racial injustice, the exploitation of minority groups, etc.)? 7/What are *a*-God's and *b*-the people's parts in ratifying the *covenant*?

day 21 Δ *Deuteronomy 27*
1/What is involved in the solemn ceremony which is to follow the renewing of the covenant in Canaan (cf. 11:26-32; Ex. 24)? 2/What would be a permanent witness to their commitment? 3/Describe the geographic arrangement of the tribes for the

ceremony (locate the mountains on a map). What is the significance of this arrangement? 4/What part do the priests have? 5/Compare or contrast these curses with the ten commandments (chap. 5). What areas of life are violated?

day 22 △ Deuteronomy 28

1/Imagine you are an Israelite listening to Moses. How do the *a*-blessings and *b*-curses affect you (blessing and curses in the call to loyalty are a formal part of all Near Eastern treaties during this time)? 2/Describe and visualize Israel's *a*-foreign, *b*-domestic, and *c*-personal affairs if the people obey. 3/Imagine the responses of the surrounding nations to the blessing (v. 10) and cursing (v. 25) of Israel. 4/Imagine Moses' feelings as he recites the curses (relate to his past experience with the Israelites). 5/What areas of life do the curses include? 6/How does this chapter reveal the ultimate folly and horror of rebellion against God? 7/What is your response to a God who *delights* in *a*-doing good and *b*-bringing ruin? What is the basis of this paradox?

day 23 △ Deuteronomy 29

1/List reasons that this chapter is crucial to the whole meaning of the covenant. 2/Who is included in the covenant? 3/How has God called you to personal commitment? 4/Compare idolatry with *a root* (v. 18). 5/In what ways have you been tempted to substitute mere conformity to Christian ethics or conduct for the inner reality of true commitment? What effect, do you think, does your superficiality have on others? 6/Relate verse 29 to verses 10-15.

day 24 △ Deuteronomy 30

1/Contrast the life and death promised here. 2/What is the total meaning of the life offered in this chapter? What are its *a*-causes, *b*-conditions, and *c*-results? 3/Contrast the characteristics of the Israelites in the past with their characteristics when the Lord will *restore* them. 4/What are God's actions in this change? 5/What attributes of God are revealed in his continued dealing with Israel even after he judges her? 6/For what reasons is Israel's disobedience inexcusable? 7/What is *a*-God's and *b*-your part in your *loving* God? 8/What is the significance of *heaven and earth* witnessing the covenant (Near Eastern covenants include witnesses—often a pantheon of deities—to stand behind the covenant commitment)?

day 25   Δ   *Deuteronomy 31:1-29*
1/What are Moses' most pressing concerns before his death? 2/What charges does he give? To whom? 3/What is to be the continued role of *Deuteronomy* in the life of Israel (Near Eastern treaties are read at periodic intervals)? 4/Why, do you think, is the year of release during the feast of booths (cf. Lev. 23:42-43) chosen for the reading of *Deuteronomy*? 5/What about God's patience is revealed in this chapter? 6/What is the purpose of the song Moses is to write? 7/In what ways have you been *learning to fear the Lord* from your study of *Deuteronomy?*

day 26   Δ   *Deuteronomy 31:30–32:25*
1/In what ways is this song a reflection of the total message of *Deuteronomy*? Do you see anything new in the song? 2/How are God's love and justice related in this song? 3/Circle and explain the metaphors. 4/Contrast the qualities God manifests to Israel with the qualities they return to him. 5/What is your response to God in view of what he feels toward you? 6/In what ways is Israel's sin *foolishness* and *senseless* ingratitude (Jeshurun is a name of reproach for Israel)? 7/How can you avoid similar folly today?

day 27   Δ   *Deuteronomy 32:26-52*
1/For what reason does God limit the power of the *foolish nation* over Israel? 2/Contrast the enemies' *rock* with Israel's *Rock.* 3/For what reasons will God preserve a *remnant* of Israel? 4/What is the basis of your hope of preservation? 5/What is significant about Joshua's involvement with the song? 6/Why,

do you think, does God emphasize the reason Moses cannot go into Canaan?

day 28 Δ Deuteronomy 33
1/Compare and contrast Moses' blessing here with Jacob's in Genesis 49 (cf. especially the predictions and prayers for each tribe). 2/Compare the Lord's appearing with a sunrise in Sinai. 3/In what ways is God unique? 4/Summarize his relationship with *a*-Israel and *b*-you. 5/In what ways does your assurance of your relationship with God affect the attitudes and actions of your daily living?

day 29 Δ Deuteronomy 34
1/Imagine Moses' feelings on Mount Nebo. 2/What is Israel's response to *a*-Moses' death and *b*-Joshua's new leadership? Why? 3/Summarize Moses' qualities of character (cf. Ex. through Deut.). Contrast the "end product" with his first confrontation with God (Ex. 3–4:20). Account for the drastic change. 4/How has *Deuteronomy* altered your *a*-values, *b*-view of God, and *c*-view of your relationship to him? 5/Summarize the main themes of the book.

day 30 Δ Mark 10:1-16
1/Investigate the contrasts of Galilee and Judea as to *a*-geography and *b*-population. 2/What, do you think, do the Pharisees expect or want Jesus to say? 3/What does the existence of divorce (cf. Deut. 24:1-4) in Moses' time reveal about human nature? 4/Relate Jesus' view of marriage with God's initial purpose in creating two sexes. Describe the essence of the marriage bond. 5/Contrast this teaching with the generally accepted view of *a*-vows and bonds and *b*-morality today. Compare or contrast your views. 6/What is Jesus' attitude toward his standards in view of human weakness? 7/What qualities of children *a*-are necessary to enter the kingdom and *b*-need to be part of your life?

Month 22

day 1 Δ Mark 10:17-31

1/What, do you think, prompts the man to ask Jesus this question? 2/Relate *goodness* and God. 3/What have been the man's relationships with others? 4/What prevents the man's relationship with God? 5/Contrast Jesus' use of the verb *lack* with the man's wealth. 6/Imagine Jesus' feelings as he watches the man go away. Imagine the man's feelings. 7/What about *riches* makes entering the kingdom *hard* (relate to the metaphor)? 8/What is the paradox about anyone being *saved*? 9/What have you *left* to follow Jesus? Why? What will be your gain? 10/How will this promise (vv. 29-31) encourage the disciples as they contemplate the previous event?

day 2 Δ Mark 10:32-45

1/What, do you think, makes the disciples *amazed* and *afraid*? 2/What additional facts about his future does Jesus divulge (cf. 8:31; 9:12, 30-32)? 3/What do James and John *a*-understand and *b*-misunderstand about Jesus' kingdom? What are their aims? 4/What are your aims in regard to Jesus' kingdom? 5/Determine the meaning of *cup* and *baptism* (add to your understanding in subsequent chapters). 6/In what ways have you participated with Jesus in regard to his *cup* and *baptism*? With what manifestations in your daily living? 7/What is Jesus' concept of leadership (cf. 9:33-37)? Contrast the actions and attitudes of the rulers (v. 42). 8/Summarize how Jesus exemplifies the concept. 10/How does Jesus *exercise authority*? 11/Explain the metaphor of *ransom*.

day 3 Δ Mark 10:46-52

1/Locate Jericho on a map (note its relation to Jesus' final destination). 2/Imagine Bartimaeus' feelings as he hears the crowd approach (relate to his occupation). 3/What qualities does Bartimaeus reveal? 4/What are the reactions of the crowd to him?

Why, do you think? 5/In what ways have you *rebuked* someone's progress to Jesus? Why? 6/Explain the significance of the title Bartimaeus uses for Jesus. 7/What do you want Jesus to do for you? Why? 8/What is the *a*-cause and *b*-result of Bartimaeus' healing?

day 4 Δ *Mark 11:1-11*
1/Imagine Jesus' feelings as he begins the last week of his life here (cf. 14:1; establish the chronology of this last week in this and subsequent chapters). What Jewish feast is being observed? 2/Imagine the disciples' feelings as they find everything as Jesus has said. In what ways do they act in faith? 3/What *a*-qualities of character and *b*-views of Jesus prompt the people to *a*-give the colt and *b*-spread the garments and branches? 4/Imagine you are a disciple. What are your feelings about all this commotion? 5/In what way do the Jewish people here understand the coming of the *kingdom*? 6/What does Jesus' acceptance of the honor reveal about his view of the shouts (cf. Ps. 118:26)? 7/Contrast his acceptance here with 8:27-30 and 9:9. 8/What does Jesus do when he gets to Jerusalem?

day 5 Δ *Mark 11:12-25*
1/For what reason does Jesus perpetuate the state in which he finds the fig tree (a pre-crop of small figs usually appears with the leaves)? 2/Relate verse 11 with Jesus' actions in the temple. 3/How does Jesus justify his actions to those he turns out? 4/According to Jesus what is the purpose of the temple? 5/Imagine the reactions of those who usually buy, sell, and change money in the temple. 6/Account for the reaction of the priests and scribes. 7/Find out who the chief priests are. Why do Jesus' actions make them *fear*? 8/In what ways does Jesus use the fig tree to illustrate *prayer*? 9/To what extent are *a*-faith and *b*-forgiveness problems for you? Why? In what ways do you make God's forgiveness possible for you? Whom do you need to forgive today?

day 6 △ Mark 11:27-33

1/Find out what the priests, scribes, and elders claim as their authority. Find out the function of the elders. 2/What, do you think, is their purpose in asking Jesus to prove his authority (cf. their attitudes toward him previously—2:6-7, 16, 24; 3:2, 6, 22; 7:1-5; 10:2; 11:18)? 3/In what ways does Jesus relate himself to John? 4/What are the alternatives for the scribes' answer? Why do they reject each? 5/What is the ultimate irony of their answer to Jesus' question? 6/What is your view of the source of Jesus' authority? How do you know?

day 7 △ Mark 12:1-12

1/Contrast the characteristics of the *a*-vineyard owner and *b*-tenants. 2/Are the tenants fully aware of what they are doing? What is their motive? 3/What will happen to the tenants? 4/How do the priests, scribes, and elders know what the metaphors of the parable represent (cf. Is. 5:1-7)? 5/In what way does the parable make plain their attitude toward Jesus? 6/Create a parable which describes your real attitude toward Jesus. 7/In what ways are the *others* (v. 9) particularly unpalatable to these religious leaders? 8/How does the parable relate to 11:27-33? to Psalm 118:22-23?

day 8 △ Mark 12:13-17

1/Investigate the political beliefs of the Herodians (cf. 3:6). What is their opinion of Caesar? 2/Relate the trap they plan for Jesus with the political situation in Palestine at this time. 3/What do the Pharisees and Herodians "know" about Jesus? 4/What is Jesus' reaction to their "knowledge"? 5/How does the trap fail? 6/Define *render*. Paraphrase Jesus' teaching here to fit your situation. 7/What benefits do you accept from your government? List the responsibilities demanded of you in return. What is your attitude toward *a*-the benefits and *b*-your responsibilities? Why?

day 9 △ Mark 12:18-27

1/Investigate the religious beliefs of the Sadducees (especially about *a*-the resurrection and *b*-angels). 2/How do they hope to trick Jesus? 3/On what law do they base their question (cf. Deut. 25:5-10)? 4/Imagine the undercurrent of the listeners as the Sadducees finish reciting their situation-question. 5/In what ways does Jesus embarrass them? In what way is their question meaningless? 6/Given these criteria (v. 24) what questions of yours are meaningless? 7/How does Jesus validate belief in the resurrection?

day 10 △ Mark 12:28-34

1/What prompts the scribe to question Jesus? 2/What place does Scripture have in Jesus' answer (cf. Deut. 6:4-5; Lev. 19:18)? 3/What does the scribe (cf. his knowledge of Scripture) think of Jesus' understanding and answer of his question? 4/From your study of the *law* (Gen.–Deut.) what do you think of Jesus' answer? 5/What is involved in love to *a*-God and *b*-your neighbor? 6/How will you show your *love* to *a*-God and *b*-neighbors today?

day 11 △ Mark 12:35-44

1/Relate Jesus' question here to the Jewish opinion about the kingdom (cf. 11:10). 2/How does Jesus explain the quotation from Psalm 110? 3/How does Jesus characterize the scribes (contrast with their self-opinion)? 4/Find out the *a*-location and *b*-purpose of the *treasury*. 5/Contrast the characteristics which the scribes (especially v. 40) and the poor widow reveal. 6/Explain Jesus' evaluation (*more* in v. 43) regarding the contributions. 7/How does his evaluation here *a*-encourage or *b*-shame your giving?

day 12 △ Mark 13:1-36

1/List Jesus' forewarnings about future happenings. 2/How will this knowledge equip *a*-the disciples and *b*-you to face the future with *endurance*? 3/What will the Son of man do when he comes in the future? What is your responsibility in regard to his coming?

day 13 △ *Mark 14:1-9*

1/What is the priests and scribes' concern as to the timing of their plan? 2/How do the people in Simon's house feel about the woman's act? 3/Imagine the woman's feelings *a*-as she pours the ointment on Jesus and *b*-as Jesus defends her. 4/Contrast this situation with 12:41-44. Compare Jesus' evaluation of each. 5/In what areas are God's values different from yours? 6/Contrast the attitudes of *a*-the chief priests and scribes and *b*-the woman toward Jesus. Can you account for the difference?

day 14 △ *Mark 14:10-16*

1/Compare and contrast Judas' attitude toward Jesus with *a*-the woman's (vv. 3-9) and *b*-the chief priests'. 2/Why, do you think, does Judas want to betray Jesus? 3/What preparations are made for the Passover? 4/What is the significance of *a*-the extent of Jesus' knowledge and *b*-the apparent secrecy of the upper room?

day 15 △ *Mark 14:14-31*

1/What does Jesus know about the man who will betray him? 2/How does Jesus feel about Judas? 3/How do you understand the paradox of God's sovereignty and human responsibility? 4/What do you learn about Jesus' *covenant* in verses 22-25? 5/How do *a*-the disciples and *b*-you share in this covenant? 6/What predictions does Jesus make about himself (cf. Zech. 13:7)? about the disciples? 7/Characterize the disciples' self-assurance.

day 16 △ *Mark 14:32-65*

1/Imagine Jesus' feelings as the disciples sleep while he prays. What is the disciples' response? 2/How complete is Jesus' prayer in verse 36? 3/How do you express your desires and submission to God? 4/Imagine the disciples' feelings as they watch and hear Judas. How do these feelings prompt their actions (vv. 47, 50)? 5/How does Jesus greet those who are about to arrest him? 6/Recreate imaginatively the trial in verses 53-65. 7/What kinds of reactions do the priests and scribes have? the witnesses? Jesus? 8/Who appears most composed in this whole situation? How do you account for this composure?

day 17 △ *Mark 14:66-72*
1/Does Peter keep to his commitment of verses 29-31? 2/Why, do you think, does he react in this way? What is his response when he realizes what he has done? 3/How do you handle your own unfaithfulness to God? Why? 4/Where is the source of your self-confidence?

day 18 △ *Mark 15:1-15*
1/To what extent are the priests concerned about the outcome of the trial before Pilate (cf. vv. 1, 3, 10-11)? 2/How does Pilate seem to feel about Jesus? 3/What "out" does Pilate try to make for himself and the people? 4/Does Jesus try to affect the outcome of the trial? 5/Compare this trial before Pilate with the trial in 14:53-65. 6/Summarize your feelings about both trials.

day 19 △ *Mark 15:16-32*
1/What humiliations does Jesus experience in this passage (cf. 14:65)? 2/How do the *a*-soldiers, *b*-people, and *c*-chief priests talk and act toward Jesus? 3/What is ironical about what they say about Jesus? 4/Do you think they all now have him where they want him? Why? 5/What do they ask Jesus to do (vv. 30, 32)? What do they misunderstand about *seeing* and *believing*? 6/In what areas and situations do you demand proof from God for your belief? Why?

day 20 △ *Mark 15:33-47*
1/Recreate imaginatively the sights and sounds of the crucifixion. 2/In a society where crucifixions are common what is different about the events of this crucifixion? 3/How does at least one soldier respond to this difference? 4/How is God involved in

the crucifixion? 5/What is the significance of the torn curtain? 6/How does Joseph of Arimathea involve himself in Jesus' death? What risks does he take? 7/How are you involved in Jesus' death?

day 21 △ Mark 16:1-8
1/Imagine the women's feelings as they go to the tomb this early morning. 2/What is their concern? 3/How do they feel as they go *from* the tomb? 4/What information do they receive about Jesus from the young man? 5/What message are they to tell (cf. v. 7 with 14:28)? Do they obey? Why? 6/What is your response to the fact of the resurrection? Why?

day 22 △ Mark 16:9-20
1/To whom does Jesus appear in these verses? 2/How does he *a*-scold and *b*-encourage the disciples? 3/Relate *belief* and *signs*. 4/How do the disciples carry out Jesus' commission? 5/How do you respond to Jesus' commission? Why? What makes your message authentic?

day 23 △ Mark 1–16
1/Summarize the outworkings of Jesus' authority here. What are the various reactions to that authority? Why? 2/List the questions Jesus answers. Account for his wisdom. 3/What facts recorded by Mark have been most important to you? Why? 4/What is your response to Jesus as Mark portrays him?

day 24 △ Introduction to Judges
The structure of *Judges* is biographical, dealing with the men and women God selects to judge the people of Israel during the first few centuries after they enter Canaan. Review the instructions Joshua gives the Israelites before he dies (Josh. 23–24). Keep a list of the judges as to their *a*-tribe, *b*-length of service, *c*-distinction, and *d*-defeat of each oppressor. *Judges 1–2:5* 1/In what different

ways do the various tribes of Israel treat the people of the land? 2/Which of the tribes act according to God's direction (cf. Josh. 23:4-13)? 3/What, do you predict, will develop from this state of co-existence? 4/How is God consistent with his nature when he declares judgment on his people? 5/How effective is God's judgment in dealing with their basic problem of disobedience? 6/How does this situation affect your attitude about God's commandments for you?

day 25 Δ *Judges 2:6–3:6*

1/To what extent does the people's obedience to God depend on an obedient leader (note also in subsequent chapters)? 2/In what ways is the worship of the Baals (gods of rain and fertility) and the Ashtaroth (Baal's consort) more convenient than the worship of God? 3/How does God provide a way for the people to get to know him? 4/How do the people respond? 5/In what ways can you know God? What is your response? 6/Determine the meaning of *harlot* in relation to Israel, God, and the gods. 7/What is the threefold purpose of the nations' presence in Canaan? 8/What specific commandments do the Israelites disobey (cf. Deut. 7:1-5)?

day 26 Δ *Judges 3:7-31*

1/How do the people respond to God's educational program? 2/What pressure is put on the people to make them cry out to God? 3/What picture of God's forgiveness and compassion do you see in the raising up of these judges? 4/Keep a list of *a*-the judges, *b*-the nations they conquer, and *c*-the reasons for their victory. 5/What is the prerequisite for mercy that God requires of his people? of you? 6/What pattern of God's dealings with his people do you see in this chapter?

day 27 Δ *Judges 4–5*

1/What pressures move the children of Israel to appeal to God for deliverance? 2/Describe and evaluate the relationship of Deborah and Barak as co-deliverers. 3/Account for the willingness of the people to resist the oppressors when their predicament has been so dreadful. 4/What contrasting response to the call of battle is seen among the various tribes? 5/Compare this reponse with their first war activities (cf. chap. 1). 6/How does Sisera's army *fall*? 7/Characterize Jael. 8/Relate the poignant scene of Sisera's mother to the results of judgment in personal relations.

day 28 △ *Judges 6*

1/Compare the Midianite oppression to *locusts.* How does it affect Gideon? 2/Why, do you think, does God stress his past experience with the Israelites (cf. 2:1-2; Josh. 24)? 3/What do Gideon's *a*-actions and *b*-conversation reveal about his character? 4/In what way is Gideon prepared by the angel for his assignment? 5/Contrast Gideon's need for the *a*-first (v. 17) and *b*-second (vv. 36-40) signs. 6/What do you learn about guidance from Gideon's experience? 7/How does Gideon's call to be responsible in his home and community parallel what God has called you to do? 8/To what extent will you claim God's faithfulness to enable you to do these things today?

day 29 △ *Judges 7*

1/In what way are the selected soldiers more qualified than the ones sent home? 2/Imagine Gideon's feelings about the reduction in his army and the size of the Midianite camp. 3/How does God continue to be the controlling influence in Israel's battle preparations and strategy? 4/What causes the Midianites' panic? 5/How is God's role in the victory acknowledged? 6/What do you learn here about the way God's strength works through human weakness? 7/How can you know God's strength in your life today? 8/What is the effect of the dream (cf. the oriental regard for dreams)?

day 30 △ *Judges 8*

1/What motive is reflected in the actions of the men of Ephraim? How is this action contrary to the goals set for them by God (cf.

7:2)? 2/How does Gideon appease them? 3/What potential
threat to Gideon's victory is represented in the taunts of Succouth
and Penuel? 4/How is Gideon able to handle these threats? How,
do you think, does he justify his actions? Are they simply revenge? 5/To whom do the people give credit for the victory? 6/How does Gideon encourage this? 7/How does their failure to give God credit relate to the people's turning away from
a-God and *b*-Gideon's family when Gideon dies? 8/How do the
motives for your actions relate to your response to the honor you
gain from them?

Month 23

day 1 Δ Judges 9
1/What basic argument does Abimelech use to persuade the people
to accept him as their leader? 2/What makes this appeal agreeable
to the people? 3/What is the meaning of *a*-the fable that Jotham
presents and *b*-his subsequent remarks? Who is the judge? 4/How
are the selfish motives of Abimelech demonstrated repeatedly in
the events recorded here? 5/Locate the cities on a map. 6/How
does Abimelech become a victim of the methods that make him
king? 7/When have you experienced a similar boomerang effect?
What have you done? 8/In what way do Jotham's remarks (vv.
7-20) come true?

day 2 Δ Judges 10
1/How do the judges Tola and Jair differ from their predeces-
sors? 2/Describe their positions in the nation. 3/What, do you
think, is the appeal of the nations' gods for Israel? 4/Contrast the
appeal and the result of following other gods for *a*-Israel and
b-you. 5/Imagine the kind of oppression Israel endures.
Why? 6/Determine the meaning of *sold* in verse 7. 7/What, do
you think, provokes them to finally cry to the Lord? 8/How long
is the usual interval between your sinning and crying to the Lord?

Why? 9/What indicates that the people have a definite change of heart?

day 3 Δ *Judges 11*
1/Explain the difference in behavior of the Gileadites toward Jeph-thah before and after the declaration of war. 2/In what way does the condition of Jephthah's leadership (cf. v. 9) make possible his challenge to the Ammonite king? 3/How does Jephthah deter-mine the ownership of the land? How certain is he that he is right? 4/In what ways is Jephthah's sacrifice of his daughter an unnecessary tragedy? 5/What is your view of making and keeping vows to the Lord (cf. Lev. 27)?

day 4 Δ *Judges 12–13:1*
1/Contrast the ways *a*-Jephthah and *b*-Gideon (cf. 8:1-3) handle the resentment of the men of Ephraim. With what results? 2/What does Jephthah's burial place reveal about the promise made to him by the elders of Gilead? 3/Locate on a map the lands of the judges in this chapter. What kind of coverage do they have? 4/What is noticeable about the impact of their death upon Israel? 5/To what extent are you dependent on the leadership of another person for your spiritual stability? Why?

day 5 Δ *Judges 13*
1/How is the calling of Samson as a judge different from the other callings thus far? 2/What is involved in being a Nazarite (cf. Num. 6)? 3/Describe Manoah's concern for the future of this promised son. 4/Imagine the wife's feelings. 5/Explain the difference of the husband's and wife's actions when they learn the identity of the angel. 6/Imagine how you would have reacted. 7/What in Samson's childhood shows that the Lord confirms his calling of Samson?

day 6 Δ *Judges 14*
1/How does Samson's basis for choosing a wife differ from that of

232

his parents? 2/How does God guide the choice? 3/List the specific experiences on the way to Timnah. 4/Account for Samson's silence both times (cf. Num. 6 with vv. 8-9). 5/How does the nature of these events make the riddle impossible to solve? 6/Imagine the mixed emotions of Samson's wife. What do her actions reveal about her character? 7/How does God continue to be the victor in Samson's life even though he yields to pressure? 8/What provokes Samson's anger? 9/In what ways has God given you victory over pressured crises?

day 7 Δ Judges 15

1/Compare the events of this chapter with 14:4. 2/What marital arrangement accounts for Samson's separation (cf. 8:31)? 3/Compare the Philistines' revenge with their threats in 14:15. 4/What policy have the Jews adopted in regard to their suppression under the Philistines? 5/How is Samson able to take a different stand than they have and defy the Philistines? 6/How recently have you asked God to meet a need of yours? Why?

day 8 Δ Judges 16

1/What is the difference between Samson's relationship with *a*-the harlot and *b*-Delilah? How does the nature of his relationship with Delilah set the stage for his enticement by her? 2/What is the source of Samson's strength? 3/List the incidents in which he has shown strength. With what results for the Philistines? 4/What factor in Delilah's series of appeals makes Samson weaken? 5/On what other occasion has he faced the same temptation (cf. 14:15-18)? With what results? 6/How is Samson's treatment deliberately designed to show his total loss of strength? 7/Speculate on the *sport* Samson performs. 8/How is Samson's final prayer related to God's purpose in his life? 9/How can you pray according to God's purposes in your life?

day 9 Δ Judges 17

1/Try to determine the period of these events and those following in chapters 18–21. What is the recurring phrase (cf. 17:6; 18:1; 19:1; 21:25)? 2/Describe the relationship of the son to his mother at the outset of this incident. How does it become what it should be? 3/List the actions of the mother, Micah, and the Levite. 4/Why, do you think, doesn't the author evaluate these actions? Can you evaluate the actions in view of God's commands through Moses to his people? 5/Describe the relationship of Micah and the Levite. 6/Do you ever feel that your relationships to others will *prosper* you? Why?

day 10   Δ   Judges 18
1/How does this incident give you specific information about the relationship of the Jews to their priests in this period of history? 2/On what evidence do the men decide that Laish is given to them by God? How do their actions show their confidence? 3/What element seems to be missing in the anxious demands of the Danites to have the religious items and the priest? 4/Imagine Micah's feelings. 5/Who is responsible for the victory at Laish? 6/How does the Danites' behavior after the victory show their token relationship to God? 7/What is your relationship with God in your daily life and special undertakings? Why?

day 11   Δ   Judges 19
1/Describe the life of this unemployed Levite. 2/Try to determine the meaning of his actions (cf. especially vv. 3, 12, 29). 3/Account for the difference in his attitude toward his concubine in verses 3 and 25-29. 4/What is the effect of the Levites' action on the people of the tribes? 5/Compare the happenings at Gibeah with Genesis 19:1-11. What is the value placed on hospitality? regard for women? Compare or contrast with your values (especially under pressure).

day 12   Δ   Judges 20
1/How effective is the Levites' communication of the disaster that

has corrupted Israel? 2/How does the action of the people show that even without a king they have a certain amount of judgment and control? 3/What progression in the people's dependency on God takes place here? 4/In what ways are you dependent on God in your activities? 5/Contrast the loss of the Benjamites at the end of the battle with what they would have lost in the beginning.

day 13 Δ Judges 21
1/How do the people get their guidance about the problem of wives for the Benjamites? 2/How does the solution to the problem of the shortage protect the law of agreement made at Shiloh (cf. v. 7)? 3/Have the people learned anything about depending on God? 4/Summarize the religious atmosphere of Israel during *a*-the time of the judges and *b*-the period of anarchy (chaps. 17–21). 5/What is the religious atmosphere of your society? 6/What have you learned from *Judges* about the necessity of obedience to God and the consequences of rejection of God?

day 14 Δ Introduction to 1 Peter
Peter writes this letter (63-64 A.D.) to exiled Christians who live scattered among non-Christians throughout the provinces of Rome. The letter arrives about the time of inquisitions and Nero's general persecution of Christians. *1 Peter 1:1–2:10* 1/Skim the passage. 2/Jot down the topics and themes. 3/What do you recall about Peter and his experiences with Jesus (cf. Luke and Mark)? 4/What are the roles and ministries of *a*-God the Father, *b*-Jesus Christ the Son, and *c*-the Holy Spirit? 5/Contrast the conditions of *a*-Christians and *b*-non-Christians.

day 15 Δ 1 Peter 1:1-5
1/Contrast the exiles' earthly and spiritual positions in verses 1-2. 2/What specific work does each Person of the Trinity have in a believer's life? 3/From this passage list what God has done for you. In what ways have these facts changed your life? 4/For what

have you been *sanctified?* To what have you been *born anew?* 5/How is *a-obedience* and *b-hope* expressed in your life? 6/In what specific areas do you experience God's *guarding* power?

day 16 △ *1 Peter 1:6-12*

1/In what should you rejoice (cf. vv. 3-5)? Why? 2/How can you *rejoice* while you suffer? 3/What is faith's purpose in a Christian's life in relation to self? in relation to Jesus Christ? 4/How is faith to be expressed actively? 5/What are the *a*-prophets' and *b*-angels' attitude toward your salvation? What is their self-awareness? 6/What, would you say, is the basic purpose of the Old Testament and the prophets? 7/Compare and contrast the *grace* you have received with the *sufferings* of Christ.

day 17 △ *1 Peter 1:13-25*

1/What two thoughts does *therefore* connect? 2/Who has called you? 3/What characteristics should be yours once you are called? Why (cf. Lev. 11:44-45; 19:2; 20:26)? 4/What difference has being *ransomed* made in your life? 5/What event gives confidence to your faith? Why? 6/How are God and the *word* related (cf. Is. 40:6-8)? 7/Why is your mental understanding so important to your faith (underline and explain the verbs in vv. 13, 18, 21)?

day 18 △ *1 Peter 2:1-10*

1/How would the attitudes and actions of verse 1 affect a Christian group? Relate 1:22 with 2:1. 2/What is the source of a Christian's nourishment? What should initiate his *hunger?* 3/In what specific ways is God's Word making a difference in your relationships with others? 4/List the phrases describing *a*-Jesus Christ (cf. Is. 28:16; Ps. 118:22; Is. 8:14-15) and *b*-your relationship to him. 5/Explain the relationship of the metaphors. 6/Compare and contrast your *priesthood* and *sacrifices* with the Old Testament priesthood and sacrifices (cf. especially Ex. 25–30; 35–40; Lev. 1–9; 16–17; 21–22). 7/What was your former condition (cf. Hosea 1:6-10;

2:23)? What is your present condition? 8/Who has made this change for you? For what purpose? 9/What *wonderful deeds* of God will you declare to others today?

day 19   Δ   *1 Peter 2:11–5:14*

1/Skim the rest of the letter. 2/Jot down topics and themes. 3/What relationship has Peter been discussing? Now what relationship does he address? 4/Why, do you think, is the former relationship discussed first? 5/Which relationship do people today emphasize? Why, do you think? What problems does this emphasis leave unsolved? 6/List some attitudes and actions which need to change in the relationships directly involving you (continue on subsequent days).

day 20   Δ   *1 Peter 2:11-17*

1/What motivations does Paul suggest for *a*-personal and *b*-public good conduct? 2/What specific passions of the flesh *war against* you? 3/What attitude does Peter express toward social institutions? Why? 4/To what human institutions are you subject? Check your daily subjection to their rules, traffic laws, work hours, etc. 5/What is the situation of the Christians Peter addresses? 6/How can you change social injustices? 7/Relate *subjection and freedom* for the Christian. 8/Discuss today's attitudes toward "states' rights," "bucking the system," "centralized government," "civil disobedience," etc. in view of this scriptural position.

day 21   Δ   *1 Peter 2:18-25*

1/Investigate the social institutions of Peter's day concerning the relationship discussed here. 2/Who are your *masters?* What characteristics do they show toward you? 3/To what extent do you *submit* to them? Why? 4/Give examples of *unjust suffering.* What would be your contemporaries' attitudes and actions toward these examples? What are your attitudes and actions in similar situations? Why? 5/What is God's response? 6/In what ways is Christ an example in this area (cf. Is. 53)? 7/For what purpose has Christ suffered? With what effect for you?

day 22 △ 1 Peter 3:1-12

1/What are the *a*-basic roles and *b*-duties of a wife/husband who is a Christian to her husband/his wife? For what reasons? 2/Deliberately compare or contrast your feelings and values concerning marriage relations. 3/How has this passage modified your views? Why? 4/How is the scriptural portrayal of marriage different from today's "democratic" or "50/50" concept? 5/Summarize the principles for Christian living Peter gives in 2:11–3:12 (cf. Ps. 34:12-16). 6/To what have you been *called* (cf. v. 9 with 2:21)? 7/In what specific ways are you going against your *calling*? Why?

day 23 △ 1 Peter 3:13–4:6

1/How do verses 13-14 relate to the preceding passages? Why should a suffering Christian not fear or panic? 2/What two aspects of Christ's life are mentioned? 3/How is Christ's lordship and authority related to your suffering (cf. 1:6-7)? What difference does this relation make in a Christian's attitude toward himself? toward his persecutors? toward the devil (cf. 5:8-9)? toward God? 4/How is a *clear conscience* involved with suffering (cf. vv. 16, 21 with 2:12, 20)? 5/How does the example of Christ relate to the practical aspects of daily suffering: *a*-your attitude, *b*-your practices, and *c*-your hope? 6/What is the purpose of Christ's death in relation to *a*-your past and present life, *b*-non-Christians, and *c*-people already dead? 7/How and when has suffering helped you live by the will of God instead of by human passions?

day 24 △ 1 Peter 4:7-19

1/How is verse 7 related to 4:3-5? How does the fact of Christ's return keep you *sane and sober* in difficult situations? 2/List the exhortations in this passage. Which is mentioned first? How does it affect each of the others? 3/What does Peter say about gifts? about their use? 4/What gifts do you have? How do you use them? 5/List the responses of attitude and action that a Christian *a*-should   and *b*-should not have when suffering comes to him. 6/What are the results (explain the paradox) of godly response to suffering (cf. 3:12, 16; 4:4)? 7/What do you now share with Jesus Christ? What will you share with him? 8/What judgment does God bring on *a*-Christians and *b*-non-Christians? Why?

day 25 Δ 1 Peter 5
1/What relationship does Peter discuss now? On what basis (cf. John 21:15-17)? 2/What characteristics of *a*-leadership and *b*-subjection are mentioned? Describe and contrast the right and wrong methods of leadership. 3/Define *humility*. How does God respond to the attitude of humility? 4/What responses are you exhorted to make during suffering? How can your responses aid other Christians? What will God do? Why? 5/Summarize what Peter teaches should be your responses to *a*-others and *b*-your circumstances. In what ways has studying *1 Peter* increased *a*-your understanding of your *calling* and *b*-your ability to cope with life?

day 26 Δ Introduction to 1 Samuel
1 Samuel highlights Israel's history from the birth of the last judge Samuel to the death of the first king Saul. 1/Skim the first eight chapters. 2/List the important characters. Describe them briefly. 3/How does the Lord involve himself in the daily affairs of the people of Israel? List examples. 4/How do you expect him to reveal himself to you today?

day 27 Δ 1 Samuel 1:1-20
1/Describe Hannah's state of mind. Who is responsible for her barrenness? How does Elkanah respond to her situation? Peninnah? 2/Is any situation causing you similar frustration? Does wanting something very much probably indicate that it is not God's will? Do you pray regularly and specifically about your desires? 3/How does Hannah respond to Eli's accusation and reprimand? Do you have the right to tell anyone off (even if they deserve it)?

day 28 △ *1 Samuel 1:1-28*

1/How does this passage show that God begins his sovereign work in imperfect people and situations? 2/What kind of man is Elkanah? 3/Contrast Hannah's feelings and behavior in verses 8 and 18. Does God have a purpose in what he allows? 4/What is the significance of the name of the child? 5/Do you acknowledge answers to prayer, as Hannah does in verse 27? Do you back down when a promise is difficult or inconvenient to keep?

day 29 △ *1 Samuel 2:1-11*

1/According to Hannah's prayer, what is God like? What conditions or situations are subject to his sovereignty? 2/Contrast the destinies of the faithful ones and the adversaries. 3/What does the Lord do for the hungry, the barren, the poor, and the needy? 4/Contrast Hannah's feelings in verses 2:1 and 1:10. What makes the difference? 5/Do you worship the Lord spontaneously as Hannah does?

day 30 △ *1 Samuel 2:12-36*

1/What are Eli's sons doing with the sacrifices (cf. Lev. 7:28-36)? What other sin are they committing? 2/Imagine Elkanah and Hannah's worry and doubt about raising Samuel in such an environment. 3/How does Eli describe his sons' actions? What inconsistent action of Eli negates the force of his reprimand (vv. 29b, 36)? What is God's judgment of Eli's attitude toward his sons? 4/Whom do you try to please? Ask God to reveal your sin and inconsistency. 5/How does verse 35 define faithfulness?

Month 24

day 1 △ *1 Samuel 3*

1/Describe the religious situation at Shiloh. 2/How does God reveal himself and his Word to Samuel? How does Samuel know who is peaking to him? How does God speak to you? 3/How does verse 13 amplify Eli's inconsistent attitude and action toward his sons? 4/What does Eli's response in verse 18 show about God? Do you accept God's judgment? 5/How does Israel know that the Lord is with Samuel?

day 2 Δ *1 Samuel 4*
1/In what ways is the action of the elders (vv. 3-4) commendable? In what ways is it superstitious? 2/Is your faith or conduct superstitious? 3/Do the Israelites honestly believe the presence of the ark will guarantee victory? How do the Philistines respond to news of the presence of the ark? 4/How does news of the defeat and capture of the ark affect Eli? the wife of Phinehas? 5/Is a Christian guaranteed success?

day 3 Δ *1 Samuel 5*
1/Describe the situation in Israel before and after the Philistine capture of the ark (cf. Ps. 78:56-64). 2/Explain what happens when the ark is in the house of Dagon. 3/How do the people of Ashdod, Gath, and Ekron respond to the God of Israel because of the ark? 4/How has God shown you his power recently? How have you responded?

day 4 Δ *1 Samuel 6:1-18*
1/What is the significance of the phrase *with what* in the Philistines' inquiry to the priests and diviners? What do the priests recommend? 2/According to the priests, what will the guilt offering accomplish (cf. God's law for a guilt offering: Lev. 6:6-7; 7:1-7)? 3/How is your guilt removed? 4/What is the final test to distinguish God's actions from chance? How do verses 9 and 12 show God's graciousness and desire that men will realize his power and come to him?

day 5 Δ *1 Samuel 6:19–7:14*
1/Why does God kill men who have just worshiped him? Will he

overlook your casual ethics? 2/Find the last reference to Samuel prior to 7:3 and consider these silent years in his life. 3/How does the passage describe wholeheartedness toward God? 4/Why does the Philistine attack fail? Do you pray when you are afraid? Why?

day 6   △   1 Samuel 7:15–8:22

1/List some possible reasons Samuel's sons do not *walk in his ways.* 2/What two conditions do the elders of Israel point out to Samuel before they ask for a king? 3/What is God's response to their request? How will the king break up family life? 4/What is the significance of the phrase, *like all the nations?* To what extent do you allow those who do not know and honor God to be your example?

day 7   △   1 Samuel 9:1-25

1/What starts the chain of events which results in Saul becoming king of Israel? Can you determine which events in your life are important? 2/What do the young maidens tell Saul about Samuel and the sacrifice? Imagine Saul's bewilderment as he eats in the hall. 3/Do you recognize your limited understanding of yourself, others, circumstances, and the future and trust God's sovereignty?

day 8   △   1 Samuel 9:26–10:27

1/Compare 10:1 with 9:16-17. Considering 8:7 what does the repetition of *my people* reveal about God? 2/Into what areas of human affairs does God's sovereignty extend so that the signs to Saul are fulfilled? 3/What happens to Saul after he leaves Samuel? 4/What has God done for the people of Israel? What have the people of Israel done to God? 5/Do you place people in a God-like position (v. 19)?

day 9   △   1 Samuel 11

1/How does Israel's response to the crisis show that they have rejected God? To whom do you turn in crises? 2/How does God use the people's desire for a king to deliver them from enemies? Have you seen God use your mistakes and sins in his plan for good? 3/To whom do the Israelites attribute victory? To whom does Saul attribute deliverance? 4/What do Saul and all the men of Israel do in Gilgal?

day 10 △ 1 Samuel 12

1/Why does Samuel listen to the people (cf. w. 8:7, 9, 22)? 2/List the incidents Samuel emphasizes to show what God has done and been in the past and to stimulate Israel's present confidence and obedience. What may the people and their king expect if they serve the Lord? if they rebel? 3/In spite of Israel's past evil, why will the Lord retain his people? What is Samuel's responsibility to them? 4/For whom should you pray regularly, specifically, and earnestly?

day 11 △ 1 Samuel 13

1/How do the Philistines react to the Geba defeat? What do the Israelites do when the Philistines camp in Michmash? 2/How does Saul act foolishly? What is the result of his impatience? Have you ever acted foolishly because of impatience? 3/What are the odds of the battle? What is the added disadvantage of the Israelites in battle?

day 12 △ 1 Samuel 14:1-46

1/What verses show Jonathan's confidence that the Lord will determine the day's outcome? What are the effects of Jonathan's confidence? 2/How have you seen God influence many because of the confidence placed in his power by a few people? 3/What oath does Saul lay on the people? Compare the responses of the people to Saul's commands in verses 36, 40, and 45. What does the priest suggest in verse 36?

day 13 △ 1 Samuel 14:47–15:21

1/What instructions does the Lord give Saul for attacking Amalek?

According to verses 8-9 who is responsible for sparing Agag and the best cattle (cf. Saul's explanation)? 2/Contrast Saul's action in verse 12 with his earlier attitude in 11:13. 3/What does Saul's insistence that he has obeyed indicate about his spiritual condition? 4/Is partial obedience acceptable to God?

day 14 △ 1 Samuel 15:17-35

1/How does Saul justify sparing the best sheep and oxen? Do you ever try to justify partial obedience? 2/What is the Lord's attitude toward sacrifice and obedience? What are rebellion and stubbornness like? 3/Why does God reject Saul as king? 4/How does Saul respond to Samuel's comments? 5/What finally happens to Agag?

day 15 △ 1 Samuel 16

1/Does the Lord answer Samuel's question and objection? What instructions does the Lord give Samuel? 2/Explain how David is chosen to be king (cf. 13:14). 3/How is verse 7 important in your attitude? 4/Describe David before and after his anointing (cf. Saul's change in chaps. 9–10). How does the young man describe David to Saul? What assurance do these chapters give that God will prepare you?

day 16 △ 1 Samuel 17

1/Describe the psychological condition of Saul and the Israelites (cf. 16:14). How long has Goliath challenged the Israelites? 2/How does verse 15 amplify 16:14-23? 3/Contrast the responses of a-the men of Israel and b-David to Goliath's challenge. 4/What preparation does David have to fight Goliath? 5/Do you trust in *swords, spears, and javelins* (v. 45) instead of God?

day 17 △ 1 Samuel 18

1/In verse 1 what is the significance of the metaphor *knit* and the use of the passive voice? To what extent do you pray for God's

guidance in your friendships? 2/How does Saul react to David's
success? What saying makes him especially angry? 3/Why is Saul
afraid of David? Why do all Israel and Judah love David? 4/Do
you break your promises (cf. vv. 17-19)?

day 18   Δ   1 Samuel 19
1/How does Jonathan convince Saul that he should not kill
David? 2/Contrast verses 6 and 10. Do you live according to principles you know are right or according to your mood of the
moment? Pray that your spiritual life will not be determined by
your erratic and unstable emotions. 3/How does Michal assist
David (Ps. 59 gives insight into David's thinking and praying during
the decisive period of v. 11)? 4/What happens to the messengers
and Saul at Naioth?

day 19   Δ   1 Samuel 20
1/In what ways is Jonathan's friendship with David remark-
able? 2/How do David and Jonathan plan to find out Saul's attitude toward David? 3/How does verse 22b show Jonathan's faith
in God's sovereignty? Do you trust God to overrule in your circumstances? 4/Why does Saul think Jonathan's friendship with David
is shameful? Imagine Jonathan's feelings as he meets David.

day 20   Δ   1 Samuel 21
1/What does David need now? How does he answer Ahimelech's
question? 2/What does Ahimelech give David? Does David break
the Old Testament ceremonial law (cf. Mk. 2:23-28)? 3/What is
David's conviction concerning his actions in verses 10-15 (Ps. 34,
56 record David's prayers)? 4/What does God want you to do
when you are in trouble? Will he permit lying to relieve some
situational pressure on you?

day 21   Δ   1 Samuel 22
1/Who gathers with David at Adullam? 2/How does David show

concern for his parents? How can you? 3/What does Doeg the
Edomite disclose to Saul at Gibeah (cf. Ps. 52)? 4/Does Ahimelech say anything about having been deceived? What does Ahimelech tell Saul? Pray that God will make you a person of integrity
and character. 5/For what reason does Saul order Ahimelech and
the priests of Nob killed? Who kills them? Who takes the blame for
their death?

day 22 Δ 1 Samuel 23
1/What happens at Keilah? Do you pray specifically for guidance
before you make decisions? 2/Why is Saul's persistence thwarted? 3/What kind of friend is Jonathan? 4/What is ironic about
Saul's blessing of the Ziphites (Ps. 54 describes David's feeling at
this time)? How does God deliver David?

day 23 Δ 1 Samuel 24
1/How do David's men try to persuade him to kill Saul? For what
reason does David insist on sparing Saul? 2/How does David show
his respect for Saul? 3/Do you "get even" when a wrong is done
to you or do you repay good for evil (even in little
things)? 4/What makes Saul realize that David is *more righteous*
than he?

day 24 Δ 1 Samuel 25
1/Review Samuel's faithful life (especially w. 1:28; 2:35;
12:2-5). 2/What is the request of David's men? What is Nabal's
answer? 3/Contrast David's attitude in verses 21-22 and 24:11-12
(cf. 24:17). What makes the difference? 4/What kind of woman is
Abigail? 5/Do you trust God to take vengeance on wrong or do
you try to avenge yourself (cf. w. 38-39)?

day 25 Δ 1 Samuel 26
1/Compare verses 8-12 with 24:3-7. What additional reason does
David give for refraining from killing Saul (cf. 25:39)? 2/What

does the miraculous event of verse 12 reveal about God? 3/What does Saul confess after he recognizes David's voice? 4/For what does the Lord reward a man? Pray that you will develop these characteristics.

day 26 Δ 1 Samuel 27–28:2
1/What reason does David give for going to the land of the Philistines? Contrast David's words in verses 1 and 17:37. 2/What does David gain from his raids? Describe his procedure. Why does Achish trust David? 3/What does Achish want David and his men to do in the war against Israel? In what predicament does this request put David? When have your casual ethics put you in a similar predicament? What have you done?

day 27 Δ 1 Samuel 28
1/What is Saul's predicament? Have you ever felt you were in a similar situation? What have you done? 2/How does the woman respond to Saul's request and identification? 3/What happens when Samuel appears? 4/What does Samuel tell Saul? How does Saul respond to Samuel's prediction?

day 28 Δ 1 Samuel 29
1/What is David's predicament? Imagine his thoughts. 2/What is the extent of David's reputation (cf. v. 5 with 18:6-7; 21:10)? 3/Do you subtly seek to appear better than you actually are in the eyes of others (vv. 6-9)? 4/In spite of David's dishonesty, how does God honor his former concern to spare Saul? How has God delivered you from situations you have gotten yourself into because of unbelief and sin?

day 29 Δ 1 Samuel 30
1/How does God use the Amalekites' raid in David's life? In what three areas is he affected? How do the people react to the raid? Pray that tragedy and disappointment will cause you to strengthen

yourself in the Lord.   2/Are you learning to pray before you make decisions?   3/Why are the Amalekites unprepared for attack?

day 30 Δ 1 Samuel 31
1/What is the outcome of the battle between Israel and the Philistines? What happens to Saul and his sons (cf. 28:19)?   2/To whom do the Philistines proclaim their victory?   3/Review and summarize Jonathan's life (especially 14:6-10, 43; 18:1-4; 19:2; 20:13, 34, 42).   4/Review and summarize Saul's life (especially 10:1, 9, 24; 13:13-14; 15:10; 18:12; 28:6-7).   5/Pray that God will give you obedience to him for today and throughout your life.

YEAR
THREE

Month 25

day 1 Δ *Introduction to Ruth*
The author of *Ruth* records a story of the common people of Israel
caring for each other while the leader-aristocrats of the land are
involved in wars, intrigue, and rivalries. *Ruth 1:1-14* 1/Establish
the historical setting. Skim *Judges* and *1 Samuel* again. 2/Who are
the people involved in the story? How are they related? 3/Why
does the family leave Judah? How does this move affect the sons'
lives? 4/Imagine the effect of the tragedy on the three
women. 5/Why does Naomi urge Orpah and Ruth to return to
Moab when she starts to go back to Judah? What are their prospects for marriage in Judah? 6/How do you react when God's
actions toward you involve hurt to other people? 7/Why does
Orpah obey Naomi? Why does Ruth disobey?

day 2 △ Ruth 1:6-22

1/What is Naomi's argument to her daughters-in-law? 2/What will *a*-Orpah's and *b*-Ruth's decision mean socially, religiously, and economically? 3/Imagine the change in Naomi's appearance that causes such a stir in Bethlehem. How does she describe the change (contrast the reason for her initial departure in 1:1)? 4/What is Naomi's view of God and his dealing with people? 5/How is God related to the affairs of your life? When have you felt *full? empty? Why?*

day 3 △ Ruth 2

1/What is the immediate need of Naomi and Ruth? How can they meet this need (cf. Lev. 19:9-10; 23:22; Deut. 24:19-21)? 2/Imagine Ruth's feelings as she goes out in the morning to work in a strange land with customs she doesn't know. 3/What kind of person is Boaz? 4/What special privileges does he offer Ruth? How does he insure these privileges for her? 5/What are the provisions for the poor in your society? What is your part in meeting the needs of the poor? 6/Who has shown you special kindness recently? How have you responded? 7/In what ways does Naomi share Boaz's kindness to Ruth? 8/Contrast what Naomi says about God here with her earlier feelings (cf. 1:13, 20-21). What makes the difference? 9/How do you respond when you suddenly become aware of God's caring for you?

day 4 △ Ruth 3

1/What does Naomi now do for Ruth (cf. 1:11-13)? 2/Review the obligations of *kin* in these times (Deut. 25:5-10) and the order of family ties (Lev. 25:48-49). What indicates that Boaz has already done some checking into these obligations? 3/Imagine Ruth's fears and hopes as she comes to the threshing floor. What are her needs? 4/How does Boaz respond to her identity? What do you learn about him from his handling of the whole situation? 5/How do you respond to people who come to you with emotional and social needs? Why? 6/To what extent do you let other people know your emotional and social needs? Why? 7/What is Ruth's reputation (cf. 2:6, 11-12)?

251

day 5   △   Ruth 4:1-12

1/What legal procedure does Boaz now follow (the gate is the center of social and communal life)? 2/What does Boaz's knowledge of the field indicate about his knowledge of Naomi and Ruth's situation? 3/What is the family obligation to land (cf. Lev. 25:23-28)? 4/Considering the times, how would redeeming both a field and a widow affect *a*-the kinsman and *b*-Boaz (cf. 2:1) economically? 5/What qualities about *a*-the kinsman and *b*-Boaz are revealed in their dealings with each other? 6/How do the people and elders relate God to the affairs of the marriage? 7/How has God been active in your life in the past? today?

day 6   △   Ruth 4:13-22

1/Compare and contrast Naomi's and Ruth's situation now with the events in chapter 1. 2/In what areas of life has God cared for their needs? 3/In what areas of life do you have needs? Do you admit them to God? 4/What do the women say about *a*-the new baby and *b*-Ruth (cf. the importance of sons in these times)? 5/Summarize the outstanding qualities of Naomi, Ruth, and Boaz. How does each think of God? 6/What is the author's main theme in this story? 7/What is the significance of the genealogy at the end of the book? 8/To what extent is this story important for an understanding of Israel's history?

day 7   △   Introduction to Ephesians

Paul sends this letter to a cluster of churches in Asia Minor (the church at Ephesus being the most important). Read the ent re letter at one sitting several times during these studies. Note the fulfillment of God's purpose in the church, the corporate people of God. *Ephesians 1:1-14* 1/What has God the Father done for you? 2/How are you to acknowledge his gracious acts? 3/What should be your response to the benefits which have been provided by *a*-Jesus Christ and *b*-the Holy Spirit? 4/What is the focal point of God's plan for all history? 5/How does this fact help establish priorities for the furthering of God's purpose in *a*-your life and *b*-the world today? 6/How can you express today the unity that is in Christ?

day 8 Δ Ephesians 1:15-23
1/List the specific things Paul prays God will do in the lives of these Christians. 2/To what extent do you desire that such things be incorporated into *a*-your life and *b*-the lives of your Christian friends? 3/What means do you expect God to use in developing these things in your life? 4/Will you pray that God will do this for you and others? 5/How does Paul describe the immeasurable greatness of the power in believers? 6/What is Christ's present relationship to *a*-the Father, *b*-other authorities, *c*-the universe, and *d*-the church? 7/What is your present relationship to Christ?

day 9 Δ Ephesians 2:1-10
1/What are the consequences of following the *prince* mentioned here? 2/What is the scope of his domain? 3/What evidences his present work? 4/Who has taken the initiative in saving you from these consequences? Why? 5/What is your response for the *gift?* 6/In what ways have you been made *alive?* How would you explain this in practical terms to another person? 7/How can you demonstrate to those around you that you are *God's workmanship?* What are the contrasts to your former life? to those who still follow the *course of this world?*

day 10 Δ Ephesians 2:11-22
1/Contrast the Gentile condition prior to Christ's death (relate to the metaphors Paul uses) with the Jewish condition prior to Christ's death. How does this account for the hostility between them? 2/Why does the blood of Christ make unity possible for the Gentile and Jew (relate to the purpose of God—cf. 1:9-10)? 3/How extensive is the unity which has been effected? 4/What are some practical ways in which you, as a part of the church, can show this unity on your campus? in your neighborhood? in your fellowship group? 5/Contrast God's former (cf. Ex. 25:8; 1 Ki. 8:27) and present dwelling places (relate to the Jewish-Gentile unity). 6/What is the foundation of the church? How do you build on the apostles and prophets?

day 11 △ Ephesians 3:1-13
1/What is the *mystery* of which Paul speaks (cf. 1:9-10)? 2/How has Paul obtained his knowledge of the now openly declared secret? 3/What responsibility has been given Paul because of his knowledge of the mystery? 4/How does this help explain the content of Paul's prayer in 1:15-23? 5/What is the role of the church in unfolding the purpose of God? 6/To what extent are you committed to active participation in the work of the church? Why? 7/What specific steps are you taking to make all men see the *wisdom* of God as known through the gospel? 8/For what specific people are you praying?

day 12 △ Ephesians 3:14-21
1/What is the *reason* (cf. v. 1, 14) Paul talks about? 2/List the petitions which are part of this prayer. 3/How do they relate to *a*-the Father, *b*-Christ, and *c*-the Holy Spirit? 4/How can this insight add depth and content to your prayers? 5/Why is Paul justified in praying that these Gentiles might be filled with *all the fulness of God* (cf. 2:19-22)? 6/To what extent are your prayers based on what God has done in Christ or has promised to do by the Holy Spirit? 7/What is the extent of the power now within you? 8/For whom are you praying in this (vv. 16-19) way? 9/In your prayers who places the limits on what God can do?

day 13 △ Ephesians 4:1-16
1/What is your *calling* (cf. 1:3-14; 2:19-22; 3:14-19)? 2/Are the traits listed in verses 2-3 considered strengths or weaknesses in the various groups you associate with? 3/Is your life shaped more by your *calling* among men or by your *calling* in Christ? 4/Why has Christ given various gifts to those in the church? 5/Are the gifts for the benefit of the individual or the group? 6/To what extent are you preparing yourself to minister to your fellow Christians? 7/Distinguish between the unity (vv. 3-7) already existing among Christians and the unity (vv. 13-16) which must be

sought? 8/Relate the metaphors of children and a boat to the theme of unity here. 9/What is the relationship of *truth, love,* and *growth?*

day 14 △ *Ephesians 4:17-32*

1/Contrast the introduction to this section (vv. 17-19) with that of yesterday's section (vv. 1-3). 2/Why are people alienated (cf. 2:1-3; review Rom. 1:18-25)? 3/How should this knowledge determine the content for some of your prayers (cf. 1:17-18a)? 4/List the traits which characterize the *a-old* and *b-new* natures. 5/List the reasons given for these traits. 6/Is the *new nature* to be discerned in acts of worship and personal piety, or in social conduct? Why? 7/As you examine your life considering these lists, what indicates that you are *a-putting off the old nature* and *b-putting on the new nature?*

day 15 △ *Ephesians 5:1-20*

1/How can you possibly take the admonition of verse 1 seriously (cf. 3:14-21)? 2/Considering verse 5, how can anyone hope to have an *inheritance* in Christ (cf. 2:3-9)? Yet considering 2:8-9, why does Paul demand rigorous righteous conduct from Christians (cf. 2:10)? 3/What is the basis for your conduct? for your inspiration (v. 18)? 4/How does this relate to Paul's admonition to give thanks (v. 20)? 5/What does Paul urge beyond separation from evil? How can you do both? 6/How do the admonitions to *walk in love* (v. 2) and to *walk as children of light* relate? 7/In what ways are you *light* to your society? 8/What indicates that walking in the light requires participation in group worship and fellowship? To what extent is this a regular part of your experience? 9/How is your study in *Ephesians* giving you a growing understanding of what *the will of the Lord* is (cf. 1:9-12)?

day 16 △ *Ephesians 5:21-33*

1/List what this section teaches about *a*-Christ, *b*-the church, *c*-the husband, and *d*-the wife. 2/What is the right motive for submission? 3/Why does unsubmissiveness in the *a*-home and *b*-church show lack of reverence for Christ (cf. 1:9-10; 4:15-16)? 4/In what way does the carefully stated universal principle of relationships between husband and wife allow for variation in individual temperament yet maintain a necessary order under Christ's lordship? 5/Considering this principle, where is your area of potential weakness? 6/List several specific ways you can fulfill your responsibility in this area today. Write out goals for the future. 7/If your family were deficient according to this standard, where might you find a standard to follow in establishing your home? 8/Within your web of relationships, what will be required of you today to show reverence for Christ?

day 17 Δ *Ephesians 6:1-9*
1/What are the orders of authority in this passage? 2/How does Paul enforce the imperative to children? 3/Distinguish what is involved in the commands to *obey* and to *honor.* Considering these words, evaluate your feelings toward your parents. 4/What guidelines are available for fathers in fulfilling their essential responsibilities within the family unit (cf. 1:3-6; 3:14-19; 4:1-3, 15-16; 5:1-2)? 5/What are the requirements of Christians who are *a*-serving others and *b*-supervising others? 6/In what ways are you prepared to fulfill these responsibilities in your activities today? 7/Account for the understanding Paul, a free Roman citizen, shows for the plight of a slave (cf. 3:1). 8/How does Paul emphasize the common level between the slave and master? 9/How does this fact undermine the structure of slavery and all injustice within society? 10/What guidelines does this give for dealing with problems in your society?

day 18 Δ *Ephesians 6:10-24*
1/Determine the *a*-identity and *b*-characteristics of the enemy (cf. 2:1-2). Analyze his tactics (define *wiles*). Who are his allies? 2/What resources of protection and strength are available to you as you face such a formidable enemy? What is your responsibility? 3/List each item of armor. What is the reality of each metaphor? 4/How does each item relate to Christ? 5/What are

the practical ways of *putting on* each item? 6/To what extent are you actively equipped? 7/How are the dual provisions of the Holy Spirit related? 8/Explain the defense against Satan as an *a*-individual and *b*-corporate responsibility (cf. 4:11-14). 9/What should be your attitude about the necessity of a personal quiet time and group prayer and Bible study? How are both related to the spread of the gospel?

day 19 Δ Ephesians 1—6

1/Summarize the *a*-basis and *b*-purpose of a church. 2/Compare and contrast the accomplishments of your church with the purpose of a church in this letter. 3/List the gifts of the people in your church. What are your gifts? 4/How do diverse gifts contribute to the unity of your church? 5/Compare and contrast your present personal and interpersonal standards with the qualities Paul urges here. 6/How is your will involved in your Christian life (relate to the imperatives in the letter)? 7/Summarize how the power of Christ is evident in *a*-the universe, *b*-the church, and *c*-your life. 8/In what ways are you equipped today to resist Satan's assaults upon the unity of your family and the Christian community? 9/What is your part in the final working out of God's purpose in this world?

day 20 Δ Introduction to Job

The unidentified author of the book of *Job* is a poet, a thinker, and also a teacher. The book treats realistically the problems of human suffering and divine justice, struggling with questions as: Why do the innocent suffer? What sort of God permits suffering? Try to feel Job's anguished passion as he gropes for the truth about himself and God. Watch the emergence of Job's faith—sturdily born of real-life experience and consistent with the total biblical picture of God. Assess the understanding of Job's friends. *Job 1* 1/What kind of man is Job according to the author? according to God? Find evidence in the chapter for God's characterization of Job. 2/What blend of qualities and facts in Job's life and situation makes him the target of Satan? 3/What do you learn here about

Satan's activities? 4/What is God's role in the test to be imposed
on Job? 5/Put in contemporary language the cunning suggestion
of Satan. 6/Is Satan here in mere ignorance or willful opposition?
What is your evidence? 7/Does Satan really know your
heart? 8/What does this passage teach you about the exercise of
God's providence in times of tragedy? 9/In his affliction what is
Job's response to things? to his family? to God? 10/What are your
responses in similar situations? Why?

day 21 Δ Job 2
1/Contrast *a*-God's and *b*-Satan's estimates of Job's character after
the test. 2/What does this chapter reveal about Satan's character? 3/How does Job respond to the second test? How does his
wife respond? 4/Is Job's view of God changed in any way? 5/Try
to imagine a day in Job's life during his second test. 6/What evidences that Satan has access to the heart of Job's wife? 7/How do
the lips reveal the true self? 8/What is the theological significance
of your lips? 9/What is the strongest sign of the sympathy of
Job's three friends? 10/What is the significance of their silence? 11/What does this suggest about your bedside manner
when you visit the suffering? 12/To what extent are you concerned about the problems of others? What forms does your concern take?

day 22 Δ Job 3
1/What is the common element of the questions Job asks (vv.
11-12, 16, 20-23)? 2/Why should success followed immediately
by tragedy provoke thought? 3/Contrast what death and life offer
Job. 4/What about death fascinates Job? Why? 5/To what extent
do you sympathize with the desperate? 6/What kind of answer do
you have for such people? By what authority? 7/How has your
counsel been proved in your life?

day 23 Δ Job 4–5
1/What do the opening verses of chapter 4 reveal about

Job? 2/What is the emphasis of Eliphaz's speech? 3/What is the
implication of 4:7-9 regarding Job? 4/What is the calculated
effect upon Job as Eliphaz dwells on the exalted purity of
God? 5/Do you agree with the logic of 5:6-7? In what sense is
man *born to trouble?* How, if at all, does this apply to
Job? 6/How does Eliphaz counsel Job? 7/What has Eliphaz
learned about God in 5:8-16? 8/What assumption underlies the
eloquent pronouncements of 5:17-27? 9/Would this kind of advice (or rhetoric) help you through suffering? 10/What do you
learn from this about helping others? 11/In what ways is Eliphaz
guilty of a preconceived diagnosis of Job's troubles?

day 24 Δ Job 6
1/What evidences the intensity of Job's sorrow? 2/What does Job
expect from his friends? 3/What in his speech suggests that he is
getting less? 4/What are his challenges to his friends? 5/What are
the connections between your friendships and your relationship
with God? 6/Does impatience ever have a rational basis? 7/Why
do you think Eliphaz doesn't take Job's side? 8/How do you
know that Job isn't merely complaining of pain (physical and mental)? 9/To what extent does he maintain his powers of reason? 10/To what extent are you teachable when suffering?

day 25 Δ Job 7
1/What wish dominates Job's thought in the first part? 2/To what
does he compare the life of mortal man? To what extent is the
comparison just? Where does the likeness stop? 3/What is always
open to a man in despair (note change in form from v. 6 to v.
7)? 4/What is the implied comparison of verse 12? To what extent
is it apt? 5/Can your cry of distress ever become so intense that it
indicates lack of faith? 6/Do you think Job really wants to be left
alone by God? In such circumstances would man become *less* a
problem to himself? to God? 7/In what sense is God's trusting
Job with this affliction an "intolerable compliment?" 8/To what

extent is God a *watcher of men?* 9/What is incomplete about Job's understanding of sin and God here?

day 26 △ Job 8

1/Compare and contrast the speeches of Bildad and Eliphaz (chaps. 4–5). What does Bildad emphasize? 2/When does tradition become a prison? 3/What is the implication of Bildad's conditional promise in verses 4-6? 4/How would the reference to his children strike Job (cf. 1:5)? 5/Can you *always* find the clue for the present in the past? Why? 6/How well does Bildad's sermon (vv. 13-18) apply to Job? 7/Do you readily moralize on the misfortunes of others? on your own? Why? To what extent are you consistent in what you think or say? 8/Do the sorrows and suffering of others lessen your load? 9/What are the characteristics of a person in whom you would confide? To what extent do those with problems find you ready to empathize with their woes? 10/Do verses 21-22 sound like a promise? 11/Explain in what ways Bildad totally misunderstands Job's problem.

day 27 △ Job 9

1/If the *fact* of God's justice doesn't bother Job, what does? 2/What is Job's conception of God in verses 3-12? 3/Imagine you must reply to Job. How do you answer? 4/What would you do and say in Job's situation? Why? 5/How can the justice of God be an antidote to despair? 6/How does Job conceive of God in relation to *a*-good and *b*-evil? How do you? 7/What can you now say to Job's classical complaint in verses 32-33 (review 1 Tim. 2:5)?

day 28 △ Job 10

1/What mystery agonizes Job? 2/Contrast Job's expectation from God because he is *not* a man with the situation resulting if he *were* a man. 3/How do the first clauses of verses 8-9 qualify the second clauses? Do these truths (in the first clauses) strengthen you? 4/What does Job think has been the purpose of God's preservation in the past? 5/Do you think verse 13 reflects a guess, positive knowledge, or some other possibility? Why? 6/How do you respond when you can't understand the reason for your suffering? Why? 7/Show that Job's list of "if I_____" 's is incomplete by citing what God anticipates in his behavior (cf. chaps. 1–2). 8/What does Job seem to believe about what happens after death? 9/Attracted again to the idea of non-being (cf. chap. 3), what does Job think now?

day 29 Δ *Job 11*

1/Why do you think Zophar has such a stake in God's answer (v. 5) to Job? 2/What is Zophar's judgment of the situation and Job's understanding of it? 3/What is the reasonable action of a creature when the wisdom of God is so great? 4/Determine the meaning of *understanding* in the sense of verse 12. 5/List the effects of *setting your heart aright*. 6/How much of this picture (vv. 13-19a) reflects your life? 7/Contrast the *hope* of the righteous (v. 18) with the *hope* of the wicked (v. 20).

day 30 Δ *Job 12–13*

1/Describe the frustration of Job in 12:1-5. What are the issues? 2/When have you felt similarly frustrated? What have you done? 3/Have his friends really heard Job? What does he think explains their lack of sympathy? 4/How should 12:11 affect your response to the opinion of others? 5/List the realms of God's sovereignty in chapter 12. Which of them impresses you most? Why? 6/Why does Job think his friends are guilty of a deceitful defense of God? 7/What does Job say about God under such circumstances (cf. 13:10 with 42:7)? 8/How do you think sincere, passionate doubt or opposition to God fares in relation to insincere support of God? 9/How do you account for Job's courageous assurance (13:18)? 10/Can man rightly demand what Job asks in 13:23? 11/How is the silence and self-restraint of God related to the cry of your times? 12/When have you endured conditions that made you wonder if God's treatment is capricious and arbitrary? What finally brought you to understanding? Does God owe you any explanation for his action or lack of it?

Month 26

day 1 △ Job 14
1/How does Job's mood in verses 1-6 mold his thought about God? 2/Mark the contrast and comparison in the parable of the tree. 3/How would you answer Job's question in verse 14? 4/Does Job think that suffering and sin are related? Why? 5/Have you ever felt as Job: If I can just know that this life isn't all, then I can stand up to the bludgeonings of life? How can you know? 6/Summarize what has been accomplished in the first round of speeches.

day 2 △ Job 15
1/Look for the change in intensity during the second round of speeches. 2/Are you in sympathy with Job or Eliphaz after verses 1-6? Why? 3/How would you answer the question of Eliphaz in verse 9? 4/What argument would you use to refute Eliphaz in verses 12-16? 5/How does Eliphaz now try to convince Job of his errors? What illustrations does he use? 6/Does your experience bear out Eliphaz's dogma about the wicked (cf. Job's experience in 9:24)? Why do you think he clings to this idea (esp. vv. 18-19)? 7/Have you unconsciously inherited a dogma that doesn't fit the facts of life?

day 3 △ Job 16:1-21
1/How does Job counter the accusations of Eliphaz (esp. 15:2-6)? 2/What do you think is the tone of *could* in verses 4-5? 3/Try to feel Job's despair. How would you describe it? What metaphors does Job use? 4/What is Job's convict on concerning himself and his life? concerning God? 5/What causes the change in tone in verses 18-21? What does Job seek in his predicament?

day 4 Δ Job 16:22–17:16

1/Compare the state of Job's body (cf. chap. 16) and spirit (cf. 7:11). 2/What is Job's continual appeal (cf. v. 3 with chap. 9; 13:13-23)? 3/How does verse 6 show that Job will not find what he wants among men? 4/What is Job's answer to his friends' promises of a bright tomorrow (cf. 5:19-27; 8:6-7, 21; 11:15-20)? 5/Does Sheol (the grave) offer a solution to Job?

day 5 Δ Job 18

1/What is Bildad's explanation for Job's frustration (vv. 1-4)? 2/Cite four illustrations from this chapter that picture the ruin of the wicked. 3/Show how each metaphor can, from a different point of view, illustrate the life of a righteous man. 4/Why do you think Bildad chooses the negative aspect of each metaphor? 5/To what extent does your mood determine how you view a given situation? What is your mood today? Why?

day 6 Δ Job 19

1/What does Job think is the source of his troubles? 2/What is the extent of Job's needs? 3/What is the attitude of Job's servants, family, and friends? Why? 4/What human feelings are being inundated by the friends' belief about Job? Why don't they *pity* him? 5/How do you respond to people in miserable circumstances? Compare and contrast what you usually say in such situations with what Job's friends have been telling him. 6/What is Job's emotional tone before and after verse 23? 7/What is his desperate hope? 8/How does the thought of a judgment affect him?

day 7 Δ Job 20

1/What theme does Zophar reiterate? 2/What is the emotional tone throughout (cf. vv. 2-3 with the verbs he uses)? 3/How is Zophar's God an extension of his emotional reaction? 4/What illustrations does he use this time? 5/Imaginatively put Zophar in Job's place. What do you think is the effect of his words on himself? 6/To what extent do you find these metaphors fulfilled in your society?

day 8 △ Job 21
1/How does Job regard the second speech of Zophar? 2/What is all Job wants from his friends? 3/What are the facts as Job sees them? 4/How does Job answer the anticipated defense (v. 19) of his friends? Of what does he accuse them? 5/Contrast Job's observations with his friends' speculations (esp. what they would say about the two examples in vv. 23-25)? 6/Do you attempt to judge similar examples? Why (cf. v. 22)? Would this state of affairs be reasonable if existence ended at death? 7/Do you have to understand God's ways of doing things? Why? 8/Summarize what has been accomplished in the second round of speeches.

day 9 △ Job 22
1/Look for the change in intensity during the third round of speeches. 2/What concept of God does Eliphaz have? 3/What answer does he expect to his questions in verses 3-4? 4/What specific charges does Eliphaz bring against Job (contrast God's judgment in chaps. 1–2)? 5/Who is the truly wealthy man? Although this is a beautiful passage, why doesn't it apply to Job's situation? 6/When have you misapplied truth? Why?

day 10 △ Job 23–24
1/What is Job's main concern in chapter 23? 2/What will Job plead in front of God as judge? 3/How does Job feel God will answer him? 4/What are your feelings toward *a*-God and *b*-yourself when life seems to tumble in on you? 5/What makes the difference between Job's confidence (23:4-7, 10-12) and his dread (23:13-17)? 6/How can Job attribute to God such unfeeling arbitrariness and yet not curse him? What does this reveal about the range of faith and understanding? 7/How has God taken the initiative to *find* you? 8/What social injustices does Job cite? 9/What is his response to all this injustice? 10/In what way

is Job limited by time here? 11/To what extent are you willing that God be vindicated after you are gone from the realm of time? 12/Compare evil men and darkness. 13/How are reality and struggle related in your life? 14/How does your understanding of the world relate to God's reality? How do you know?

day 11 Δ Job 25–26
1/What is the emphasis of Bildad's third speech concerning *a*-God and *b*-man (cf. 4:17-21; 15:14-16)? 2/How can Job understand both parts of Bildad's argument (cf. 14:4) without using it against himself? 3/What is the point of Job's sarcasm in 26:2-4? 4/How does the world have being? 5/In what different ways does God use his power (relate to 26:14)? 6/How are you involved in the greatness and power of God? Compare or contrast your view of man with Bildad's (25:6).

day 12 Δ Job 27
1/Considering that Job and his friends have access to the same facts, account for the different conclusions. 2/What is ironical about Job's oath in verses 2-4? 3/What is Job's final word to his friends (vv. 5-6)? 4/What can you do when you are pressured (even by religious friends) to be deceitful or ignore facts you know? 5/When have you asked God to expose flaws in your thinking? Why? 6/Considering Job's previous thoughts about the wicked (cf. chaps. 21, 24), do you think verses 7-23 are Job's or Zophar's (cf. chap. 20)?

day 13 Δ Job 28
1/What is the purpose of this description of mining? 2/Contrast the *a*-growing (v. 5a) and *b*-mining processes. 3/What are the three specific contrasts of wisdom with the objects of mining, fishing, and trading. 4/Why doesn't technological advancement bring moral wisdom? 5/What kind of perspective brings wisdom? 6/What is the connection between religious belief and morality in verse 28? in your life? 7/How and where have you found *wisdom?*

day 14 △ Job 29

1/What have been the sources of Job's happiness in the past? 2/In what areas does Job claim integrity? What have been his relationships with *a*-God and *b*-men? 3/What have men thought of him (relate to the metaphors)? 4/Contrast his statements here with the friends' charges (esp. 22:5-11). 5/What had been his thoughts about the future? 6/To what extent can you trust God for your future prosperity or adversity? 7/What is the irony of the last line of this chapter?

day 15 △ Job 30

1/Contrast Job's former prosperity (chap. 29) with his present condition. 2/What are his relationships to *a*-God and *b*-men now? 3/What do people think of him now (cf. 19:13-22)? 4/Can you feel the utterly helpless despair of Job? 5/How does he feel God has "rewarded" him? 6/Imagine you are in his situation. What do you do? How do you respond to your friends' arguments? to God's "reward"? 7/If virtue results in honor, does it follow that the virtuous escape evil? Why?

day 16 △ Job 31

1/In what areas does Job claim integrity? 2/What is Job's evaluation of faults in these areas? 3/What reasons are given for his right attitudes and behavior? 4/Compare or contrast your attitudes and behavior in sex ethics (relate to magazines and TV), social consciousness, etc. 5/What is Job's plea? 6/Summarize what has been accomplished during the third round of speeches.

day 17 △ Job 32

1/What is the focus of Elihu's anger toward Job? toward the three friends? 2/How does Elihu justify his intervention? Why has he been silent so far? 3/Toward what conclusion does the renewed silence of the friends point? 4/What characteristic that Job has objected to in the other friends will Elihu try to avoid? 5/Try to catch his emotion.

day 18 △ Job 33
1/How does Elihu establish contact with Job's situation? 2/Can you discern in Elihu a different feeling toward God that hasn't been evident in the other friends? 3/What error does Elihu see in Job's contention against God? 4/What does the chapter teach about God's initiative toward man? 5/Has God spoken to you in either of these ways recently? How do you know? 6/What is the progression in restoring man from the depths of suffering? 7/In what ways does this progression parallel your experience?

day 19 △ Job 34
1/Into what two complaints does Elihu summarize Job's speeches? 2/Do you think his summary is accurate? 3/What is Elihu's view of *a*-the universe and *b*-God? Compare and contrast these with the views of the other friends. 4/What would be the result of God's reneging any of his control of the universe? 5/What quality in God does Elihu extol? 6/What effect will this quality have on a person inclined toward evildoing? on one inclined toward good works? 7/What is Elihu's estimation of Job's speeches so far? 8/To what extent does Elihu relate his arguments to Job's questions? 9/To what extent do you think Elihu is right?

day 20 △ Job 35
1/What question of Job does Elihu now proceed to answer (cf. 7:20-21)? 2/Compare Elihu's and Eliphaz's (chap. 22) feelings on this subject. 3/What reasons does Elihu give for God's disregarding man's cries for help? 4/To what extent do you think these reasons apply to Job's cries? 5/Try to determine why some of your prayers are "unanswered." 6/How does Elihu view God's relation to man (cf. v. 11 with 36:22)? How does this differ from the views of the other friends? 7/What is Elihu's summary of Job's speeches?

day 21 △ Job 36:1-23
1/List the attributes of God which Elihu has discovered. 2/Ac-

cording to Elihu what is the purpose of affliction? 3/How should these facts qualify criticism of even the wicked? 4/Can you know a person (considering his past, future, and present) well enough to judge him justly? 5/According to Elihu how should Job regard his affliction? 6/To what extent do you think Elihu understands Job? 7/Has Job said of God: *Thou has done wrong?*

day 22   Δ   Job 36:24–37:24

1/How is the greatness of God expressed in nature? What is God's relation to nature? 2/List the specific items in the descriptions that picture God anthropomorphically (in the form of man). 3/How should winter make people respond to God? 4/According to Elihu what are God's two uses for nature? 5/How is all this *a*-an account of God's ways and *b*-a challenge to Job?

day 23   Δ   Job 38:1-38

1/Recreate imaginatively what happens now. 2/Compare God's challenge with Job's self-evaluation (cf. esp. 31:35-37; 23:4-7). 3/Categorize the questions, condensing them to key ideas when you can. 4/Now go through them, imagining that you, like Job, must answer God. 5/How involved is God in the affairs of the world? 6/Can you be ignorant of nature's ways and yet hope to understand God's ways? 7/What are the specific realms of God's sovereignty?

day 24   Δ   Job 38:39–39:30

1/In what areas here are God's power and sovereignty revealed? 2/Try to frame additional questions that are appropriate to contemporary man with his vaunted knowledge of certain aspects of nature, computers, space travel, etc. 3/What is the purpose and logic of God's argument with Job in chapters 38–39? 4/How do you think God would challenge a contemporary Job? 5/Project your response to these two chapters as if you were Job.

day 25 Δ *Job 40*

1/What is the effect of God's first speech on Job? 2/Does God charge Job with moral fault? What is God's indictment (vv. 1, 8)? 3/In what areas does God challenge Job's ability? What is the relation of Job's inability in the *a*-natural and *b*-moral orders of the universe? 4/Contrast the forms and content of Job's friends' previous speeches with God's speech. Why have the friends' speeches failed to convince or comfort Job? 5/How have you been convinced of the sovereignty of God?

day 26 Δ *Job 41*

1/Trace the irony in this passage (cf. chaps. 38—40). 2/How does God describe *Leviathan* whom he has made? Contrast *Leviathan's* effect on *a*-God and *b*-man. 3/Distinguish the two explanations God gives Job in verses 10-11. 4/Does God explain why he does what he does? why he doesn't do what he doesn't do? 5/Recall those times in the last month when you have asked God *why?* Why? 6/What has God told you about himself? yourself? his ways?

day 27 Δ *Job 42*

1/Precisely what is Job convinced of regarding God? What has convinced him? 2/Compare verse 3a with 38:2 and verse 4 with 40:7. 3/What confession follows (cf. 40:3-5)? 4/Has God justified Job or his arguments? 5/What do you think makes vindication superfluous? 6/What does this reveal about the ultimate significance of philosophical problems (even considering their existential urgency)? 7/What is your response to God when he comes to you personally? 8/Imagine the feelings of the friends considering *a*-God's judgment and *b*-what they have to do for restoration. 9/What does this reveal about the dishonest defense of God? 10/Can your faith be robust if it isn't founded on facts? 11/In what way is your honest doubt a means to an end? What end? 12/Go back through the book. Summarize what you have learned. How can you put your new and reinforced knowledge into practice today? Write out goals for the future.

day 28 △ Introduction to Psalms 42–51
The *Psalms* are personal and public poems of worship used as hymns. They represent a range of emotional tones, subjects, and authors. Read the psalms aloud and imagine the experiences and feelings which prompted their writing. Keep a list of the metaphors. Relate their aesthetic and spiritual values. *Psalm 42* The word *Maskil* in the title is related to the verb meaning "to have insight"; hence a *Maskil* is a poem of insight. 1/What does the psalmist desire? To what extent? 2/Reflect on the images of the thirsty deer and the flowing streams. What do they depict? 3/When have you felt the same desire? How has it been fulfilled? 4/What has been the psalmist's past spiritual experience? 5/What does his past and present experience suggest about the Christian life? 6/When and why do you feel cut off from God? 7/Compare the refrains of verses 5 and 11. How does each answer the problems raised in the preceding verses? 8/What is the hope of the godly man?

day 29 △ Psalm 43
1/How does this psalm continue and complete the theme begun in Psalm 42? 2/Describe the psalmist's situation. 3/What are his requests? 4/What does he then promise to do (in the Old Testament, communion with God before his altar is the method of worship)? 5/What specifically can you do to praise God now? 6/Read Psalms 42 and 43 together. 7/Write out a prayer expressing your desire to commune with and praise God.

day 30 △ Psalm 44
1/What experiences have these people and their forefathers had with God? How have these experiences made them feel toward God? 2/What is their present situation? What do they feel toward God now? 3/Why can't the psalmist explain their estrangement from God? 4/How do you react to apparently undeserved suffering? to the suffering of groups of people and nations? 5/To what extent does this psalm offer a solution or explanation for the sufferings of people who trust in God? 6/Summarize the feelings in this psalm.

Month 27

day 1 Δ *Psalm 45*

This psalm is set to the ancient Hebrew tune *Lilies*. 1/Read the psalm first as a poem celebrating the marriage of a Hebrew king to a foreign princess. How is the king described? 2/What is the psalmist's attitude to the king? By reading the psalm aloud and by reflection, try to capture some of the excitement of the psalmist. 3/How is the king's bride described? 4/Read the psalm again as a graphic type of the Messiah and his bride. 5/What is the bride asked to do? 6/What *beauty* would the king see and *desire* in you? 7/Reread the psalm as a song of praise to Christ.

day 2 Δ *Psalm 46*

1/How is God described in this psalm of praise in memory of national deliverance? 2/What in your world makes you fearful? Why? 3/Compare the imagery and tone of verses 4-5 with that of verses 6-7 and 9. What variations are there in the ways God acts? 4/To what extent are you aware that God is with you, that he is your *present* helper? 5/How may a person become aware of God's majesty? 6/Obey the command of verse 10a for five minutes—not praying but meditating on *knowing* that God is God. 7/What are appropriate responses to your knowledge now?

day 3 Δ *Psalm 47*

1/List the ways God is shown to be king of all the earth. 2/What does the psalm reveal of God's *a*-power, *b*-character, and *c*-relation to the world and his people? 3/How are the people to respond to their God? 4/How can you respond? 5/Write a song of praise you can *shout* to God now. For what earthly and heavenly inheritance can you praise him?

day 4 Δ *Psalm 48*

1/What is the focus of praise in this psalm? 2/List the characteristics of Zion. 3/According to the psalmist what specifically has God done for the city? How are the city and God related in the people's minds? 4/What have the people heard? seen? 5/What specifically have you *seen* of God's majesty? 6/What request does the psalmist make of all the people? 7/What about God can you convey to those around you?

day 5 △ *Psalm 49*

1/To whom is this psalm directed? For what purpose? 2/What is the great equalizer for all men? 3/What makes the difference after all men are equalized? 4/What happens to those whose confidence is in riches? 5/To what extent do you trust in material wealth? What do you expect it to do for you? 6/Where is the psalmist's confidence? (This is one of the few intimations of personal immortality found in the Old Testament.) 7/How do verses 7-20 answer the question of verses 5-6? 8/In what ways will this *wisdom* help you overcome *fear?* 9/Summarize the content of this psalm in a title.

day 6 △ *Psalm 50*

1/What is the dramatic action here? Who is judge? Who are witnesses? the accused? 2/Whom does God *a*-reprove and *b*-rebuke? For what reasons? How does each regard God? 3/What is wrong with the worship of the Israelites? Why are sacrifices beside the point? 4/Explain the difference between formalism and righteousness. 5/What sort of worship does God desire? 6/What does this psalm add to your concept of true worship? 7/How can you worship God now?

day 7 △ *Psalm 51*

1/Review the background for this psalm in 2 Samuel 11:1–12:15. 2/Carefully list the requests David makes of God (cf. what he already is assured in 2 Sam. 12:13). 3/What beyond simple forgiveness does he request? 4/Against whom has David sinned? Why? 5/What does David know about true worship?   6/When are you likely to come to God with an "offering" for sin instead of a broken, contrite heart? Why?   7/Use the whole psalm as a pattern for confessing your own sin now.

day 8 Δ Introduction to 2 Samuel
2 Samuel (originally undivided from *1 Samuel*) continues the history of Israel. Review the events, people, and their interaction in *1 Samuel*. *2 Samuel 1*   1/Contrast the young man's version of Saul's death with 1 Samuel 31:1-13. Why do you think he changes the story? What mistake does he make in his estimate of David? 2/What is David's reponse to the news? How does he refer to Saul (recall the way Saul had treated him)?   3/Do you evaluate people according to their relationship to God or to yourself? Why?   4/To what extent do you practice saying what is positive about others who have hurt you?

day 9 Δ 2 Samuel 2
1/What principle of guidance can you learn from David in verses 1-2? Do you prefer to be independent about details? Why? 2/What do you learn about David's character from his response to the brave deed of the Jabesh-gilead men (cf. 1 Sam. 31:8-13)?   3/Compare and contrast Abner and Joab. 4/What causes Abner to stop running and sue for peace?

day 10 Δ 2 Samuel 3
1/What do you think causes the trend in verse 1?   2/Why does Abner change his plan of action? What indicates that he has known all along what the Lord's plan is?   3/When do you act out of mixed motives? Why? How do you respond when your faults are pointed out? Why?   4/Contrast David and Joab. What does Joab want David to think?   5/Why does Joab kill Abner? Is he justified (cf. 2:18-23)?   6/What is David's response to the murder? What does this response reveal about his attitude toward other leaders?   7/How far does your forgiveness extend? Why?

day 11   △   2 Samuel 4

1/What is the status of Ishbosheth now? 2/What solution do Rechab and Baanah think their plan will bring? 3/How will David's consistent response to opportunists affect the people as the kingdom is established (for his attitude toward treachery cf. v. 11; Ps. 5:4-10)? 4/In what ways do the *a*-nurse and *b*-doorkeeper fail? 5/Are you careless and undependable in "minor" things? Why?

day 12   △   2 Samuel 5

1/What two reasons do the tribes of Israel give for anointing David king? Why do you think they take more than seven years to act on what they know? 2/**Are** you entangled with secondary motives in some area and as a result are putting off doing God's will? Why? 3/What is the Jebusites' opinion of David's strength (esp. v. 6)? 4/How does David capture the fortress of Jebus? (Modern archaeology has found the tunnel made by the Jebusites to get water from a spring outside the city walls.) 5/Characterize David's spiritual life (esp. vv. 10, 12, 19, 23, 25). What accounts for his greatness? 6/What is your standard of greatness for yourself? for others?

day 13   △   2 Samuel 6

1/Review the history of the ark in 1 Samuel 5:1–7:2. 2/Why is Uzzah killed (cf. Num. **4:15**)? 3/What do David and the people learn about God from this experience (cf. 1 Chron. 15:11-13)? 4/In what ways does David express his zeal in this parade? 5/What motivates Michal's objection? 6/What is the extent of David's response? What will this mean for her? 7/Do you scorn people with "excessive" zeal? Why?

day 14   △   2 Samuel 7

1/What precipitates Nathan's vision? How does it supercede his first inclination? 2/Are you able to publicly retract a statement or opinion if God shows you an error? 3/What does **God** want David to remember? What does he promise (cf. v. 11b with David's original proposal)? Find other indications of divine initiative. 4/What does David's response reveal about his character? God's character? prayer? 5/List specific things that God has shown you for which you can dare to pray.

day 15 △ 2 Samuel 8
1/To what does *after this* (v. 1) refer? 2/What is David's task now? 3/Contrast the status of the tribes (think back on the content of *Exodus* through *1 Samuel*) with the status of the nation now. What is their influence on the Mediterranean world? 4/What does David do with the spoils of war? 5/Characterize David's administration. 6/Account for Joab's prominence in view of 3:26-39 (cf. 1 Chron. 11:4-9). 7/In what place does God want you now? How are you fulfilling your obligations there?

day 16 △ 2 Samuel 9
1/What motivates David's kindness to Mephibosheth (cf. 1 Sam. 20:14-17, 42)? 2/Why does Mephibosheth refer to himself as a *dead dog?* Why might he fear David? 3/What is the extent of David's generosity? 4/Imagine you are Mephibosheth. What do you tell Mica about your past and present life? 5/To whom do you show *the kindness of God?* Why?

day 17 △ 2 Samuel 10
1/Why does David's generous move lead to war? 2/What have you done when a well-meaning deed of yours has been misinterpreted? Why? 3/Are you prone to mistrust the motives of others or, like Haman, to listen to those who do? Why? 4/What indicates that Joab is an able leader? What are the elements of *a*-challenge and *b*-comfort in his words to Abishai? Are they valid? 5/How do the Syrians get involved? What does it finally cost them?

day 18 △ 2 Samuel 11
1/How does verse 1 imply that David is not in his place of responsi-

bility? What is he doing instead? 2/Analyze the progression in David's disobedience through this chapter. 3/What is David trying to do when he sends for Uriah? 4/Contrast verse 15 with 4:11—both the words of the same man. What has changed him? 5/What does Joab know about the situation? What does he do? 6/What should be the criteria for what you do? In what areas are you operating unethically and disregarding these criteria? Why? What can you do today to change?

day 19 Δ 2 Samuel 12
1/How and by whom is action initiated in this chapter? What does this indicate about God's dealings with someone who sins? 2/How does God interpret David's actions (esp. vv. 9-10, 14)? 3/How does David respond to judgment? 4/How do you respond to just correction? Why? 5/Is David forgiven? What are the consequences? 6/What can you learn from David's attitude toward sickness and death?

day 20 Δ 2 Samuel 13
1/What judgments (chap. 12) are fulfilled here? 2/What kind of influence is David as a father and leader? 3/What is the character and quality of Jonadab's friendship to Amnon? What do verses 32-33 indicate? 4/What is the quality of your advice to friends? Why? 5/What weakness in David contributes to the death of Amnon? 6/What are the consequences of Amnon's death for Absalom?

day 21 Δ 2 Samuel 14
1/How does Joab's action compare with Nathan's (cf. chap. 12)? 2/According to the woman what is Joab's reason for sending her to tell this story? 3/What does this chapter show about Absalom? To what lengths is he willing to go to get his way? Why does he want to see the king? 4/Imagine how David as king and father feels in this situation. How is his feeling complicated by his sin? 5/When have intimate relationships of yours been severed by your sin? What have you done to rectify the situation? Why?

day 22 Δ 2 Samuel 15
1/What does Absalom set out to do? What means does he use? What influences the people toward him? 2/What lies and deceptions does Absalom use? 3/What is the basis of his appeal to David? 4/Do you ever give spiritual reasons for wrong or selfish actions? Why? 5/In what ways should the reply of Ittai (a Philistine) mirror your response to God? 6/Why does David send the priests, ark, and Hushai back to Jerusalem?

day 23 Δ 2 Samuel 16
1/Who are the key men in this chapter? What stand does each take? Why (review chap. 9 regarding Ziba)? 2/What is the point of Ahithophel's advice? How does it fulfill 12:11? 3/What sort of influence does Ahithophel have? 4/What two terrible humiliations does David suffer in this chapter? How does he respond? 5/How do you respond to humiliation? Why?

day 24 Δ 2 Samuel 17
1/Contrast the advice of Ahithophel and Hushai. How does each picture David and his men? What psychological effect will each have on Absalom and his men? 2/Why is Hushai's counsel accepted over Ahithophel's (cf. v. 14 with 15:31; 16:23)? 3/Why does Ahithophel hang himself? 4/What is your response when your advice is not taken and you foresee the worst for yourself and others? 5/Visualize verses 27-29. Imagine how David and the people feel when they see these men come with provisions. 6/What refreshment has God sent you during periods of weariness and discouragement? What has been your response?

day 25 Δ 2 Samuel 18
1/List what this chapter reveals about David's character. 2/What are possible reasons for Joab's killing of Absalom against David's orders (cf. 3:26-39; chap. 14)? 3/Contrast Joab's and the soldier's attitudes. 4/How is Absalom's pride indicated in this section? Contrast the monument and the burial pit. 5/What is David's pri-

mary concern (review chap. 12)? What are the elements of his lament? 6/What have been consequences of your past sins? What have you learned?

day 26 Δ *2 Samuel 19*

1/What is David's problem? What duties does he have as king? 2/Is Joab's judgment of the situation valid? 3/What is the national problem described in verses 8b-10? How is it complicated by the rivalry between Israel and Judah? 4/Compare and contrast Shimei (cf. 16:5-13), Ziba (cf. 16:1-4), Mephibosheth, and Barzillai (cf. 17:27-29). What has each done for David? What does David do in return? 5/To what extent do you help people because they need help, regardless of whether you get recognition?

day 27 Δ *2 Samuel 20*

1/In what ways is Sheba an opportunist? 2/What can be inferred about the men of Israel and their powers of discernment? What may have motivated them? 3/When are you guilty of party spirit? 4/What does Joab accomplish for himself by killing Amasa (cf. 19:13)? What is the point of stationing the soldier beside Amasa's body with the message? 5/How is the woman of the city wise? What is the basis of her appeal to Joab?

day 28 Δ *2 Samuel 21*

Six miscellaneous appendices finish the book. 1/What drives David to seek God? 2/What covenant, made in the name of the God of Israel (cf. Joshua 9), has been broken? What great issue is at stake here? 3/List some examples from modern life in which the sins of the fathers take their toll on following generations. 4/How is David influenced by Rizpah's action? 5/What is his attitude toward the house of Saul? 6/What does this section teach you about God—his righteousness, judgment, time, and the honor of his name?

day 29 Δ   2 Samuel 22

1/Compare this poem and Psalm 18. Look for the divisions of thought. 2/What is described in verses 8-16? What are the spheres of God's activity? 3/What reasons are given for David's deliverance? 4/What do verses 26-31 reveal about God's character? How does this affect David? 5/What has God done for David? 6/In what areas of David's life has God worked on his behalf? 7/For what does David praise God? 8/Can you, from experience, take any of his words for your testimony?

day 30 Δ   2 Samuel 23

1/Compare and contrast David's reign with his portrayal of the just ruler. 2/In what sense can David speak of God's prospering all his desire? 3/To what extent do you meet your responsibilities in such a way that God can illumine and bring growth through you? 4/Characterize the mighty men who have fellowshipped with David. 5/What do you learn about David from his sense of what belongs to God? 6/Review David's conquests. What part have these men and Joab had?

Month 28

day 1 Δ   2 Samuel 24

1/Compare verse 1 with 1 Chronicles 21:1, which sheds light on David's sin in this chapter. Why is numbering the tribes wrong? 2/What is Joab's wise advice? 3/What is David's estimate of the numbering? 4/What three choices is he given? On what basis does he make his choice? 5/What evidences of David's greatness are indicated in verses 17, 19, 24? 6/To what extent are intercession, obedience, and sacrifice part of your daily life with God? 7/Summarize David's a-strengths and b-weaknesses. What are the consequences of his sins? 8/Summarize what David has accomplished for Israel.

day 2 △ Psalm 52

1/Identify and characterize the *mighty man* (cf. 1 Sam. 21:1-9; 22:1-23). What is his main weapon? 2/To what extent do you similarly use this weapon? Why? 3/What will be the end of the mighty man? Why? 4/What will be the reaction of the righteous? 5/What qualities do you think David has in mind when he describes himself as a tree? What is his response to God's working? 6/For what can you thank God now? in whose presence? 7/Summarize this psalm in a title.

day 3 △ Psalm 53

1/Compare and contrast this psalm with Psalm 14. Account for the similarities and differences. 2/List and consider the characteristics of the sons of men. How are these characteristics an extension of their basic attitude toward God? 3/What is God's future for such people? 4/What kinds of attitudes about life and God do you consider foolish or wise? Why? 5/With what does God equate wisdom and understanding? By this definition to what extent are you wise?

day 4 △ Psalm 54

1/What situation does David face here (cf. 1 Sam. 23; 26:1-4)? 2/What emotions does he express in this situation? Toward whom? against whom? Why? 3/What is the basis for his plea for safety? 4/What descriptive names of God does he use? 5/What does David anticipate? What will he do in response? 6/What is your feeling about God's name? Why? 7/From what trouble has God recently delivered you? What has been your response? 8/Write out a prayer of thanksgiving to God.

day 5 △ Psalm 55

1/Determine the divisions in David's thought here (by subject or person addressed). 2/What is his first reaction to the horror of his suspicions? 3/What is the change in his emotions as his suspicions become more well-founded? 4/What does he want from God for the enemy? for himself? On what basis? How can he be so sure of the outcome? 5/Reread the psalm imagining that your friend has turned against you in an extremely vital situation. In what ways do your emotions parallel David's? What is similar and different in your communication with God about the matter? Do you finish with the same confidence as David has? Why?

day 6 △ Psalm 56

This psalm is set to the ancient Hebrew tune *The Dove on Far-off Terebinths.* 1/Picture the scene of verses 1-6 (cf. 1 Sam. 21:10–22:1). 2/When have you been in or felt such a position? To what extent, then, have you felt the tension between fear and trust in God? 3/How does the image David uses reveal God's intimate concern for him? 4/What is David's necessary response to God's care for him? 5/In what ways has God been *gracious* to you recently? What has been your response? 6/What reason for deliverance is given in verse 13? 7/What is the theme of this *Miktam* (probably sung during the rite of the sin offering)?

day 7 △ Psalm 57

Do Not Destroy is the tune. 1/Compare and contrast (in theme and style) this *Miktam* with the previous one. 2/What are David's present circumstances (cf. 1 Sam. 22:1)? 3/What images does he use to describe himself? his enemies? 4/What is his confident hope? 5/What are the themes of his praise to God? 6/How is God fulfilling his purpose for you in regard to your studies, vocation, marriage, friends? When do you tend to work out your own purposes? Why? 7/Write down qualities of God for which you can praise him now.

day 8 △ Psalm 58

1/Determine the identity of the *gods.* Of what does the writer accuse them? How does he characterize them? 2/On what basis does David demand obliterating vengeance? How do you answer the accusation that this call for vengeance is a spiteful end-justi-

fies-the-means revenge? 3/Why is widespread evil so detrimental
to godly men? 4/How do godly men respond to the downfall of
evil men? 5/What do you do when surrounded by flagrant injustices brought about by evil men? What should be your attitude
toward their defiance of God? 6/Do you pray for destruction of
the wicked, as David does here? Why? 7/What is the theme of this
Miktam?

day 9 Δ Psalm 59
1/What does David desire for himself? On what basis (cf. 1 Sam.
19:1-18)? 2/In what capacity does David want God to intervene
internationally? On what basis? 3/To what extent do you long for
international vindication when you are in a desperate personal situation? 4/How does David describe his enemy? his relationship
with the enemy? Which of their sins does he find most damaging? 5/Why is David so sure of triumph (note the verb
tenses)?   6/Why is the obvious, but not-too-swift (the meaning of
slay them not in v. 11) punishment of the enemy essential? 7/Summarize the characteristics of God which David praises.
8/In what ways is God a fortress to you today? 9/What is the
theme of this *Miktam?*

day 10 Δ Psalm 60
1/What has happened to Israel in the midst of their military prowess (cf. 2 Sam. 8)? How do the people interpret God's part in the
disaster? 2/What do the images reveal about the depth of the
people's emotions as a result? 3/What promises of God does David
recall? How does he interpret the event since God's promises aren't
fulfilled? 4/What do you think about these interpretations of
God's responsibility for man's success and failure? To what extent
do you tend to feel similarly about God in the successes and failures of your life? Why? Should you? 5/How important is God's
help? 6/Why do you think this *Miktam* is designated *for instruction?* 7/Look again at Psalms 56–60. What is their common
theme?

day 11 Δ Psalm 61

1/What are David's feelings now in his relationship with God? How does he express his feeling of distance from God? 2/What does he request? For what reasons? What metaphors does he use? 3/What do you do when you feel distant from God? 4/What has God given David as king? Imagine his feelings as he rules day after day. 5/When have you felt the need for security and strength recently? How have you expressed your need to God? How has he responded? 6/Sing a song of praise to God now.

day 12 Δ Psalm 62

1/How does David regard the necessity of God in his life (note the use of *alone* and *only*)? 2/Contrast the effects of *a*-God and *b*-men on his life. 3/What is David's advice to his subjects watching the power struggle in the kingdom? 4/What do your actions and advice reveal about the source of your strength? 5/How would you describe your relationship with God? Why? 6/Contrast the qualities of God which show he is trustworthy with the qualities of men who are untrustworthy. What makes the drastic difference?

day 13 Δ Psalm 63

1/What are David's circumstances now? 2/What especially does he miss? 3/With what is he satisfied? How? 4/To what extent have you similarly experienced God alone? To what extent are you dependent on Christian friends and services for your joy? 5/What is the future of the men who try to overthrow him as king? 6/Summarize the content of this psalm in a title.

day 14 Δ Psalm 64

1/List the characteristics of the wicked men. 2/How does David react toward their schemes and assaults? Imagine his feelings as a hunted man. 3/Why do you think David keeps emphasizing the evil of their tongues (cf. 52:2-4; 55:21; 57:4; 58:3-6; 59:7, 12; 62:4—list the metaphors he uses)? 4/What will be the end result of God's intervention? 5/What is your major concern when you are wounded by *bitter words?* Do you complain to God? Why? 6/Summarize this psalm in a title.

day 15 △ Psalm 65

1/How are words and action related in this song of praise? What is the basis for a person's praise to God? 2/In what ways do you think God's *house* is good? Can you specify to him what the *goodness* should include? 3/To what extent has God been involved in the world in the past? How do these deeds give hope for the future? 4/What is God's present involvement in Israel? What is the response of the people? of nature itself? Savor the picture of this bounty. 5/In what ways has God provided for you in the past? now? What is your hope for the future?

day 16 △ Psalms 66–67

1/What is the stimulus for the call to praise God here? Who participates in the praise? 2/How is God related to Israel's history? Why? 3/What will the nations see that God has done for Israel? What will be their response? 4/What qualities of God are revealed by his actions toward Israel? 5/What are the appropriate *a*-individual and *b*-corporate responses? How have you responded? 6/Why does a consideration of God's nature and a review of his activity in the world lead naturally to a re-evaluation of man's personal responsibility?

day 17 △ Psalm 68:1-18

1/Review the probable occasion for this majestic psalm in 2 Samuel 6:2-18. Of what historical event does the present festive procession remind David? 2/How does David regard God's part in the reasons for celebrating? 3/How are his requests and his thanksgiving related? On what basis? 4/What different aspects of God are extolled here? 5/How can you *exult* before God today? 6/To what extent do you thank God in anticipation of his goodness to you? Why? What gifts can you give him?

day 18 △ *Psalm 68:19-35*

1/List additional aspects of God from these verses. 2/What effect do his characteristics have on his people? 3/To what extent is Israel assured of victory? Why? What do they ask God to do in regard to their enemies (note their description—esp. v. 30)? 4/Contrast God's attitude toward his people with his actions toward their enemies. To what extent are these necessarily coexistent? 5/Write a short poem titled *Blessed be God!*

day 19 △ *Psalm 69*

1/Compare the themes of this psalm and Psalms 22 and 35. 2/How does David picture himself? What intense emotions do these pictures reveal? What are their causes? 3/How do people regard David? What have they done? 4/Why is he concerned about those who back him in spite of his predicament? 5/How are his requests related to his feelings about *a*-himself, *b*-his enemies, and *c*-God? 6/What do you request from God when you are in despair? Why? How do you usually feel about God in such a situation (cf. v. 33)? Why? 7/What is David's assurance for the future?

day 20 △ *Psalm 70*

1/Compare and contrast this psalm with Psalm 40:13-17. 2/Why do you think this is a separate psalm? 3/What is the basis of David's appeal to God for himself? his enemies? 4/Account for the urgency expressed. 5/To what extent are your desires centered in seeking and loving God? Why? 6/What recent experiences have caused you to say, *God is great!*

day 21 △ *Psalm 71*

1/What is the tenor of verses 1-9? 2/What is the author's age? What has been his experience with God? 3/How has his experience with God affected others? Define *portent*. 4/Imagine how the dogged pursuit of enemies (look back through the psalms in this section) would affect your actions and feelings. Account for the author's hope and praise in this situation. 5/Why is God's past action a basis for David's hope? 6/What has God done for you in the past? What do you anticipate for the future?

day 22 Δ Psalm 72
1/What are the characteristics the king should have (note esp. the metaphors; cf. God's characteristics) in regard to *a*-his own nation and *b*-all men? 2/To what extent do they characterize Solomon's reign (cf. 1 Ki. 1–11)? 3/In what ways have you experienced these characteristics in Christ as divine king? 4/What is the natural effect of a righteous national administration? To what extent do you pray that your government will be righteous? Why? 5/Are national prosperity and righteousness related? Why? 6/In what ways are verses 18-20 a fitting doxology for Psalms 52–72?

day 23 Δ Introduction to 1 Kings
1 and *2 Kings* show various kings of Israel and their people either obeying or rejecting God's covenant (promises and commands) and God's corresponding judgment. Political aspects are not the main concern, but rather how God deals with his people in history is the emphasis. As you study make a chart of the kings: their response to God (consider the role of the prophets), personality, leadership ability, relationship to people, successes, failures, and the lessons for you. *1 Kings 1* 1/What does Adonijah's choice of friends suggest about his character (cf. 2 Sam. 3:27; 20:8-10; 12:1-15; 20:23; 23:20-23)? 2/What is Adonijah's motive? Trace his attitude and emotion through the chapter. What makes the difference? 3/What place do you secretly desire in your Christian group? Why?

day 24 Δ 1 Kings 2
1/Why does David charge Solomon in this way (cf. chap. 1)? 2/How does Solomon follow through (cf. vv. 26-27 with 1 Sam. 2:27-36)? What is the result? 3/What does this show about *a*-God's desire for man and *b*-the result of obedience? 4/What response does God want from you? To what extent are you trusting God to fulfill his word in time?

day 25 △ *1 Kings 3:1-15*
1/Why do you think Solomon makes a marriage alliance with Egypt? Compare and contrast this incident with the comment in verse 3. 2/In what ways does your love for God need to be more consistent? 3/What is Solomon's request? What does he say about *a*-God, *b*-David, and *c*-himself? 4/What may a Christian leader learn from this request? 5/How does God respond? What will God do if you ask him for wisdom? What are the stipulations?

day 26 △ *1 Kings 3:16–4*
1/How does the story of the harlots illustrate the fulfillment of God's promise in 3:12? 2/To whom does Israel give credit for Solomon's wise judgment? 3/What qualities in your life are God-given? Who receives the praise? 4/List the *a*-personal and *b*-national benefits of God's fulfilled promises in chapters 3–4. What do these benefits reveal about God? 5/What is the basic source of Solomon's prosperity?

day 27 △ *1 Kings 5*
1/What is Hiram's relationship with *a*-David and *b*-Solomon? What qualities of friendship are apparent? 2/How can you express these same qualities in your life today? 3/What does Solomon tell Hiram about God in verses 2-5? 4/What does Hiram's reply indicate about his relationship to God? 5/Compare and contrast Solomon's treaty with Hiram and his alliance with Egypt. 6/What kind of friendships should you *a*-seek and *b*-avoid?

day 28 △ *1 Kings 6–7*
1/Visualize the temple (a cubit=about 15 inches). What quality of workmanship and materials goes into God's house? 2/What sort of worker is Hiram? 3/How long does the job take? 4/What can you learn about serving God from Solomon and Hiram? 5/What does God say is his major interest? 6/How does God *dwell* with you? Why?

day 29 Δ *1 Kings 8:1-21*

1/When the temple is finished, what must then be brought to God's house? What place does it occupy there? Why? 2/What occupies the inner core of your life? Why? 3/Who then comes to dwell in the house? 4/In what specific ways is God's indwelling evident in your life? 5/What causes Solomon to bless God in verses 14-21? 6/What promise of God applies to your life today?

day 30 Δ *1 Kings 8:22-53*

1/What is Solomon's concept of God? What characteristics does he emphasize in verses 22-30? 2/What is Solomon's opinion of mankind? To what extent is this opinion true of you? 3/What is necessary if man is to enter God's presence? What is God's response? 4/How do you express a sense of sin and repentance when you talk to God? 5/For whom does Solomon pray? 6/For what friends and associates will you pray specifically today?

Month 29

day 1 Δ *1 Kings 8:54-66*

1/On what basis does Solomon bless the assembly (cf. vv. 51, 53)? 2/Imagine you are there. What blessings do you receive? 3/What application does Solomon make at the end of his blessing? 4/How is the house of God dedicated? 5/How are you dedicating your life to the Lord? 6/How do the people feel as they go home? 7/What is your response to God?

day 2 Δ *1 Kings 9*

1/What does God say about Solomon's prayer? What conditions does God lay down for the future? What promises does he make? 2/Compare and contrast these words (vv. 3-9) with the exhortations in 3:14 and 6:11-13. What progression do you see? Consider why. 3/To what extent are you now heeding God's words to you? 4/Compare and contrast verse 25 with 3:3. 5/What growth and improvement is evident in your worship of God from the time you became a Christian? from a year ago? from yesterday? How do you know?

day 3 Δ *1 Kings 10*

1/What types of activities does the queen of Sheba (probably southern Arabia) observe? 2/To what extent can others tell that you love God by your ordinary actions as well as by your worship activities? 3/How does she react to Solomon? to his God? 4/Are those you meet led to praise God or do they see only you? 5/How does Solomon use the gifts God gives him? 6/How do you use God's gifts to you?

day 4 Δ *1 Kings 11:1-8*

1/What is a major cause of Solomon's spiritual decline? Where does the decline begin? How far does it extend? 2/Are you in similar danger now in relationships with the opposite sex? Why? 3/Assess Solomon's character in these eleven chapters. What are his strengths? his major weaknesses (esp. 3:1-4)? 4/What tendencies, weaknesses, or sins in your life should you bring to God as you pray now?

day 5 Δ *1 Kings 11:9-43*

1/What knowledge does Solomon have that destroys any excuse (cf. 9:6-9)? 2/To what extent are you obeying the knowledge that you possess? 3/What do verses 9-13 indicate about God's character? 4/What type of people does God use to implement his word? 5/Describe the implications of God's actions in verses 14 and 23 for the world today. How does this affect your concept of God and your faith in him? 6/What balance should you maintain in *a*-trusting God to do his work and *b*-taking active initiative in his affairs? 7/What major principles have you learned from this account of Solomon's life?

day 6 Δ *1 Kings 12:1-24*

1/What causes the rebellion of the people against Rehoboam? How might he have prevented it? 2/To what extent do you heed the counsel of older believers? Why? 3/What basic elements of good leadership are lacking in Rehoboam's decision? 4/How does God use the circumstances to carry out his purpose? 5/Does the fact of God's providence relieve you of responsibility? Why? 6/Imagine the feelings of the assembled army. What makes them go home again?

day 7 Δ *1 Kings 12:25-33*

1/What is God's desire for Jeroboam (cf. 11:26-43)? 2/List the ways he departs from God's ways. What do verses 26 and 33 indicate about the cause of his defection? 3/What types of situations or thoughts make you doubt God's promises to you? How can you prepare yourself to cope with these situations or thoughts? 4/Compare and contrast Jeroboam's self-conceived religion with the commands for worship originally given Israel. 5/What warning is here for you?

day 8 Δ *1 Kings 13*

1/How does God seek to change Jeroboam? What is the effect? 2/Compare and contrast the behavior of the man of God in the two incidents. Why do you think he disobeys God? 3/Do you seek or accept advice from others, even respected elders, when you have an explicit command from God? 4/Imagine the old prophet's feelings as he *a*-relates God's judgment to the man of God and *b*-finds the body. 5/Contrast the man of God's experience with Rehoboam's experience in chapter 12. 6/How will the study of these experiences change or improve your method of making decisions?

day 9 Δ *1 Kings 13*

1/Why does disobedience warrant severe punishment? 2/What issues are at stake here? 3/What motivates you to lie? What sectional or professional rivalries might be motivations here? 4/To what extent are you faithful to God where he has placed you? 5/What is your attitude toward the work and success of others? 6/How does the older prophet's attitude change? Why? 7/How does the failure of these men of God contribute to Jeroboam's hardness of heart? 8/To what extent do your attitudes and actions affect whether people around you obey or disobey God?

day 10 Δ *1 Kings 13:33–14:20*

1/Contrast how Jeroboam and Ahijah carry out their respective commissions from God. 2/What seems to be Jeroboam's concept of God (note his dealings with the prophet of God)? 3/How does Jeroboam's sin affect *a*-his family (cf. the feelings about a decent burial at this time) and *b*-Israel? 4/As you think over Jeroboam's life, evaluate your faithfulness to God's commands.

day 11 Δ *1 Kings 14:21–15:8*

1/Characterize the two kings of Judah mentioned here. 2/What influence does Rehoboam's mother have (cf. 11:1-2, 5, 7-8)? 3/How does your parental heritage affect your spiritual life? 4/How does Judah repay the favor of God (contrast v. 21b with vv. 22, 24b)? 5/Why is the invasion and plundering by Shishak permitted by God? 6/In what ways have you provoked God to *jealousy?* How can you be *wholly true* to him today?

day 12 Δ *1 Kings 15:9-24*

1/What reforms does Asa institute? What is his basic heart attitude? 2/How does he handle his mother's sin? 3/To what extent do you let personal relationships stand in the way of obeying God? 4/Contrast Asa's actions in verses 17-24 with his earlier actions. 5/How do you handle threats from God's enemies?

day 13 △ *1 Kings 15:25—16:34*

1/Compare the *a*-lives and *b*-ends of Baasha and Jeroboam (cf. 11:26—14:20). 2/What seems to be the common denominator of all the kings of Israel here? How does Ahab add to the blasphemy? 3/Describe the political, religious, and moral climate here. Imagine yourself a prophet during these times in Israel. 4/While Omri is one of Israel's most important kings politically, how does his dismissal here point out the important issues of Israel's history? 5/To what extent do you profit from observing the lives of these kings?

day 14 △ *1 Kings 17*

1/What seems to be the religious and moral climate now? 2/What brings Elijah to the foreground? 3/Describe Elijah's relationship with *a*-God and *b*-the widow at Sidon. 4/How does the fact that she is heathen highlight her faith? How does her faith mature? 5/What are you learning about God's work through the events of your life? 6/How is God using you in other people's lives? How do you know?

day 15 △ *1 Kings 18*

1/What is unusual about Obadiah in contrast to Ahab's government? 2/To what extent do you pray for men similar to Obadiah in today's governments? 3/What is Ahab's attitude toward Elijah? 4/Imagine yourself in Elijah's position at Mount Carmel. What are the odds? 5/What is the ratio where God has placed you? 6/To what extent do you speak God's words?

day 16 △ *1 Kings 18*

1/How does Elijah's question in verse 21 compare or contrast with modern statements that all roads lead to the same God? Why? 2/Compare and contrast the approach of *a*-the prophets to Baal and *b*-Elijah to God. 3/How do you approach God?

Why? 4/Why do you think Baal doesn't answer? 5/Imagine the effect of the event recorded in verse 38. 6/What recent experience in your life has caused you to say, "The Lord, he is God"?

day 17 △ 1 Kings 19

1/What is Jezebel's reaction to the Mount Carmel incident? 2/What contrasting facet of Elijah's personality emerges as a result? What are the reasons for his depression and sense of failure? 3/Which of Elijah's needs does God meet first? 4/How do you respond to persons in need? To what extent do you try to meet their needs? 5/How does God answer Elijah's charge against Israel? 6/What is your feeling about being a prophet in your generation? Do you ask God to show you companions in the faith? 7/How does Elisha respond to God's call?

day 18 △ 1 Kings 20

1/Trace the downfall of Ben-hadad. Why does God give him into Ahab's hands (vv. 10, 23-25, 28)? 2/To what extent do you try to departmentalize God's power? 3/What is God seeking to teach Ahab? 4/What is the place of the prophets now (cf. 19:10, 14, 18)? 5/Why do you think Ahab spares Ben-hadad (consider esp. the political implications)? 6/What is Ahab's attitude toward God's judgment?

day 19 △ 1 Kings 21

1/What qualities of life does Jezebel reveal in this incident? 2/How does Naboth suffer for his obedience (cf. Lev. 25:23-28) to God? Why? 3/To what extent do you obey God in spite of possible consequences? 4/What further do you learn about Ahab—his weaknesses, ability to lead, attitude toward God? 5/For what reasons do you let other people influence you to do evil? 6/How does Ahab's repentance affect God's announced punishment?

day 20 Δ 1 Kings 22
1/Contrast Micaiah's prophecy with that of the others. What does
his allegory teach about God? 2/What does Zedekiah believe
about his relationship to God? What warning is here for
you? 3/What do verses 8, 16, 18, 26-28, 30 reveal about Ahab's
real attitude to truth? How do you react to parts of scripture that
reprove and correct you? 4/Contrast Jehoshaphat's and Ahab's
lives. 5/How do verses 51-53 summarize a theme in *1
Kings?* 6/Review the chart you have kept. Summarize the effect
of the *a*-kings and *b*-prophets on Israel's political, socio-economic,
and religious life as seen in *1 Kings.* 7/What main lessons have you
learned from *1 Kings?*

day 21 Δ Introduction to the Gospel of John
John's purpose in writing is definite (20:31). He presents Christ as
the Son of God. He shows that Jesus makes *himself,* not the truths
he announces, the center of his message. *John 1:1-18* 1/Who is
the Word? What has the Word done? 2/Who is the light? What
does the light do? Who bears witness to the light? 3/How is the
true light received? 4/Who are the children of God? How can or
how have you become a child of God? 5/What is the purpose of
the Word's appearance in flesh?

day 22 Δ John 1:1-18
1/Contrast *light* and *darkness.* Explain how the Word's life is man's
light. 2/How are *receiving* and *believing* related? 3/Compare and
contrast the reasons or sources of birth in verse 13. 4/Contrast
what is given to man through *a*-Moses and *b*-Jesus Christ. 5/What
has the Son revealed about the Father to you recently?

day 23 Δ John 1:19-34
1/How does John the Baptist bear witness to Christ? Do you proclaim Christ as a voice (v. 23) or do you proclaim yourself? How
can you bear witness to Christ? 2/How does John identify himself? Jesus? What is John's relation to Jesus? 3/Compare the bap-

tisms of John and the Christ.   4/What does John say the Christ will do?   5/Who are present at Jesus' baptism?

day 24 Δ *John 1:35-51*
1/Compare how John's two disciples, Simon Peter, Philip, and Nathanael meet the Christ. Compare the ways John, Andrew, and Philip identify Jesus.   2/How does Philip answer Nathanael's question? How does Jesus overcome Nathanael's prejudice?   3/What have you learned from these examples to help you present Christ to your friends?

day 25 Δ *John 2:1-12*
1/What power of Christ does the miracle at Cana reveal (cf. 1:3)? What power do you expect him to reveal to you today?   2/Explain Jesus' statement in verse 4.   3/What does Jesus' mother tell the servants? What is the result of their obedience to Jesus' command?   4/How does the steward of the feast respond? Whom does he call?   5/What does Jesus' first sign manifest (cf. 1:14)? What is the result of Jesus' first sign?

day 26 Δ *John 2:13-25*
1/What happens in the temple? Describe Jesus' character and emotion. What command does he give?   2/What sign does Jesus give the Jews for his actions? How does he refer to *temple* in verse 19?   3/For what reason do many people in Jerusalem believe in Jesus' name?   4/How does Jesus know all men? How does his knowledge affect the openness and honesty of your prayers?

day 27 Δ *John 2:23–3:21*
1/How does Nicodemus know Jesus comes from God? Can this knowledge get him into the kingdom of God?   2/How does Jesus explain being *born again?*   3/Compare the significance of what was done to the serpent with what will be done to the Son of man (cf. vv. 14-15 with Num. 21:4-9). For what purpose has God sent his

Son into the world? 4/To what does *light* refer (cf. 1:5, 9)? Contrast the responses of *a*-those who do evil and *b*-those who do what is true to the light. What is your response to the light?

       day 28 Δ *John 3:22-36*

1/What does John reply to the complaint of his disciples (cf. 1:19-23)? How can this apply to people today? 2/How does John explain his relationship to the Christ? Explain your relationship to Christ. 3/Why is John's joy full? 4/In verses 31-35 what distinguishes the Son of God from others? What do these verses reveal about the relationship of Father and Son? 5/How do you obey the Son (cf. v. 36)?

       day 29 Δ *John 4:1-26*

1/Why does Jesus leave Judea? 2/What does verse 6 reveal about Jesus? 3/How is the woman's interest in Jesus aroused? List the items of conversation. Does Jesus answer the woman's questions in verses 9 and 12? Contrast the statements of Jesus and the woman about *water*. How does Jesus answer the woman's request of verse 15? 4/What makes the woman realize Jesus is a prophet? 5/What does Jesus say about worship? about God? 6/When does Jesus identify himself? 7/What does this incident show you about personal witness?

       day 30 Δ *John 4:27-42*

1/What does the woman consider the most important part of her conversation with Jesus? 2/What does Jesus say about *food?* Can Jesus live without this food? Can you? 3/How can the *sower* and *reaper* rejoice together in the harvest? 4/In what is the Samaritans' belief initially based? What reason do they give for their belief after Jesus has stayed with them? 5/Why do you believe in Jesus?

Month 30

day 1   Δ   *John 4:43-54*
1/Why does Jesus go to Galilee? Why do the Galileans welcome him (cf. 2:23)?   2/How does Jesus test the basis for the official's request? What is the result?   3/How does the official confirm the cause of his son's healing? What is the result?   4/How has Jesus tested the basis of your faith recently? What is the result?

day 2   Δ   *John 3:1–4:54*
1/Are theological education and spiritual insight necessarily related?   2/Compare the characteristics of *wind, water,* and the *new birth.*   3/How does God express his love to *a*-the Son and *b*-the world?   4/Contrast the way Jesus talks with *a*-Nicodemus and *b*-the Samaritan woman. What have you learned from these conversations about your approach in witnessing? What is the result of each conversation?   5/Summarize what these passages reveal about *a*-God, *b*-Jesus, and *c*-man.

day 3   Δ   *John 5:1-18*
1/How does the sick man answer Jesus' question? How does Jesus' question apply to problem areas in your life? What is your answer?   2/What two commands does Jesus give the man (vv. 8, 14)? What happens between these two commands?   3/For what action is the man reprimanded by the Jews? How does the man answer?   4/How does Jesus explain and defend his healing on the Sabbath?   5/What do verses 17-18 reveal about the Jews' understanding of the relationship of Jesus and God?

day 4   Δ   *John 5:19-29*
1/What can the Son do? List two things he does (vv. 21-22). Why can he do these two things (vv. 26-27)? Who will experience the finality of the Son's two actions (vv. 28-29)? In which group will you be?   2/Distinguish how *hour* is used in verses 25 and

297

28. 3/What are two prerequisites in obtaining eternal life? two **results?**

day 5 △ John 5:30-47
1/To what five witnesses does Jesus refer? Which are valid? Which do the Jews accept? 2/Do the scriptures give life? To whom is life related? 3/List at least five accusations Jesus makes against the Jews. Do any of these characterize you? 4/What is ironical about the source of accusation against the Jews? 5/From whom do the Jews receive glory? From whom does Jesus? From whom do you?

day 6 △ John 5:1-47
1/What does this passage reveal about the relationship of the Father and Son? 2/Whose authority does Jesus claim for his actions? Summarize the reasoning he uses to establish the truth of his testimony. Why is his claim valid? 3/How is life related to Jesus? How is Jesus' life related to you? 4/How is Jesus' judgment related to his authority?

day 7 △ John 6:1-15
1/Why does the multitude follow Jesus? 2/Why does Jesus question Philip? 3/Contrast Andrew's remark in verse 9 with the events of verses 10-13. 4/Have you ever felt like Philip and Andrew? What has Jesus done? What is your response? 5/How do the people identify Jesus? What makes them say that? 6/Where does Jesus go?

day 8 △ John 6:16-40
1/What power does Jesus reveal in verses 16-21? 2/How does Jesus answer the people's question in verse 25? 3/Do you ever ask the question of verse 28 and expect to receive an answer of "Go here" or "Do this"? 4/Contrast the statements of Jesus and the people about *bread* (relate to vv. 1-15). 5/List the claims Jesus makes in verses 25-40. What two basic needs does Jesus fulfill?

day 9 △ *John 6:41-59*

1/How do the people respond to Jesus' claims of verses 25-40? 2/What are the prerequisites and results of coming to Jesus (cf. v. 37)? 3/List the claims Jesus makes in verses 43-58 (cf. vv. 25-40). 4/How are Jesus' *flesh* and *blood* connected with eternal life? Who abides in Jesus? 5/Can Jesus live apart from the Father (v. 57)? Can you?

day 10 △ *John 6:53-71*

1/How does Jesus answer the disciples' murmuring? 2/Contrast the *flesh* and the *spirit.* 3/Who can come to Jesus? 4/How are Jesus' words connected with eternal life? 5/How does Jesus' penetrating knowledge of you affect your relationship with him (cf. his knowledge of Judas)? 6/What is the response to Jesus' words (cf. v. 63) by many disciples? by Peter? How have the twelve realized Jesus' identity? How have you?

day 11 △ *John 6:1-71*

1/What in Jesus' miracle and statements do the people and Jews misunderstand? Relate the disciples' experiences of Jesus' power with their response to his words. 2/Compare and contrast the barley loaves, *manna* (Ex. 16:14-21), and the *bread of life.* 3/What does this passage reveal about the relationship of God, Jesus, and you? 4/How are *seeing, believing, eating, drinking, knowing,* and *living* related? 5/How do Jesus' repeated statements of who can come to him (vv. 37, 44-45, 65) and what he will do for them (vv. 39-40, 44, 54) relate to his claim, "I am the bread of life"?

day 12 △ *John 7:1-24*

1/Why do Jesus' brothers urge him to go to Judea? 2/Why does the world hate Jesus? What does Jesus mean by *my time* and *your time* (vv. 6-8)? 3/What do the people at the feast say about Jesus? 4/How does Jesus answer the Jews' question of verse 15? 5/How can a man know the source of Jesus' teaching (cf. vv.

16-19 with 5:30-47)? 6/Why do the Jews sometimes circumcise a man on the Sabbath? 7/What principle of judging does Jesus give? How can you apply this principle today?

day 13 △ *John 7:25-36*
1/Trace the Jews' desire to kill Jesus. Why are they unsuccessful? 2/Do the people have a basis for their claim in verse 27 (cf. v. 42)? How does Jesus answer the questions about his origin? 3/List four different responses to Jesus in verses 25-36. 4/What about Jesus' statement in verses 33-34 do the Jews misunderstand? 5/How can you discover the meaning of Jesus' statements?

day 14 △ *John 7:37-52*
1/Compare *water, living water,* and the *Spirit.* How are *drinking* and *believing* Jesus related? What is the result? 2/How do you respond to Jesus' words in verses 37-38? 3/What is the source of the people's confusion in verses 41-44? 4/Why don't the officers arrest Jesus? 5/What is Nicodemus' relationship to the Pharisees? According to the chief priest and Pharisees, who are the only people who believe in Jesus (cf. Nicodemus' statement in 3:2)?

day 15 △ *John 7:1-52*
1/What false conception of Jesus do his brothers have? 2/In what ways does Jesus claim authority? What authority do the Jews claim for their actions (cf. v. 26)? 3/How are knowing Christ and knowing God related? 4/Group the responses of the people and compare these responses to similar contemporary opinions. 5/Have you received the Spirit? How do you know?

day 16 △ *John 7:53–8:11*
1/Why do the scribes and Pharisees bring the woman to Jesus? Do they keep Moses' law (cf. v. 5 with 7:19)? 2/How does Jesus bring the accusers to the same level as the accused? Describe the actions of the accusers before and after Jesus' words. 3/Who finally con-

demns the woman? Compare Jesus' statement in verse 11 with 3:17. What is your attitude to a "sinner"?

day 17 Δ John 8:12-30
1/How are *light* and *life* related to Jesus? to you? 2/How do the Pharisees try to prove that Jesus' words are false? How does Jesus fulfill the law's requirement for proof of truth? How does the Father bear witness to the Son? 3/Why doesn't anyone arrest Jesus (cf. 7:30)? 4/With what part of Jesus' statement in verse 21 are the Jews most concerned (cf. 7:35-36)? What part does Jesus reemphasize? 5/When will the Jews know who Jesus is and on whose authority he acts? 6/How can you please God today?

day 18 Δ John 8:31-47
1/What action identifies a disciple (relate specifically to your actions)? 2/Who are slaves? How do they become free? How can they continue free? 3/What two fathers do the Jews claim? Why can neither of their claims be true? Who does Jesus say is their father? Who is your father? How do you know? 4/What does Jesus claim in verse 46? 5/What reason does Jesus give for his misunderstood statements?

day 19 Δ John 8:48-59
1/Compare Jesus' answers to the Jews' three questions in this passage. 2/How do the people respond to Jesus' words of verses 31-47? 3/What does Jesus claim in verse 51? How do the people respond? 4/How can you *keep* Jesus' words? What will happen if you do? 5/How does Jesus relate himself to God? to Abraham? How do the people respond? How does Jesus escape them?

day 20 Δ John 8:1-59
1/What does this passage reveal about the relationship of Father and Son? 2/Contrast the two spiritual families. 3/Summarize the claims Jesus makes about *a*-himself and *b*-man. Trace Jesus' claim

to *truth*. What is offensive about his claim? 4/What freedom does Jesus offer? 5/Summarize the response to Jesus' actions and words. What is your response?

day 21 △ John 9:1-17

1/List the setting, characters, and events of the passage. What is the man's occupation? 2/Is the man's blindness a result of sin? Is sickness always caused by sin? 3/Explain Jesus' statement in verse 4. Relate Jesus' statement in verse 3 with the events of the passage. 4/What happens to the blind man? How does he answer the neighbors? the Pharisees? 5/What reason do some of the Pharisees give that Jesus is not from God (cf. 5:9-18; 7:21-24)? How have you similarly passed judgment recently (cf. 7:24)?

day 22 △ John 9:18-41

1/Why do the man's parents refuse to give information about the transformation of their son? Does the son answer how and by whom he sees? 2/Compare the reasoning of *a*-the Jews and *b*-the man. How do the Jews respond to the man's reasoning (vv. 24-34)? What happens to the man? 3/How does the man respond when he finds out who Jesus is? 4/By what evidence do you know that Jesus is God? 5/Relate Jesus' statements in verses 39-41 to the events of the passage.

day 23 △ John 9:1-41

1/State in columns what the man, the Jews, and the parents claim *a*-to know and *b*-not to know. Which are facts? opinions? lies? 2/How does the man evidence progressive belief in Jesus? 3/Relate the characteristics of sight and blindness in this passage to Jesus' claim, "I am the light of the world." 4/What have you learned from this incident to help you in personal witness?

day 24 △ John 10:1-21
1/Contrast the true and false shepherd (actions, intentions, purposes). 2/In what two ways does Jesus identify himself with the sheep? What characterizes his sheep? How do the sheep distinguish the true and false shepherd? 3/List the things which Jesus as the good shepherd has done for you. 4/How do the Jews respond to Jesus' words (cf. 8:48)?

day 25 △ John 10:22-42
1/How does Jesus answer the Jews' question in verse 24? 2/Describe the sheep's relationship to the shepherd and the shepherd's relationship to the sheep. 3/Who are Jesus' sheep? How do you know that you *a*-are and *b*-always will be among them? 4/Why do the Jews want to stone Jesus (cf. 5:18)? To what does Jesus appeal? What argument does he use to refute the Jews' charge? 5/What do the people around the Jordan River say about John the Baptist?

day 26 △ John 11:1-16
1/How do Mary and Martha identify Lazarus in their message to Jesus (cf. vv. 5, 36)? 2/What reason does Jesus give for Lazarus' illness? What does Jesus do when he hears Lazarus is sick? 3/How does Jesus answer the disciples' concern for his life? Why is he unafraid of the Jews? 4/Why is Jesus glad for the delay? 5/Summarize reasons for Jesus' actions (cf. vv. 9-10 with 9:4-5). How can you have similar confidence for your actions?

day 27 △ John 11:17-44
1/Compare the conversations of Jesus with Martha and Mary. Do you believe that Jesus' timing is always right (relate to specific examples in your life)? 2/Distinguish *resurrection* and *life*. 3/What are two responses of the people to Jesus' weeping? 4/For whose benefit does Jesus pray? When? What request? What happens? 5/Group the statements assuming *a*-human re-

sources or *b*-supernatural resources. 6/How have you seen the *glory of God* recently?

day 28   △   *John 11:45-57*

1/What are two responses to Jesus' raising of Lazarus? 2/What do the religious leaders fear? 3/How does the author John explain the high priest's statement? What is your attitude toward statements by opposition? 4/What is the purpose of Jesus' death? 5/Why does Jesus stay with the disciples? 6/What is the extent of Jesus' reputation?

day 29   △   *John 9:39–11:57*

1/What does this passage reveal about the relationship of Father and Son? about Jesus' power and authority? 2/List Jesus' claims. 3/Relate Jesus' statements about *life* in chapter 10 with the events of chapter 11. How do these statements and events affect your life? 4/Compare Jesus' words in 10:3-5, 27 with the response of *a*-the Jews in 10:20, 24 and *b*-Lazarus in 11:43-44.

day 30   △   *John 12:1-11*

1/How is Lazarus identified? 2/Contrast the actions of Martha and Mary (cf. 11:2). 3/Contrast the attitudes of Mary and Judas. Is Judas concerned for the poor? Is Jesus unconcerned? What do your attitudes and actions reveal about your character? 4/Why do the chief priests want to kill Lazarus? What is ironical about their plan (cf. chap. 11)?

Month 31

day 1   △   *John 12:12-19*

1/Why does the crowd go to meet Jesus (cf. 11:56)? How do they act? What do they say about him? Why do you follow

Jesus? 2/Compare verse 15 with Zechariah 9:9 (kings use the ass for errands of peace). 3/When do the disciples understand the significance of the event? 4/How do the Pharisees react to this event (cf. 11:57)?

day 2 ∆ *John 12:20-36*

1/How are the Greeks' request and Jesus' comments (vv. 23-26) related? 2/How will the Son of man be glorified? 3/How can your life bear much fruit? Explain Jesus' statements in verses 25-26 (apply specifically to your actions). 4/What is Jesus' predicament in verses 27-28? 5/What is the purpose of Jesus' death (cf. 3:14-15)? 6/How does Jesus answer the question of the identity of the Son of man (cf. 1:4-8; 3:19-21; 8:12; 9:5; 11:9-10)?

day 3 ∆ *John 12:37-50*

1/Contrast the responses to Jesus in verses 37-43. 2/In what areas of your life do you love the praise of men rather than the praise of God? 3/What claims does Jesus make in verses 44-50? Contrast the results of belief and unbelief. To what does Jesus equate belief in him and seeing him? 4/Contrast the roles of Jesus as savior and judge. How will a person who rejects Jesus be finally judged?

day 4 ∆ *John 1:1–12:50*

1/Trace John's emphasis on Jesus as the Messiah (esp. 1:41; 4:25-29; 7:25-52; 10:24; 11:27). 2/What does Jesus emphasize in telling people who he is? 3/What emotions have you seen Jesus express here? In what situations? 4/To what extent can you identify with him as a man? 5/Imagine that Jesus is alive in your society. What would you expect him to be discussing in the dorm, in homes, on buses, on farms, and in churches in your area of the country? Would you be afraid for his safety? Why? Would you follow him? Why?

day 5   △   Introduction to 2 Kings
1/As you study *2 Kings* make a chart of the kings: their response to God, personality, leadership ability, relationship to people, successes, failures, and the lessons for you. Distinguish the kingdoms of Judah, Israel, and the surrounding nations. *2 Kings 1* 1/List what you learn about Ahaziah. What indicates that he knows Elijah? 2/What characteristics of Elijah are shown? 3/What is the effect of Elijah's two demonstrations of God's power and reality? 4/What is your attitude toward God and his messengers? Why?

day 6   △   2 Kings 2
1/How is Elisha tested in this chapter? 2/What qualities do his actions reveal? 3/Why is his one request of Elijah granted? Are your requests of God so clear and confident? Why? 4/Where do you find a source of power for your daily life? 5/When Elisha comes to Bethel, bald because of mourning for Elijah, what attitude toward God and his messenger do the young men show? Why, do you think?

day 7   △   2 Kings 3
1/What causes the attack upon Moab? 2/When do the kings seek the prophet of the Lord? 3/What is the Lord's response to them? 4/How does this event show the part of one man in saving many people? 5/How does it reveal God's mercy and faithfulness to his inconsistent people? 6/For what experiences of mercy can you thank God today?

day 8   △   2 Kings 4
1/List the demonstrations of God's faithfulness in *a*-keeping his word and *b*-providing the material needs of those who trust him. 2/List some of the ways in which God has done these two things in your life. 3/What do you learn about faith from the two women in this chapter? 4/How can you follow their example today?

day 9   △   2 Kings 5

1/Describe Naaman's position, personality, relationship with his servants, and character. 2/What example does the maid set for you? 3/How have you, like Naaman, hesitated to submit to God's way of working because it hasn't matched the way you thought he should work? 4/What further effect does the healing have on Naaman (vv. 15-19)? 5/What warning is in Gehazi's example?

day 10   △   2 Kings 6

1/List the areas in which Elisha has authority and power. 2/To what limits have you confined God's power recently? How has he enlarged your concept? 3/In whose power does *a*-the king of Syria and *b*-Elisha trust? 4/What makes the difference between the servant's fear and Elisha's confidence? 5/Have you learned to conquer fear? How can you? 6/When he sees the plight of his people, what is the king of Israel's attitude toward God? 7/What is your attitude when you see pain and suffering? Why?

day 11   △   2 Kings 7

1/How are the prophecies in verses 1-2 fulfilled? 2/How are the unwanted lepers wiser than the king? 3/Are you willing to accept wisdom from someone who is repulsive to you? Why? 4/Compare the four lepers and a Christian witness in *a*-need, *b*-discovery, and *c*-action. 5/What is the lepers' negative motivation in telling the good news? What is your motivation in telling the good news you know?

day 12   △   2 Kings 8

1/How does the incident in verses 1-6 show God's care for his people (cf. 4:8-37)? 2/To what extent are you trusting God for your security and your future? 3/What is Elisha's part in Hazael's rise to power (cr. 1 Ki. 19:15)? God's part? Hazael's? 4/List common characteristics in Ahab's descendents. 5/How can one man's attitude toward God influence history? 6/What heritage are you leaving your descendents?

307

day 13 Δ *2 Kings 9*

1/What part does God have in the revolution of Jehu against Joram? 2/What instructions does God give Jehu? Why? 3/List the events which fulfill the word of God. 4/How seriously do you regard God's warnings in the Bible? 5/To what extent do you believe God will accomplish what he says he will? Why?

day 14 Δ *2 Kings 10*

1/Contrast Jehu with the sons of Ahab as rulers. 2/How does Jehu explain his actions? 3/What reforms does he introduce? Do they please God? 4/Account for Jehu's keeping of God's word so carefully in one area and ignoring it in another. 5/In what areas are you guilty of this inconsistency? Why?

day 15 Δ *2 Kings 11*

1/Contrast the motives of Athaliah with those of Jehosheba and Jahoiada. 2/What relation are these people (cf. 2 Chron. 22:11)? 3/What spiritual influence do you have over children near you? 4/Describe Jehoiada as to *a*-leadership ability, *b*-spiritual influence, and *c*-practical insight. 5/What is his first concern after Jehoash is king (vv. 17-18)? 6/How do the people respond to his leadership? 7/After you have made promises to God, what rival attitudes or things do you need to destroy? Why?

day 16 Δ *2 Kings 12*

1/For what actions can Jehoash be commended? 2/In what ways does he fail to fully please God? 3/What divided loyalties and confidences are struggling in your life? What should you do? 4/How long does Jehoiada's influence and kindness last (cf. 2 Chron. 24:15-22)? 5/Is your obedience to God dependent on another person or on your relationship to God?

day 17 Δ *2 Kings 13*

1/Contrast the actions of Jeroboam and Jehoahaz. What is God's response to each? 2/What prompts Jehoahaz to seek God? 3/Why has Israel fallen to such poverty? 4/How does God respond to Israel's oppression? Why (vv. 22-23)? 5/What do you learn of God's character for which you can worship him today? 6/What effect do his holiness and mercy have on you? 7/Review and summarize the deeds and attitudes of Elisha recorded in *2 Kings.*

day 18 Δ *2 Kings 14*
1/Characterize Amaziah's reign in several words or phrases. 2/What motive in Amaziah does Jehoash recognize? 3/Describe Jeroboam's strengths and weaknesses as one of his subjects might. 4/Why is Israel now so successful in contrast with the time before Jeroboam? 5/What evidences of God's faithfulness, in spite of your failure, can you see in your life?

day 19 Δ *2 Kings 15*
1/List in parallel columns the kings of Judah and Israel: the length of their reigns, special events, and their responses to God (Azariah and Uzziah are the same man). 2/How long does Jehu's family reign? Why (cf. 10:30 with 15:12)? 3/Compare the evaluations of Uzziah and his son. 4/To what extent is the summary *he did right in the eyes of the Lord . . . nevertheless* true of your life so far? Why? What changes can you begin to make today? 5/What happens to the freedom of Israel when her leaders turn from God?

day 20 Δ *2 Kings 16*
1/Add to your list of the kings. 2/Contrast Ahaz with his father Jotham and his grandfather Uzziah. 3/List the foolish actions of Ahaz. 4/To what extent do his family and nation suffer because of his sin? 5/When are you tempted to think that your actions affect only yourself?

day 21 Δ *2 Kings 17*
1/What does God finally do with Israel? Why? 2/Outline the

things Israel does against God. 3/After whom do they pattern themselves? After whom do you? 4/Why can't they plead ignorance of God's will? 5/What do you see of God's mercy and judgment in this chapter? 6/Describe the religious confusion and hypocrisy in verses 29-41. 7/To what extent is this confusion descriptive of your life? Why?

day 22 Δ 2 Kings 18

1/List the eight actions for which Hezekiah is commended. With what national benefit? 2/Contrast these with the reason for Israel's destruction. 3/Which is a better description of you—verse 6 or 12? 4/Imagine that you are an inhabitant of Jerusalem listening to Rabshakeh. How does he shake your confidence in your only source of help—Egypt or Jehovah? 5/How have you been conquered by the fear of men? Why?

day 23 Δ 2 Kings 19

1/In face of threats and dangers what is Hezekiah's attitude? Where does he go? Whom does he seek? 2/What command and promise does God give him? 3/In trouble have you learned to trust God's promise before circumstances change? 4/How does Hezekiah describe God in his prayer? What are the requests? How does God differ from other gods? 5/What explanation does God give for Assyria's success and her impending failure? What happens (cf. vv. 7, 32-34)?

day 24 Δ 2 Kings 20

1/Imagine that you are Hezekiah. What emotions do you experience in verses 1-11? 2/Since events of this chapter precede chapters 18–19, how would this experience strengthen Hezekiah's faith to face Sennacherib? 3/What repeated reason does God give for his action (cf. v. 6 with 19:34)? 4/Though Hezekiah stands well the tests of illness and danger, how does he respond to the temptation of pride? 5/To what extent can you face flattery as well as criticism with spiritual victory?

day 25 Δ *2 Kings 21*
1/How old is Manasseh? During what time in his father's life was he born (cf. 20:6)? What influence do Hezekiah's bonus years have on his family? 2/Contrast Manasseh with his father. 3/What promise and warning does he ignore? 4/What responsibility does God put on the people? 5/Summarize the argument in verses 11-15. 6/What is the summary of Manasseh's life? 7/What summary could be written of your life as it has influenced others in the past month?

day 26 Δ *2 Kings 22*
1/What is the initial action of a king who does *right in the eyes of the Lord* (cf. previous chaps.)? 2/What great discovery does the high priest make? 3/How does the reading of the scroll affect the king? Why (review the content of *Deuteronomy*)? 4/How does the reading of God's word affect you? 5/How does God's message to Josiah show his justice and mercy?

day 27 Δ *2 Kings 23*
1/What are the specific items in Josiah's covenant with God? 2/List what Josiah does to keep his covenant *a*-positively to establish right worship and *b*-negatively to destroy false religion. 3/How is Josiah's life summarized? 4/Summarize your relationship with God so far. What reforms, negatively and positively, does your life need? List specific ways you can act in reform today. List goals of reform for the future. 5/Why is Josiah's reform not adequate to divert God's judgment? 6/How do verses 28-37 fulfill God's promise to Josiah in 22:20?

day 28 Δ *2 Kings 24*
1/What four kings rule Judah after Josiah? For how long? 2/How do they act considering the covenant made in chapter 23? 3/How does the writer account for Judah's political and military defeat (vv. 3, 20)? 4/Would more warning have averted Judah's destruc-

tion? Give reasons. 5/How should you and your country take warning from Judah's history?

day 29 Δ 2 Kings 25
1/Why does Nebuchadnezzar have to come a second time against Jerusalem? 2/Compare and contrast his treatment of the city, people, leaders, and temple these two times (cf. 24:10-17 with 25:2-21). 3/What does the history of Judah show about the result of continued refusal to acknowledge God? 4/Where and how do you see God's *a*-justice and *b*-mercy displayed in the world today? 5/Evaluate the religious-political-moral situation in Judah during her last 400 years. 6/In spite of the short duration of the religious-social reforms, of what value are they to the nation? 7/How can Christians work for similar reforms today?

day 30 Δ John 13:1-11
1/Review what Jesus has accomplished during his life. Describe Jesus' state of mind as the time of his death approaches. How can you have similar composure when you face threatening situations? 2/What action does Jesus perform during supper? In what garb? Does he wash Judas' feet? 3/How does Peter misunderstand? 4/How does Jesus use the word *clean* inverse 10?

Month 32

day 1 Δ John 13:12-20
1/How does Jesus apply the significance of his actions in verses 4-11? How can you obey verse 14 in modern time? 2/What is the relationship between teacher and disciple, master and servant, one who sends and one who is sent? 3/To whom do you feel superior? How can you serve that person? 4/How are *knowing* and *doing* related in your life? 5/What scripture will be fulfilled (cf. Ps.

41:9)? 6/What, according to Jesus, is the purpose of sharing his foreknowledge with the disciples?

day 2 △ *John 13:21-35*
1/Do the disciples realize who will betray Jesus? 2/Describe Jesus' character and attitudes during this incident (his action in v. 26 is a sign of friendship). 3/What do verses 31-32 reveal about the relationship of God and Jesus? Define *glorify* (cf. 8:54; 11:4; 12:27-28). 4/What is the identification of a disciple? What is the standard of love to one another? How can you fulfill this commandment?

day 3 △ *John 13:36–14:11*
1/Compare the questions of Peter, Thomas, and Philip. What questions do you have? 2/How does Jesus answer the disciples' questions? What claims does he make (cf. vv. 2-4 with 13:33)? What does he say about knowing God? 3/What has he revealed to you about the Father recently? 4/How does he establish his authority? his relation to the Father?

day 4 △ *John 14:12-21*
1/Why will the person who believes in Jesus do greater works than Jesus does? 2/What four promises does Jesus give? 3/How can you know if you love Jesus? 4/What inter-relationship do the Father, Son, and you have? 5/What will the Holy Spirit do? Why can't the world receive the Holy Spirit? What counsel has the Holy Spirit given you recently? 6/Why is your existence, present and future, dependent upon Christ's being risen and alive (v. 19)?

day 5 △ *John 14:18-31*
1/How does Jesus answer Judas' question? Contrast one who loves Jesus with one who does not. 2/How will the disciples remember Jesus' words after he has gone? 3/How does Jesus *leave peace*? How do you experience this peace in your daily living? 4/What do

313

verses 28-31 reveal about the Father, Jesus, the *ruler of this world* (cf. 12:31), and the world?

day 6 △ *John 13:1–14:31*

1/In what ways does Jesus manifest awareness of his approaching death? How does he prepare the disciples for his absence? 2/How are Jesus' actions and your actions related? Jesus' love and your love? your love and your actions? 3/How will the coming of the Holy Spirit affect the disciples' lives? In what ways does the Holy Spirit influence your daily living?

day 7 △ *John 15:1-17*

1/Identify the *vine, vinedresser,* and *branches.* How are they related? 2/Define *bear, fruit, prune, clean* (cf. 13:10), *abide, joy.* 3/Why must the branch abide in the vine? What happens to those who abide? to those who do not? 4/How can you abide in Jesus' love? How can you glorify God? List specific examples. 5/How does having Jesus' joy within make your joy full? 6/What is the greatest example of love (cf. v. 12 with 13:34-35)? 7/How are the privileges of slaves and friends different? How can you be Jesus' friend? 8/For what purposes has Jesus chosen and appointed you (cf. v. 16b with v. 7)? 9/List the ways *love* shows in your relationship with *a*-Christ and *b*-others.

day 8 △ *John 15:18-27*

1/What three reasons does Jesus give for the world's hatred of his disciples (cf. v. 25 with Ps. 35:19; 69:4)? Why should the disciples expect persecution? Why should you? 2/What does this passage reveal about the relationship of Father, Son, and disciple? 3/For what reasons is the world inexcusable for its sin? 4/How is the Counselor related to *truth?* How does the presence of the Counselor stabilize your life against the world's hatred? 5/To what two witnesses does Jesus refer (cf. 5:30-47)?

day 9 △ *John 16:1-11*

1/What is the purpose of Jesus' discourse with his disciples? 2/What will happen to the disciples in the future? Why? What attitudes and actions should you expect non-Christians to show toward you (compare with your present experience)? 3/Why are the disciples full of sorrow (cf. v. 20)? Why will they benefit when Jesus goes away? 4/Who will take Jesus' place? What will he do in the world? Why?

day 10 △ *John 16:12-24*

1/List three aspects of the Spirit's work with the believer. Is he working in your life? How can you know? 2/What do verses 13-15 reveal about the relationship of Father, Son, and Spirit? 3/What is the disciples' problem in verses 16-19 (cf. v. 5)? What promise does Jesus repeat (vv. 16, 20, 22)? 4/Compare the feelings the disciples will have with those of a woman delivering a child. 5/When will the disciples establish a direct relationship with the Father? 6/How are *asking, receiving,* and complete *joy* related?

day 11 △ *John 16:25-33*

1/What is Jesus' relationship to the Father? the disciples' relationship? yours? 2/When will the disciples pray to the Father? 3/Contrast the disciples' assertion in verses 29-30 with Jesus' answer in verses 31-33. 4/What will happen to the disciples? What is to be their attitude? Why? 5/Define *peace.* How can you have peace?

day 12 △ *John 15:1–16:33*

1/Contrast the emotions in this passage. What is the source of each? its reason for expression? 2/In what ways are the Father, Son, and Spirit related? How are you related to them? 3/In what ways will the disciples' lives change when Jesus goes away? 4/Summarize Jesus' teaching about prayer.

315

day 13 △ *John 17:1-19*

1/To what *hour* does Jesus refer? 2/What power has the Son received from the Father? 3/How does Jesus define *eternal life?* 4/What is the result of Jesus' manifesting the Father's name to the disciples? 5/List the requests Jesus makes for the disciples. What has he done for them? 6/What is the purpose of your being *in the world* but *not of the world?* 7/Define *truth* (cf. 8:32). 8/How are the Father, Son, and disciples related?

day 14 △ *John 17:20-26*

1/For whom does Jesus pray? What requests does he make for them? 2/How are the Father, Son, you, and the world related? What will be accomplished through believers manifesting their oneness of life with the Father and Son? 3/In verse 22 what does Jesus give them (cf. v. 5 with 1:14)? Why? For what reason does Jesus want believers to be with him? How is Christ's glory revealed in your daily living?

day 15 △ *John 17:1-26*

1/How has Jesus glorified the Father? How will the Father glorify Jesus (cf. 12:27-28; 13:31-32)? How is Jesus glorified in the disciples? in you? 2/Compare how the Father has sent Jesus into the world with how Jesus sends *a*-his disciples and *b*-you into the world. 3/What do the two adjectives Jesus uses in addressing God (vv. 11, 25) reveal about the Father? 4/How are God's *name*, *word*, and *love* related?

day 16 △ *John 18:1-27*

1/Describe Jesus' attitude as Judas and the soldiers come. What indicates a voluntary surrender by Jesus? 2/How does Jesus' identification of himself affect the men? How does he show concern for his disciples? 3/What reason does Jesus give for his command to Peter? 4/What two disciples follow Jesus? What happens to the disciples? to Jesus? 5/How has Jesus taught? 6/How does Jesus distinguish right and wrong? How can you?

day 17 △ *John 18:28-40*
1/Why don't the religious leaders go into Pilate's judgment hall? 2/How do the Jews answer Pilate's question in verse 29 and his command in verse 31? 3/Contrast Pilate and Jesus (attitudes, position, character). 4/Describe Jesus' kingship (cf. 6:15; 12:13-15). For what purpose is he in the world? you? Should you fight about it? 5/Contrast Jesus and Barabbas.

day 18 △ *John 19:1-16*
1/Contrast Pilate's statement about Jesus (18:38b; vv. 4, 6) with his actions. 2/For what reasons do the Jews want to kill Jesus (cf. 5:18; 10:30-38 with Lev. 24:16)? 3/What prompts Pilate's question of verse 9? 4/How does Pilate misunderstand his power? What finally causes him to yield to the Jews' demands? 5/What power do you have over circumstances? over others? What power do others have over your circumstances? over you?

day 19 △ *John 19:17-30*
1/What is the significance of *a*-Pilate's title and *b*-the chief priests' complaint? 2/What scriptures are fulfilled (cf. vv. 23-24 with Ps. 22:1-8; 14-18; vv. 28-29 with Ps. 69:21)? 3/Describe Jesus' state of mind while on the cross. For whom does he show concern? 4/What is commendable about John's obedience? Imagine the change in the household. How can you show obedient concern for others when you observe their grief or suffering? 5/What indicates a voluntary death (cf. 10:17-18)? What has Jesus finished (cf. 17:4)?

day 20 △ *John 19:31-42*
1/What happens to Jesus after he dies? Why don't the soldiers break Jesus' legs? How do they make sure he is dead? What scriptures are fulfilled (cf. vv. 33, 36 with Ps. 34:20; vv. 34, 37 with Ps. 22:16; Zech. 12:10)? 2/Why is Joseph a *secret* disciple? Can he remain secret? Do your associates know that you are a disciple? 3/How do Joseph and Nicodemus (cf. 3:1-15; 7:50-52) reveal

their devotion to Jesus? How can you show devotion to Jesus today?

day 21 Δ John 20:1-10
1/Who come to the tomb? When? What do they discover? How do they react? Imagine their feelings. 2/List evidences that Jesus' followers are not expecting the resurrection (cf. v. 9 with 10:17-18, 11:25-26; 16:16-22). 3/What produces belief in the other disciple (John)? 4/What difference does Jesus' resurrection make in your daily living?

day 22 Δ John 20:11-18
1/Describe Mary's feelings. How does she respond to the question of *a*-the angels and *b*-Jesus? 2/What makes her realize Jesus' identification? 3/How does Jesus refer to his followers? 4/How does Mary respond to Jesus' revelation and command (cf. vv. 2, 13, 15)? 5/How has Jesus revealed himself to you today? How have you responded?

day 23 Δ John 20:19-31
1/Describe the disciples' feelings. 2/How does Jesus greet his disciples? What command follows his greeting? By what power and authority will this command be fulfilled? 3/How are *seeing* and *believing* related for Thomas? for you? How does Jesus relate *seeing* and *believing?* 4/What is John's purpose in writing this book? 5/How are *believing* and *life* related? On what basis do you believe? have life?

day 24 Δ John 21:1-14
1/Describe Peter. How does Peter's decision (v. 3) influence the other disciples? 2/When do the disciples recognize Jesus? 3/What power of Jesus does this incident reveal? 4/What does this passage reveal about Jesus' concern for his disciples? What needs does he

fulfill? 5/How does Jesus show concern for you? What needs of yours has he fulfilled recently?

day 25 Δ John 21:15-25

1/Imagine Peter's feelings. How does he respond to Jesus' question and command? What action has your love for Christ produced? 2/How does Jesus show insight into Peter's character? How has Jesus shown understanding of your character recently? 3/Relate Jesus' command in verse 19 with Peter's question in verse 21. 4/What does John's explanation of the rumor reveal about his reliability in writing this book? 5/What is John's basis for selecting *these things* to write (cf. 20:30-31)?

day 26 Δ John 1:1–21:25

1/Summarize the purpose and character of John the Baptist. 2/Describe Jesus as the light of the world, bread of life, good shepherd, resurrection and the life, true vine, and Son of God. How does Jesus manifest these claims in your life? 3/What have you learned about God and the Holy Spirit by observing Jesus? 4/Summarize Jesus' claim to authority (relate to the meaning of his death and resurrection).

day 27 Δ John 1:1–21:25

1/Summarize in columns the *signs* Jesus performs. For what purpose is each done? What does each reveal about Jesus? How do the people respond? How do you respond to Jesus because of these signs? 2/Distinguish Jesus' methods of public teaching. List examples. 3/Distinguish Jesus' methods of private teaching. List examples. What have you learned from these examples about personal witness? 4/How do *a*-the people, *b*-the leaders of the people, and *c*-the disciples respond to Jesus' teaching? 5/Summarize Jesus' teaching about belief and eternal life (relate to John's purpose in writing). How does having eternal life affect your daily living?

day 28 Δ *Introduction to Isaiah*
Isaiah writes about charges, countercharges, and paradoxes. Jerusalem is the safest place on earth in one sense and the most vulnerable and violently desolate in another. Nations around Jerusalem are charged with Israel's same folly–a deafness and blindness that obstinately refuses to hear or see–and each in turn are consigned to similar dire consequences. But Israel receives the Lord's repeated attentions, not to press the charges against them the more villifyingly, but to accomplish the purpose of God–to forgive transgression! Israel seems determined *not* to be the case study of God's mercy; but she also fears the anger of unrighteous, not-about-to-be-corrected nations. So she prefers sharing their rebellious stance and eagerly turns to their mean gods as her Refuge and Redeemer. 1/During what period is Isaiah prophesying (cf. 1:1 with 2 Ki. 15–21)? 2/Leaf through the book. What kind of plot seems to be developing? 3/What qualities about God do you anticipate will come out as this plot unfolds? 4/Who stands to win the conflict intimated here? 5/Watch Isaiah's feelings and the language in which he expresses them. 6/What do you expect to learn about yourself from this record of God's dealings with a nation?

day 29 Δ *Isaiah 1:1-17*
1/Whose message is Isaiah giving? 2/What is the charge against Israel? How have the people responded to God? 3/How does Isaiah refer to God here? 4/How extensive a beating is Israel sustaining? What is its effect? Is it doing any good? 5/How is God's mercy revealed even in the desolation? 6/What about Israel's religious activities is so nauseating to God? What does he demand instead? 7/In what ways do you identify with Israel here? with Isaiah? 8/In what specific ways will you relate today to the imperatives in verses 16-17?

day 30 Δ *Isaiah 1:18-31*
1/Is the matter discussed in the first 17 verses still open with God? What are the alternatives? 2/Describe the state of the society. Is it seriously interested in a comeback? 3/What is God's response?

Does he seem at all stymied or disillusioned? 4/What is his plan? 5/Do you sometimes think that God has reached the end of his patience, interest, and resources in recovering what is his? When? Why? 6/How can you and your society be *redeemed?*

Month 33

day 1 Δ *Isaiah 2*
1/What objective does God have clearly in mind for the closing chapter of man's history? How extensive is it? 2/What will men find so inviting in contrast with their contemporary society? 3/What invitation is given to Israel (Jacob)? 4/What three sins has Israel committed? 5/If they turn from their sin, what general and extensive disaster will they escape? 6/What in particular is scheduled to fall? 7/To what extent are you taking to heart the plea made to Israel? How urgent is it today?

day 2 Δ *Isaiah 2:22–4:1*
1/Answer the question of 2:22 by comparing 3:1-5. 2/Where is help among men? 3/What will be the attitude of capable men about being leaders? Who will fill the vacuum of leadership? How will the people be affected? 4/What charge is God reversing and handing back to the rulers? 5/What about the women of Jerusalem is Isaiah assailing? 6/What will be the ultimate punishment for them (relate to their culture)? 7/What are you telling people (and God) daily in your posture, bearing, and outward decor?

day 3 Δ *Isaiah 4:2–5:17*
1/In contrast to decaying human culture what will make a gorgeous comeback from its once burned-out stump (4:2-4; cf. 1:30-31)? 2/As the first to be judged, what help will Israel be to the nations (4:4)? 3/What evidences the concern with which God

has established Israel? 4/What is Israel's response to righteous cultivation? What does she yield? 5/In what ways has God "cultivated" you? For what purposes? What have been the results? 6/Where does all Israel's evil lead? 7/How do God and his world look when he is finally done?

day 4 Δ *Isaiah 5:18–6:13*

1/What mocking is being aimed at God here? How do the mockers "flirt" with their denial of a judgment of consequence? 2/When the judgment comes, what will check any reconsideration or recovery (relate to the metaphors)? 3/Considering what he knows about Israel's future, imagine Isaiah's feelings when Uzziah dies (cf. 2 Chron. 26). 4/Where does he go? 5/In what ominous scene does he find himself inescapably surrounded? What call does he hear? 6/What awesome truth impresses him? Into what experience does his searing judgment lead? 7/If you were Isaiah, what would be your response to your burning lips and to the pronouncement of verse 7? Why? 8/Examine the difficult assignment ahead. Who will mock now? Whose mouth is to be used? How satisfying is the assignment? 9/To what extent do you think the *burning* (cf. 6:6-7 with 4:4) is appropriate? indispensable? for yourself?

day 5 Δ *Isaiah 7*

1/Although the attempted attack against God's city fails, what is the response of the city and king? 2/What is the meaning of the name of Isaiah's son? 3/Compare and contrast the *heads* of *a*-Damascus, *b*-Samaria (Israel), and *c*-Jerusalem (Judah). 4/What is King Ahaz to hear and see? About what offense is he strictly warned? 5/When God invites Ahaz to preview a sign, how does Ahaz respond? 6/What sign does God give? For what reason (cf. 2:2)? 7/Who alone is effective against the rage and fury of war? 8/Add to your understanding (cf. the metaphors) of what will happen to Ahaz and his city. How soon will this happen? 9/Does God have enough time to solve your most pressing problems?

day 6 Δ *Isaiah 8:1-15*

1/What occasions the birth certificate, reliable witnesses, and the visit to the prophetess (cf. 7:14)? 2/What will the next months demonstrate indisputably, as the child's name so plainly dramatizes? What two subsequent events will illustrate this (the *River* is the Euphrates)? 3/What possible failure of his lips (cf. vv. 11-13 with chap. 6) is Isaiah cautioned about? How can you avoid this failure in your socio-political situation? 4/In what two guises will God make himself known according to men's *fear?* How does God appear to you in the day of imminent national catastrophe?

day 7 Δ *Isaiah 8:16—9:7*

1/To what *teaching* and *testimony* do Isaiah's disciples and children (cf. 7:3; 8:3) draw attention? 2/Considering the circumstances of God's clear word, what rebellion is indicated in Judah's unabashed appeal to the dead? 3/Does this rebellion stand a chance of succeeding? 4/Who will break through the gathering darkness? 5/How has the *anguish* come about (cf. 2:5, 22; 4:4; 6:6-7; 8:11-15)? 6/Into what beautiful and glorious way (cf. 4:2) are they to be "lighted"? 7/What will come about? How? By whom (his name is two—the Singular Counsel for the Defense, and Prince of Peace; contrast 2:22)? 8/In the darkness in your nation, where can you find dawning light and hope? Is it hidden (cf. 8:16-22)?

day 8 Δ *Isaiah 9:8—10:19*

1/What sentence is passed down on Israel? 2/On what four counts does this awesome Attorney General take up the case for justice and righteousness on behalf of the world's plaintiffs? 3/Why can't Israel's case be finished up and set aside (9:12b, 17b, 21b; 10:4b)? 4/To what extent is your stubborn waywardness checked by legal correctives? Why? 5/What point is God proving here? 6/What other case is in this Judge-Advocate's brief? What is the charge? What is the mocking rebuke? 7/To what extent are you enjoying credit that belongs to someone else? 8/What is your attitude toward success?

day 9 △ Isaiah 10:20–12:6

1/Locate on a map these suburban towns and villages. 2/How would you as an inhabitant choose to respond to the promise of verses 24-27? 3/While Assyria reduces Judah to a hewn-down and burned-over stump (cf. 1:30-31; 5:24; 6:13), what incredible phenomenon will appear from the wretchedness and perfidy that has been Israel-Judah (cf. 11:1 with 1:21-26)? 4/How does this passage bring out more clearly the significance of the child's names in 9:6? 5/What are your misgivings about the future? To what extent can you join in the invitation of 12:5-6? Can you make 12:2 your reply? 6/Summarize Isaiah's message so far. What is Isaiah's relation to his message?

day 10 △ Isaiah 13

1/What signal is being raised for all to see? 2/Who are being waved in from their hiding places? 3/At what target is God taking well-timed aim? 4/List and describe (esp. note the imagery) the details in this disaster arena. 5/What are the characteristics of the plundering nation? of the plundered nation? 6/How are you related to this sovereign God?

day 11 △ Isaiah 14

1/What is to be the repercussion from the collapse of the mighty empire that holds Israel captive? What is finally at an end? finally begun? 2/What terrible truth and irony will be public and plain? 3/What will God's victory over Assyria notably demonstrate? 4/What erroneous interpretation of events (cf. 2 Chron. 28:16-27) is Philistia making? 5/How are the messengers (from nations that ask: Is Judah to be similarly defeated?) answered? 6/With Assyria looking like a sure winner, what would be your response to this oblique advice?

day 12 △ Isaiah 15–16

1/Investigate the background of Moab-Judah-Israel relations (cf. 2 Ki. 3 with chap. 15). 2/Summarize the characteristics of

Moab. 3/To what is Moab suddenly reduced? Where does that leave the surviving populace? 4/Having heard the counsel sent out from Jerusalem (14:32), what are the refugees seeking in earnest (notice the quote in 16:3-5)? 5/What is the general lot of the nation? 6/To what extent do you feel the sorrow of a national tragedy abroad? Why?

day 13 Δ Isaiah 17–18

1/Who is the ally of Syria at this time? 2/What will enjoy the peace in a land where men cannot work it out? 3/How do the two metaphors in verses 10-11 depict Israel's situation? 4/How far will the enemy get in their conquest of Israel? What will happen then? 5/What procession will the arrogant, would-be captors join instead of their scheduled triumphal march? 6/Compare and contrast the destruction which will happen to Damascus, Israel, and Ethiopia. What is different about the end result for Israel? 7/To what extent do you think God is working in the history of nations today? Why? 8/Do you expect any of God's enemies to bring him *gifts* at the end of history? Why?

day 14 Δ Isaiah 19–20

1/How is mighty Egypt to collapse? 2/From what beleaguered (by Assyrians) place will her fears arise? 3/On what premises will a reconciliation in the Middle East be established between these mutually suspicious and hostile parties? 4/What does major highway construction in the area (19:23) suggest about the traffic patterns? 5/What feelings of Israel toward Egypt at this time make Isaiah's *sign* necessary? 6/How important is Egypt in the coastland's defense plans? 7/If your favored Big Power were to disintegrate under a combined internal and external pressure grip, where would you turn? 8/Is Jerusalem still to be considered safe (cf. 14:32)?

day 15 Δ Isaiah 21

1/Having often pointed to a dawning of peace and international

recovery for the nations (cf. chap. 9; 19:19-25), what happens to
Isaiah's own twilight-dawn (cf. 8:20-22)? 2/What does the festal
celebration (v. 5) indicate about their readiness for judgment? 3/What is the watchman to observe and report? 4/With
Assyria and Egypt reduced to impotence, what hope of dawn is left
when the third Big Power is darkened? 5/What answer is given the
call about the blackout (v. 11)? Is the answer encouraging?
Why? 6/Are refugees, already on the move south and west from
Jerusalem, headed into any greater safety? 7/When God is judging, where is the only safe place for you?

day 16 △ Isaiah 22

1/Who is now in convulsive tears? 2/What is the rest of Jerusalem
up to (cf. Babylon on her last night—21:5)? What makes this celebrating particularly churlish? 3/What are Jerusalem's "defenses"? 4/What has made "safe" Jerusalem into the most disastrous place? 5/What insult is added by the king's steward? 6/What reforms within the city does Isaiah demand (cf. 2 Ki.
18:18)? 7/Contrast Shebna and Eliakim. What is the warning to
Eliakim? 8/To what extent do you make yourself responsible to
God in any position of authority you have? Why?

day 17 △ Isaiah 23

1/What remaining great city will feel the destructive
wrath? 2/What are Israel's relations with this city (1 Ki. 5:1-12;
Ps. 83:1-7)? 3/Who is waiting to pick up the lucrative business of
being an international trade center? 4/What is your attitude
toward money? business? 5/Can Sidon go anywhere for security? 6/Why will Tyre be restored to service? 7/What is a proper
use of material wealth?

day 18 △ Isaiah 24:1-20

1/What is to happen to the unwarranted mirth in a once-gay
world? 2/Who is bringing this on? What justification does he
give? 3/How inclusive will the wasting be? Is there any basis for

exclusion? Does the happening make you want to sing any more? 4/Who bursts into song? What has dawned beautifully on them? 5/Why can't Isaiah join in right now? 6/What frustrates Isaiah? What will frustrate the person experiencing the desolation of the earth?

day 19 Δ Isaiah 24:21–25:12

1/Who are the prisoners here? Into what darkness and prison are all to descend? What light shatters their darkness? 2/Account for Isaiah's singing here when he could not sing before over the smoldering ruins. 3/What is about to be abolished? Where? For whom? 4/At what merry-making feast will all peoples be gathered? What will happen at the festival? 5/What makes you jubilant: political and national gains that favor your people over another? fulfillment of your nation's destiny? world peace? something else?

day 20 Δ Isaiah 26:1-19

1/What causes the singing here? 2/What are the characteristics of the people who enter the city? 3/For what are the righteous waiting? 4/While earth's proud rulers perish (cf. v. 14 with 14:9), what is going on inside Jerusalem? 5/With Israel trying hard to bring forth deliverance herself, how does God grant it (contrast vv. 14 and 19)? 6/When have you been aware of God's deliverance as a *dew of light*? What has been your response?

day 21 Δ Isaiah 26:20–27:13

1/With fears and futility their routine lot these days, imagine how these Jerusalemites comtemplate the invitation of verse 20. 2/What assurances does God give to encourage them? 3/What frustration confronts God? What characterization of Israel could "release" God? To do what? 4/Instead, not willing to break faith himself, what promise does God give? 5/What evidence of God's restraint does Isaiah present? 6/What assessment does Isaiah make of the people and their readiness to be taught? 7/Do any of these

metaphors characterize your state of life now? Why? What do you
think is God's assessment of you now? 8/Does God's method of
instruction achieve final success?

day 22 △ Isaiah 28

1/What sort of festivities have filled the time scheduled for sobriety
(cf. 22:12; 26:20)? 2/What does God have for proud Samaria (cf.
8:7-8)? for the remnant? 3/How does Isaiah describe the priests
and prophets? What is their opinion of Isaiah's attitude toward
them? of his teaching? 4/Therefore, how will God teach them
(note the irony and relate to the educational style)? 5/To what
alliance and contract have they just drunk a toast? 6/By building
his *refuge* (where? what qualities?) and flooding theirs, what proud
mockery of the Jerusalemites will God dispense with? 7/Deter-
mine the meaning of the imagery in verse 20 (cf. v. 18). 8/Is the
harrowing of men an end in itself? How does God's *wonderful
counsel* and *excellent wisdom* relate to the harrowing of men?

day 23 △ Isaiah 29

1/How does God view Jerusalem's activities (cf. v. 1 with 22:1-2a,
13; 28:15)? 2/Taking up the seige, as David once has done to
make the city his, what will God hear all muffled and ghostlike?
Where does this signal cry come from? 3/At that instant what
becomes of the enemy trampling overhead? 4/Imagine you have
to tell this fantastic story to a Jerusalem audience. In what condition to hear and see are they (vv. 9-10)? What excuses will they
make to disown acquaintance with the message? 5/What are the
causes of their reaction here? How seriously are they taking
God? 6/What in your relationship with God is *upside down?*
Why? 7/What will God do so they can't thwart his purposes? 8/Who can see and hear God without the slightest problem? 9/Have you any hide-outs?

day 24 △ Isaiah 30:1-17

1/Where will Israel seek immediate sanctuary? 2/Contrast Israel's and God's views of Egypt. 3/How will God tolerate this policy of alliance with Egypt? 4/What mocking tragedies will overtake the people before they reach their *refuge?* 5/How does God characterize Israel? 6/Where do you turn for protection? What attracts you to this protective refuge? 7/What orders does Jerusalem receive while in wild flight (from Assyria's encirclement)? How do the people respond? With what consequences?

day 25 △ *Isaiah 30:18-33*
1/What is God waiting for? 2/List the areas of life in which God will manifest himself. 3/In what area of your life today do you need God's healing? 4/What glorious transformation, what appropriate song and fest, is scheduled in beleaguered Jerusalem? 5/How will God manifest himself to the Assyrians?

day 26 △ *Isaiah 31*
1/What folly is Jerusalem involved in? 2/Who is the only one not currently frightened and in flight? Characterize him in relation to the metaphors used. 3/What must those in flight immediately do? 4/Are you running from anything? What qualities about God commend him as someone to turn to? 5/What is to become of the great threat that frightens Jerusalem?

day 27 △ *Isaiah 32*
1/What is coming to transform the whole social order of things? In what ways will the society be transformed? 2/What part of the social order is singled out for special attention (cf. 3:16-26)? 3/In what ways is your society striving for peace, quiet, and productivity? Assess the receptivity and success of such strivings. 4/What do you foresee for your society? What would you like to see? In what way and to what extent can you influence or change your society? 5/What is the point of the little proverb in verse 20?

day 28 △ *Isaiah 33*
1/Why is the destroyer going to be destroyed? 2/What is the ap-

propriate stance of prayer within the city? 3/What word of comfort comes resounding back? 4/What is the situation outside the city for those who abandoned her? 5/What happens to the people when God begins to manifest himself? 6/What is promised those who survive the terror of heart? 7/What is the basis of your view of the future? From a similar hope? from something more temporary and contemporary? 8/What is the ultimate fulfillment for those whose hope is too great for fear?

day 29 △ Isaiah 34

1/For all the scathing judgments against Jerusalem, how does God feel about behavior in the rest of the world? 2/How does this chapter depict universal judgment? 3/Choose a few of the images and visualize more fully what will occur. 4/Do you feel God is justified in making a wasteland out of the earth in which mankind has invested so much? Why?

day 30 △ Isaiah 35

1/However much beyond recovery it appears, how does the wasteland respond? To what event? 2/How do you think this message will affect the people (It is the last message before Jerusalem is enveloped by Assyrian armies)? 3/In what situations do you tend to be *weak, feeble,* and *fearful?* Why? 4/What encouragement is given to the people? 5/What hope and joy do you have in the midst of your society? Why?

Month 34

day 1 △ Isaiah 36

1/What last hope has just given out (cf. 2 Ki. 18:13–20:11)? 2/What tactics does Rabshakeh use to try to soften up Jerusalem before the assault? 3/Between what two men is this preliminary battle for the mind? 4/Whose faith is more keenly at stake than any other in the city? 5/Which of Rabshakeh's foils is most pointed and damaging? 6/How formidable is the defense Jerusalem is able to raise? 7/What kinds of tactics are most devastating in undermining your faith in God? How can you prepare for these attacks?

day 2 Δ *Isaiah 37*
1/What do verses 1-3 reveal about Jerusalem's extremity? 2/In spite of the convincing sound of the enemy's speech and letter, how does Hezekiah describe them? 3/What unpopular person is the king's most trusted confidante? What does the king seek in him? 4/What is Hezekiah concerned about even more than his own safety and survival? 5/How is Hezekiah's faith borne up in the last spirit-breaking hours? 6/In what ways are your times *a day of distress, of rebuke, and of disgrace?* In what ways do you see manifestations of the sovereignty of God in these times? 7/What happens to Assyria? Why?

day 3 Δ *Isaiah 38*
1/What happens to Hezekiah now? How does Isaiah comfort him? 2/On what basis does Hezekiah *beseech* God? 3/How do you consider your requests when they seem to contrast with God's announced intentions? 4/What does Hezekiah want to live to see? Why is life important to him? 5/Why is life important to you? 6/What kinds of events or feelings make you bitter? How can bitterness be for your *welfare?*

day 4 Δ *Isaiah 39*
1/How does Hezekiah's recovery affect the international situation? 2/Contrast Hezekiah's response to the king's son with his earlier concerns (37:20; 38:19-20). What are his interests now? 3/To what extent do you notice a fluctuation in your spiritual interests parallel to the ebb and flow of adversity? 4/What makes you concerned today? Can you determine the motives of

this concern? 5/To what extent does the future influence your daily actions? Why?

day 5 Δ *Isaiah 1–39*
1/Summarize the situation in Israel and in the neighboring nations. 2/How does God look on *a*-the people of Israel, *b*-their activities, and *c*-their city Jerusalem? How do the people regard *a*-themselves, *b*-their city, and *c*-God's assessment of their situation? 3/What joyful hope is interspersed throughout the indictments? How does Isaiah respond to this hope? 4/What qualities of God have been revealed here? 5/To what extent are you aware of God at work in history today? 6/To what extent have you been able to enter into Isaiah's feelings as he struggles with the actual and the ideal situations in his society?

day 6 Δ *Introduction to 1 John*
This letter was probably written by the apostle John (about the same time he wrote his gospel) to counteract false teaching that denied Jesus' incarnation and asserted the supremacy of knowledge over righteousness. *1 John 1:1-4* 1/Read the whole letter as though you have just received it. 2/List the repeated words. 3/Why is John writing this letter? 4/What evidence does John give for the certainty of his presentation? 5/What evidence do you have for Jesus' becoming man? Why is the issue important? 6/What do you have in common with other Christians?

day 7 Δ *1 John 1:5–2:6*
1/How is God like *light?* 2/What are the four false assumptions John warns against? 3/What are the contrasting truths? 4/What then is the basis of fellowship? How is fellowship between individuals related to the fellowship of each one with God? 5/Since John does not teach sinless perfection nor a life of licentiousness, what does he teach? 6/To what extent are you experiencing God's forgiveness when you sin? 7/What criteria does John give for knowing you are a Christian? 8/How did Jesus Christ *walk* (v. 6)?

day 8 Δ *1 John 2:7-17*

1/What is this commandment which is neither old nor new? 2/What does your attitude toward your brother reveal? 3/What are the advantages of being *in the light* (relate to your interpersonal relationships)? the disadvantages of being *in the darkness?* 4/What is the Christian experience of the people to whom John writes? 5/How does love for the world in verses 15-17 differ from the love in verses 7-11? 6/List examples of the three kinds of lust mentioned. To what extent are any present in your life? What will you do about it (cf. v. 12)? 7/How can you tell if you love God?

day 9 Δ *1 John 2:18-29*

1/What are the distinguishing characteristics of antichrists (cf. the teaching in John's day that God could never contaminate himself by becoming human)? 2/To what extent do you know people with similar beliefs on your campus? in your neighborhood? in your church? 3/In contrast what are the characteristics of one who knows God and has eternal life? 4/What is your relationship with God? 5/In the face of false teaching who is the Christian's true teacher? Have you asked him to teach you today? 6/What will *abiding in the Son* mean in the specific attitudes and actions of your life today?

day 10 Δ *1 John 2:29–3:10*

1/What has happened to you because of God's love? 2/How will *seeing God* affect you? What is the result of this hope in your daily living (cf. the teaching in John's day that knowledge is superior to pure living)? 3/What is the source of sin? What is the logical conclusion about a person who habitually sins? 4/Why did Christ become man?

day 11 Δ *1 John 3:11-24*

1/What happens to evil when confronted by righteousness? 2/What are some "civilized" ways to "murder" your brother? 3/How does God regard hatred? 4/In contrast, if you really love your brother, how will you express it? 5/According to this criteria, whom do you love? 6/How do you respond to the fact that God knows everything about your love for your brothers? 7/What characteristics are essential in your life to give you *confidence* before God and the assurance that your prayers will be answered?

day 12 Δ 1 John 4:1-12
1/What three tests does John give for determining whether a person truly knows God? Do you know him? 2/How can you distinguish truth from error? 3/Why is error accepted and propagated? 4/How is God related to *a*-truth, *b*-error, and *c*-love? 5/What is the highest expression of God's love? In what context is his love expressed? 6/If you have submitted to God's love, how has your life been affected?

day 13 Δ 1 John 4:7-21
1/What should be the result of God's love to you? 2/Compare verses 13-14 with 1:1-2. 3/What are the two basic tests for knowing that God abides in your life? Can you have one without the other and truly belong to God? 4/List the effects of love in a person's life. What is the source of this love? 5/What is the source of *confidence* here (relate to the source in 3:21-24)? What is the context here? 6/Why are loving God and hating your brother incompatible?

day 14 Δ 1 John 5:1-12
1/Who is a child of God? 2/How is loving God related to loving the children of God? 3/What is the source of faith? 4/What does John mean by *world* (cf. 2:15-17)? 5/To what extent do you triumphantly overcome the temptations and discouragements of the world? Why? 6/What are the five witnesses in verses 8-9? To what do they all give testimony? 7/How can you know that Jesus is the Son of God? that you have eternal life?

day 15 △ *1 John 5:13-21*
1/Has John's purpose in writing this letter been accomplished in your life? 2/How can you be confident that God will answer your requests (cf. 3:22)? 3/How do you react when you see a brother sin? Why? 4/How are John's emphasis on love for your brother and the recommended prayer in verse 16 related (cf. v. 16b with Luke 12:10)? 5/What three great truths does John *know*? Can you include yourself with John in this knowledge? 6/What kind of idols do you need to keep yourself from today?

day 16 △ *1 John 1–5*
1/Summarize John's arguments and teaching in the two main areas the false teachers attacked. 2/Summarize the *a*-requirements and *b*-results of fellowship with God. 3/How can you renew fellowship with God today? 4/What will your fellowship with God involve in relationships with your brother and sister? your roommate? your neighbor? your employer? 5/How can you recognize false teaching about God and the world? What should you do about false teaching? 6/What is God commanding you to do today? What is your response? Why?

day 17 △ *Introduction to 2 John*
The second letter of John concerns traveling teachers and evangelists who are welcomed into homes as guests because the inns are few and seldom of good repute. 1/How does the author relate himself to those he is writing to? 2/Why does he commend them? What does he find lacking? 3/How are truth and love related in your daily living? 4/Characterize the *deceivers* warned against here. 5/According to John what should be the basis for hospitality to traveling teachers? Why is John concerned that his readers make this distinction? 6/How can you reconcile the attitude toward *deceivers* with John's reminder to *love*? 7/What similar struggle do you find in your attitudes toward such people today?

> *day 18* Δ *Introduction to 3 John*

This letter furthers the discussion of hospitality to strangers. 1/Compare and contrast the *a*-basis and *b*-practical outworking of the hospitality spoken of here with that in *2 John.* 2/List the characteristics that make Gaius so well beloved. 3/What do you think people outside the early church would think of this practice of hospitality? 4/How might people outside the church regard such practice today? 5/In contrast describe Diotrephes as you might find him on campus or in your neighborhood today. What seems to be at the heart of his dissension? 6/What is the testimony concerning Demetrius? How extensive is it? 7/Write out specific ways you can be hospitable in your situation while following truth and love (cf. *2 John*).

> *day 19* Δ *Isaiah 40:1-11*

1/Review and summarize Jerusalem's state of affairs. 2/What message are the prophets to speak to her now? Why? 3/Who is coming to occupy the throne in Jerusalem? What is he like (cf. esp. the verbs)? What will be the result? What should be the people's response? 4/What was Isaiah's whimpering response to the tender voice? Despite Jerusalem's recent deliverance, what has Isaiah clearly heard and bemoaned (cf. 39:6-7)? 5/How would you respond to such a message? 6/Contrast the qualities of the Lord and man. What is the relationship of man's qualities and the Lord's actions? 7/Has the *glory of the Lord* been revealed in your society? Why? 8/What is your part in preparing *the way of the Lord?*

> *day 20* Δ *Isaiah 40:12-31*

1/From high up in the mountain (radio antenna country) comes the voice of Zion. Listen! Contrast this "boasting" for God with the boasting vaunted for Assyria's god-king (chaps. 36–37). 2/To what extent is God threatened by the nations around Israel? by nations today? 3/What have the Israelites seen and understood about God? 4/What do you see when you *lift up your eyes* to God? 5/What is the prophet's answer to the people's complaint that they are disregarded by God? 6/In waiting for the Lord, what suspicions about God and your life do you notice taking root and growing in you? 7/What happens when you are spiritually exhausted? What do you do about it?

day 21 Δ *Isaiah 41:1-20*
1/Who else is to listen to this manifesto? What are they invited to do to settle who really is in charge of the earth? 2/Identify and locate on a map the *one from the east* (cf. 44:28; 45:1-5). What happens as he comes west? How does his coming affect idol manufacturing? 3/To what extent does Israel seem to like being chosen to fight on God's side? Does she feel confident and motivated? 4/How will God help Israel? Why? 5/In what way are you God's *servant?* How can God help you?

day 22 Δ *Isaiah 41:21–42:17*
1/What does God challenge the idols to prove? 2/What is God's proof? 3/How is God going to carry out his proof (cf. 41:2, 15-16, 25)? 4/What specific assignments is the servant given? How is he to achieve this without martial cry? How will he respond to weakness? 5/What makes the difference in the commands to be silent (41:1) and to sing (42:10)? 6/After his prolonged restraint what is God going to do? 7/How can you *give glory to the Lord* today? How do you feel about being God's servant?

day 23 Δ *Isaiah 42:18–43:13*
1/What is the servant (Israel) actually like? 2/What happens to the mass exodus in its panic flight? 3/In what ways have you as God's servant become *robbed, trapped, a prey?* Why? 4/Who is making his point good? 5/Contrast 42:25 with 43:2. What makes the difference? 6/Since God is unwilling to dismiss his recalcitrant servant, to what truth must the people now witness? 7/What knowledge of the kindness and salvation of God is bottled up, silent, inside you? Why?

day 24 Δ *Isaiah 43:14–44:23*

1/In plainest terms what does God say he will do for these people? Why? 2/What is Israel's past history in serving God? To what extent has the servant called for help in following God's orders? Have the people made any servant-like approaches? 3/What have they brought to God so obligingly? What other matter has God as obligingly received and removed? Why? 4/What is Israel's only hope for the future? 5/When recently have you been aware of God's *doing a new thing* in your life? How have you responded? 6/Lest any servant complain of the impassible desert road as an excuse for not returning to Jerusalem, what is plainly promised? 7/Contrast the Lord and gods made from metal and fuel wood. 8/How does a man know which half of a tree he should use to make an idol? 9/How does Isaiah characterize people who make these gods? 10/Which god is worthy of your service? Why?

day 25 Δ *Isaiah 44:24–45:19*

1/What all-embracing truth about himself does God want understood here? 2/What is the irrefutable proof that God's purposes literally materialize? 3/What purposes, secret or otherwise, do you have which compete with or contest God's? 4/What purpose of God's is to be significantly fulfilled in his plans for his servant-nation? 5/How does God parry objections to his choice of a foreigner to do this gracious thing? 6/What obvious problems for residents of Jerusalem do prophecies of the city's rebuilding from depopulated ruins create? 7/To what extent does God accept responsibility for what he does? Does it seem to embarrass God to admit the chaos? 8/From what charge is God "protecting" himself (vv. 18-19)? What plain truth, not hidden in the complexities of international affairs, does God mean to establish thoroughly (vv. 5-6, 18)? 9/What is your responsibility to this God today?

day 26 Δ *Isaiah 45:20–46:13*

1/Confronted with impending international crisis, what truth about God will the surrounding nations be asked to admit, as had

Israel? 2/What same invitation is theirs to heed? 3/To what extent will God's purpose be accomplished? What will happen to Israel? 4/How will the power symbols of mighty Babylon be exposed and shamed? 5/Contrast the uses of *carry* in the discussion of idols and God (46:1-7). 6/What, by all reason and evidence, are the transgressors to know certainly about God? 7/Who really is the recalcitrant? the perseverer? Who stands to win out in the impasse? 8/How does all this relate to your ideas of "The Good Life"?

day 27 △ *Isaiah 47*

1/Whether or not contemporary Israel thinks their God could reduce great Babylon to ignominy, what does Jerusalem's invitation to Babylon suggest will happen? 2/List the metaphors used to depict Babylon's fate. Contrast these pictures with Babylon's self-image. 3/What is Babylon's ultimate folly (cf. vv. 8, 10 with 45:18, 21-22; 46:9)? 4/As she maintains her reckless course, what is Babylon the Great converting her soulish substance into? 5/How do you feel about powerful modern nations? your nation? 6/What does or could make you feel secure? Why?

day 28 △ *Isaiah 48*

1/What are these "big talkers" unwilling to talk about? 2/What do they *a*-know and *b*-not know? 3/On what basis does God go ahead, against their wishes, with plans to act in their favor? 4/To what extent do you hope to escape God's purpose by claiming you don't know it? Why? 5/Who will see that, like it or not, Jerusalem gets back home? 6/What could have been Israel's? 7/Because captivity is rather to their liking, on what explicit command will they hold back? How would they have fared on the return journey? 8/Are you aware of a command you are ignoring or holding back on because obedience seems a hardship to you? What may be the benefits if you obey? the consequences if you disobey?

day 29 △ *Isaiah 49*

1/What is the servant's assignment? 2/Does Isaiah think that he had made much progress toward bringing forth this servant? 3/What other servant is called (v. 5)? How well does he do? 4/What happens to the original servant who has given Isaiah so much trouble (v. 7)? 5/What is God's purpose for other nations? 6/What rebellious dejection of Israel is overruled as groundless? 7/Returning from their scattered graveyards abroad, what **will the** Israelites discover overcrowding their little land (vv. 19-21)? 8/Who is their escort on the return journey? 9/What further objection is dismissed (vv. 24-26)? 10/To what extent do you feel that God has too big a job on his hands? Why?

day 30   Δ   Isaiah 50–51:8

1/In putting their questions back to them, what answer does God give stubborn Israel? What question does he put to them? 2/Do you gather that God's relations with his people are improving as his promises are spelled out? 3/Who agrees to a costly assignment? 4/In less than conciliatory tones what challenge does this listening servant put forth to Israel? 5/What invitation does he extend? To whom (notice the rebuff to interrupting hecklers—50:11)? Since he is to sustain the weary (50:4), to what example of God's activity does he point to encourage them when little of consequence seems to be happening? 7/What further encouragements does he add? 8/In what situations do you feel *weary* and *dismayed?* What perspective do these verses give you (consider your past, present, and future)?

Month 35

day 1   Δ   Isaiah 51:9–52:2

'What cry of help goes back in response to God's call (50:2)? ᵗhat is weighing down the spirits of these weary people? What is ᵗtle rebuke to them? 3/Along with their release what re- ᵗity are they assigned? 4/Whom does God think needs to wake up? Why? What metaphors does he use? 5/What is seriously missing (51:18)? 6/What are the unpleasant reminders of their affliction (cf. vv. 19-21 with v. 9 and 52:1-2)? 7/What are the results of rousing? 8/When have you needed a demonstration of God's wide-awake strength? What inner strength have you discovered?

day 2 Δ *Isaiah 52:1–53:3*

1/Why aren't the people already awake? 2/Since God has not traded them into captivity at any personal profit (cf. 52:3 with 50:1a), how does he regard their slur about not being able to raise capital to reestablish his claim on death's slaves? 3/Since they will not let God act for their benefit, on what basis is he determined to take action? 4/How does this triumph in the debate (vv. 5b-6) strike discouraged Isaiah? 5/How will the people welcome these omens of success? 6/Who will accompany the people out of Babylon? Are they eager to leave? 7/Do they find their leader particularly attractive? 8/To what extent do you find your Lord attractive? What about him irritates you?

day 3 Δ *Isaiah 52:13–53:12*

1/How is God's servant slated to make out? 2/What will the nations—or even any world leaders—say about God's servant not "looking the part" (esp. v. 15)? 3/If the nations see and understand without being told in advance, what is Israel's problem in understanding? 4/To what extent do your opinions about Christ coincide with his revelation of himself? Why? 5/What is so terribly ironic about the situation of 53:4? 6/What is the cause and effect in 53:5? 7/Even though Israel is explicitly told why their leader, God's servant, will not "look the part" of a conquering soldier (53:5-6), will anyone take it to heart (53:8)? 8/What is God's own overruling objective in the matter? With what results? 9/Of the world's vast population, chiefly in graves, what "cut" is God's servant to get from the Great Tyrant over human life? 10/What should be your response to what you have learned today about this servant (cf. 53:12 with 51:17; 52:1, 11)?

day 4 △ Isaiah 54

1/Review the situation in Isaiah 53. Can you possibly restrain yourself from joining in this song here? 2/Describe the condition of Israel in the past. 3/Whose efforts of all the nations have been so futile in populating and possessing the earth (vv. 1-3)? What will happen now? 4/Has God ever really broken with his people and his purposes for them (cf. 50:1)? 5/How does God describe his relationship with them? 6/What are God's feelings toward you? 7/Having been on such shaky foundations for so long, on what lovely rock-basis will the people now rest (vv. 11-12)? 8/What new attitudes are forthcoming? 9/Why won't they need military hardware to survive? 10/To what extent do the qualities of righteousness and truth "protect" you in your daily living?

day 5 △ Isaiah 55

1/To those still reluctant to begin the journey, what call comes from down the road? 2/What are those in lush captivity invited to find out on the wilderness highway to God's city? 3/What kind of witness has David been to the nations in the past? How will the nations repond to Israel now? Why? 4/When God calls Israel first, what should they do? What will they find? 5/With a preferring of his ways to theirs, what will God do to the dry, barren wilderness-barrier to their return? 6/How will they be accompanied back (cf. v. 12 with 52:12)? 7/To what extent can you identify with Israel's comfortable circumstances? 8/How would you respond to a call to forbiding prospects? 9/How do you *come* and *seek* God today?

day 6 △ Isaiah 56–57

1/What obligations do the people have in order to be delivered? 2/To what extent are you obliging in these areas? 3/What people are unsure about whether the invitation embraces them? What do they fear? 4/What can't the bachelor contribute? What can't the proselyte claim? 5/On what basis will God accept them? 6/Relate what God will do for each with the fear each has

expressed. 7/In contrast describe Israel's real impotence and fatu-
ous claims (56:9-12). 8/Who looks the loser in the midst of this
situation? Who is the real loser (57:20-21)?   9/What is so appealing
in their captivity (57:3-10)?   10/What fear has led them to their
unholy style of "righteous doings"?   11/Why is God continuing
with preparations for their true home?   12/To what extent does
God find himself "at home" with you (57:15)?   13/What characteristics of God are revealed here?

   day 7 Δ Isaiah 58
1/What potentially dangerous assignment falls on the servant with
the taught-of-God lips (cf. 50:4)?   2/What kind of people don't
like having their sins rehearsed to them?   3/Listen to their own
rehearsal of their deeds (cf. vv. 2-3a with 57:10b, 12).   4/How
does God interpret their righteousness (vv. 3b-5)?   5/Thoughtfully
consider each part of God's *fast* (cf. 56:1-2). Which are you used to
doing? Which sparingly? Any not at all?   6/How will God show his
acceptance of this *fast* (note esp. the metaphors in vv.
8-12)?   7/How have you experienced this acceptance? What has
been your response?

   day 8 Δ Isaiah 59:1-19
1/What is the cause of separation from God? What is its effect
a-personally and *b*-socially?   2/Characterize your society. Which
injustices most upset you? What has society done to try to right
them? What have you done? What has happened?   3/From Isaiah's
turning the catalog of accusations back to God as a confession,
what do you learn about true piety?   4/Is God content with things
as they are? What is his problem (cf. vv. 15-16a with
51:18)?   5/Who is suddenly on the scene in the crisis? How does
he win over evil?   6/What qualities protect him (cf. 56:1-2;
58:6-14)?   7/To what extent is your "protection" a privately
arranged affair with God that has no relation to daily grievances
and ills in life around you?

day 9 Δ *Isaiah 59:20–60:22*

1/How does the Redeemer expect Israel to demonstrate that they embrace his promise (59:21)? What must the nation do when he arrives (60:1)? 2/How does the promise (60:2-3) involve all other nations? What is their response (note the metaphors)? 3/To what extent do you think these promises and fulfillments will command universal attention from world leaders? 4/Contemplate the expansive details until you feel the writer's mood. 5/Who are being gathered? 6/With all this wealth is it safe to leave the gates open? 7/Will people know where they are going? 8/Summarize the *a*-personal and *b*-societal changes in the presence of the Redeemer. 9/How do you reconcile striving for a better society now and waiting for a revealed glorious society in the future?

day 10 Δ *Isaiah 61*

1/What is the assigned servant's part in the covenant (cf. 59:21 with 52:13; 55:4-5)? How will it transform society? 2/What is the focus of attention? In what areas does the servant invite energies from Israelites loath to leave the boon of captivity in a pluralistic society? 3/What inheritance will all the people of the Lord enjoy? 4/Compare and contrast Israel's ultimate relationship with the nations with their present desire for coexistence with them (cf. 57:3-13). 5/Distinguish the two metaphors (and their sources) used to illustrate righteousness. 6/To what extent are you aware of the source of your righteousness? How do you respond? 7/With all the scoffing going on, how do you imagine the gracious portents of marriage are greeted?

day 11 Δ *Isaiah 62:1–63:6*

1/What are the servant's feelings toward Zion? 2/If the people don't care to be the Lord's, how will the wedding announcement (cf. 61:10) affect them? 3/Why is the servant determined to keep speaking (cf. 62:1 with 59:21)? 4/If the people manage to silence him anyway, who else is to be on the job? 5/What are the *new names* given? 6/Why does the Lord *delight* in you? What is your name? 7/What emotions would speaking with this certainty

(62:8-12) tend to arouse in an other-minded crowd? 8/Who suddenly appears in his wedding outfit? 9/What has he been up to with all Israel's "friends"? Why can't he find any help?

day 12   Δ   Isaiah 63:7–64:12
1/What is the servant resolved to do yet? 2/In what ways has God been good to Israel? 3/As Israel's former behavior testifies, what can the current leader expect to contend with? 4/For what relief does Isaiah cry (note the progression in intensity)? 5/What does Isaiah feel toward God?   What relationship does he reiterate? 6/For whom does Isaiah speak in bearing the burden of the confession? 7/What responsibilities of God does Isaiah claim are unrenounceable (63:14b; 64:2b, 9-12)? 8/What are the desperate needs in your life today? What is your question to God now (cf. 64:12)?

day 13   Δ   Isaiah 65
1/How does God answer Isaiah's questions? Does God feel that the pleading for him to act is justified? 2/What will happen in Israel when God does answer such a prayer? 3/What have you earnestly prayed for recently? On what basis? 4/What partial deliverance will God work now (vv. 8-12)? 5/What relationship to God will the majority forfeit? Why? 6/Whatever the scale and rage of the rebellion now in Jerusalem, what purpose is established beyond their retrieving? 7/Imagine the effect of this newness. How would you feel in such a situation? Why?

day 14   Δ   Isaiah 66
1/What great hypocrisy are the religious zealots carrying on in Jerusalem (cf. 1:12-15)? 2/What does God want from you? 3/What contempt does God show for Israel, his once and future servant? 4/Where is the showdown to take place? 5/What will be unexpected and unusual? With what results (v. 14)? 6/What metaphor is used to picture the event? 7/What will point the way to God clearly? 8/What parting word to his audi-

ence probably clinched Isaiah's destiny as a martyr (as tradition has it)? With what vision did he perish? 9/Do you hope to awaken to such a gathering of nations in worship of the living, true God?

day 15 Δ *Isaiah 40–66*

1/Contrast Jerusalem's present condition with her future glory. 2/Distinguish the redemption from foreign exile and the final redemption of the homeland. 3/What is the servant's part in this ultimate liberation? What qualities enable him to fulfill what servant Israel can't? 4/Account for the shift in these chapters to God's inclusive purposes for the world. What is the result of exclusion from these purposes? 5/What qualities of God have been revealed here? 6/How has your relationship with God deepened as a result of your study of *Isaiah*?

day 16 Δ *Introduction to Philippians*

Paul writes this letter to thank the Philippians for their gifts to him and to adjust some disorders in the church. *Philippians 1:1-11* 1/From the introduction what is important to know about this letter? 2/What does Paul's prayer reveal about his relationship to the Philippians? 3/How would you respond to a person who wrote this to you? 4/List the qualities Paul prays for in the Philippians. 5/Can you list three people that you will pray for like this over the next two weeks? How do you think *a*-you and *b*-they will be changed?

day 17 Δ *Philippians 1:12-18*

1/What two things have resulted from Paul's imprisonment? 2/Do you respond to similar situations which happen to *a*-you and *b*-other Christians with optimism or with pessimism? Why? 3/What does Paul tell about the two motives for preaching? 4/How could you justify any good resulting from preaching out of a motive as described in verse 17? 5/In your dorm, church, or fellowship do you ever have splits over differences of opinions? How can you handle them in view of this passage?

day 18   △   Philippians 1:19-30
1/What is Paul's dilemma in verses 19-26? What are the alternatives?   2/Determine the meaning of *gain* in verse 21 (relate to the context).   3/What seems to be the aim of Paul's ministry?   4/What emotional tones and moods do you find expressed here? Do you think Paul is boasting in verses 24-26? Give reasons.   5/What is Paul urging the Philippians to do in the rest of the chapter?   6/As you review the chapter, can you see two or three dominant themes?   7/What part should *a*-defending the gospel, *b*-suffering, and *c*-unity have in your local fellowship? Why?

day 19   △   Philippians 2:1-11
1/In what ways do verses 1-4 relate to the preceding paragraph?   2/What is the basic principle involved in 1:27 and 2:2?   3/How does *this mind* (v. 5) unite the thought of the rest of the section?   4/What progression do you find in Christ's *a*-humiliation (vv. 5-8) and *b*-exaltation (vv. 9-11)?   5/In what ways is Christ a perfect example of the principle of 1:27?

day 20   △   Philippians 2:12-18
1/In what ways does this passage relate to the preceding paragraph?   2/Relate the imperative of verse 12 to the situation in the Philippian church (cf. 1:28).   3/What is *a*-your and *b*-God's part in restoring unity in your fellowship?   4/In what way is verse 16a related to verses 14-15?   5/How is Paul using himself as an example?   6/What is the essence of his challenge to the Philippians?

day 21   △   Philippians 2:19-30
1/How is Timothy used as an example to the Philippians (cf. 1:27)?   2/What are Paul's motives in sending Timothy?   3/What credentials does Timothy have to recommend him to the Philippians?   4/What qualities does Epaphroditus reveal?   5/What credentials do you have to recommend you to your campus or church? What qualities do you reveal?   6/What does this chapter

add to the themes found in the first chapter? 7/List specific areas
of *action* to make these themes more real for your life.

day 22 Δ *Philippians 3:1-11*

1/Considering the basic themes you have found and the good
examples of chapter 2, explain the two kinds of zeal pictured
here. 2/What phrases does Paul use to describe the two kinds of
people? 3/What gives evidence that these people are or are not
Christians? 4/What does Paul contrast to *flesh?* How does he develop the basis of this idea here? 5/Relate these ideas to *gain* and
loss. 6/What have you counted loss for the surpassing worth of
knowing Christ?

day 23 Δ *Philippians 3:12-16*

1/Why do you think Paul is concerned to show that his zeal isn't
perfect (cf. previous passage)? 2/What is Paul seeking to *make his
own* (relate to the goal of v. 14)? Compare or contrast your intense
desires and goals in life. 3/How does Paul use *forgetting what lies
behind and straining forward to what lies ahead* in his argument? 4/In verses 15-16 how is Paul claiming to be right in his
analysis of the problem? 5/How is he using *mature* here?

day 24 Δ *Philippians 3:17-21*

1/In view of what has preceded in the chapter, how can Paul give
himself as an example? 2/List the phrases that contrast the true
and false person. 3/What additional evidence is here concerning
who the false believers are? 4/Considering the truths of chapters
1–3, how could you become an example for others to follow? 5/How can you recognize *suffering* when it comes to you?
How have you responded to recent suffering on your campus or in
your church? Why?

day 25 Δ *Philippians 4:1-7*

1/In what way does this paragraph begin a summary of what Paul has been trying to say in his letter? 2/Imagine the situation which prompts Paul's mention of the two women. 3/In what way do 1:27 and 2:2 give you help in understanding this paragraph? 4/Trace the theme of *rejoice-joy-thank* through the letter to see what it teaches. Relate it to the themes you have seen previously. 5/What progression do you see in these themes? 6/Think of some practical ways and occasions in your life in which to practice these themes.

day 26 △ *Philippians 4:8-13*
1/How do verses 8-9 help you in your thought life? 2/What do you do with untrue, dishonorable, unjust, impure, etc. thoughts that come into your mind? Why? 3/Which of the principles in verses 11-13 is hardest for you to learn? Why? 4/What is the basis for Paul's statements in this paragraph? Relate verse 13 to verses 11-12.

day 27 △ *Philippians 4:14-23*
1/In what way is the idea of *giving* related to the basic themes of this letter? 2/What makes a gift *acceptable* to God? 3/Summarize the principles and attitudes which Paul urges in this chapter. 4/List several specific, practical courses of *action* that will build the basic themes of this letter into your life. To what extent are you willing to commit yourself to them?

day 28 △ *Introduction to Jonah*
Jonah, a prophet of the Lord in Israel (cf. 2 Ki. 14:25), prophesies while Israel and Judah are divided, prior to Israel's defeat in 721 B.C. by Assyria (Nineveh is its capital). *Jonah 1* 1/What is God asking Jonah to do? 2/Locate the cities on a map. 3/Has God called you to a similar place? What has been your candid response? 4/How does God recapture Jonah's attention? 5/What is God telling you through your present circumstances? 6/How do Jonah's *a*-disobedience and *b*-identity affect the lives of the mari-

ners? 7/What characteristics of *a*-God and *b*-Jonah are obvious in this passage?

day 29 Δ *Jonah 2*

1/What attitudes toward God lead Jonah to pray during his difficult circumstances? 2/What alternatives to prayer do you use when distressed? Why? 3/For what is Jonah thankful in this awkward situation? 4/What *vows* to God will you *pay* today? With what emotion?

day 30 Δ *Jonah 3*

1/Distinguish God's and Jonah's responsibility in the mission to Nineveh. 2/How might God use you to such an extent in your campus, office, or community? 3/What types of people respond to God's message? 4/Have you ever judged certain groups of people as "impossible cases"? Why? 5/What does this chapter reveal about God?

Month 36

day 1 Δ *Jonah 4*

1/Why had Jonah fled to Tarshish in the first place (relate to his concept of God)? 2/In what ways is Jonah's prayer here different from the one in chapter 2? 3/In what kinds of circumstances do you tend to be angry with God? Why? 4/What is Jonah's concern as he sits outside the city (contrast God's chief concern)? 5/How does God use the plant to illustrate the rightness of his actions toward Nineveh? 6/Why doesn't Jonah *pity* the people and animals of Nineveh as he does the plant (relate to his religious belief)? 7/Summarize what God has taught you through your study of this book. What will you do about it?

day 2 Δ *Introduction to Joel*

Joel is apparently among the first of the prophets, a contemporary of Hosea and Amos, living in Jerusalem about the time of Joash or Uzziah. He speaks to Judah. *Joel 1* 1/What has happened in the land? 2/Who is affected? 3/List the responses urged by God. 4/What does this plague preview? In what ways? 5/How is religious worship affected by the plague? 6/What response is urged? 7/How do you respond when circumstances prevent your participation in corporate worship? Why?

day 3 Δ *Joel 2:1-17*

1/What is Joel describing (review 1:4, 6-7)? 2/In what ways does this plague preview the *day of the Lord* (consult the section in the *New Bible Dictionary*)? 3/In the midst of this chaos what does God urge? 4/Why can the people have confidence in this solution? 5/Compare and contrast the purposes of the solemn assemblies in chapters 1 and 2. Who are involved in each (cf. 2:16 with Deut. 24:5 to see the urgency of the assembly)? 6/How do you *rend your heart and not your garments?* 7/How does your concept of God affect the quality of your repentance?

day 4 Δ *Joel 2:18-32*

1/How does this section grow out of yesterday's reading? 2/How has God acted in restoration (note the first person singular verbs)? What is the result (note the second person plural verbs)? What are the imperatives for the people? 3/What time element is involved in the restoration? 4/How is the *day of the Lord* motif woven into the picture (cf. Acts 2:1-21)? 5/How will God's *a-jealousy* and *b-pity* affect you today?

day 5 Δ *Joel 3*

1/How does this chapter add to yesterday's section? to your understanding of the *day of the Lord?* 2/Summarize what you learn here about God's *a*-judgment and *b*-restoration. What metaphors are used? 3/What is the fate of the nations? Do they have ade-

quate defenses (cf. the elaborate systems of nations today)? 4/What is the personal climax to the *day of the Lord* activities (v. 17)? 5/What in your value system reflects God's desire for
a holy people who know him personally? 6/Go back over the
entire book and outline the major *a*-stages of God's actions toward
his people and *b*-concepts of God that come through Joel's prophecy.

day 6 △ Introduction to Zephaniah

Zephaniah prophesies during the reign of Josiah following the long
reign of wicked king Manasseh (cf. 2 Ki. 21–23). *Zephaniah
1* 1/What is significant about Zephaniah's autobiogra-
phy? 2/What is the situation in Jerusalem at this time (cf. v. 5
with 2 Ki. 23:13)? 3/What does the *great day of the Lord* (cf.
Joel) reveal about God's nature? Why is a special day necessary? 4/What kinds and classes of people will be punished (cf. v. 9
with 1 Sam. 5:1-5)? 5/What can you say to people today who
believe and act as if God were morally indifferent (v. 12)?

day 7 △ Zephaniah 2

1/How should the people respond to warning? 2/Locate on a map
the peoples and nations under judgment. 3/Investigate the prosperity of these lands at this time and their subsequent
ruin. 4/What is promised to the remnant of Judah? 5/What are
the characteristics of a faithful remnant in your society? 6/What
is the consequence of taunting the people of the Lord?

day 8 △ Zephaniah 3

1/Summarize the religious climate in Jerusalem. 2/Contrast the
nature of the Lord with the quality of leadership in the
city. 3/What qualities in man does the Lord desire? 4/Which of
these qualities has God begun to develop in your life? 5/What is
the purpose of God's judgment? 6/Summarize the characteristics
of the remnant. 7/What is the tone of verses 14-20? What do these
promises reveal about God's plan for the future?

day 9 Δ Introduction to Nahum
Nahum prophesies the fall of Nineveh, capital of Assyria, the great enemy of Israel. He is a contemporary of Zephaniah and Habakkuk. Investigate the historical setting for this period between 666 B.C. (defeat of Thebes by the Assyrians—3:8-10) and 612 B.C. (fall of Nineveh). Find out who finally defeats Nineveh. *Nahum 1* 1/What is the theme of this poem (acrostic in Hebrew)? 2/What is God like according to Nahum's description? 3/What in nature does Nahum cite to support this view of God? 4/Describe the enemy. Why are they God's enemy? 5/What will happen to them (cf. the metaphors)? How will this affect oppressed Judah (cf. 2:2)? 6/What characterizes an enemy of God today?

day 10 Δ Nahum 2
1/Is Nahum's word to Nineveh characterized by confidence or uncertainty? Support your conclusion. 2/What analogies does Nahum use to describe the defeat of Nineveh? 3/What is the Lord's purpose in the destructive work? 4/What happens to Nineveh's wealth? her prowess? 5/What effect does this action of God have on the people of Nineveh? 6/Why does God seem to delay his discipline?

day 11 Δ Nahum 3
1/What are some symptoms of a sinful nation? 2/In what ways can a person or nation practice *harlotry* today? 3/What analogies describe how God will deal with Nineveh? Describe the battle. 4/What do spectator nations conclude about Nineveh? 5/What basic principles for the God-man relationship do you observe in Nahum's writing? What consequences for ignoring these principles?

day 12 Δ Introduction to Habakkuk
Habakkuk, probably a contemporary of Jeremiah, seeks an explanation of God's justice toward Judah. *Habakkuk 1:1-11* 1/What is

the situation in Judah at this time? 2/What about the situation provokes Habakkuk? 3/Why do you think Habakkuk questions God? 4/What answer does God give him? 5/Compare or contrast your attitudes toward your society with Habakkuk's attitudes. 6/Have you ever asked God the same question? What has been his answer? 7/Characterize the Chaldeans (Babylonians).

day 13 Δ Habakkuk 1:12–2:5

1/What is Habakkuk's concept of God? 2/How does his concept prompt the next question? 3/How does Habakkuk feel God must view man to carry out justice in this way? 4/What answer does God give? 5/List God's promises and warnings. 6/What aspects of this answer are at the heart of God's concern for you today? 7/How has Habakkuk handled his personal questions and complaints? How is his example helpful to you?

day 14 Δ Habakkuk 2:5-20

1/List the *woes*. To whom does each apply? What type of evil does each involve? 2/Which warnings can you apply to your society? 3/What is your responsibility in righting such evils? 4/What are the prospects for justice and righteousness (relate to each *woe*) in the future? 5/What significance does verse 20 have in this message?

day 15 Δ Habakkuk 3

1/Describe Habakkuk's attitude toward God as he prays. 2/Contrast his tone here and in chapter 1. What has Habakkuk learned about God? 3/How does he draw on past history (esp. cf. Ex. 7–15; Judg. 4–5) to build his confidence for the present? 4/What have you learned from *a*-your past experience with God and *b*-your study of *Habakkuk* which applies to your present relationship with God? 5/What is Habakkuk's attitude toward the future? 6/Where does Habakkuk find stability when the world around him is unproductive? 7/In what ways is your relationship to God similar to Habakkuk's?

day 16 △ *Introduction to Obadiah*
Obadiah prophesies doom and a bright future. 1/How does God look upon Edom? Why? 2/List the things in which the people of Edom put their confidence. 3/What will be their punishment? On what basis (cf. Gen. 25:19-34; 36:8-9; Deut. 23:7)? 4/What should be your attitude toward the disaster of other people (even those who have wronged you) and other nations? 5/Contrast Edom's future with the promise given to God's people. 6/List the attributes of God which Obadiah's vision reveals.

day 17 △ *Introduction to Colossians*
Paul counterattacks the false teaching which is confusing the Christians at Colossae by writing about Christ. 1/Skim the letter. 2/List statements made about Christ. 3/Describe problems in the false teaching. 4/List positive commands for the true Christian life. 5/How does your doctrine relate to your daily living?

day 18 △ *Colossians 1:1-8*
1/Define *apostle*. How does Paul greet the Colossians? 2/Describe the Colossian Christians. What is the source of their hope? To what extent are the Christians you know like the Colossian Christians? Are you? 3/What is happening to the gospel? Who had told the Colossians about the gospel? 4/What is Epaphras like? What has he done? Ask God to use you in a similar way.

day 19 △ *Colossians 1:9-14*
1/What do these verses teach about prayer? Who is praying? when? for whom? 2/What are the specific requests to God for the Colossians? What things has God done for them? 3/Why do you pray? Are you praying regularly and specifically for anyone?

day 20 △ *Colossians 1:15-23*
1/Who is Jesus Christ? What is his relation to God, creation (heaven and earth), and the church (note prepositional meanings and verb

tenses)? Worship him.   2/What place does Jesus Christ have in your life today (cf. v. 18b)?   3/What is the purpose of the cross? Define *reconcile.*   4/What is Christ's final goal for you? What is your part in the realization of this goal?

day 21   Δ   *Colossians 1:24-29*

1/Why does Paul rejoice in his sufferings? What is his *divine office?*   2/What is the revealed mystery? To whom is it revealed? What are its implications for you? for your friends?   3/What is Paul's goal in his ministry? How does he accomplish this goal? How can you?

day 22   Δ   *Colossians 2:1-7*

1/Define *strive.* For whom does Paul pray? What specific requests does he make for them?   2/To what *riches* and *treasures* does he refer (cf. vv. 2-3 with 1:27)?   3/Why is Paul writing this letter?   4/What two characteristics of the Colossians make Paul rejoice?   5/How can you *live in* Jesus Christ today? in the future?

day 23   Δ   *Colossians 2:8-15*

1/How can you distinguish true and false teaching?   2/What has happened to you in Christ? Compare verse 9 with 1:19. Of what is Christ the head (cf. 1:18)?   3/Explain the *circumcision of Christ.* What is the relation between circumcision and baptism?   4/What has happened to *a*-you and *b*-principalities and powers because of the cross?   5/What has happened to you because of Jesus' resurrection?

day 24   Δ   *Colossians 2:16-19*

1/How does verse 16 relate to the preceding passages?   2/In what ways are the Colossians being judged and disqualified? How does Paul describe those who advocate such practices? Why are these practices unnecessary?   3/Compare your part in the Christian community with the functioning of a body. Who is your head? How are you nourished? How are you held together? How do you grow?

day 25 △ *Colossians 2:20–3:4*
1/What does this passage teach regarding abstinence from certain things? What is the source of these regulations? In what ways do they appear wise? Why are they valueless? 2/Are you concerned with similar negative regulations? What is the basis of your principles for action? 3/What is the positive answer to the problem of "worldly" regulations (cf. v. 20 with 3:1-4)? What commands are given to the person who has been raised with Christ? 4/Commit your thought life to Jesus Christ today.

day 26 △ *Colossians 3:5-11*
1/How does verse 5 relate to the preceding passages? 2/What sins does Paul enumerate? What is God's attitude toward these sins? What is your attitude? Are any of these sins in your life now? 3/Compare the *old* and *new* natures. What is happening to your new nature in Christ? 4/Relate verse 11 to the various backgrounds of the members of the Christian community.

day 27 △ *Colossians 3:12-17*
1/List the positive commands Paul gives the Colossians. How do they relate to 2:20 and 3:1? 2/What qualities are to be "put on"? List specific situations in which these qualities can show in your life today. 3/What is the example for forgiving one another? 4/In what two places is the peace of Christ to rule? What is the standard for your actions?

day 28 △ *Colossians 3:18–4:6*
1/What is the proper relationship between husband and wife? child and parent? slave and master? List the specific commands and reasons. 2/How do verses 23-25 apply to your work today? 3/How and for what are the Colossians commanded to

pray? 4/List specific situations in which you can obey the commands concerning conduct and conversation.

day 29 Δ Colossians 4:7-18

1/Describe the Christians in this passage. What have they done for Paul? For what purpose does Paul send men with his letter? 2/Compare verses 12-13 with 1:7-8. What are the characteristics of Epaphras' prayer life? Paul's? How do you pray for other Christians? 3/With whom are the Colossians to share this letter? With whom will you share what you have learned from this letter?

day 30 Δ Introduction to Philemon

Paul writes this letter in 61 A.D. while imprisoned in Rome. 1/What do you learn about the characters of Paul, Philemon, and Onesimus from this letter? 2/What is the reason for the letter? 3/Why do you suppose Paul sends Onesimus back? What will the experience do for Onesimus? for Philemon? 4/What is the new relationship between Philemon and Onesimus? 5/Show how this letter works within the system of slavery and yet undermines it at the same time. 6/To what extent do you make restitution to someone you have wronged? To what extent are you willing to forgive and receive one who has wronged you? Why? 7/Do you ask other people to *refresh* you in Christ? Why?

YEAR FOUR

Month 37

day 1 ☐ *Introduction to Jeremiah*
Nearly a hundred years have passed since the northern kingdom collapsed. When God calls Jeremiah to preach to the southern kingdom, it too is in danger. For forty years Jeremiah warns the people and urges a return to faithful obedience and trust. But they do not listen. They have turned away from God . . . and Jeremiah lives to see the result: the destruction of Jerusalem. *Jeremiah 1:1-10* 1/What is Jeremiah's family background? 2/Review the political, social and moral situation before and during Josiah's reign (cf. 1 and 2 Kings, esp. 2 Kings 22:1—23:25). 3/What is the basis of God's task for Jeremiah? 4/What is the basis of Jeremiah's response? 5/Do you know what task God has in mind for you? How has he made it known? What are you doing about it today?

day 2   ☐   *Jeremiah 1:11-19*

1/What two visions does God give to Jeremiah?   2/What attributes of God do you see in verse 12 (the almond tree is first to bud in the spring)?   3/Why is God going to destroy Judah?   4/Why does God expect Jeremiah to obey?   5/How is God going to change Jeremiah's personality?   6/What changes have you seen in yourself recently that have enabled you to better fulfill God's desire for his kingdom?

day 3   ☐   *Jeremiah 2*

1/Compare and contrast the picture of Israel presented in verses 1-3 with the picture drawn in verses 4-13.   2/Who is responsible for the change?   3/What has been every other nation's relationship to its ancestral gods?   4/What are the consequences of the two evils Israel has committed?   5/In what ways has Israel attempted to deal with her evil (esp. vv. 18, 22-24, 35)?   6/In what ways has God tried to correct her?   7/What characteristics do you find in Israel that are common to human nature? With which do you identify?   8/Which are you determined to change? Why? How?

day 4   ☐   *Jeremiah 3:1-4:4*

1/Read the poem of 3:1-5, 19-25 and 4:1-4 aloud. Imagine the feelings of Jeremiah and his listeners.   2/Why do you think the broken loyalties described in verses 1-2 are not re-established easily?   3/How has Judah's sin affected her daily life?   4/Why is Judah's guilt before God greater than that of her sister Israel?   5/What is Judah's attitude toward her own actions?   6/What is involved in true repentance?   7/What will be God's response to such repentance?   8/How will Judah's returning to God affect other nations?   9/How do you know you will be faithful to God?   10/What will you do if you are ever unfaithful?

day 5   ☐   *Jeremiah 4:5-31*

1/What is the tone of this passage?   2/How is the enemy described?   3/Locate Dan and Mount Ephraim on a map. What is their relationship to Jerusalem?   4/What is Jeremiah's response to God's judgment?   5/What will be the enemy's effect on Jerusalem?   6/How does Jeremiah describe Jerusalem's behavior in the crisis?   7/Imagine you are one of the people in Jeremiah's day. What are your concerns? What are your feelings as you listen or hear about his message?

day 6   □   *Jeremiah 5*

1/Recall your feelings of yesterday. To what extent are you included in the indictment?   2/What is the condition of Jerusalem?   What three classes of people does Jeremiah single out because of their evil?   4/What is the attitude of the rank and file in Jerusalem toward their leaders?   5/Compare and contrast God's control over his creation in nature with man's free will.   6/Compare the last half of chapter 5 with 2:11-13; 3:6-10 and 4:18. What theme runs through these passages?   7/How can you distinguish true and false prophets today?

day 7   □   *Jeremiah 6*

1/Locate Tekoa on a map. What is its relation to Jerusalem?   2/What is Jeremiah's interest in the tribe of Benjamin (cf. 1:1)?   3/How does God picture the coming disaster?   4/What will be the plight of unrepentant Judah (examine esp. the metaphors in vv. 24-26)?   5/What is Jeremiah's role in this drama?   6/How would you evaluate the situation in Judah during Jeremiah's time?   7/What parallels do you find with your own nation?   8/What role do you have in your nation's ultimate destruction or salvation?

day 8   □   *Jeremiah 7:1–8:3*

1/Where is Jeremiah as he delivers this address?   2/Why do the people think they are safe from enemies and God here?   3/What is Jeremiah's warning?   4/What social as well as moral evils have been a matter of course (cf. Deut. 14:29; 24:19-22; 27:15-26; Lev. 20:2-5— *queen of heaven* is the Assyro-Babylonian goddess Ishtar)?   5/Why are their ritual sacrifices useless (cf. Is. 1:10-17)?   6/Imagine Jeremiah's feelings as he delivers God's message and as God speaks specifically to him (esp. 7:16, 27).   7/What in your practices and life style must be changed if you are to *truly execute justice* with people in your land?

day 9   □   Jeremiah 8:4–9:1
1/What metaphors does God use to describe Judah's unnatural behavior? Why is it possible for a people to turn away and never repent? 2/How have the scribes deceived the people?   3/When will they come to their senses? What will happen then?   4/Describe Jeremiah's emotional reaction. What causes his conflict (cf. 8:22 with Gen. 37:25)?   5/Try to imagine how you would respond in Jeremiah's position.

day 10   □   Jeremiah 9:2-26
1/How does Jeremiah describe his countrymen? Compare this with the way God describes his people.   2/Describe Jerusalem after its ruin.   3/What characteristics does God ascribe to himself? Compare or contrast these with what has been revealed in the first nine chapters of *Jeremiah* and with what you have experienced.   4/How can one be circumcised but yet uncircumcised (cf. v. 26 with Lev. 19:27)?

day 11   □   Jeremiah 10
1/Contrast the nature of idols with the revealed nature of the Lord (cf. Is. 40:18-20; 44:9-20; 46:5-7).   2/In what specific ways are idols powerless?   3/In view of their worthlessness, how do you account for Judah's preference for them?   4/What metaphor is used to describe the impending doom?   5/What plea does Jeremiah make now? 6/What could be the result of God's anger?   7/To what extent are you responsible for God's present feelings toward you?

day 12   □   Jeremiah 11
1/What are the terms of God's covenant with Judah (cf. Deut. 29—30)?   2/How has Judah kept this covenant?   3/How effective had Josiah's sweeping religious reforms been (cf. v. 10 with 2 Kings 23:34-37)?   4/What does God forbid Jeremiah to do? Why?   5/What do the people in his hometown think about Jeremiah and his message? 6/How does God respond?   7/How do you know you are one of God's people?

day 13 ☐ *Jeremiah 12*
1/With what paradox does Jeremiah confront God? 2/What concept of God is revealed by the confrontation? 3/What answer is offered Jeremiah (vv. 5-6)? 4/Account for the change in verb tenses in verses 7-13. 5/With what metaphors does God describe Judah? 6/What is the future for Judah's evil neighbors? 7/How would you answer *Why does the way of the wicked prosper?* Does God's answer satisfy you?

day 14 ☐ *Jeremiah 13*
1/What does the waistcloth (a thigh-length underskirt) symbolize? 2/What warning is given to Judah in the parable of the wine jars? How will they react in the crisis time? 3/How is their arrogance toward God pictured? 4/What will happen to Judah's leaders (cf. 2 Kings 24:8-9)? 5/Why is doom and desolation to come to Jerusalem? 6/What "little" sins of yours have already become habitual?

day 15 ☐ *Jeremiah 14*
1/Who has been affected by Judah's drought (cf. Deut. 28:23-24)? 2/Imagine Jeremiah's feelings as he intercedes for his people. 3/What is God's answer? 4/Whom does Jeremiah blame for the people's waywardness? What is God's reply? 5/How much do you identify with your nation? To what extent do you intercede for the people of your land? Why?

day 16 ☐ *Jeremiah 15*
1/What is God's response to Jeremiah's plea (cf. Ex. 32:11-14; Num. 14:13-24; Deut. 9:18-20, 25-29; 1 Sam. 7:5-11; 12:19-25)? 2/Account for God's being so adamant here. 3/What destroyers will God send as punishment? 4/What did Manasseh do in Jerusalem (cf. 2 Kings 21:1-18; 23:26-27; 24:3-4)? 5/How does Jeremiah view his place in society? Why? 6/Has God ever been to you like a *deceitful brook* (summer-dry wadi) or *waters that fail*? 7/What promise does God give Jeremiah (cf. v. 12)?

day 17 ☐ *Jeremiah 16*
1/Why is Jeremiah forbidden to marry? 2/What is God taking away from the people? What is left (cf. v. 6 with Deut. 14:1)? 3/What does God tell Jeremiah to say to the people of Judah who demand a reason for their trouble? 4/What is to be the ultimate result of the exile? 5/How do you *know* God's power and might?

day 18 ☐ *Jeremiah 17*
1/What picture does Jeremiah paint in verses 1-2 (cf. Deut. 16:21)? 2/Contrast the man who trusts in man and the man who trusts in God (cf. v. 13 with 2:13). 3/What metaphor does Jeremiah employ to describe a rich man? 4/Imagine your feelings if you had been prophesying disaster for years and nothing had happened. 5/What additional specific chance to repent does Jeremiah relate? 6/Why is the observance of the sabbath so important?

day 19 ☐ *Jeremiah 18*
1/Compare the relationship between a potter and his clay with God and his people. 2/What characteristics of God befit him for such a role? 3/Account for the constant tension of *if* and *I will* of God's judgment (cf. esp. 2:35; 4:1-2; 6:21; 7:5-7, 14-15, 34; 8:10; 9:7, 11, 15-16; 11:11; 12:14-17, 24-26; 17:24-27). 4/What is Jeremiah's reaction to his enemies' attempt to secure treasonable evidence against him (cf. 11:18—12:6; 15:10-21)?

day 20 ☐ *Jeremiah 19*
1/Contrast the acting out of this parable with the actions of 18:1-11. What is its significant difference for the people this time? 2/What does the empty, broken flask symbolize? 3/Who are witnesses? 4/What is in store for the valley of Topheth (cf. 7:31—8:3 with Lev. 20:1-5)? 5/What warning does Jeremiah give the people at the temple? 6/What reaction might be anticipated? 7/To what extent do you deliver God's message in religious circles which have *forsaken* God? Why?

day 21   ☐   *Jeremiah 20*
1/What is Pashhur's status in the temple? What does he do as a result
of Jeremiah's message?   2/How long is Jeremiah confined?   3/What
might Pashhur have expected to accomplish?   4/What will happen to
Pashhur and his house? When will this occur (cf. v. 6 with 14:13-16)?
5/Read verses 7-18 aloud.   6/In what areas and ways does Jeremiah
feel and express his tension?   7/To what extent can you identify with
Jeremiah's position? What have you done?   8/Summarize the people's response toward God and Jeremiah's words during the reign of
Josiah (chaps. 1—10; 18—20) and of Jehoiakim (chaps. 11—17 so far).

day 22   ☐   *Jeremiah 21*
1/Contrast and compare the messages to King Zedekiah (cf. 2 Kings
24:17—25:2), the people of Judah and the house of the king of Judah.
2/Imagine the reaction of each.   3/Account for the change of attitude
toward Jeremiah.   4/What would surrender to the enemy mean?
5/To what extent are the religious leaders responsible for the social
injustice as well as the moral degradation in the land?   6/What is
your understanding of the *justice* God requires?

day 23   ☐   *Jeremiah 22*
1/What is involved in doing *justice and righteousness* (cf. v. 13 with Lev.
19:13)?   2/What are the consequences of obedience? of disobedience?   3/To what extent will other nations understand the consequences?   4/Contrast the life of Josiah with those of his two sons and
grandson (Shallum is Jehoahaz, Coniah is Jehoiachin; cf. 2 Kings
23:28—24:9; 1 Chron. 3:17).   5/What metaphors does God use?
6/What about your life reveals that you *know* God?

day 24   ☐   *Jeremiah 23*
1/Who are the shepherds that have led the flock astray?   2/What is
their fate?   3/Contrast these false shepherds with the character of a
true shepherd.   4/What will be the benefits for the people?   5/Char-
acterize the false prophets and their moral and political messages.
6/Contrast the characteristics, content and reliability of the prophet's

word and God's Word. 7/Why should Jeremiah no longer use the phrase *the burden of the Lord* as part of his proclamations? What will happen to those who still use it? 8/What do you think true prophets of God would be saying now to religious leaders in your land? to you? Why? 9/Compare and contrast the association of religion and politics in Jeremiah's time and today.

day 25 □ *Jeremiah 24*
1/What is the political situation at this time (cf. 2 Kings 24:10-20)? What vision does Jeremiah have? 2/Who are the captives? Why do you suppose they were chosen? 3/What do the figs symbolize? 4/What is the future for those in exile? Why? for King Zedekiah? Why? 5/How do you know God is the Lord? What is your response to him?

day 26 □ *Jeremiah 25:1-11*
1/Summarize Jeremiah's message of twenty-three years (review chaps. 1—24). 2/What has been significant to you about Jeremiah's humanness from his background and personal life? about his consciousness of his role as a prophet of God? about his feelings toward his vocation? 3/What metaphors have been used to describe the people of Judah? to describe God? 4/Whom is Jeremiah addressing here? 5/How have the people responded thus far to the message? 6/What is the consequence? To what extent? 7/Contrast the *servants* of verse 4 with the *servant* of verse 9.

day 27 □ *Jeremiah 25:12-38*
1/What nations are included in the indictments here? Locate as many as possible on a map. 2/What does the wine cup symbolize (cf. 13:12-14)? 3/Where does its journey begin? 4/What poetic images are used of God here? of the people? What are the sound effects? 5/What attributes of God have been revealed thus far in Jeremiah? What has been your response? 6/To what extent are you involved in your nation's destiny? Why?

day 28 ☐ *Introduction to Matthew*
The apostle Matthew writes for the Hebrew Christians in the early
church. He presents Jesus Christ as the Messiah long promised by
God. With its references to Old Testament law and prophecy, this
Gospel effectively links the Old and New Testaments. God's purposes
continue in every century. As you read Matthew, try to imagine your
reactions if you were reading it in the first or second century. *Matthew 1:1-17* 1/What is the significance about Matthew's record of
Christ's genealogy? 2/Into what three sections is it divided?
3/Identify the three women cited. 4/Consider Christ's family tree.
What things do you remember about his ancestors? 5/What is your
lineage? What is your place?

day 29 ☐ *Matthew 1:18-25*
1/In your own words describe the factors surrounding the birth of
Jesus Christ. 2/What does Matthew say about Mary? about Joseph
(a betrothed couple could be separated only by divorce)? 3/What is
Joseph's part in being Jesus' father? 4/Consider the meaning of the
name Emmanuel (cf. Is. 7:14). To what extent is God with you?
5/Why is the child called Jesus? 6/Which prophecy has been fulfilled? 7/How do you answer the charge that Jesus was born out of
wedlock? 8/Where would Matthew have gotten his information?
9/Do you know if anyone ever confronted Jesus directly with the
charge of being illegitimate? Why?

day 30 ☐ *Matthew 2:1-12*
1/How do these Gentile astrologers find out about the birth of a Jew?
2/Contrast the responses of Herod, the wise men and the people of
Jerusalem in anticipating the birth. 3/Investigate the history of
Herod the Great's political life, character and methods of rule. 4/List
everything Herod finds out about the birth of the king of the Jews.
5/Where do the priests and scribes go for their answers to Herod's
questions? Follow their reactions as the gospel unfolds and as things
once revered as prophecies become personal present tense demands.
6/Add to your list of fulfilled prophecies. How has Matthew changed
Micah 5:2? Why, do you think? 7/What do the wise men do when

they reach the end of their quest? 8/How do you know you have found the true God?

Month 38

day 1 ☐ *Matthew 2:13-23*
1/Characterize Joseph's relationship with God (cf. 1:18-25). 2/Imagine his feelings about bringing up a boy who was the Son of God. 3/How do you think the baby affects Mary and Joseph's relationship? 4/Compare and contrast the significance of Egypt in the Old Testament (cf. Ex. 4:21-23; Hos. 11:1) and its purpose here. 5/How seriously does Herod regard the birth of a king of the Jews? To what extent do you think his actions result from revenge on the wise men? 6/How does Matthew view Herod's actions (cf. Jer. 11:4-5; 31:1-25)? 7/How would you feel if your son were hunted to be killed and you knew that other children were being slaughtered on account of him? 8/How is Nazareth regarded (cf. Jn. 1:46)?

day 2 ☐ *Matthew 3:1-17*
1/Who is John the Baptist? What is his relationship to Jesus (skim Lk. 1:5-80; 3:1-17)? 2/What is John's message? 3/How do the people signify their acceptance of his message? 4/Why do you think the Pharisees and Sadducees come for baptism? 5/What is involved in repentance? 6/How does John's baptism differ from Christ's? 7/Why does Jesus come to be baptized? 8/How would you answer the charge that Jesus became the Son of God only when he was baptized (cf. Ps. 2:7; Is. 42:1-4)? 9/How do other people know you are a child of God?

day 3 ☐ *Matthew 4:1-11*
1/How do you think Matthew got this information? 2/Why is Jesus in the wilderness? 3/What aspects of man does the devil attempt to

exploit in his temptations? 4/To what is Satan limited in his offers to Jesus? 5/To what extent does Jesus submit to God's purpose in the temptations (cf. Deut. 8:1-4; 6:16; Ex. 17:1-7)? 6/What phrase is used by both? 7/What difference do you see in their use of Scripture (cf. v. 6 with Ps. 91:11-12)? 8/To what extent are you prone to latch on to lone verses or details and take them out of context? Why? 9/What would be involved in worshiping Satan? 10/How do you worship God? 11/Why do you think the devil left Jesus?

day 4 ☐ *Matthew 4:12-24*
1/Locate Jesus' residence on a map (cf. Is. 9:1-2). 2/What is its relation to Jerusalem? 3/How can a person be in *darkness*? In what areas of your life and circumstances are you in darkness? Why? What light do you need? 4/What is the content of Jesus' preaching? 5/Compare and contrast the preaching and activities of John the Baptist and Jesus. Where do they preach? To whom? 6/How does Jesus call the disciples here? How do they respond? 7/To what extent does God's word come to you in your daily occupations? 8/Locate on a map the extent of Jesus' influence.

day 5 ☐ *Matthew 4:23-7:28*
1/Read this passage rapidly to get the continuity of Christ's teachings. 2/Note the promises, demands and conditions. 3/What is the theme of this teaching? Summarize it briefly in your own words. 4/What is the kingdom of heaven like? 5/What is the *will of the Father*? 6/To what extent do you practice the ethics of the kingdom of God? 7/Compare and contrast the law of Moses (cf. Ex. 20—23) and the teachings of Jesus. 8/What are you saying when you cry *Lord, Lord*?

day 6 ☐ *Matthew 4:23-5:16*
1/For whom is *the gospel of the kingdom* intended? 2/What qualities characterize the blessed? 3/What is the significance of the verb tenses? 4/To what extent do you need God's assistance in your activities and future? 5/To what extent do you *mourn* for your own sin? for the evil of others? for the suffering in the world? 6/To

what extent are you furthering God's purposes for his kingdom in the areas of truth, justice and purity?   7/In what ways are you distinctive from your non-Christian friends? How can you restore your *saltness*? 8/In what ways are you arresting the moral decay surrounding you? 9/What places and situations around you need God's light?

day 7   □   *Matthew 5:17-37*

1/What is Jesus' relation to the law of Moses?   2/In what ways are the scribes and Pharisees righteous? In what ways must you go beyond their limiting regulations?   3/When do you get angry? sarcastic or insulting (cf. Deut. 16:18)? How do you deal with these feelings? Why? 4/What things do people have against you?   5/What part does a right attitude toward Christian brothers play in your service and worship? 6/How do you handle your lust? What rationalizations do you use for its enjoyment?   7/Relate divorce and adultery. How are your views distinctive from national consensus (cf. 5:3-13)?   8/How does Jesus argue that all oaths are binding (cf. Deut. 23:21-23; scribes would disregard oaths if God's name were not actually mentioned)? Then why do you think he condemns taking oaths?   9/What subsequent feelings or circumstances generally cause you to disregard or forget promises? Does a simple yes or no from you carry any weight with your friends?

day 8   □   *Matthew 5:38-48*

1/What is the original intent of the Mosaic law in verse 38 (cf. Ex. 21:22-24; Lev. 24:13-23; Deut. 19:15-21)? in verse 43 (cf. Lev. 19:17-18, 33-34)?   2/How should you treat *a*—a brother and *b*—an enemy who has personally wronged you?   3/How would you apply Jesus' principles here to burglary? legal suit? kidnapping? combat? assault? rape? Why?   4/How do you think God regards such evil (cf. esp. v. 45)?   5/To what extent does your attitude show you are a son of your Father?   6/In what practical ways do you *love* your friends? your acquaintances? people who do not turn you on? your enemies? 7/What exceptions do you make?   8/How can you be perfect (note *therefore*; cf. Lev. 19:2)?

day 9   ☐   *Matthew 6:1-6, 16-18*

1/What does Jesus say about external shows of righteousness? List the examples he uses. Add to this list some that are particular to your circumstances.   2/Reconcile 5:14-16 with today's passage.   3/Contrast the rewards of ostentation and secrecy. What are the limits of each? 4/How do people *reward* you? On what basis? How do you respond to reward?   5/How do you give alms, pray and fast? Why?

day 10   ☐   *Matthew 6:7-15*

1/Why are terminology, phrasing and wordiness in prayer unessential?   2/What does Jesus' example of prayer reveal about its purpose? 3/What indicates that the Lord's prayer is for corporate use?   4/What attitude is revealed toward the Father? his kingdom? his will? our daily situations? List the things for which you are dependent on God. 5/How is God's will done in heaven?   6/How would *a*—your life and *b*—the world be different if God's kingdom would come?   7/For what do you need God's forgiveness?   8/Who has wronged you? In what ways have you forgiven them? Why?   9/Pray this prayer now.

day 11   ☐   *Matthew 6:19-34*

1/Contrast the treasures of earth and heaven. Are they mutually exclusive?   2/How do these principles relate to the good life?   3/What metaphor is used of the *eye*? How can it become darkened (cf. 5:29)? 4/In what ways are you an *eye* to the rest of the world?   5/Contrast the characteristics of the two masters. Which would you rather serve? Why?   6/Describe the concerns of birds and flowers.   7/What things have made you anxious this past week?   8/Who benefits from your anxiousness? Who is hurt? Why?   9/To what extent do you really believe God is interested in your life and daily activities? Why? 10/What are the ultimate goals in your life? How do your daily activities relate to them? To what extent?

day 12   ☐   *Matthew 7:1-12*

1/Define *judgment* here. What is its purpose?   2/Why do we tend to be unaware of our own faults? Account for the hypocrisy of judgment.

3/What should be the greatest deterrent to judgmental attitudes toward others? 4/Distinguish between judging a person and removing a speck from his eye. 5/Write a paraphrase of verse 6. 6/What part does judgment play in this principle? 7/How would swine react to pearls when expecting food? 8/Identify your *pearls.* How do you regard them? 9/What two conditions are given for receiving good gifts (vv. 7, 12)? 10/Compare and contrast *a*—bread and a stone and *b*—a fish and a serpent.

day 13   □   *Matthew 7:12-28*

1/Contrast the description, availability, process and destiny of the two gates. 2/How are false prophets characterized? What is especially deceiving about them? How can they be distinguished eventually? 3/What is the relationship between verbal confession and ethical conduct in your life (cf. chaps. 5—7)? 4/How does the parable of the wise and foolish men illustrate verses 21-23? How does it summarize Jesus' ethical teaching of chapters 5—7? 5/What are the attributes and actions of a wise man? 6/How do the people respond to Jesus' teaching? What authority do you recognize? 7/Summarize the law and the prophets (cf. v. 12 with chaps. 5—7).

day 14   □   *Jeremiah 26*

1/Review the political situation in Judah at this time (cf. 2 Kings 23:24-37). 2/Review the religious and moral problems. 3/What is Jeremiah commissioned to say now (cf. 7:1-15)? 4/How do the priests, cultic prophets and people react to his speech? 5/How do the princes judge the situation? 6/Now, how do the people respond? 7/Compare Micah's prophecy (cf. Mic. 3:12). 8/What was the fate of the prophet Uriah? 9/What saves Jeremiah from an untimely death (cf. 2 Kings 22:12-20)?

day 15   □   *Jeremiah 27*

1/What is the political situation now (cf. 2 Kings 24:10-17)? 2/Explain the presence of envoys in Jerusalem. 3/What does Jeremiah portray to the envoys? 4/Contrast this with the popular message of their prophetic and occult men.   5/What will happen to those who believe the lies?   6/What does God call Nebuchadnezzar (cf. 25:9)? 7/Compare Jeremiah's message to the Gentile kings with his message to *a*—the king of Judah and *b*—the people and priests.   8/Of what significance are the temple vessels (cf. 1 Kings 7:13-51)?

day 16   □   *Jeremiah 28*

1/What is Hananiah's message? How does his message differ from Jeremiah's?   2/What is Jeremiah's response? his criteria for discerning the true prophet?   3/How does Hananiah demonstrate his point? What does his act symbolize?   4/Why do you think Jeremiah *went his way* after the confrontation?   5/What is Jeremiah's ultimate answer to Hananiah?   6/How do you know that messages from God to you are true? What messages have you questioned lately? How were they settled?   7/How do you judge what other people claim to have received from God? Why?

day 17   □   *Jeremiah 29*

1/What is the content of Jeremiah's letter to the Jews exiled in Babylon? What should be their attitude toward their new home?   2/How long will these Jews remain in exile? What will be their destiny? 3/What will happen to their kinsmen who did not voluntarily submit to Babylon?   4/What will be the consequence of Ahab's and Zedekiah's prophecies?   5/What recommends God to be a judge of people? 6/What is Shemaiah's complaint to Zephaniah about Jeremiah? 7/What is Zephaniah's position (cf. 20:1-2)?   8/What is Jeremiah's answer?

day 18   □   *Jeremiah 30*

1/What is God's promise to both Israel and Judah?   2/What images are used to depict the agony of the captivity?   3/How will they be restored?   4/What will be the political, religious, economic and social situations then in Israel and Judah?   5/What will be the final situation of the neighboring countries?   6/Which attributes of God revealed here have you experienced and found true in your individual and corporate life?

day 19   □   *Jeremiah 31*

1/Read verses 1-25 aloud. What emotional atmosphere is created with Jeremiah's dream?   2/How does he envision the time of restoration? 3/How would the exiled Jews respond to a vision like this?   4/What characteristics of God are shown to his people?   5/How will they respond to him?   6/What will be the terms of the new covenant? 7/What is the great difference between the old and the new covenants in regard to forgiveness for deliberate sin (cf. Num. 15:27-31)? in regard to personal instead of corporate responsibility for sin?

day 20   □   *Jeremiah 32*

1/What is the historical setting of this chapter?   2/What might Zedekiah have feared from pro-Babylonian Jeremiah?   3/What is the significance of Jeremiah's buying a field now under enemy possession (cf. Lev. 25:25)?   4/In his prayer, what characteristics does Jeremiah attribute to God?   5/In your own words, summarize Judah's history as unfolded in God's answer.   6/However, what is Judah's future? 7/To what extent is what God requires of his people an extension of his character (esp. vv. 40-41)?   8/To what extent does God's justice involve evil and good? To whom?

day 21   □   *Jeremiah 33*

1/What is Jeremiah's situation in this chapter?   2/How anxious is God to reveal the future to Jeremiah?   3/What does God promise to do to Judah?   4/What will be involved in the restored true worship of God? 5/How strong is the covenant with David (cf. 23:5; 2 Sam. 7:12-16)? 6/Compare God's faithfulness with the consistency and order of nature (cf. 31:35-37).   7/List specific things you have thanked God for in the past week. What were your reasons?

day 22 ☐ *Jeremiah 34*

1/What is the situation in Jerusalem? 2/What will happen to King Zedekiah (cf. 32:3-5)? Who controls the historical events of the time? 3/What covenant does the king make with the people of Jerusalem? Where is it made? What might have been the motivation? 4/What historical precedent does this covenant have (cf. Deut. 15:12-15)? 5/In what two ways do the people violate the covenant (cf. v. 16 with Ex. 20:7)? 6/What are the immediate consequences? 7/What motivates you to make promises (covenants, pacts, etc.) to God? To what extent do you remember and carry out promises made in crisis situations?

day 23 ☐ *Jeremiah 35*

1/What incident does Jeremiah recall? 2/Who witnesses the object lesson? 3/Compare and contrast the nomad Rechabites with the citizens of Jerusalem. What has been their past relationship (cf. Judg. 1:16; 1 Chron. 2:55; 1 Sam. 15:6)? 4/Why is God going to bless the descendants of Jonadab? 5/How do you explain your behavior? What do you say when tempted to disregard your behavioral values? Why? 6/What is the significance of the placement of this chapter in the book of Jeremiah?

day 24 ☐ *Jeremiah 36 and 45*

1/How have Jeremiah's words survived in writing? 2/What is the date of the first compilation (cf. 2 Kings 23:34—24:5)? What is the purpose? 3/What kind of man is Baruch (cf. 32:12-15)? What is his role in writing and reading the scroll? Why? 4/What is his reaction to what he has been writing (chap. 45)? 5/What is God's stake in the destruction? 6/Trace the progression of Baruch's audience and their responses (cf. chap. 26; esp. v. 12 with 26:22). 7/Contrast Josiah's and his son's responses to God's word (cf. 2 Kings 22:11—23:25). 8/What is added to the second draft of the scroll? Why? 9/How do you think the leaders of your nation would respond to a reading of God's word about the destruction of their nation? Why? 10/How can you distinguish God's word from either a placating or alarmist viewpoint?

day 25 ☐ *Jeremiah 37*
1/What is the situation now in Jerusalem (cf. 2 Kings 24:8—25:7)?
2/What is Zedekiah's intention in sending for Jeremiah (cf. chap. 21)?
3/How does Jeremiah portray the fate of Jerusalem?   4/What is the
charge against Jeremiah (cf. 32:1-5)?   5/Imagine Jeremiah's feelings
in confinement and when the king sends for him (cf. 1:17-19).
6/What is his message? his appeal (cf. chap. 28; Deut. 18:15-22)?
7/How is Jeremiah provided for?   8/What prediction becomes a
reality (cf. 24:8-10)?   9/To what extent are you willing to accept the
consequences of speaking God's message when it is unpopular or
considered treason? Why?

day 26 ☐ *Jeremiah 38:1-28; 39:15-18*
1/Compare and contrast the events of this chapter with chapter 37.
Give evidence to support whether they are the same or different
events.   2/What have been Jucal's (37:3) and Pashhur's (21:1) past
associations with Jeremiah?   3/What have been the effects of Jeremiah's continuing message (cf. 21:8-10)?   4/When have you found
God's words to have a demoralizing effect on you? Why?   5/What
would you, in Jeremiah's situation, feel and say to God?   6/What are
the alternatives for Zedekiah (surrendering rebel kings were usually
mutilated and killed)?   7/Summarize the king's qualities of character
as seen in his reactions to economic, political and religious pressures.
8/What is the relationship between religious vision and political sense?
Which has priority in your government? Why?   9/How will Ebed-
melech be rewarded for his actions toward Jeremiah?   10/What does
he fear (cf. 38:9)?

day 27 ☐ *Jeremiah 39:1-14*
1/How long has the city been under siege?   2/What finally happens
(cf. 2 Kings 25:1-12)?   3/Who is left in Jerusalem?   4/Contrast
Zedekiah's fears (38:19) with his actual fate (cf. 38:21-23).   5/Imag-
ine Jeremiah's feelings as he is carried away with the rest of the people.   6/Who intervenes?   7/Summarize Jeremiah's message of
destruction. How has he survived the attempts to silence him (cf.
chap. 1)?   8/Characterize his awareness of his role as a prophet.

377

9/How is he rewarded?   10/To what extent do you trust God's words before you have seen the results or outcome? Why?

day 28 □ *Jeremiah 40*

1/To what extent do the Chaldeans understand the causes of Jerusalem's fall?   2/How do they regard Jeremiah (cf. vv. 2-5 with 39:12)? 3/Contrast their regard for a prophet of God with Israel's regard for God's words.   4/To what extent has Jeremiah been vindicated in his fellow countrymen's eyes?   5/How do you handle vindication after you have been humiliated, abused and disbelieved? Why?   6/What steps does Gedaliah take to re-establish stability and prosperity in the land (cf. 2 Kings 25:22-24)? To what extent do the refugees trust him? 7/How are Johanan and Ishmael related (v. 8)?   8/What might have been Ishmael's motives (cf. 2 Kings 25:25)?

day 29 □ *Jeremiah 41*

1/Who are involved in the execution of the plot? What is the extent of their atrocities?   2/Locate the towns on a map (Mizpah may have been 4 to 8 miles north of Jerusalem).   3/How long has the pilgrims' journey been? What is its purpose?   4/Account for Ishmael's motives in the slaughter of the pilgrims and abduction of the settlers.   5/What is his destination?   6/How do you think Johanan finds out about Ishmael's actions?   7/What is the situation now facing Johanan? 8/Imagine Jeremiah's feelings in all of this.   9/How do you feel when your circumstances are controlled by other people? Why?   10/Have you ever had to plead for your life?

day 30 □ *Jeremiah 42*

1/How long has it been since Jeremiah has prophesied?   2/Who confronts him now? With what request? What is their intention?   3/What will the people have to face if they stay and try to live in Israel? if they begin the trip to Egypt?   4/What does God promise if they go to live in Egypt?   5/Account for the change of tone in verse 18.   6/What is the consequence of disobeying the voice of the Lord?   7/To what ex-

tent are you prepared to obey God without preconceived notions?
8/How do you know you are totally open to God's leading?

Month 39

day 1   □   *Jeremiah 43*
1/Account for the accusations against Jeremiah in view of his recently
fulfilled prophecies. What is the extent of the disbelief?   2/Why do
you think the leaders suspect Baruch?   3/In view of his declarations
(42:18-22), how do you account for Jeremiah's presence in Egypt?
4/Where does Jeremiah perform his parable? When?   5/Where do
the Israelites go for protection? How successful will they be? Why?
6/What metaphor is used to describe the extent of the conquest?
7/Imagine the response of the men of Judah now that they have
chosen the course of action.   8/What do you do when you realize you
have made a disastrous decision?

day 2   □   *Jeremiah 44*
1/What is the extent of Jewish colonization in Egypt?   2/What consequences of rebellion are plainly visible to all?   3/What is so serious
about their continuing disobedience (vv. 7-8)?   4/To what extent do
they carry on the tradition of past generations?   5/What are the
specific charges?   6/With which could you be justly charged?
7/What reasons would you give to God's question Why?   8/How do
you account for the *evil* (vv. 2, 11) God determines against Israel?
9/To what do the people attribute their prosperity? their hardships?
10/How do the women implicate their husbands?   11/Contrast the
people's and Jeremiah's explanations for the evil that has come on
them (cf. 7:18).   12/What does their future hold?   13/What reasons
do you give others to explain hard times that come to you? Why?

day 3   ☐   *Jeremiah 45:1–46:28*

1/What seems to be the situation that prompts God's message to Baruch via Jeremiah?   2/What does this special personal message probably mean to Baruch?   3/Locate the battle scene on a map (46:2). 4/Contrast the Egyptian confidence (vv. 3-4, 8-9) with their humiliation (vv. 5-6, 10-12).   5/What nations supply the Egyptian forces? 6/How do Pharaoh and his gods fare (vv. 15, 22, 25)?   7/What is the significance of Pharaoh's nickname in verse 17 (cf. v. 8)?   8/What metaphors are used of Egypt? of Babylon?   9/To what extent are you God's *servant*? What are your spiritual obligations?   10/How has God chastened you? For what purpose? Whom has he used to accomplish his purposes?

day 4   ☐   *Jeremiah 47*

1/What image depicts the destruction of the Philistines?   2/What will the calamity mean for family relationships?   3/How effective will the ally help be?   4/Locate the devastated cities on a map.   5/How extensive will the destruction be?   6/Account for the Babylonian strength. What territory do they gain?   7/How do you explain God's use of pagan nations to accomplish his purposes?   8/To what extent does he work in a similar way today? Why?

day 5   ☐   *Jeremiah 48*

1/Locate the land of Moab on a map. What natural resources and products add to its desirability?   2/What is the Moabites' ancestry (cf. Gen. 19:36-37)?   3/What has been the relationship of Israel and Moab (cf. Num. 25:1-3; Judg. 3:12-30; 1 Sam. 14:47-48; 2 Sam. 8:1-2)? 4/Who had been given these cities as an inheritance (cf. Num. 32:33-38; Josh. 13:15-23)?   5/How do the land, gods (cf. 2 Kings 23:13) and people fare?   6/How can you be described as *at ease*? What are the dangers of such a state? Why?   7/Contrast the strength and pride of Moab with its fate. Describe the metaphors used.   8/Whom do you tend to deride? Why?   9/Characterize the conquerors.   10/What is the reason for Moab's fall (cf. Num. 21:26—24:25)?   11/What is the relationship between God's judgment and his mercy?

day 6   □   *Jeremiah 49*

1/What countries and tribes are judged in this chapter? Locate each area and major cities on a map.   2/What has been their past relationship with Israel (cf. Gen. 19:38; 1 Kings 11:5; Num. 20:14-21; 1 Kings 15:16-22; Is. 21:16-17; 60:7; Judg. 6:3 with 25:15-29)?   3/What are the charges against each country?   4/How is God's judgment personified? How certain is it?   5/Describe the emotions and actions of the people as judgment comes.   6/To what extent can your nation be described as *at ease, that dwells securely?*   7/What is the *pride of your heart?*

day 7   □   *Jeremiah 50*

1/What is eventually in store for Babylon? How has God used this empire in the past?   2/How will God continue to assert his supremacy over other gods?   3/Describe the extent of the punishment Babylon will be given.   4/How will the Israelites react to the destruction of their conqueror?   5/How have past enemies understood their responsibility for Israel's destruction?   6/How would your nation fare if others did to her *as she has done?*   7/Contrast the future situation of Israel with Jeremiah's diatribes against her.   8/Characterize Babylon's destroyer (cf. 6:22-24).   9/How do you justify God's use of violence and force to accomplish his purposes?

day 8   □   *Jeremiah 51*

1/What metaphors are used to depict Babylon's destroyer? How extensive is the destroyer's power (vv. 27-28)?   2/How would you explain Babylon's guilt in view of God's use of her?   3/How has Babylon treated Israel?   4/What command is given to the Israelites (cf. 50:8)?   5/Contrast what has happened to the Lord during Israel's punishment and what will happen to other national gods during their country's punishment (cf. chaps. 46—50). Account for the difference.   6/How extensive is the damage to the Chaldean countryside?   7/What qualities of God are revealed in his building up and overthrowing of nations?   8/What is the date of these prophecies?   9/Who is Seraiah (cf. 32:12)?

day 9 ☐ *Jeremiah 52*

1/Review the historical setting for Jeremiah's message. 2/Characterize his awareness of his role in God's plans. 3/What is your place and purpose in God's plan for today's world? 4/Enumerate the momentous historical events and powers in the Near East which Jeremiah has witnessed. 5/Summarize his understanding of the political, social, religious and moral conditions of the time. 6/What has been Israel's regard for her covenant with God? Why? 7/What does Jeremiah predict for Israel and the surrounding nations? What prophecies does he see fulfilled?

day 10 ☐ *Introduction to Lamentations*

In the wake of Jerusalem's collapse when the Babylonian armies devastated her in 586 B.C., this book mourns the suffering sin has brought—and affirms the mercy of God in the midst of bitter circumstances. These five poems are acrostics and have a dirge-like rhythm in the Hebrew. As you read, picture your nation trampled and your countrymen taken away prisoners. How would such a situation affect your understanding of God? *Lamentations 1:1-11* 1/Read the poetry aloud. What is the mood? 2/How is Jerusalem depicted? 3/Contrast her before and after pictures. 4/What has happened to her lovers and friends (cf. Jer. 2:33—3:5; 18:21; 27:3)? to her princes (cf. Jer. 39:4-5)? 5/Why have Jerusalem's lovers rejected her? What have been the consequences of her indifference? 6/In what areas of life do you tend to ignore the consequences of unethical behavior? Why? Which do you excuse in others? Why? 7/How do others react to the exposure of your sin? 8/What has happened to Jerusalem's sacred places (cf. v. 10 with Jer. 52:17-23)? 9/How does she address the Lord now? 10/How do you approach God after you have sinned?

day 11 ☐ *Lamentations 1:12-22*

1/To whom does the grieving woman appeal? Why? 2/What imperatives does she use (vv. 12, 18, 20)? 3/What can those who observe learn from her sorrow? 4/What images show the extent of the suffering? 5/Who is the agent of destruction? 6/What is the basis of her claim to virginity (cf. vv. 8-9 with Jer. 2:2-3)? How has she become

contaminated? 7/What do you do when you become *filthy*? 8/To
what extent does she accept her fate? Why? 9/Contrast her intent
here with that portrayed in Jeremiah 44. 10/Account for the attitude of the enemies toward Jerusalem's suffering. 11/To what
extent does revenge gratify you? Why? 12/What is the cause and
effect of sin? 13/On what basis does Jerusalem pray for divine vengeance? Why is she concerned about retribution? 14/How do you
react when others gloat over your punishment? Why?

day 12 □ *Lamentations 2:1-13*
1/Who is responsible for the devastation? 2/How is his wrath pictured (esp. vv. 1-2, 4, 8, 13)? What is the effect of its unleashing?
3/What verbs show the extent of its power? 4/What is left in its wake?
5/What has happened to the structure of religious life in Jerusalem?
6/To what extent do you depend on ritual or religious procedure and
other people in your relationship with God? Why? 7/How do you
think God feels about his victory? 8/Can you picture the scene of
suspended life in the city? 9/What are the consequences of the
adults' actions for their children? 10/How do you live for your children's sake?

day 13 □ *Lamentations 2:14-22*
1/What have the prophets seen (cf. Jer. 14:13-16; 27:8—28:17)?
2/To what extent do the enemies savor revenge (cf. vv. 15-16 with
1:2, 21)? 3/What threat has the Lord made (cf. Lev. 26:14-39)?
4/To what extent do you understand the consequences of sin?
5/What has happened to the Lord's chosen people? 6/What is particularly devastating about the slaughter and deportation of the youth
(cf. v. 21 with 1:4, 15, 18)?

day 14 □ *Lamentations 3:1-20*
1/How does the poetic structure in this lament differ from the first
two chapters? 2/What is the point of view here? 3/Read verses 1-20
aloud. To what extent can you identify with the feelings? 4/When
have you experienced affliction? What has been your response?

5/What images depict the effects of God's wrath (underline the verbs)? its personification?

day 15   ☐   Lamentations 3:1-39
1/Read the entire section aloud. Account for the change in mood and response.   2/On what basis is there hope for restoration?   3/What is required to experience it?   4/In what ways have you learned submission to God?   5/Relate judgment and love.   6/What are the basic rights of man? What are you doing to see that these rights are assured to *all the prisoners of the earth*?   7/Who arbitrates all human affairs? 8/How do you respond to unjust accusation? just accusation? Why? 9/Compare or contrast God's faithfulness to you and your faithfulness to God.

day 16   ☐   Lamentations 3:40-66
1/What is the responsibility of people for God's redemption? 2/What is revealed about how God reacts to sin? What images are used?   3/How is the nation's predicament described?   4/Account for God's different responses in verses 43-45 and 55-58.   5/Account for God's distance (v. 50) and nearness (v. 57).   6/What is especially humiliating about the aftermath of war?   7/What has been God's promise about Israel's enemies (cf. Deut. 32:34-43; Jer. 51:34-44)? about Israel because of her enemies (cf. Jer. 30:17; 49:1-2)?   8/How do you know your enemies will not ultimately triumph?   9/When have you recently heard God say, "Do not fear!"? What has been your response?

day 17   ☐   Lamentations 4:1-22
1/Contrast the before and after conditions of Zion.   2/What was her former self-estimate?   3/How powerful and safe do you consider your nation? Why?   4/Enumerate the political, economic, social, psychological and spiritual repercussions of Israel's rude awakening (cf. 1:7; 2:5-13, 19-21; 3:13-18 with Jer. 19:7-9).   5/Account for the degree of punishment she experiences (cf. the result of surrender in Jer. 21:8-10).   6/What occasions the exposure of the false leaders (cf. Jer.

8:10; 23:11, 13)?   7/What do verses 17-20 add to the account of the conditions of the poor people left in Jerusalem (cf. Jer. 39:10) and those who try to escape?   8/Who is the Lord's anointed (cf. Jer. 52:7-11)?   9/How does Edom share the joy of Israel's enemies? To what extent will she share Israel's grief?   10/To what extent do you try to hide your sins from God? Why?

day 18   □   *Lamentations 5:1-22*

1/What is the Lord to *remember* and *behold*?   2/What has been Israel's inheritance (cf. Lev. 20:24)?   3/How do they explain their desire to ally with Egypt or Babylon here?   4/What has Jeremiah stressed about the present generation's responsibility for its sin (cf. Jer. 31: 29-30)? Why is the statement in verse 7 also true (cf. Ex. 20:4-5)?   5/Summarize the political, moral, economic and emotional disruptions of the captivity (cf. with the actions of aggressor nations in war today).   6/Relate war and lack of respect.   7/On what basis is the appeal to God made?   8/Contrast the Lord's reign with the royal status of Israel at this time (vv. 12, 16-17).   9/Account for the Lord's rejection and restoration of Israel.   10/How have you been restored and renewed?

day 19   □   *Jeremiah and Lamentations*

1/Review the life and ministry of Jeremiah. What have been his feelings and response to God throughout his life?   2/Contrast the past, present and future of Israel in each of these areas: religious, political, economic, social and moral (cf. 1 and 2 Sam.; 1 and 2 Kings).   3/Summarize the major causes for Israel's downfall. Who is responsible?   4/What qualities of God and his dealings with nations and people have you seen here?   5/What is your response to this God?

day 20   □   *Matthew 8:1-17*

1/Account for Jesus' fame (cf. 4:24-25).   2/Where is he now?   3/Characterize the three persons involved in these three miracles. In what ways are they different? alike?   4/Imagine the leper's feelings when Jesus touches him.   5/What must he do to certify his healing (cf. Lev. 13—14)?   6/What is the servant's condition?   7/What does the centurion understand about Jesus' authority?   8/How does this Gentile have such faith?   9/What is the basis of participating in the kingdom of heaven?   10/How do you understand and show your faith in God?   11/What evidences the cure of Peter's mother-in-law? 12/How does Matthew apply Isaiah's prophecy (cf. Is. 53:4)?

day 21   □   Matthew 8:18-34
1/Why do you think Jesus leaves the crowds?   2/How do you express your desire to follow Jesus?   3/To what extent do you consider yourself settled? Why?   4/What obligations have highest priority in your life?   5/What form does your "let me first" take?   6/What evidence is there that the disciples' faith is growing? Why the rebuke? What indicates their need for further growth?   7/What sort of man is Jesus? 8/Who recognizes Jesus as the Son of God? What is his response? 9/What events precede the people's begging?   10/What happens to the demons? to the swine? to the demoniacs?   11/When have you been convinced of the supernatural power of God? What has been your response?

day 22   □   Matthew 9:1-8
1/What is Jesus' *own city*?   2/Who is involved in the healing here? Who are witnesses?   3/Imagine the paralytic's feelings. What do you suppose he is hoping?   4/What is the scribes' reaction?   5/Imagine your response there now.   6/How would you answer Jesus' question in verse 5?   7/How does Christ answer their charge of blasphemy? 8/What authority is involved in forgiveness?   9/Does the crowd think Jesus is blaspheming?   10/Why is forgiveness important to you?

day 23   □   Matthew 9:9-17
1/Describe the rapport between Jesus and sinners. Why is this possible?   2/How do sinners react to you? Why?   3/What are the political implications of tax collecting at this time?   4/How would the Pharisees identify *sinners*?   5/What have the Pharisees misunderstood about the law?   6/Are you well or sick?   7/What is the purpose of

fasting?   8/What would the Jews do if they knew the Messiah had come among them?   9/Have you ever wondered about someone's lack of "spirituality"?   10/What do the Pharisees and the disciples of John have in common?   11/What does Jesus understand about his future?   12/Describe the old and new Israel. What situation does the new one require?   13/Is your situation old or new? Why? How do you handle it?

day 24   □   *Matthew 9:18-34*
1/List the people who approach Jesus in this passage. What does each want?   2/How do they approach Jesus?   3/In what terms do they state their requests? To what extent do they recognize who he is?   4/How does Jesus respond in each situation? In what ways do his actions toward each differ? Why, do you think?   5/What complications come up?   6/Compare and contrast the reactions of the bystanders.   7/On what basis does Jesus heal? What part does the sick person play in his or her healing?   8/How do you answer the charge that the healings are only psychological?   9/How would you approach Jesus if you needed healing? Why?

day 25   □   *Matthew 9:35-10:4*
1/Categorize Jesus' activities. How are they inseparable?   2/What is *the gospel of the kingdom*?   3/What is Jesus' reaction to the crowds?   4/To what extent do you think of the crowds around you as harassed and helpless—or do you feel as if you are the harassed one?   5/Are you praying for laborers?   6/What might be the answer to this prayer?   7/Recall your first meeting with some of the disciples. What have they seen and learned?   8/How does their *authority* relate to their responsibility?   9/How do you think they are given this authority?   10/How would you feel if someone gave you authority like this? Why?

day 26   □   *Matthew 10:5-15*
1/Who is to know first about the coming of the kingdom? Why?
2/What is involved in the coming of the kingdom (cf. Is. 29:18-19;

35:5-6; 61:1)?   3/What have the disciples *received* (v. 8)?   4/Which of Jesus' instructions for the disciples are temporary? List these. 5/What general principles given here are applicable to your present situation? to your thinking about future possibilities?   6/Distinguish the actions commanded for those who accept and reject the message of the kingdom.   7/What happens when you tell someone about the kingdom of heaven?

day 27   ☐   *Matthew 10:16-23*
1/List the commands Jesus gives his disciples.   2/List the warnings. 3/Why will they be persecuted? How are the disciples to react? 4/What words of comfort are included?   5/Compare and contrast wisdom and innocence.   6/To what extent are you finding the Lord's promises true in your experience?   7/What divisions does the message of the kingdom cause? Why?   8/Describe contemporary feelings about the message of the kingdom.   9'How do people respond to you when you are loyal to Jesus' name? Why, do you think?

day 28   ☐   *Matthew 10:24-33*
1/Why does Jesus say the disciples can expect trouble? Remember his warning here as the rest of Matthew's account unfolds.   2/To what extent do you act according to your position in the Christian family (v. 24)? Yet how are you treated (vv. 30-31)?   3/What is *enough*? Why? 4/How does Jesus understand his place in God's plan (cf. 9:34)? 5/What is the Christian's basic advantage in the warfare between God and the ungodly?   6/What result should this have in your emotional-physical life (vv. 26-28)?   7/Whom do you fear? Why?   8/How do you *acknowledge* Jesus *before men*? Why? How do you deny him? When? Why?   9/What major strategy is being taught in this chapter?

day 29   ☐   *Matthew 10:34–11:1*
1/What is Jesus' intention in coming to earth (cf. 5:9; Is. 9:6)? What are the consequences of his coming? Why? 2/What divisions have you experienced because of Jesus' coming?   3/How can you love a member of your family *more than* Jesus?   4/To what extent are you *worthy*

of Jesus?   5/Why is life under Jesus' orders a paradox?   6/Have you
ever saved your life by denying your faith?   7/What is God's attitude
toward those who show kindness to a true prophet and righteous man
(the reward is according to the merit of the prophet or man)?   8/Do
you think the converse is true, i.e., that there is less reward or no reward for befriending a false prophet or unrighteous man (cf. Jeremiah's denunciations of false prophets)?   9/Why then is even an "insignificant" kindness to one of Jesus' "insignificant" disciples rewarded?

day 30   □   Matthew 11:2-19
1/Imagine John's feelings in prison.   2/How could he get information about Jesus' activities?   3/How have you asked and answered
John's question?   4/What evidence have you seen and heard?
5/When do you question a previous affirmative answer (cf. 3:16-17)?
6/When have you lost confidence in Jesus? Why? What has restored
your confidence?   7/How have the people regarded John?   8/How
does Jesus affirm their regard?   9/What is John the Baptist's role in
history (cf. Mal. 3:1; 4:5-6)? How is it unique from that of the Old
Testament prophets? from the New Testament disciples?   10/Com-
pare and contrast John the Baptist and Elijah.   11/How are Jesus'
contemporaries like children playing games?   12/How do Jesus and
John the Baptist differ?   13/How do the people react to each?
14/How is each vindicated?   15/What is your personality type? How
do you fit into God's plan?

Month 40

day 1   □   Matthew 11:20-30
1/List the towns which Jesus talks about here. What does he say about
each? Locate each on a map.   2/What appears to be one reason for
Jesus' mighty works? What is your response to his works?   3/Why do
you think the present cities reject Jesus' message of repentance?

4/What does the fact that the New Testament writers do not record the *mighty works* done in Chorazin tell you about the writers' intentions (cf. Jn. 21:25)? 5/Contrast the *wise* and *babes* here. 6/What about Jesus has the Father revealed to you? 7/What are Jesus' and God's parts in revelation? 8/What kinds of yokes have the Pharisees been imposing on the people? Why? 9/What claims does Jesus make about his *yoke*? What are the responsibilities? the results? In what ways has your soul been relieved?

day 2 □ Matthew 12:1-14

1/What is the problem here? Who are the judges (cf. 7:1-5)? Where do the two incidents take place? 2/How does Jesus respond to the Pharisees' charges (cf. 1 Sam. 21:1-6; Hos. 6:6)? 3/In what areas do you have tendencies to be legally correct, but far from God in attitude? 4/What does Jesus mean in verse 6 (relate to v. 8)? 5/What has the temple represented? 6/What mercy do you show? 7/Why would the Pharisees rescue a sheep? Why do they argue about whether a man should be healed on the sabbath? Which requires more effort? 8/How does Jesus value human life (cf. 8:28-34)? 9/Account for the reaction of the Pharisees to Jesus' *mercy*.

day 3 □ Matthew 12:14-21

1/How far has the Pharisees' antagonism gone? What is their avowed intent? Why? 2/What is Jesus' reaction? Why? 3/Why does Jesus forbid the people to witness to his powers? 4/What has Isaiah prophesied about the Messiah (cf. Is. 42:1-4)? What qualities characterize him? 5/Which have you seen thus far in Matthew? 6/Is there any indication that Christ's teachings, claims, demands and values are to be universally applied? How?

day 4 □ Matthew 12:22-37

1/Note the two reactions to the same objective act. 2/What do the people hope? How do the Pharisees squelch the hypothesis (cf. 9:33-34)? 3/What is the logical rebuttal offered by Jesus? 4/Have you ever considered your response to Jesus as a choice between re-

garding him as God's Son or as an agent of Satan? Contrast the
fruits of Jesus and Satan. 5/To what extent does Jesus have dominion
over Satan? 6/Relate verse 30 to verses 23-24 (cf. Is. 5:20). 7/How
serious is the Pharisees' criticism (cf. v. 31 with v. 28)? 8/Relate verse
34 with verse 24.

day 5 □ Matthew 12:38-50

1/Considering what has preceded, what is ironical about this request?
2/What kind of sign are they seeking (cf. 16:1)? Why are they only
going to be given the sign of Jonah? 4/When will God vindicate the
Son of man? 5/Compare and contrast the messages of Jonah and
Jesus. How did the people of Nineveh respond? 6/What did the
queen of Sheba want to find out (cf. 1 Kings 10:1-13)? 7/Compare
and contrast the wisdom of Solomon and Jesus. 8/What is the
danger of preaching moral order without Jesus Christ? 9/Contrast
this evil generation with Jesus' relationship to those who do the will of
the Father.

day 6 □ Matthew 13:1-9

1/Picture the scene. 2/Contrast Jesus' method of teaching here with
his previous methods (cf. chaps. 5—7, 11—12). 3/Account for his
change in policy. 4/What are the four alternatives? 5/From whose
perspective is this parable told? 6/Are aspersions cast on the sower
because of the unfruitful sowings? 7/List ways that a gardener might
be of help here. 8/Do you take opportunities to pull weeds? 9/In
what ways has your heart been prepared to receive God's words?
10/What is the significance of Jesus' concluding statement?

day 7 □ Matthew 13:10-17

1/How do the disciples react to the change in Jesus' presentations?
2/How does Jesus explain his change of method? 3/What do some
have and some not (v. 12)? 4/What would happen if the situation
were reversed? 5/What do the have-nots lack? 6/Add to your list
of prophecies (cf. Is. 6:9-10). Account for the difference in tone and
wording. 7/What are the disciples seeing and hearing? 8/What is
your place in the unveiling of God's plan for the world?

day 8   □   *Matthew 13:18-23*
1/Compare Jesus' explanation of the parable here with the original telling in verses 1-9. Who makes up each audience?   2/To what extent has the word of the kingdom taken root in your heart? Why? 3/In retrospect, can you think of instances when you have not understood and truths have been snatched away?   4/How does the explanation relate to current understanding of subconscious memory? 5/What powers do you have over recall?   6/Take time now to thank God for his patience and faithfulness in repeating lessons that should have been learned long ago.   7/What is your reaction to trouble or persecution?   8/What care do you take to help others get their roots in?   9/What are the requirements for bearing fruit?   10/Account for the barrenness or fruitfulness in your life.

day 9   □   *Matthew 13:24-35*
1/What else besides type of soil causes a poor crop?   2/How real is the enemy in your thinking? actions? attitudes toward others?   3/To what extent do you care for any new seed in your group, despite the ravages of its contact with weeds?   4/What will the enemy ultimately accomplish? When is the day of reckoning?   5/Will any weeds get into the barn? Why?   6/What characteristics of the kingdom of heaven are illustrated by a seed and leaven?   7/How will the truth of the kingdom proclaimed in Israel influence the world?   8/Why do you think the good news of the kingdom has been hidden (cf. v. 35 with vv. 11, 17, 33)?   9/What Old Testament passage finds its fulfillment in Jesus' new way of teaching (cf. Ps. 78:2)?

day 10   □   *Matthew 13:36-52*
1/In what ways do the sons of the kingdom and the sons of the evil one coexist (cf. vv. 37-42 with vv. 47-50)? How do they affect each other? What makes each *good* or *bad*?   2/When will the enemy no longer be able to permeate the righteous?   3/What will be involved in the purge?   4/What will be the place of the sons in the Father's kingdom?   5/Did you suddenly come upon Christianity or did you search diligently before you found the truth?   6/Why do you think the response of each man in verses 44-45 is the same?   7/How much do

you value the kingdom of heaven?   8/In what ways is the teaching of the kingdom old? new?

day 11   ☐   *Matthew 13:53–14:13*
1/How would you react to a tradesman who had never been to seminary but criticized the pastors and elders of the community and performed many healings and exorcisms, teaching in your church about a new kingdom of God? Now imagine he is your son's playmate and buddy—or your own son.   2/How do you think Jesus' sisters and brothers regard him?   3/Imagine Jesus' feelings in the situation. 4/How does Herod react to Jesus' fame?   5/How does he explain Jesus' powers?   6/How does Jesus respond to his home prejudice and Herod's fear (v. 13)?   7/Who is Herod concerned to please? Who pleases him?   8/What motivates Herodias' request?   9/Imagine the relationship between Herodias and her daughter.   10/Imagine what Jesus might have wanted to explain to John the Baptist about his destiny.

day 12   ☐   *Matthew 14:13-21*
1/Remembering who Jesus is, think about the continual restraint that is necessary as he moves about in the world.   2/What is Jesus' intention? What takes precedence?   3/What in this passage shows Jesus' regard for man? How is his love expressed in action?   4/What resources do the disciples have?   5/What have you received from God to minister to others?   6/Imagine your response.   7/To what extent do you honor God because he supplies your material needs? 8/In what way is the crowd *satisfied*?

day 13   ☐   *Matthew 14:22-36*
1/Consider the physical strain of Jesus' ministry.   2/How does he maintain his spiritual "strength"?   3/What is the sequence and timing here? How long has the boat been *beaten*?   4/List what you can learn from the disciples' behavior during the storm.   5/To what extent is God with you in your circumstances even though physically separated?   6/Imagine the strength of the wind. How does it feel to walk

into a head wind on land?   7/What powers does Jesus have?   8/How do people respond to Jesus' presence in their land here (locate on a map)?

day 14   □   Matthew 15:1-20

1/Where are the Pharisees and scribes from?   2/What is the nature of this controversy?   3/How are the Pharisees trying to defeat the purpose of the law (cf. Ex. 20:12; 21:17; Lev. 20:9)?   4/What relationship between knowledge, response and God's judgment do you see in Jesus' dealings with the Pharisees?   5/How are the Pharisees like the people in Isaiah's time?   6/Define *defile.* Relate verse 11 with verses 2 and 8. How does Jesus amplify this with his disciples?   7/What *precepts of man* are part of your beliefs? Why?

day 15   □   Matthew 15:21-28

1/Where does Jesus go now (locate on a map)? Why?   2/Contrast the words of Jesus to this Gentile woman with those to the Pharisees in the earlier part of this chapter.   3/What is the basic difference?   4/On what grounds does Jesus refuse this woman's request?   5/What is Jesus' understanding of his earthly role in God's plan?   6/How do the Jews regard the Gentiles?   7/What can you learn from these verses about compassion, humility and faith?

day 16   □   Matthew 15:29-39

1/In view of Jesus' statement in verse 24, how do you explain his healing in non-Jewish territory (cf. v. 31)?   2/Compare and contrast this account of a large feeding with 14:13-21.   3/How do Jesus' actions reflect his feelings?   4/Account for Jesus' choice of locations for his ministering (cf. 14:13).   5/Imagine the scene on the hill. What do you suppose the disciples do during the healings?   6/In what ways has Jesus supplied your needs?

day 17   □   Matthew 16:1-12

1/Who try to test Jesus now?   2/What sign in the natural world do

they interpret?   3/What distinguishes its different interpretations?
4/What is the sign of Jonah (cf. 12:40)?   5/Of what does Jesus tell the
disciples to beware? What religious teachings in these times should
you be on guard against? Why?   6/Why does Jesus rebuke the disciples for worrying about the lack of bread? What is their failure?
7/What past examples of God's provision are you forgetting in the
needs of the moment?   8/What important prophecy is found in these
verses?

   day 18   ☐   *Matthew 16:13-20*
1/Locate this district on a map.   2/Compare Jesus with John the Baptist, Elijah and Jeremiah.   3/What is the major difference between
who the majority of men are saying Jesus is and who Peter says he is?
Imagine the reaction of the other disciples.   4/What is Jesus' response to what Peter says? Why is such a revelation to be kept secret?
5/What three statements does Jesus make about the future?   6/What
authority will Peter have?   7/How would you summarize what Jesus
is?

   day 19   ☐   *Matthew 16:21-28*
1/What new teaching is introduced? Why do you think Jesus has
waited?   2/What does he make plain that he has only hinted before
(cf. 12:40; 16:4)?   3/To what extent are the disciples and Christ now
thinking as one? In what area is there still a major misunderstanding?
4/What is Peter forgetting about the Christ?   5/Why does God's
side involve death?   6/What do the disciples have to look forward to?
How will the kingdom come?

   day 20   ☐   *Matthew 17:1-13*
1/Compare and contrast this event with Exodus 34:29-35.   2/Ima-
gine the scene. What do you think the three *a*—men and *b*—disciples
talk about? Why?   3/What is the primary purpose of the visit?
4/Compare and contrast God's words about Jesus with Peter's declaration.   5/How do the disciples respond?   6/What example of Jesus'
love can you find here?   7/What is the teaching of the scribes re-

garding the time of the coming of the Messiah (cf. Mal. 4:5-6)?
8/What does Jesus say about the preparation for his coming (cf.
11:14)?

day 21 □ *Matthew 17:14-27*
1/What has happened while Christ and the three disciples were gone?
Why are those left behind powerless to help?   2/Describe the boy's
condition.   3/How does Jesus handle the situation?   4/What is the
result of faith? Why? What is the quality and intent of your faith?
5/Where does the party go now? 6/What prophecy is in this reading?
How do the disciples react to it? What are they forgetting?   7/Ima-
gine Jesus' feelings about the future in the midst of the demands of
the present situation.   8/What is the purpose of the tax (cf. Ex.
30:11-16)?   9/Contrast the tax obligation on earth with the obligations of the kingdom.   10/What does this incident show of your legal
and Christian responsibilities?

day 22 □ *Matthew 18:1-14*
1/Think about your attitude toward your Christian friends.   2/To
what extent are you self-confident? To what extent do you seek after
greatness? Why?   3/Characterize the values of the kingdom of heav-
en.   4/In what ways is a child humble?   5/How can you be a temptation for a fellow believer (v. 6)? for yourself (vv. 8-9)?   6/How do
verses 10-14 reflect the other side of verses 5-9?   7/How can you
show Jesus' concern for a straying member of the kingdom?

day 23 □ *Matthew 18:15-22*
1/Compare Jesus' teaching about your sin against a brother with a
brother's sin against you.   2/What should be your efforts in solving
interpersonal problems?   3/At what point does the telling stop?
4/What kind of people do you choose to accompany you in settling
problems? in petitioning God?   5/What great promise is inserted in
verse 19?   6/What is the extent of your identification with the corporate body of the kingdom? Why?   7/What should be your incentive
to forgive your brother?

day 24   □   *Matthew 18:23-35*
1/Why is forgiveness so important to the Christian community? 2/How does Jesus illustrate the kingdom of heaven here?   3/Contrast the debts of the two servants.   4/What is the logical result of being shown mercy? What is the relationship between mercy and forgiveness?   5/What are the consequences of failing to forgive our brothers? Why?

day 25   □   *Matthew 8–18*
1/Review the mighty works Jesus has done. For what purpose? Who have been involved?   2/Summarize the confrontations between the Pharisees and scribes and Jesus. What do the Pharisees seem intent on proving? How has Jesus avoided their traps thus far?   3/Trace Jesus' progressive revelation about himself and his relationship with the Father and with the great prophets of the past.   4/Differentiate the reactions of the people to Jesus' teaching and works.   5/Summarize what the kingdom of heaven is like.   6/Which of your values, attitudes and actions need to be changed to align them with the message of the kingdom?

day 26   □   *Introduction to Ezekiel*
The prophet Ezekiel is a contemporary of Jeremiah and, like him, one of the temple priests. His call as a prophet comes after his deportation to Babylon in 597 B.C. (cf. 2 Kings 24:8-16). God leaves Jeremiah the more difficult post in besieged Jerusalem but gives Ezekiel a series of more strenuous prophetic ecstasies. They both insist that the future of Israel is with the exiles. The situation for the deported Jews is therefore better than for those who have stayed behind and continue to fortify Jerusalem and rebel against God's servant Nebuchadnezzar. Ezekiel's prophecies reassure the exiles of the complete destruction of the life they have left behind and warn those who persist in their sin against God.   1/What is the historical setting of Ezekiel's ministry?   2/Skim chapter 1. Compare the succeeding appearances of this same vision in 3:23; 8:2-4; 10:1-22; 11:22-24; 43:1-5; 48:35.   3/Why has God's glory left Jerusalem? What occasions its return?   4/What do you learn about the condition of the

place where God dwells? 5/Compare the visions of God as witnessed by Moses (Ex. 3:1-6) and Isaiah (Is. 6).

day 27   □   *Ezekiel 1*

1/Familiarize yourself with the details of this vision without trying to visualize it specifically. 2/What are the sights and sounds (note the repetition of *likeness* and *appearance*)? 3/What happens to the character of metal alloy in a furnace? 4/What is special about living creatures? 5/What does a face represent? What do these faces have in common? What distinguishes them? 6/What are wings and wheels for? What is peculiar about the wheels? 7/Who is on the throne? 8/Why is this vision given? What is its effect?

day 28   □   *Ezekiel 2:1–3:15*

1/How is Ezekiel addressed? 2/What will be his ministry? How is his mission field described? 3/In what specific ways does it compare to your modern setting? 4/What *words* and *looks* do you get when you speak God's words in face-to-face encounters? 5/Distinguish Ezekiel's message, his manner and authority, the reason for his persistence, his conduct and endurance, and his own necessary response.

day 29   □   *Ezekiel 3:16-27*

1/How is Ezekiel addressed (contrast the majesty of God in chap. 1)? 2/What is Ezekiel's relation to Israel (cf. Deut. 18:15-22)? 3/Under what circumstances is his responsibility excusable? 4/Why does the righteous as well as the wicked man need warning? 5/What stumbling blocks have you encountered? To what extent have you chosen to stumble? 6/What comfort would Ezekiel find in the experience of verse 23? 7/What is the significance of the seemingly contradictory experiences of verses 25-26? 8/How are you to speak God's words? When? For what purpose?

day 30   □   *Ezekiel 4*

1/How does Ezekiel attract attention? 2/Why is it necessary to demonstrate siege and length of punishment to people already in exile? What would their contrary optimism be based on?   3/Why do you think Ezekiel uses symbolism instead of direct interpretation? 4/What are the restrictions placed on his life? To what extent do you question the limitations God puts on your life as a Christian witness? 5/What evokes Ezekiel's complaint? To what extent is it justifiable (cf. Ex. 22:31; Lev. 7:19; 22:8)?   6/What do you learn about God by divine accommodation?

Month 41

day 1   □   *Ezekiel 5*
1/Imagine the reactions of the crowd gathered around Ezekiel. 2/What will happen to the inhabitants of Jerusalem? Why?   3/How have they responded to God's favors?   4/How will surrounding nations view Israel's punishment?   5/How do you think this portrayal affects the prophet's reputation?   6/How does God regard sin? 7/How do you regard your own sin? Why?

day 2   □   *Ezekiel 6*
1/What has taken place in the hills of Israel?   2/How does God try to make plain the folly of false objects of worship?   3/Why is destruction coming upon the people (cf. Lev. 26:23-33)?   4/To what extent are you convinced that the pleasures and adornments of life which you pursue will not endure nor have power to preserve you from judgment for worshiping them?   5/Relate God's mercy to his judgment. 6/What is the purpose of God's judgment?

day 3   □   *Ezekiel 7*
1/What relationship is stressed between sin and judgment?   2/What is your attitude toward God about sin which is not punished immediately or that which is without seeming evil consequence (relate to the

Israelites' belief that God would not destroy his temple or city)? 3/How will the doom affect economics? other securities? 4/What will, in fact, happen to the temple? 5/To what extent is God involved in the suffering of judgment? 6/Is God's judgment capricious? Why?

day 4 □ *Ezekiel 8*

1/How long has Ezekiel been prophesying? To what extent has he been recognized as a prophet? 2/What identifies this vision as of God? 3/What four abominations does Ezekiel witness (Tammuz is a Sumerian god of vegetation associated with mourning and fertility rites)? In each instance, note the location, type of wickedness, and station and number of participants (cf. Deut. 17:2-7; 13:1-11). 4/Characterize the religious leaders of your nation. What is the extent of their followings?

day 5 □ *Ezekiel 9*

1/What do you learn about the character of God's justice from his destruction of the people of Jerusalem? 2/How is the judgment executed? 3/What is the criteria for exemption? 4/How do you account for God's attitude toward the temple? toward his people? 5/How does Ezekiel respond to the execution? 6/Summarize God's case (cf. chaps. 5—8). 7/Do you wish that God would be more lenient? Why?

day 6 □ *Ezekiel 10*

1/Contrast the tasks of the man in linen here and in chapter 9. 2/Compare the vision of the glory of God here with that in chapter 1. 3/What might be your reaction to repeated visions of God's glory? 4/Trace the movement of the glory of the Lord (cf. 9:3 with 10:1, 18-19). 5/In what way do you approach God? Why? 6/How sensitive are you to the reaction of God's holiness to places and occasions which you cherish?

day 7 □ *Ezekiel 11*

1/Where does Ezekiel stand as he witnesses this final scene in the city (cf. 10:19)? 2/How do the princes regard themselves? 3/What image of protection for themselves do they cite? How does Ezekiel show its futility? 4/What is his message to the political group at Jerusalem? to his fellow exiles? 5/Contrast the view of the people in Jerusalem and God toward his chosen people. 6/What is Ezekiel's attitude toward his people? 7/What hope is introduced? 8/To what extent does your self-opinion coincide with God's knowledge of you? Why?

day 8   □   *Ezekiel 12*

1/What does Ezekiel do by day? at evening? 2/How important is it that Ezekiel be obedient in every detail? In his position, at what point might you have balked? Why? What is your price for discipleship? 3/When is the action explained? 4/Who is the prince involved (cf. 2 Kings 24:18—25:7)? 5/How is God personified? For what purpose? 6/What is emphasized about God's judgment? 7/Distinguish the two false notions about Ezekiel's prophecy. How do God's answers parallel each phrase of the quoted sayings? 8/Relate these sayings to current feelings about Christ's coming again.

day 9   □   *Ezekiel 13*

1/Characterize the source, content and effect of the false prophet's message. 2/What is God's attitude and consequent action toward the false prophets (note esp. the threefold punishment in v. 9)? toward his own people? Why (vv. 9, 14, 21, 23)? 3/How do the prophetesses captivate the people? What power do they claim? 4/Why do the people succumb? 5/To what extent do you turn against falsehood? Do you fear the division which truth brings? Why?

day 10   □   *Ezekiel 14*

1/Why can't God give direction to the inquiring elders? What must they do? If they refuse, what action must a holy God take? 2/Distinguish the presence of idolatry in the environment and the action of these men. 3/To what extent does your inward allegiance to God coincide with your outward profession? How can God guide you?

4/What is the further indication of false prophecy (cf. vv. 7, 9)? 5/What is God's primary concern? 6/What quality would deliver only Noah, Daniel and Job from judgment? What does this teach of God and his attitude toward the individual? 7/Why may there be a few survivors? 8/How can the sight of evil men suffering punishment *console* you?

day 11   □   *Ezekiel 15*

1/What metaphor is used to characterize Israel? 2/What usual quality of a vine does Ezekiel ignore? Why? 3/What is Israel's value to God? What makes her value even less? 4/How does God answer the prevalent belief that budding and flourishing would come again before long? 5/Do you expect God to forgive you or remove your judgment because of some human merit? because of his love for you? because of your association with righteous people? What is his standard?

day 12   □   *Ezekiel 16:1-42*

1/What literary form does Ezekiel use here? 2/Describe the state of the baby in the story. 3/Characterize the traveler's kindnesses, provisions and covenant with her. 4/How has the bride regarded her marriage and adornment? 5/Distinguish the reactions of her husband, her paramours and herself. 6/How are her actions different from an adulteress and harlot? 7/Relate her actions with the moral, political and religious prostitution of Jerusalem (cf. Deut. 7; 2 Kings 23:7, 10; Lev. 18:21; Is. 30:1-5; 31:1). 8/To what extent are you *satisfied* with your sin? 9/Who will be the agents of Jerusalem's devastation? How? 10/Relate God's love and anger.

day 13   □   *Ezekiel 16:43-63*

1/How is Israel portrayed here? 2/Characterize her *sisters.* What are their attitudes and actions toward their husbands and children? 3/How has Israel formerly regarded her sisters? 4/What is God's assessment of the three? 5/How will the sisters regard Israel after the restoration of all? 6/How do you feel about your unfaithfulness to God? How do you think others regard it?   7/Distinguish the covenant in the days of Israel's youth and the everlasting covenant. What will be Jerusalem's response to the new covenant?   8/Relate forgiveness and shame.   9/Which of your sins has God forgiven? For which do you still feel shame? For what purpose?

day 14   □   Ezekiel 17
1/From the parable, identify the eagles (vv. 3, 7), the top of the cedar, the seed of the land and the fertile soil where it is planted (cf. 2 Kings 24:8—25:7; 2 Chron. 36:9-14).   2/What sin is God rebuking through Ezekiel here?   3/To what extent are contracts signed by men binding with God?   4/How do you view the contracts and agreements you make? Why?   5/How will God accomplish his purpose in spite of the ideas and schemes of men? What reversals will come about?   6/What do you think are God's purposes for your nation?   7/To what extent is God involved in history today? Why?

day 15   □   Ezekiel 18
1/What is the meaning of the proverb? How will its acceptance affect the children's actions?   2/How does God refute it (contrast Ex. 20:5)?   3/What is characteristic of the just man in his life and relationship to God? What areas of life are included (cf. Ex. 22:26; Lev. 18:19-20; Deut. 23:19-20)?   4/How will God deal with individuals? What three examples are given to illustrate the principle?   5/What direct result must come to the sinner?   6/What will happen to the wicked man turned righteous? vice versa? Why?   7/Have you ever felt like Israel in her complaint to God (v. 25)? Why?   8/How does God analyze the problem and demonstrate his mercy and justice?   9/To what extent will you keep doing what is *lawful and right*?

day 16   □   Ezekiel 19
1/What two metaphors are used of Israel?   2/What is the mood?   3/Identify the three kings and their activities (cf. vv. 2-4 with 2 Kings 23:31-34; vv. 5-9 with 2 Kings 24:8-15; vv. 10-19 with 2 Kings 25:4-11).   4/What changes have occurred in the nation? Why?

5/How does a leader's relationship with God affect a whole nation? 6/Over what have you lost your hope recently? How have you tried to remedy the situation?

day 17   ☐   *Ezekiel 20:1-44*

1/What is the time now?   2/How is the story of Israel's past related here (contrast chaps. 15—17, 19)?   3/How does God bind himself to Israel (note the phrase *I swore* throughout)?   4/What has God given Israel? For what purpose? What stipulations are cited?   5/How have the Israelites responded?   6/What characteristics of God are revealed?   7/Trace God's actions in terms of the tension of consequences and restraint.   8/Seeing that Israel has completely disregarded God's covenant (even when she came into Canaan), what is God's motive for restraint?   9/What is God's word for the present house of Israel? How will he accomplish his purpose (cf. v. 3 with Lev. 27:32)?   10/How will God deal with Israel in the future? Why? 11/What is God's ultimate purpose for you? How do you know?

day 18   ☐   *Ezekiel 20:45-21:32*

1/What is the reaction of the people to Ezekiel by this time?   2/What two symbols are used to depict the destruction of Israel?   3/What is the extent of the destruction? Who is the agent? For what purpose? 4/How have the Israelites responded to past punishment (v. 13)? 5/What contrasting emotions is Ezekiel to display? Why?   6/What symbolic performance does Ezekiel give in verses 18-27?   7/What three methods of divination does the king of Babylon use (names of people or places are marked on the arrows, shaken and drawn out)? 8/How will the Israelites regard the answer the king receives? 9/What will happen to the king of Israel (cf. 2 Kings 24:18-20; Gen. 49:10)?   10/What does this passage reveal concerning God's methods of working out his purposes?   11/Do you look for his hand in the happenings of your daily life? Why?

day 19   ☐   *Ezekiel 22*

1/List the types of sins for which judgment is passed on the city.

2/What groups of people are guilty of those sins? To what extent do those in similar responsible positions disregard God today?   3/How does the people's attitude toward the Lord affect their total lives (cf. v. 26 with Lev. 10:10-11)?   4/What is the extent of the judgment? 5/What metaphor is used to depict the process? Why is the refined product conspicuously lacking (cf. v. 18 with v. 30)?   6/What is the result regarding God himself?   7/To what extent do you aspire to be a political, religious, judicial or social leader in your country? Why (cf. v. 30)?   8/How can you influence present and future national leaders for God?

day 20   □   Ezekiel 23
1/Compare the allegory of this chapter with 16:44-63.   2/Compare and contrast the behavior of the two sisters. What about their lovers attracts them? What do they expect to gain?   3/Characterize the lovers in appearance, actions and attitude toward the sisters.   4/What is involved in political liaisons at this time (cf. v. 7 with 2 Kings 16)? 5/To what extent do you learn from the examples of others? (Must you have the experience before you can understand the consequences?)   6/How do the former lovers turn against each of the sisters? Why?   7/Compare the punishment of the two.

day 21   □   Ezekiel 24
1/What day has come at last (cf. 2 Kings 25:1? How does Ezekiel know? 2/What common cooking utensil and procedure is used as a symbol? 3/What kind of residue is revealed in the boiling? Why is removal of the residue insufficient? What means are used to try to get rid of it? Are they successful?   4/What is Ezekiel's response to God in the personal loss of his wife (cf. 1 Sam. 4:12; 2 Sam. 15:30)?   5/How is she described in comparison with Israel's value of Jerusalem?   6/What sign would Ezekiel thus be to the people?   7/Why is this incident a turning point in Ezekiel's life and ministry?   8/What is *the desire of your soul*? What would happen to your trust in God if the object of this desire were taken from you? Why?

day 22   ☐   *Ezekiel 25*

1/What four nations are judged here (cf. 16:23-29; 21:28-32 with Judg. 10—11, 13—16; 1 Sam. 11; 2 Sam. 10; Num. 22:1—25:5; Gen. 25:23-34)? Locate them on a map of the times.   2/From each oracle, describe the nation's attitude toward Israel, the action which God must take and the result he desires (note the *because* and *therefore* pattern).   3/Why does God have something to say about nations who make no profession of allegiance to him as their god?   4/How will God deal with adversaries of his truth and his people?   5/To what extent do you allot God his rightful place as judge and avenger of wrong?

day 23   ☐   *Ezekiel 26*

1/Why does the Lord pronounce such complete destruction on Tyre? Who will be the agent of judgment?   2/Visualize the ruin which will come to her. Contrast her original greatness.   3/What will be the effect of her destruction on God's reputation? on the surrounding nations? on her own national renown?   4/What warning does this give not to place confidence in your possessions or position?   5/To what extent do you look for personal gain from the defeat or failure of another?

day 24   ☐   *Ezekiel 27*

1/How is Tyre personified? Describe her construction, crew and merchandise.   2/Identify the countries of the trade directory on a map. What benefits do they gain? What do they contribute to the trade? 3/How is the destruction foretold in the previous chapter depicted here?   4/How does the rest of the world react?   5/To what extent are you brought to a holy fear of God through catastrophe in lives of others? in your own life?

day 25   ☐   *Ezekiel 28*

1/How does the king of Tyre regard himself, his empire and his possessions?   2/Compare and contrast God's view.   3/Compare Adam in the garden of Eden with the king of Tyre in his empire.   4/What is the reason for Tyre's downfall? How will it be accomplished?   5/To what extent do you regard your possessions as provisions of your work and wisdom? as gifts from God?   6/What is the purpose in God's judgment on Sidon for himself? for his people?   7/What will be the future of Israel? When? Why?

day 26 □ Ezekiel 29
1/What is the date of this oracle?   2/What metaphors are used of Egypt (dragon probably refers doubly to the Egyptian crocodile and the mythological monster of the deep, Tiamut)?   3/Why does God bring judgment to her?   4/What has been Israel's relationship to her (vv. 6-7, 15-16)?   5/What does God show of his own power and authority?   6/To what extent is your confidence today in God or in people who make great claims for themselves?   7/How has Nebuchadnezzar worked for God (cf. 28:7-8)? What will be his reward?   8/How do you explain God's sense of justice in his dealings here?   9/What is the basis of your concern for justice among nations (cf. vv. 6, 9, 16, 21)?

day 27 □ Ezekiel 30
1/What will the day of the Lord mean for nations other than Israel (cf. 7:2-12)?   2/Visualize the completeness of judgment on Egypt. What will be its effect on Egypt's allies?   3/What is a basic cause of Egypt's destruction (vv. 6, 18)?   4/Who is responsible for the devastation (underline the *I will* phrases)?   5/Why can't anyone who trusts in his own resources and achievements ultimately prosper?

day 28 □ Ezekiel 31
1/What is the date of this oracle?   2/Picture the cedar described. What has made for its greatness? What is its relationship to the others?   3/Why is judgment called for? How extensive will be the natural and political reaction to judgment?   5/What nations might the accompanying *trees of Eden* represent?   6/Have you been given a position of authority and leadership with respect from others? How can you avoid the fate of being cast down?

day 29 ☐ *Ezekiel 32*

1/How much time has elapsed since the last oracle about Egypt? 2/List the images used of her (cf. 29:3, 6; 31:3). 3/Compare the destruction described here with her former majesty (cf. 7:20-24; 10:21-23). How will this disaster affect other nations? 4/What is Ezekiel's part in the oracle? 5/What role does God have in the development of history? Over what realms does he assert dominion (cf. v. 32)? 6/Summarize the ways Ezekiel has drawn attention to his messages. How can he speak fearlessly and with authority? 7/Summarize Ezekiel's view of God. What have you learned about God from *Ezekiel?*

day 30 ☐ *Psalm 73*

1/Who is Asaph (cf. 1 Chron. 16:4-7; 2 Chron. 29:30)? 2/Contrast the psalmist's positive attitude now with his previous doubts. 3/What has caused him to start slipping? 4/How do you react to the prosperous wicked who often seem to enjoy life more than you do? How do they affect the joy and understanding of your life (relate to v. 22)? 5/Characterize their positive and negative distinctions. 6/How do people respond to them? 7/What seems to be the psalmist's concept of ultimate justice? 8/How can you gain God's perspective on a problem that is causing you doubt and worry? 9/To what extent are you careful in expressing your doubts openly? Why? 10/Contrast those *far from* and *near* God. How does God deal with each? 11/How has the psalmist overcome his doubt? What has he learned in the process? 12/Summarize this psalm in a title.

Month 42

day 1 ☐ *Psalm 74*

1/How does the psalmist react to the destruction of Jerusalem (cf. Lam.)? 2/On what grounds does he appeal for deliverance? 3/Why do you think God should help you? 4/What is the basic question of this psalm? 5/Describe the scene at the sanctuary. 6/What does the psalmist know about God's character? What acts afford proof of his power? 7/Review some of the things God is and has done for you in the past. 8/Contrast the psalmist's plea for God to honor his covenant with the Israelites' "honoring" of the covenant.

day 2 ☐ *Psalm 75*
1/Account for the psalmist's attitude now. 2/What qualities of God is he especially thankful for? 3/Who is speaking in verses 2-5? 4/What is the image used? 5/What right does God have to speak to people as in verses 4-5? 6/Name one area where pride is a particular problem in your life. Where do you belong in the overall picture of history? 7/To what extent do you rejoice in this kind of God? 8/Summarize this psalm in a title.

day 3 ☐ *Psalm 76*
1/How is the honor of God's name bound up with victory over enemies? Why (cf. the anguish of defeat in Ps. 74)? 2/What images show God's majesty? his actions? 3/What is the effect of God's judgment? 4/How do people respond to seeing wicked individuals and nations subdued? Why? 5/To what extent do you include God's justice and holiness in your witness? 6/What vows have you made to this God? 7/Summarize this psalm in a title.

day 4 ☐ *Psalm 77*
1/What is the psalmist's problem? Why? 2/To what extent can you identify with his feelings? 3/What does he remember? Why does the memory add to his grief? bring him out of his despondency? 4/What single deed exemplifies God's graciousness (cf. Ex. 13—15)? 5/How does nature react to God? 6/How do you recover from depression? 7/Summarize this psalm in a title.

day 5 ☐ *Psalm 78:1-41*
1/What is the purpose of this national hymn? 2/What image does the

psalmist use to depict Israel's disloyalty?   3/Trace the pattern of human conduct and divine intervention here.   4/Enumerate the marvels.   5/What are the specific actions of rebellion? What are God's responses? Why?   6/What resources does God use?   7/When have you been guilty of forgetfulness and thanklessness? Why?   8/Reflect on the power God has shown to you.

day 6   □   Psalm 78:42-72

1/How would this recounting stir the Israelites' memory?   2/Underline the verbs which reveal God's actions.   3/To what extent have the Israelites been aware of God's purpose in his actions?   4/What has been their response? What images portray it?   5/Review God's rejection of Israel. How does he intervene?   6/Summarize the effectiveness of David's reign.   7/What quality of God is most predominant in this hymn? Title the hymn in your own words.   8/What kind of hymn to God could your nation write? Why?

day 7   □   Psalm 79

1/What has happened to the people of Jerusalem?   2/Describe the battlefield.   3/How are the Gentile nations reacting to Jerusalem's defeat?   4/Compare and contrast the Lord's anger toward his chosen people and the Gentile nations.   5/Does God's temporary withholding of judgment on the Gentile nations mean that he is pleased with them?   6/What is the basis of the psalmist's plea for compassion?   7/Why will deliverance be an occasion for praise?   8/To what extent do individuals and nations *taunt* God today?   9/Summarize this psalm in a title.

day 8   □   Psalm 80

1/Describe God as the *Shepherd of Israel.* How can he *shine*?   2/What does the psalmist want from God? To whom is he attributing the national misfortunes?   3/How has the nation been like a vine? How has God prepared and tended it?   4/How has it grown? Why?   5/Why has he abandoned it?   6/How is God's intervention necessary for life?   7/What is the purpose of the strength God gives you?   8/Summarize this psalm in a title.

day 9 □ *Psalm 81*

1/Describe the celebration called for. What is its purpose? 2/What does the fact that God schedules times of joy (there are many more feast days than fast days) tell you about God and the kind of life he wants you to live? 3/How does the exodus from Egypt reveal God in a new way? 4/What is the major commandment and desire of God? 5/What does God promise if Israel will listen to him? 6/When do you not want God around (vv. 11)? Why? 7/Why is verse 12 the worst possible punishment? Do you believe that following your *counsels* is a punishment? Why? 8/Summarize this psalm in a title.

day 10 □ *Psalm 82*

1/Contrast God's justice with the judgment of Israel's ruler and judges. 2/What is the charge? the command? 3/To whom have they shown partiality (cf. Lev. 19:15)? 4/Why are the cases of the poor and weak often neglected? 5/What honor is inherent in the office of judge? 6/How will God's kingdom be established? 7/Are you concerned enough about injustice to call on God to judge the earth or do you just talk about it with other people? 8/How does your attitude toward injustice reveal your concept of God? 9/What area of injustice do you think God wants you to be concerned about? 10/Summarize this psalm in a title.

day 11 □ *Psalm 83*

1/What is Israel's plight? Characterize those involved. 2/On what basis does the psalmist call for help? 3/How serious is the threat? 4/What is the psalmist's ultimate reason for calling down God's judgments on the opposition (cf. Judg. 4—8)? 5/What images of destruction are cited? 6/How has Israel reacted in her shame (cf. Ps. 74)? 7/What is the purpose of shame? 8/Is your motivation for judgment that of verse 18? Why? 9/Summarize the psalm in a title.

day 12 □ *Psalm 84*

1/Read this psalm aloud. 2/What is the psalmist's response to the opportunity for worship of God? 3/What is his desire? How does he feel about coming into God's presence?   4/What images express his joy?   5/Describe Zion as anticipated and seen by the pilgrims. 6/What images express God's attributes?   7/What is so appealing about being close to God?   8/Summarize this psalm in a title.

day 13   ☐   *Psalm 85*
1/What are the thoughts of the returned exiles as they begin the task of reconstruction? Imagine the scene of devastation that greets them. 2/What is God's part in the return?   3/What reassurance do they need? Why?   4/How does God *speak peace to his people*? What is the individual's responsibility?   5/How will God's glory dwell in Israel? Enumerate the aspects of his glory that will be present.   6/What will the future hold?   7/How have you experienced God's blessing as seen in his attributes here? Why?   8/Summarize this psalm in a title.

day 14   ☐   *Psalm 86*
1/What does David request? Enumerate and relate his reasons for believing God will answer each request.   2/What are your needs? What resources of God correspond to each need?   3/How has David learned about these characteristics of God?   4/What is the basis of David's faith in God?   5/To what extent do you feel unified? Why? 6/For what can you thank God?   7/Choose parts of this prayer to use as you pray today. Why will God answer?   8/Summarize this psalm in a title.

day 15   ☐   *Psalm 87*
1/What is God's relationship to his city (review its history)? How is his presence felt?   2/How will those born in other nations claim citizenship in Zion? Why? What jubilation will accompany the claim? 3/What would international allegiance to God mean for society? 4/Will God say of you "This one was born there"? Why?   5/Summarize this psalm in a title.

day 16   ☐   *Psalm 88*
1/Whom does the writer ultimately blame for his troubles?   2/Why

412

then does he turn to God for help?   3/To what extent can you identify with his experience?   4/Describe his condition. In what ways is he alienated from God? from other people?   5/What does God stand to gain by his death?   6/What is the extent of his affliction?   7/What happens to your view of God and his sovereignty when you feel forsaken? Why?   8/Summarize this psalm in a title.

day 17   □   *Psalm 89:1-18*

1/What is the mood here?   2/What qualities of God does he praise? Illustrate each attribute.   3/Read verses 5-18 aloud.   4/Over what realms does God rule?   5/What makes Israel *blessed*?

day 18   □   *Psalm 89:19-51*

1/List the promises in God's covenant with David (cf. vv. 3-4). What areas of life do they encompass?   2/How will David relate to God? 3/What will happen if his children violate the covenant?   4/How does God regard faithfulness?   5/In view of God's solemn promise, account for the psalmist's protest.   6/Contrast what God has sworn with the present situation of Israel.   7/Summarize this psalm in a title.   8/How does verse 52 summarize the third book of psalms?

day 19   □   *Ezekiel 33*

Ezekiel is still God's prophet to the exiles outside Israel's desolated land.   1/Reconstruct in your mind the temper and morale of a people unrooted from their cultural, economic, governmental and religious solidarity to be distributed wholesale throughout a virile foreign empire.   2/What duties does the Lord give Ezekiel toward the Israelites (cf. 3:16-21)? What individual responsibility do the people have (cf. 18:21-29)?   3/In what ways are you a *watchman* to your people? Why?   4/What is Ezekiel's source of boldness?   5/To what extent are the people aware of their sin?   6/What is God's view of judgment? of individual responsibility?   7/How have you been untrue to God? Why?   8/When does news of Jerusalem's fall reach the exiles? 9/What claims do the people left in Jerusalem make (cf. 11:15)? 10/How have the people responded to Ezekiel and his message (cf.

Deut. 18:15-22)?   11/To what extent do you regard God's message as entertainment?

day 20   □   *Ezekiel 34*
1/List the failures of the shepherds of Israel.   2/What judgment does God bring (cf. Jer. 10:21; 23:1-6; 25:34-38)?   3/Describe the Lord's action toward his flock.   4/What are his desires for his sheep? 5/Contrast the results for the sheep under the care of the shepherds of Israel and the Lord God.   6/What should be the concern of pastors today in their responsibility to the flock of God?   7/Who will the Lord God set over the regathered Israel?   8/What physical, social, political, economic and spiritual benefits will result from the new covenant? 9/How do you know that the Lord God is your shepherd (cf. Ps. 23)?

day 21   □   *Ezekiel 35*
1/Review the history of the relationship of Israel and Edom (cf. Gen. 25:22-34; Num. 20:14-21; 2 Sam. 8:13-14; 2 Kings 8:20-22; Is. 34). 2/Locate their territories on a map.   3/With which does God identify? Why?   4/What does this teach of God and his concern for his own? 5/Why is judgment pronounced?   6/Why has Edom rejoiced over Jerusalem? When will the earth rejoice over Edom? Why?   7/How will desolation bring knowledge of the Lord?

day 22   □   *Ezekiel 36*
1/What has been the action of enemy nations toward Israel? What action will the Lord take on these nations?   2/Contrast God's past and future actions toward Israel. Account for the difference.   3/How have the nations reacted to Israel's past humiliation? How will they react to her glorification? 4/What is God's purpose in using Israel (esp. v. 23)?   5/To what extent does the church have a similar role to play in the world today?   6/Because of the Lord's concern, what changes must be made in Israel (cf. Num. 19:17-19)?   7/Define *heart* and *spirit*. Describe your heart and spirit.   8/How will Israel view her past (cf. 16:62-63; 20:43-44)?

day 23 □ *Ezekiel 37*
1/What are the feelings of the exiles (esp. v. 11)? 2/What will God accomplish for those whose *hope is lost?* What two metaphors are used (vv. 1-10, 11-14; cf. 36:26-27)? 3/At what point does the situation change (v. 7)? 4/Distinguish the two commands to *prophesy.* What happens? 5/Underline *spirit, breath* and *wind* (the same word in Hebrew). 6/What "impossible" situation faces you? To what extent are you trusting it to a God of the impossible? 7/What symbolic action does Ezekiel take now? 8/What does God promise to his forgiven and restored people (cf. Ex. 29:45)?

day 24 □ *Ezekiel 38*
1/What will oppose God's purpose in chapter 37 (cf. Is. 29:5-8)? 2/What do you learn about its source, formidableness and objective? 3/How easily are you overwhelmed by such resistance to your peace? 4/How does God intend to deal with the situation? What weapons will be used? 5/Have you seen for yourself what God must forcibly show to these nations (vv. 16, 23)? 6/What is the extent of your awe and fear of God? Why?

day 25 □ *Ezekiel 39*
1/In view of the extent of God's victory over his enemy, what purpose does God have in allowing the situation to develop to such proportions? 2/What adverse circumstances has God allowed in your daily life? in your future plans? Why, do you think? 3/What particulars of God's victory are emphasized by the two tasks required of the people and that of the birds and beasts? 4/What is God's ultimate purpose for Israel (cf. v. 29 with 36:27; 37:14)? How will the nations learn the whole story of his purpose? 5/Explain God's jealousy. 6/Contrast verses 23-24 with verse 29. Account for the difference.

day 26 □ *Ezekiel 40:1-47*
1/What is the date now? How much time has passed since a date has been specified? 2/With the impossible achieved, imagine the questions which now arise for the newly hopeful exiles about how the new

society will be constructed in its worship, culture and government.
3/How does Ezekiel, as priest and prophet of the temple's ruin, see
and speak of the new temple?   4/What are gates for? How are the
gateways arranged?   5/What provision is made for sacrifice? for
those who minister in the temple?   6/What do you think is significant about the symmetry of dimensions and arrangement?

day 27   □   *Ezekiel 40:48–41:26*
1/What areas of the temple does Ezekiel see now? Which does he not
enter? Why?   2/Imagine the emotions of the prophet as he is given
this exclusive tour and the awe with which he looks at these rooms.
3/What place do they occupy in relation to the other plans?   4/Why
do the prophet's thoughts revert to these rooms for further detail
(vv. 15b-26)?   5/Compare and contrast the vision of this temple with
Solomon's historic temple (2 Kings 6).   6/What is the purpose of a
temple to God?   7/How are you like a temple to God?

day 28   □   *Ezekiel 42*
1/In view of his lineage and class, what would create special interest for Ezekiel during these further tours of the inner court area?
2/What significance do you see in the promixity of these buildings to
the temple proper and the altar?   3/In the light of your calling as a
Christian, what does this emphasize to you concerning the investment
of your time, the preoccupations of your life and the type of service
which must receive priority with God?   4/To what extent do you give
to the Lord God the devotion that is his due, even apart from your
inclination?   5/Why is there a separation between the *holy* and the
common? What is designated *holy*?

day 29   □   *Ezekiel 43:1-12*
1/What does the temple, with all its natural impressiveness and significance for the nation, lack?   2/During the years of the city's
waste, how must the exiles have felt about the presence of God?
3/Compare and contrast Ezekiel's vision of the glory of God and the
temple (cf. 10:18-22; 11:22-24).   4/What would it take to put you on

your face before God? Is this a voluntary reaction?   5/What is God's desire for the temple (cf. Solomon's temple in 1 Kings 8)?   6/For what purpose does God give the revelation of future glory (vv. 10-11)?

day 30   □   *Ezekiel 43:13-27*
1/What is the physical appearance of the altar?   2/What is the significance of the horns (cf. Ex. 29:12; 1 Kings 1:49-53)?   3/What must be done to consecrate the altar?   4/What is the result of all the procedure?   5/How do you know you are acceptable to God?

Month 43

day 1   □   *Ezekiel 44*
1/How is Ezekiel again affected by the presence of God's glory? 2/Does God's glory seem commonplace to you?   3/What specifically is God's complaint concerning the use of the place which bears his name?   4/Why is the east gate now shut (cf. 43:1-12)?   5/What is shown about the relation of God's mercy to the inexorable consequence of sin (vv. 9-14)?   6/What are the restrictions for the privilege of standing before God (vv. 15-31)?   7/To what extent are you careful about morally "legitimate" things which destroy this ultimate purpose? Why?

day 2   □   *Ezekiel 45*
1/What is the place of the temple in that national life?   2/What land is sacred? Why? What belongs to the royal family?   3/Over what areas of life does the king have authority? What are his dues?   4/Why are weights and measures now standarized (cf. Lev. 19:35-36; Deut. 25:13-16)?   5/What areas of temptation are suggested here? 6/What are to be restored to the national life of God's people as the center of its worship?   7/What is the focus of your corporate worship?

day 3 □ Ezekiel 46

1/What privileges are granted to the king? to the priests? 2/To what extent does God recognize levels of authority? require different levels of responsibility? 3/How do you respect this principle within your group? 4/Note the orderliness required (vv. 1-10). How does disorder affect your spirit of worship? 5/Why are safeguards necessary for someone in power (cf. vv. 16-18 with 45:9)? 6/To what extent are you respecting the bounds of confidence placed in you without stealing reputation or using it for personal advantage? Why?

day 4 □ Ezekiel 47

1/How do you account for the origin, direction and increase of the water? 2/What usually flows from the sacrifice? 3/What is the usual condition of this eastern district and of the inland sea? 4/How is the restoration of the glory of God among his people to affect a barren society and a stagnant religion? 5/What is the significance of verse 11 (cf. 43:24; Lev. 2:13)? 6/Who will share in the inheritance?

day 5 □ Ezekiel 48

1/How does the tribal arrangement differ from the first settlement of the land? 2/What does an equal quantity of trust require of all the tribes? 3/Who are farther away from the sanctuary? Who are in the favored positions? 4/On what basis does the city receive its name? Imagine the feelings and response of Ezekiel and a long-exiled people. 5/Where is the Lord now? 6/Why did God leave Jerusalem and his people in the beginning of Ezekiel's ministry? 7/Why will he return and restore them? 8/What qualities of God have been predominant in Ezekiel? Why? 9/Summarize the role Ezekiel has played in fulfilling God's purpose. 10/What is your place in God's plan? How do you know?

day 6 □ Matthew 19:1-15

1/Where does Jesus go now? 2/What is the Pharisees' test now? 3/What is the purpose of two sexes? 4/What had been the situation before Moses' legislation in Israel? in the surrounding nations?

5/What is the status of women in Jesus' time?   6/What is the divine ideal for marriage? What do people feel is the ideal today?   7/What is the disciples' reaction? Why?   8/What *precept* can some receive and some not? Why?   9/If perfection in marriage is so hard to achieve, why will you be or are you married?   10/How does society in Jesus' day regard children?   11/What qualities of children are compatible with the kingdom of heaven?

day 7   □   *Matthew 19:16-30*

1/What is involved in the attainment of eternal life? Why?   2/What do you think is the point of the man's question in verse 18 (cf. 5:19)?   3/What keeps this man from having eternal life?   4/To what extent can having riches be reconciled with loving your neighbor as yourself? Why?   5/Why are the disciples *astonished*?   6/How are privilege and responsibility related in Jesus' response to Peter?

day 8   □   *Matthew 19:30–20:16*

1/What is the policy of reward in the kingdom of heaven? Why?   2/Who are the characters in the parable? With whom does the householder make an agreement?   3/What does each man do after he is called?   4/What is the cause of the grumbling?   5/What quality of God is being illustrated?   6/How does the principle here apply to Jew and Gentile? young and old?   7/When have you been called? Why? What belongs to you?   8/What is implied about "working your way to heaven"? Why?

day 9   □   *Matthew 20:17-19*

1/What three experiences await Jesus in Jerusalem?   2/When has Jesus talked about this before (cf. 16:21; 17:22-23)?   3/How have the disciples reacted before? Why?   4/Imagine their feelings as they travel.   5/Who will be involved in the coming trials?   6/What is the significance of the verbs?   7/Imagine your reactions to Jesus' intention and explanations.   8/Write out what you would have said to him and the questions you would have wanted answered before you went.

day 10   □   *Matthew 20:20-34*

1/What part of Jesus' teaching do James and John have in mind (cf. 19:28)?   2/What is the extent of their loyalty?   3/Contrast the greatness of political rulers and members of the kingdom of heaven. How does authority relate to greatness?   4/How many of your ideas or concepts about here and heaven are in authoritarian terms? Why?   5/What is the consequence of Jesus' service?   6/How does Jesus practice what he preaches?   7/How do the blind men respond to news of Jesus' nearness? What is the result?   8/Whom do you serve? Why?   9/Who serves you? Why?

day 11   □   *Matthew 21:1-22*

1/Account for Jesus' actions here in view of what he knows in 20:18-19. What does he deliberately arrange (cf. Zech. 9:9)? What happens?   2/To what extent do the people recognize who Jesus is?   3/Who need their money changed?   4/What are the pigeons used for?   5/What is the purpose of the temple and sacrifices (cf. Is. 56:7)?   6/What else does Jesus do in the temple? Who is disturbed by the commotion?   7/What causes the disciples to marvel?   8/Relate Jesus' answer to both the natural and supernatural realms.   9/What insurmountable difficulties are you facing? Why?

day 12   □   *Matthew 21:23-46*

1/How does Jesus' question about John answer the Pharisees' question?   2/What is the issue?   3/What is the priests and elders' predicament?   4/Why do you think Jesus explains the parable of the two sons?   5/How have you become aware of your need for repentance?   6/What are the implications of the allegory of the vineyard in regard to John the Baptist? Jesus' future and destiny? the future of Israel? the religious leaders of Israel?   7/What could the people have done to the priests and Pharisees (cf. v. 46 with v. 26)?   8/To what extent do you *respect* God's Son? Why?   9/What motivates the murder of Jesus?

420

day 13 □ *Matthew 22:1-14*
1/To whom are these parables addressed? 2/What is the main theme
of the marriage feast (cf. 21:43; vv. 6-7 are regarded as later inser-
tions; vv. 11-14 are regarded as part of another parable)? 3/In what
ways does the king get ready for the celebration? 4/Why will those
invited not come? 5/Relate verses 6-7 with the parable of the vineyard. 6/Contrast the gathering in verse 10 with the point of verses
11-14. 7/What are the requirements for being chosen? 8/Have you
been *called*? *chosen*? How do you know?

day 14 □ *Matthew 22:15-45*
1/What is the intention of these questions? 2/Investigate the political beliefs of the Pharisees and Herodians. 3/What rights do
a—the government and *b*—God have? Define *render*. 4/Distinguish
the Pharisees' intention (v. 15) and response (v. 22). 5/What proof
do the Sadducees offer that Moses could not have believed in resurrection (cf. Deut. 25:5)? 6/Why do you think marriage is unnecessary in heaven? 6/What does Jesus offer as proof of the fact of resurrection (cf. Ex. 3:6)? What is the significance of *to you* in verse 31?
7/Can love of God and love of man be mutually exclusive? Why?
8/What question would you like to ask Jesus? Why? 9/What is your
view of the Messiah? Why? 10/What is the Messiah's relationship
with David (cf. Ps. 110:1)?

day 15 □ *Matthew 23:1-28*
1/To whom are these denunciations spoken? Why, do you think?
2/In what respect are the people to obey the teachings of the Jewish
scribes and Pharisees? Why? In what way are they not to follow these
men? 3/In what ways do they oppress the people? Why? 4/Con-
trast the actions of the scribes and Pharisees here with the injunctions
of chapters 5—7. 5/Why are Christians not to seek high places? ec-
clesiastical titles? 6/How could the scribes and Pharisees prevent
others from entering the kingdom of heaven? 7/What images describe the Pharisees' actions and attitudes? What hypocrisy is revealed
by each? Why? 8/What perversions and hypocrisy do you see in
yourself? in your church? in national religion? Why?

day 16 □ *Matthew 23:29-39*

1/In what ways are the scribes and Pharisees deceiving themselves? Why? 2/What tendencies of the past generations have they carried on? In what measure? 3/What will be the consequences of their own bloodthirstiness (cf. Gen. 4:8-11; 2 Chron. 24:20-22)? 4/What is Jesus' feeling for his fellow countrymen? Why? 5/How will they feel about him in the future? 6/To what extent do you believe you would have recognized Jesus as Messiah in Jerusalem at this time? How are you responding to his words now?

day 17 □ *Matthew 24:1-28*

1/What will precede the end of the age in the world? in the church itself? 2/What will mark the destruction of Jerusalem (cf. **v. 2** with vv. 15-28)? 3/What will signal the imminence of attack on Jerusalem? 4/Who will suffer most in the flight? What conditions will make flight difficult? 5/How extensive will the tribulation caused by the Romans be? What rumors will be circulated? 6/What image is used of the Roman conquest? 7/Distinguish Jesus' second coming from the destruction of Jerusalem. 8/To what extent have you witnessed the happenings predicted in verses 4-14? 9/How do you know you will be *saved*?

day 18 □ *Matthew 24:29-42*

1/Why will there be no preliminary signs of Jesus' second coming (cf. v. 27 with vv. 36-42)? 2/How is the destruction of the temple described in verses 29-30 (cf. Ezek. 32:7-8)? 3/What will be the significance of the destruction of the temple for the Gentile world (v. 31)? 4/How certain is Jerusalem's destruction? What metaphor illustrates its imminent certainty? 5/To what extent is it important to you to know whether Christ is coming back in your generation? How would you live differently? How are you living now? 6/What is the only definite "sign" Jesus gives (cf. v. 14)? What is your part in that "sign"? Why?

day 19 □ *Matthew 24:42–25:13*

1/Why is the disciples' question of 24:3b unanswerable? 2/What two commands are required because of its unexpectedness?   3/What is the point of the parable of the faithful and wicked servants?   4/What responsibility does each have? What is the wicked servant's attitude toward his responsibility? toward his own rights? Why?   5/What responsibilities have you been given? Why?   6/What interrupted tasks should you complete now? What steps can you take today? Write out those you will take today, this week, next month.   7/What will be your predicament if you are unprepared when Jesus does come again? 8/Distinguish what qualities make some maidens wise and some not.

day 20   ☐   *Matthew 25:14-30*
1/Who is the owner of the different amounts of money? Why is the money entrusted to others?   2/What is the basis on which the trust of the money is judged?   3/How do two servants make more money? What is their reward?   4/Of what is the one servant afraid? How does he misjudge the qualities of his master? Why?   5/Why is the money taken away from the worthless servant? What is his additional fate? Why?   6/With what have you been entrusted?   7/To what extent do you express and use it in your daily living situations?   8/What kind of master do you have? How do you know?

day 21   ☐   *Matthew 25:31-46*
1/What event does this passage describe (cf. 16:27; Ezek. 34:17-34)? 2/What qualities of the Son of man are illustrated?   3/What is the basis on which the separation is made? Is nationality significant here? 4/List the actions which please the King. When have you done any of these recently? Why?   5/What are the *a*—status and *b*—future of those who have served their fellowmen?   6/What characteristics do the *goats* lack?   7/Contrast for what *a*—the kingdom and *b*—the eternal fire have been prepared. Why?   8/Contrast the intent of the questions of verses 37-39 and 44.

day 22   ☐   *Matthew 26:1-16*
1/Contrast Jesus' prediction and the plot of the religious hierarchy regarding the timing of Jesus' death. What speeds up the matter?

2/Contrast the attitudes of the disciples and Jesus about the woman. What makes the disciples react negatively? 3/How does Jesus explain her action (v. 12)? 4/Why is it impossible to be neutral about the claims and demands made by the Son of man (cf. vv. 4-5, 10, 15)? 5/Contrast the actions of the woman and Judas. What do you think motivates each? 6/To what extent do you *betray* Jesus? Do you seek opportunities to betray him?

day 23   □   *Matthew 26:17-35*

1/What arrangements has Jesus made for the passover meal? 2/What is the stunning announcement? 3/What extreme reactions do the disciples have to what Jesus says (cf. vv. 21-22 and 35)? 4/Contrast Jesus' answer to *a*—the disciples' (cf. Ps. 41:9) and *b*—Judas' question. What is the significance of *to him* in verse 25? 5/How does Jesus associate himself with the actions of the meal? What explanations does he give (cf. Jer. 31:34; Is. 53:11)? 6/What will the immediate future hold for the disciples? Why (cf. Zech. 13:7)? 7/Imagine Jesus' sense of responsibility for his disciples and his feelings as they vow their loyalty. 8/Enumerate all the predictions of this passage. Which are hopeful? 9/To what extent are you anticipating communion in the Father's kingdom? Imagine your feelings then.

day 24   □   *Matthew 26:36-46*

1/Why do you think Jesus asks these three disciples to share in the sorrow? 2/Contrast their actions here with their intentions (cf. vv. 33, 35; 20:22). 3/What qualities of the Lord are revealed in his instructions to the disciples and in his prayers? 4/On what condition does Jesus accept the cup? 5/What time has come (cf. anticipation of this time in previous passages in Mt.)? 6/Imagine Jesus' feelings now. 7/In what areas is your *spirit willing*? Is your *flesh weak*? Why? 8/When do you think Jesus has been hurt by your weakness?

day 25   □   *Matthew 26:47-56*

1/Who accompanies Judas? Why, do you think (cf. v. 55)? 2/Why have they not captured him while he has been in the temple (cf. 12:14;

21:46; 26:4-5)?   3/What is the sign?   4/Imagine Jesus' and Judas' feelings at this moment. 5/Why does Jesus submit to this arrest? 6/Imagine the Father's feelings at this moment.   7/Why does Jesus prevent intervention by his disciples? How do the disciples react? What do you think they fear?

day 26   ☐   *Matthew 26:57-75*

1/Why do you think the scribes and elders are already in session? 2/How do you think Matthew gets his information about the trial? 3/What charge is the council seeking?   4/What do two witnesses finally agree on (cf. Deut. 19:15)?   5/Contrast what Jesus had said (cf. Jn. 2:19) with the accusation.   6/What are the implications of speaking against the temple? 7/When does Jesus answer the accusation? How (cf. Ps. 110:1; Dan. 7:13-14)? With what result?   8/Why do you think Jesus "condemns" himself?   9/Why is the need for further evidence no longer pursued? What is the verdict?   10/Where is Peter during the trial (v. 58)? Contrast his intention (vv. 33-35) with the actual events. 11/When do you deny Christ? Why?

day 27   ☐   *Matthew 27:1-10*

1/What time is it now? Imagine what has happened after the verdict and before the sentence. 2/Why must Jesus go to Pilate (cf. Jn. 18:31)? 3/What is Judas' reaction to the outcome of the trial? 4/How do the priests and elders react to his remorse? 5/What do the priests buy?   6/What prophecies does Matthew see this action fulfilling (cf. Jer. 32:7-9; Zech. 11:12-13)?   7/Why do you think Judas regrets his action? When have you regretted your actions? Have they been irrevocable?

day 28   ☐   *Matthew 27:11-26*

1/Contrast the political emphasis of the trial here with the religious emphasis in 26:61-68.   2/What question does Jesus answer? How? 3/Why is Pilate loath to authorize the crucifixion? What attempts does he make to free Jesus? to free himself from responsibility for Jesus' death?   4/What is the extent of Jesus' popular support? of the reli-

gious hierarchy's influence over the people? Why?   5/Who accepts
responsibility for Jesus' death? Why, do you think?   6/Who all are
responsible? Are you included (cf. 23:30)? Why?   7/Imagine the
disciples' feelings as they hear or hear of the shouting.

day 29   □   Matthew 27:27-56

1/Enumerate the things the soldiers do to Jesus.   2/What do you
think is going on in Jesus' mind during this time? Why?   3/Why do
you think the soldiers keep *watch* over Jesus?   4/What three groups
of people mock him? Which people acknowledge him?   5/What
events and actions to which Jesus submits appear to put the control of
his destiny into human hands? What signs show that God is also at
work in the crucifixion? What is the result of these signs in the lives of
some onlookers?   6/Why do you think more specific information is
not given about the event described in verses 52-53?   7/Imagine you
are a witness to the crucifixion. What are your feelings and response?
Why?

day 30   □   Matthew 27:57-66

1/Identify Joseph. How does he identify himself with Jesus?   2/Ac-
count for the presence of the women here (cf. vv. 55-56).   3/What
precautions against body-snatching does Joseph take? What do the
chief priests and Pharisees arrange to have done? Why?   4/Identify
the *first* and *last fraud*.   5/Account for the Pharisees' determination to
be rid of Jesus. Summarize the attitudes of each for the other. What
is the basis for their conflict?   6/Imagine the women's feelings as they
watch the proceedings.   7/What are your feelings? Why?

Month 44

day 1   □   Matthew 28:1-20

1/What happens in spite of all the precautions? When? Who witnesses the spectacle? 2/Who is reassured? What are the instructions (cf. 26:32)? 3/Imagine the women's emotions. 4/How do they respond to meeting Jesus in person? 5/Account for their obedience to his commands. 6/How do the chief priests and elders suppress the guards' story? How effective is the rumor? 7/What is Jesus' last command to his people? his promise? 8/What is the extent of Jesus' authority? 9/What is the extent of his disciples' mission (cf. 10:5)? 10/What difference does Jesus' resurrection make in your daily living? Why?

day 2 ☐ *Matthew 1–13*
1/How are Jesus' sayings and his actions related? 2/List areas of life Jesus talks about. Choose several and cite evidence that Jesus practices what he preaches. 3/Summarize Matthew's concerns in writing his Gospel. In what ways does he relate the Old Testament to Jesus' life? For what purpose? 4/List the titles assigned to Jesus. 5/Summarize the ethics of the kingdom of God. List parables which illustrate them. 6/How does Jesus relate with common people? with the religious leaders? Why? 7/With which saying of Jesus do you have the most problem? Why? Which of his actions here do you question? Why? 8/How are you responding to Jesus' claims to your life? Why?

day 3 ☐ *Matthew 14–28*
1/Summarize John the Baptist's role in the kingdom of God. 2/What does Jesus have against the religious leaders of Israel? 3/Characterize Jesus' relationship with his disciples. 4/Summarize the requirements to enter the kingdom of heaven. List parables which illustrate them. What is involved in righteousness (cf. 6:33)? 5/Summarize Jesus' teaching about his death and resurrection. What new age will come? What will happen in Israel? in the world? 6/Write out your resolutions as a result of studying Matthew. 7/List areas of study you would like to pursue further. Why?

day 4 ☐ *Introduction to Ezra*
Ezra, a priest and scribe, encourages the returned exiles in the re-

building of the temple. He teaches them how they are to worship God and follow his law in restoring the religious community at Jerusalem. *Ezra 1* 1/Review the history of the captivity (cf. Jer. 39—44). In what way does God intervene in the life of Cyrus, king of Persia (his reign begins in 538 B.C.)? Why (cf. Jer. 25:12; 29:10)? 2/Describe the content of Cyrus' proclamation. For whom is it intended? 3/Who responds to the call to rebuild the house of God? 4/Compare God's dealings in the life of a Persian king and in the lives of his own people. 5/To what extent is Cyrus obedient to God's promptings? 6/Whom does God use to accomplish his purposes in history? Why?

day 5 □ Ezra 2
1/What are the general categories of those who return to Jerusalem? 2/How many people make the 800-mile trip? 3/How many Levites return? 4/Imagine the feelings of the people on the way back. What would be their concerns? 5/What happens when the people arrive at the site of the house of the Lord?

day 6 □ Ezra 3
1/What is the first united activity of the Israelites after they return? 2/Who assumes the leadership (cf. 2:2)? 3/The directions for the burnt offerings come from what writings? 4/After seven months of no religious observances, what causes the returned exiles to resume a detailed schedule of offerings and sacrifices? 5/What motive prompts you to repent and worship? 6/What managerial principles are used for laying the foundation of the temple? 7/What act of obedience triggers the praise and thanksgiving of the people (cf. Jer. 33:10-11)? 8/What are the evidences that the Israelites have not forgotten instructions and forms of worship they received 70 years earlier (cf. 1 Chron. 16:4-5)?

day 7 □ Ezra 4
1/What do the adversaries ask Zerubbabel (vv. 1-5, 24 occur during the reign of Cyrus; vv. 6-23 later during the reign of Ahasuerus and Artaxerxes, 486-424 B.C.)? 2/To what extent do the adversaries

worship God (cf. 2 Kings 17:24-33)? 3/Are the Israelites willing to cooperate with the adversaries in fulfilling a command from God? 4/Can you or your church work with groups which are not obedient to the example and commands of the Bible? 5/How do the adversaries respond to Israel's refusal to cooperate (vv. 4-5)? 6/To what part of the building is the later objection aimed (vv. 12, 16)? 7/What is the "crowning blow" which frustrates the rebuilding of the city?

day 8 ☐ *Ezra 5*

1/What is the immediate response to Haggai's and Zechariah's prophecies? 2/Imagine the content of the prophecy. How long has the building of the temple been stopped (Darius' reign begins in 521 B.C.)? 3/How do the prophets authenticate their prophecy? To what extent are you willing to invest your time and energies to help Christian friends keep the will of God foremost in their undertakings? 4/Who is responsible for averting delays in the work? 5/To what extent do you rely on God's timing to fulfill commands he has given? 6/Contrast the letters of chapter 4—5 as to author, recipient, accusation and motive for having government records searched. 7/Account for the Jews' claim in verse 16 in light of chapter 4.

day 9 ☐ *Ezra 6*

1/Contrast the reply of Darius (vv. 6-7) and Artaxerxes (4:21) to the letters. 2/What are Darius' major additions to Cyrus' decree? 3/What is the Israelites' response to Darius' decree? Imagine what they say to Tettanai and company. 4/How do you react when you are justified in front of others? 5/When is the building completed? How long has it taken? 6/What follows the completion of the house of God? 7/Describe the events of the celebration (cf. Num. 3, 8 and 1 Kings 8:62-64). Who are involved? 8/What is the source of their joy? 9/To what extent are you joyful? Why? What is its source?

day 10 ☐ *Ezra 7*

1/Establish the time of this chapter. 2/What characterizes the relationship between Artaxerxes and Ezra? 3/What accounts for the

Persian king's favor toward Ezra?   4/Why does Ezra determine to study God's law? Why do you study the Bible?   5/What commission does Artaxerxes give regarding the Israelites (cf. 6:6-12)? his own treasures? Ezra?   6/How does the nature of Artaxerxes' commission reflect his attitude toward the Israelites' God?   7/What is Ezra's response to the king's action?   8/How do you respond to God's working in history? to political recognition of religious practices?   9/Who does Ezra choose to take with him?

day 11   □   *Ezra 8*

1/Who is missing from Ezra's traveling party? What kind of men does Ezra want?   2/Who is responsible for the caliber of men who join the ranks?   3/To what extent do you trust God to provide the right person for each task in your group?   4/Why does Ezra proclaim a fast?   5/Imagine the enemies which threaten Ezra's party (the value of the gifts is around $4,500,000).   6/How are the Israelites protected?   7/What threatens your safety when you travel? Do you request God's protection? Why?   8/Describe the successive actions of the exiles after they reach Jerusalem. Why do they do these things (cf. 7:14-20)?

day 12   □   *Ezra 9*

1/To whom do the officials bring their report? **Why?**   2/What is the people's offense? What underlies their misconduct?   3/Why is this an offense for God's people (cf. Deut. 7:1-4)?   4/Who are the greatest offenders?   5/How does Ezra react to the faithlessness of the people? Who else reacts?   6/What does Ezra's prayer indicate about his attitude toward sin? toward the preservation of the Jewish community?   7/What is your attitude toward God's commandments concerning your feelings and private life?   8/What pollutions of the peoples are prevalent today?

day 13   □   *Ezra 10*

1/How does Ezra's behavior and prayer affect the Israelites?   2/How does the spokesman propose that the Israelites deal with their sin (cf. Lev. 5:14-19)?   3/How long does Ezra mourn?   4/By what means is the covenant accomplished? Who must abide by the proclamation? Why?   5/What is involved in confession of sin?   6/Imagine the feelings of the foreign women and children in all this.   7/How does your group deal with corporate breaches of conduct?   8/Relate *holiness* and *worship* (cf. 2:62-63; 3:10—4:3; 6:20-21 with chaps. 9—10). 9/Summarize the progress and setbacks of the task of rebuilding Jerusalem so far.

day 14   □   Introduction to Nehemiah

Nehemiah returns to Jerusalem from exile to rally the people to rebuild the city walls in spite of great hostility. *Nehemiah 1*   1/What does Nehemiah hear about the Jews in Jerusalem? about the city? What does he do?   2/With whom does God maintain his covenant and love?   3/Compare and contrast Nehemiah's prayer (vv. 5-11) with Ezra's (Ezra 9:6-15) in regard to the situation which prompted the prayer, the extent of relationship with the Israelites, the identification with the Israelites, requests made of God and knowledge of God's Word.   4/To what extent do you claim God's promises when you pray for other Christians?   5/What does Nehemiah pray specifically for himself?   6/In whose presence does he want God's mercy? 7/What requests do you make of God for yourself?

day 15   □   Nehemiah 2

1/How does God answer Nehemiah's request for mercy in the king's presence?   2/What do you pray when a decision must be made quickly?   3/What has preceded Nehemiah's "on the spot" prayer (cf. 1:4)? 4/How does Nehemiah account for the amazing favor of the king in granting his requests?   5/How do Sanballat (governor of Samaria) and Tobiah feel about Nehemiah's arrival in the province and subsequent building? Why, do you think?   6/What is the first step of Nehemiah's reconstruction project? Who is author of the master plan (v. 12)?   7/Consider the psychology of Nehemiah's "declaration of intention" to the people. How does he assure them of the propriety of the project (v. 18)?   8/How do you respond to mockery of expressions of your faith in Jesus Christ? Why?   9/What is in your heart to do for your people? for your city? for your neighborhood? for your campus? Why?

day 16 □ *Nehemiah 3:1–4:6*

1/Who begins the rebuilding? What characterizes the beginning effort?   2/What class of people work on the walls and gates? What parts of the country are represented? What are the exceptions? Why? 3/To what extent are you willing to get involved in the work of the Lord?   4/What are Sanballat's and Tobiah's estimations of the Jews' ability at restoration?   5/What is Nehemiah's prayer for these men? What do you pray when you are taunted, ridiculed or jeered? Why? 6/What contributes to the early success of the project?

day 17 □ *Nehemiah 4:7-23*

1/What point does Sanballat's anger reach? What is their plot? 2/What defense do the Israelites employ to counter the plot?   3/What problem within the Israelites compounds the crises of impending attack?   4/Which situation receives Nehemiah's first attention?   5/On whom does Nehemiah focus the people's attention? How does God directly intervene to deal with the external threats against the rebuilding?   6/What building procedures are resumed after the threat subsides? What changes are made? Why?   7/What defenses do you maintain against Satan and his threats to your efforts to do God's will? To what extent are the precautions appropriate to the threat? To what extent do they allow for continuation in the present will of God?

day 18 □ *Nehemiah 5*

1/What triggers the outcry of the people (v. 3)? Who is the object of this disturbance?   2/How does Nehemiah take all of this?   3/What is the charge against those responsible for the situation? Why does Nehemiah make the charge (v. 9; Ex. 21:2-6; 22:25; Lev. 25:25-34; Deut. 23:19-20)?   4/How do the accused rectify their error?   5/What promises have you made to God regarding your social obligations? 6/What kind of governor is Nehemiah (give evidence to support your answer)?   7/Contrast Nehemiah's attitude and actions with those of the nobles and officials. 8/Why does Nehemiah forego his governor's allowance? Do he and his household lack food?   9/What ethical standards do you maintain? Why? Whom do you consider when you form your social and moral values? Why?

day 19   ☐   *Nehemiah 6*

1/Compare the plans of Sanballat to undermine the Israelites' defense as to the nature of the plan, the object or intention and Nehemiah's response.   2/What human emotions does the enemy play on?   3/What is the effect of fear on your ability to complete responsibilities God gives you? How do you combat fear?   4/How do the enemies react to word that the Jerusalem wall is finished? Why?   5/Does the completion of the wall assure that all is well in Jerusalem?   6/Compare and contrast the political intrigue here with your own nation.   7/How does Nehemiah discern the intentions of the enemy?

day 20   ☐   *Nehemiah 7:1–8:18*

1/After the "finishing touches" to the wall are completed, what does Nehemiah do? Why does he appoint Hananiah as co-keeper of the city?   2/Why does Nehemiah enroll the people by genealogy? What is discovered?   3/Describe the scene in the square. What is the request?   4/What prefaces the reading of God's law?   5/How do you acknowledge the author of the Bible when you read it?   6/What is the special work of the Levites and those who stand with Ezra?   7/How does God recognize the desires of the Israelites to understand his Word?   8/Describe the scene of the second day. What do they do during the feast?   9/What is the result of the people's understanding the law?   10/To what extent are you obedient to the things of God's Word which you understand?   11/What is the result of their obedience?

day 21   ☐   *Nehemiah 9:1-15*

1/Why are the Israelites assembled? What is the order of activity for the day?   2/How do you order your daily time apart with the Lord? On what basis?   3/What aspects of God's character does Ezra emphasize in his prayer (cf. Ezra 9)?   4/What have been the turning points of the history of God and his people?   5/How have the sons of Abram responded to God's commandments and goodness?   6/What is God's attitude toward their disobedience?   7/Why doesn't God forsake you when you sin?

day 22   ☐   *Nehemiah 9:16-38*

1/Determine the pattern which historically characterizes the relationship between God and the Israelites.   2/How does this pattern correspond with the relationship you have with God?   3/What qualities of God are revealed?   4/What does God use to bring his people back to himself?   5/What has God used in your life? How have you responded?   6/Do the Israelites do anything which God can not forgive?   7/Contrast the ideal (v. 24) and actual (vv. 36-37) situations of promised blessing.   8/Will you unequivocally commit yourself to God today? Why?

day 23   ☐   *Nehemiah 10*

1/What characterizes all those who sign the covenant?   2/What is the content of the oath? What areas of life are included?   3/What will determine the Israelites' behavior from now on? How much of God's law do they swear to heed?   4/What determines your behavior toward God? toward your fellow man?   5/How does the situation of 9:36-37 affect the Israelites' oath concerning the practice of first-fruits and tithing?   6/How do taxes, increased tuition and increased cost of living influence the portion of your income which God receives?   7/What do the people determine regarding the house of God?   8/Write out a statement of your specific commitment to God and sign it.

day 24   ☐   *Nehemiah 11:1–12:26*

1/What plan is adopted to populate the city of Jerusalem? What is its condition? Do the Israelites regard it as a desirable place to live?   2/Why is the habitation of Jerusalem necessary?   3/Why are cities considered undesirable today? What is your rationale for your living place?   4/How does where you live affect your opportunities for service and witness?   5/Who comes to dwell in Jerusalem?   6/What villages are occupied?   7/Who are considered chiefs among the Israelites now?

day 25   ☐   *Nehemiah 12:27-47*

1/What emotion characterizes the dedication of Jerusalem's wall?

How is this feeling accounted for (v. 43)?   2/Who is involved?
3/What preparations do the priests and Levites make for the special
occasion?   4/Describe the major corporate demonstration of joy that
day.   5/Have you ever been involved in a demonstration of praise to
God?   6/What follows the procession of thanksgiving (v. 43)?
7/How do the Israelites regard the men who minister to them? How
do they express their regard?   8/How do you demonstrate your regard for those who minister to you? Why?

day 26   ☐   *Nehemiah 13:1-14*
1/What indicates that the Israelites continue to abide by their written
covenant (cf. 10:29)?   2/Are you immediately obedient when you become conscious of sin?   3/What does Nehemiah find when he returns?   4/What violation of God's house does Eliashib (3:1) allow (cf.
2:19; chap. 4; 6:17-19)?   5/What further neglect has come upon the
house of God? How?   6/Who does Nehemiah hold responsible?
What precaution does he take against future neglect?   7/What are
your provisions for the leaders of your congregation?

day 27   ☐   *Nehemiah 13:15-31*
1/What laws of God does Nehemiah find the people violating?
2/Trace the various measures Nehemiah takes to restore obedience to
the two commandments.   3/What measures do you take to bring
fellow believers out of sin and into obedience?   4/To what extent do
you risk your reputation to see that God is glorified?   5/Contrast Nehemiah's actions in the two situations (cf. vv. 23-29 with Ezra 10).
What does this suggest about the graveness of the infractions?
6/Is God's attitude toward intermarriage between believers and non-
believers any different today (cf. 2 Cor. 6:14-18)?   7/Describe the
tension between a strict and lax interpretation of the law of God here.
8/Summarize Nehemiah's zeal and appeals to God on behalf of his
people; on behalf of himself.   9/Contrast modern regard for zeal,
purity and strictness.   10/Where do you stand? How much do you
accomplish in your position? Why?   11/Summarize what Nehemiah
has accomplished. In what areas of life?

day 28 ☐ *Psalm 90*

1/How does Moses describe the existence of God (cf. vv. 1-2 with Deut. 33:27)?   2/How does he contrast God's nature with man's nature and need?   3/How does God react to human sin? Why?   4/What does God require of you in order to experience his mercy?   5/Which verse do you want to become your prayer today?   6/Summarize the psalm in a title.

day 29 ☐ *Psalm 91*

1/To what extent is faith in God personal?   2/What is the basis for the declared security from danger expressed in verses 5-8?   3/In what ways do angels guard believers (cf. Gen. 24:40; Ex. 23:20)?   4/What is the prerequisite for this kind of protection? Why?   5/Make a list of your fears and troubles for which you want to trust God for deliverance or security. What is your part in the deliverance?   6/Title the psalm.

day 30 ☐ *Psalm 92*

1/Why is it good to praise God?   2/Do you adore God because you are an observer or partaker of his mercy and power?   3/Compare the final destination of the wicked in verses 6-9 with Psalm 1:4-6. 4/What is signified by the images of grass and the palm tree? Which is a symbol of permanence, dignity and fruitfulness (cf. with the tree in Ps. 1:3)?   5/What is the promise for success and prosperity for the Christian?   6/To what extent does your life reflect this kind of prosperity? Why?   7/Summarize the psalm in a title.

Month 45

day 1 ☐ *Psalm 93*

1/Is there any scriptural indication that God can be pronounced "dead"?   2/Compare verse 2 with Psalm 29:10. What qualities of God are being extolled? 3/On what basis is the world established? 4/What happens to God when floods come? to God's people? Why? 5/Write a poem expressing your own praise to God for the qualities of his nature cited here.

    day 2 ☐ *Psalm 94*
1/How do you reconcile the wickedness of man with the holiness of God? 2/Why does God allow wickedness to prosper? What will ultimately prevail? 3/In what ways do wicked rulers promote unrighteousness? 4/Is it common for people to lose their trust in God because he does not fully protect them from all difficulty? Why? 5/Is your attitude toward sinners a cry for vengeance against their wickedness or compassion for their lack of spiritual understanding? 6/How are righteous and wicked people described here? 7/Summarize the psalm in a title.

    day 3 ☐ *Psalm 95*
1/Enumerate the aspects of God which make him praiseworthy. 2/What gods have the Israelites worshiped in the past? Why? 3/What warning is inserted into the congregational worship? 4/When does it become difficult to praise God? How does he respond to our reluctance? 5/In what ways do you *harden* your heart before God? Meditate on the urgency of *today* in verse 7 and the finality of *rest* in verse 11. 6/Title the psalm. 7/Write a short song expressing your praise to God.

    day 4 ☐ *Psalm 96*
1/Who participates in the worship of the psalm (cf. 1 Chron. 16:23-33)? 2/What aspects of God are being praised? How does each make an impact on your life? 3/How does nature participate in the praise? 4/Underline the imperative verbs in the psalm. 5/Compare your verbal praise of God with the identity you feel with nature's praise. 6/How do you relate this sense of praise to your friends? 7/Title the psalm.

day 5 ☐ *Psalm 97*
1/Characterize the exalted position and presence of God.   2/What is
the effect of God's presence on nature? on mankind? on Zion? on
you?   3/Compare God's relationship with the earth (cf. Ps. 96) and
with Zion (cf. Ps. 95).   4/How are the recognition of God's character
and the *lives of his saints* related?   5/Enumerate God's promises and
commands for those that love him. How can you appropriate them
in your life?   6/Title the psalm.

day 6 ☐ *Psalm 98*
1/What calls for the festive joy?   2/Who is invited to join the festivities?   3/What kind of celebration has been prescribed?   4/To what
extent do you feel such an exuberant sense of joy in your life? in your
fellowship with others? during church worship? Why?   5/Title the
psalm.

day 7 ☐ *Psalm 99*
1/Characterize the aspects of God's kingship as focused in Zion.   2/In
what ways does he exercise royal judgment?   3/Contrast the verbs
describing God with the imperatives given to the earth and people.
4/How has God dealt with Israel's priests?   5/How do you extend
God's justice into your daily living? his holiness?   6/Title the psalm.

day 8 ☐ *Psalm 100*
1/Why is God worthy of thanksgiving?   2/What acts and attitudes
accompany thanksgiving?   3/How do you know that the Lord is God?
4/List at least fifteen specific things you can thank God for today.
5/What is the opposite of thankfulness? How do you get into such a
frame of mind? Why?

day 9 ☐ *Psalm 101*
1/What are the principles on which David will base his reign in Zion?
Which are personal? Which relate to ministers and officials of the
court? Which relate to society?   2/What promises have you made to

God? On what occasions? Why?   3/Examine the extent of your commitment to Christ. Write down promises you wish to make today, beginning each with "I will" or "I will not." What are the specific steps you will need to take today to begin fulfilling them?   4/Title the psalm.

day 10 □ Psalm 102
1/How does the paslmist describe his spiritual, physical, emotional and social condition in verses 3-11?   2/To what does he attribute his condition?   3/In contrast, how does he characterize the constancy and mercy of God in relation to Zion? to all mankind?   4/Contrast the nature of man and the universe with God's nature.   5/To what extent does the psalmist's prayer convey the certainty of God's help? 6/How do you react when you feel overwhelmed by problems? What complaint do you have today?   7/Title the psalm.

day 11 □ Psalm 103
1/Define *bless*. How can you bless God with your whole being?   2/For what personal reasons does David bless God?   3/What further aspects of God's character shown toward all men make him blessed? 4/How has he dealt with our sin? Why?   5/Who are God's subjects? How will you join the call for universal praise?   6/Title the psalm.

day 12 □ Psalm 104
1/Characterize *a*—God's personal majesty and *b*—his involvement with nature.   2/How does God provide through nature for the daily needs of animals and men?   3/Determine the manner in which God controls and preserves every aspect of his creatures.   4/What are the psalmist's responses when he is confronted with God's preservation of nature? with his dependence on God?   5/Attempt to grasp the greatness of God manifest in nature and in life. How do you respond? 6/Title the psalm.

day 13 □ Psalm 105
1/What is the context for the psalmist's call for thanksgiving and re-

joicing?   2/What is God's covenant and promise to his chosen people?
3/How has he protected and prospered them?   4/Trace God's working in the history of Israel.   5/How does God provide when people
ask? For what purpose?   6/Meditate on God's working, protection
and provision in your life. To what extent do you concur with this
psalm's theme of thankfulness? Why?

day 14   □   Psalm 106
1/Contrast the goodness and power of God with the infidelity and
weakness of Israel.   2/What have been the consequences of Israel's
disobedience?   3/For what reason has God saved Israel?   4/How has
disobedience affected your life? What have you learned from God's
forgiveness?   5/Title the psalm.

day 15   □   Introduction to Haggai
Haggai, a contemporary of Zechariah, rebukes the Jews for their failure to rebuild God's temple and promises God's blessing if they will
continue their work.   *Haggai 1*   1/What is the historical context of
Haggai's message?   2/What excuse do the people offer?   3/What is
the economic situation of the times?   4/Compare or contrast your situation.   5/What responsibility does God take for their plight?
6/Contrast their houses with the temple of God.   7/To what extent
are you busy with your house? Why?   8/What encouragement comes
when they begin to work?

day 16   □   Haggai 2:1-9
1/When does the message come this time (cf. Lev. 23:34)? To whom?
2/How do they feel when they contrast their present conditions with
the glories of the past?   3/What is the basis of God's promise to them?
4/What is in store for the Lord's house? Why?   5/In what way do
you need to *take courage*?   6/Who is *the Lord of hosts*?

day 17   □   Haggai 2:10-23
1/Now that they are working, what future decisions are they called on

to consider?   2/To what extent do you tend to live in the past? Why? 3/What are the channels for decision-making?   4/How is God's withholding of his blessing explained?   5/What is the relationship between obedience and prosperity?   6/What characteristics of God are revealed in verses 20-23?   7/To what do you owe the preservation of your life?

day 18 ☐ *Introduction to Zechariah*
Zechariah is a contemporary of Haggai. Both aim at encouraging the Jews in the work of rebuilding the temple which has been suspended for eighteen years. Haggai is more singular and immediate in his prophecy while Zechariah is artistic with much symbolism and long-range prophecy (chaps. 9—14 are exclusively future). Skim the first six chapters to get the feel of Zechariah's style of writing about his visions. *Zechariah 1:1-6*   1/What does this section teach about the Word of God?   2/Why would Zechariah begin his prophecy on this note?   3/List several experiences in which God's words have "caught up" with you.   4/Because of your history (and Israel's), what should be your attitude toward God's Word today?

day 19 ☐ *Zechariah 1:7–2:13*
1/List the basic message in each of the three visions. 2/What progression do you notice?   3/Describe the character of God revealed in the third vision. What is his relationship to Zion?   4/In what ways are you also the *apple of his eye*?   5/When have you experienced his care and possession of you? How do you anticipate it for today?

day 20 ☐ *Zechariah 3–4*
1/In the fourth vision, whom does Joshua represent?   2/Why are his clothes soiled?   3/What causes the change of apparel?   4/What privileges are promised? On what conditions are they based?   5/Upon what conditions are you promised access to God's presence?   6/In what way does the angel come for the fifth vision (vv. 6-10a are a separate oracle so the dialogue of 5 is resumed in 10b)?   7/Who was Zerubbabel and what would the angel's message mean to him?   8/Upon what confidence are you performing God's work?

day 21   ☐   *Zechariah 5-6*

1/How does the sixth vision differ from the previous five?   2/What aspect of God's character is seen?   3/If post-exilic Jerusalem was without a judicial system at this time, what makes this message crucial?   4/Compare the seventh vision with the fourth and then with the introduction (the *ephah* is a measure of approximately one bushel). 5/What does this vision reveal about evil and God's control over it? 6/Compare the eighth vision to the first.   7/How do verses 9-14 supplement the final vision?   8/What is said about the Branch?   9/Contrast 6:11-14 with 4:6-10.   10/How do you intend to diligently obey the voice of the Lord today?

day 22   ☐   *Zechariah 7*

1/What prompts the sending of this delegation? What does the fact that the trip took three and one-half months tell?   2/What event were the Jews commemorating with their fast?   3/What is the point of Zechariah's question?   4/When in your life have you performed acts of religious devotion for selfish reasons?   5/According to this passage, when is it wrong to pray, fast and have long quiet times? 6/What are the outward signs that are to characterize true piety? To what extent do these fit into your lifestyle?   7/What is the relationship between prayer and obedience in your life?

day 23   ☐   *Zechariah 8*

1/What does this passage add to the message begun in chapter 7? 2/How would this message have affected the delegation?   3/Contrast verse 5 with Lamentations 2:11-12, 19-20; 4:4, 10.   4/Inquire about Jewish fasts from a friend or calendar (cf. Jer. 39:2-3; 2 Kings 25:22-25).   5/How has God been firm yet tender with you?   6/Describe the role God has in store for Jerusalem.   7/How would this affect those rebuilding the temple?   8/How should your knowledge of the outcome of history affect your work on behalf of God's kingdom today?   9/To what extent does verse 23 describe your influence?

day 24   ☐   *Zechariah 9:1-10*

1/**Compare** this oracle with the second vision (relate to the conquests of Alexander the Great). 2/Contrast the before and after situation of the cities. 3/Trace the progression of the Word of the Lord through this passage. 4/How is the king described? 5/What are to be his achievements? 6/What response does the king's arrival call for? 7/To what extent does his reign meet with joy in your life? Why?

day 25 □ Zechariah 9:11-17
1/How does this passage continue the theme of yesterday's message? 2/What binds the king and his people? 3/What does it mean to be a *prisoner of hope?* 4/In what way is your hope different from that of Zechariah's contemporaries? 5/What metaphors are used in this passage? 6/What metaphors would describe your experience of salvation?

day 26 □ Zechariah 10
1/How is the program of the king (begun in 9:11) continued here? 2/What reason is given for the misdirection of the people? 3/How will the king deal with the shepherds? Why? 4/What reasons are given for the complete redemption of the king's sheep? 5/How has the king had compassion for you? When? For what reason? What has your response been?

day 27 □ Zechariah 11
1/How does the picture in this chapter differ from yesterday's passage (it seems impossible to anchor this prophecy in history, and the text is difficult)? 2/How are the sheep abused? 3/What is the prophet told to do? 4/How is his leadership received? 5/What happens when he comes to the end of his endurance? 6/Why are the merchants eager to be rid of the shepherd? 7/What is the result of his rejection? 8/Describe the role assigned to the prophet in verses 15-17. 9/Contrast the care, seeking, healing and nourishing you have experienced from the Lord as your shepherd.

day 28 □ Zechariah 12:1-13:6
1/When are the events of this passage to take place? 2/What will hap-

pen to those who attack Jerusalem?   3/Contrast the events of verses 10-14 with verses 1-9.   4/What is stressed by the descriptions of the mourning?   5/What hope is held for these who have killed God's anointed? for the false prophets (cf. 13:6 with Lev. 19:28)?   6/What is the relationship between mourning, repentance and forgiveness?

day 29   ☐   *Zechariah 13:7–14:8*
The shepherd motif of chapter 11 is resumed.   1/What do you learn about God's control over even the death of his shepherd?   2/What is the end result of Israel's purging?   3/Where is the climax in verses 1-8?   4/Contrast the scene before and after.   5/What does "Thy kingdom come" mean to you in light of this entire book?

day 30   ☐   *Zechariah 14:9-21*
1/What results when the king is enthroned?   2/How are animals and cooking utensils affected by the Lord's reign?   3/Why would a distinction between sacred and secular indicate that the king is not reigning in one's life?   4/What possessions, talents, relationships or blocks of time in your life still are not inscribed with *Holy to the Lord*? Why?   5/Review the ways in which chapters 8—14 enlarge upon the ideas of the eight visions and the immediate task of rebuilding the temple.   6/How would Zechariah's message affect you if you were an exile recently returned to Jerusalem?

Month 46

day 1   ☐   *Introduction to Malachi*
Inspired by Haggai and Zechariah, the Jews have rebuilt the temple. But years have passed and prosperity has not come. They begin to question the rewards of being righteous. On the contrary, Malachi says, it is prevalent sinfulness which blocks God's blessing.   1/Read the book through at one sitting.   2/List the Israelites' questions

throughout.   3/Does Malachi rebuke or encourage?   4/What positive approach appears?   5/What seems to be the main emphasis in the book? How is this emphasis needed today?   6/In what areas do you need the message of Malachi?

day 2   □   *Malachi 1*

1/What does Malachi emphasize as proofs of God's love to Israel? 2/To what extent do punishment and salvation equally reveal God's nature?   3/What about the people's sacrifices and the priests' offering of these sacrifices reveals their attitude toward God?   4/What do they actually say?   5/List the parallels to these *blemished sacrifices* (cf. Deut. 15:21) in your life. What about your religious practices do you find boring? Why?   6/Where is God honored? How can you honor God's name?

day 3   □   *Malachi 2*

1/Contrast the qualities in Levi with those of the priests to whom Malachi is speaking. What is God's response to each?   2/What can you learn from this contrast concerning your witness?   3/How has Judah broken God's covenant with her?   4/What questions do the Israelites have in this chapter? Which have you asked? When? Why? How have you been answered?   5/How does your attitude affect God's nearness to you?   6/Compare or contrast God's view of marriage with yours and with the consensus in your country.

day 4   □   *Malachi 3:1-12*

1/Describe the coming Lord. Who will precede him?   2/What is the purpose of his coming (a *fuller* is a bleacher of cloth)?   3/What social injustices will the revealed God correct?   4/What is your responsibility toward these injustices now?   5/How can the people again be blessed by God? What is involved in returning to the Lord?   6/How will God return?   7/From what statutes of God have you turned aside? Why?   8/When have you ever put God to this kind of *test*? What has happened?

445

day 5   □   *Malachi 3:13-4:6*

1/What two types of people are presented here? Contrast the opinion of God and the people toward these two types.   2/In what way does this encourage you to know God in fear and in fellowship with his followers?   3/What command is given? What promise?   4/Of what value to you is keeping God's law? Why?   5/What would you feel for your parents or children if their hearts were turned toward you? 6/Summarize Malachi's message to the people. When will the godly be vindicated?   7/Summarize your present understanding of God's justice.   8/On what note does the Old Testament end?

day 6   □   *Introduction to James*

This letter, probably written about A.D. 60 by James the brother of Jesus, addresses various groups of Christians—Jewish and Gentile—throughout the Roman world.   1/Investigate the climate of the times. What has become of the apostles? of Paul?   2/Read the letter through. 3/List the contrast between the Christian and the natural approaches to life.   4/Which areas do you feel need special emphasis in your life? Why?

day 7   □   *James 1:1-15*

1/Define *trial*. What trials do you meet most often? When? How do you usually handle them?   2/Why should you consider a trial *all joy*? 3/What should result from a trial? What has been the outcome of your trials?   4/Contrast faith and doubt. What is the meaning you derive from the simile?   5/How does true Christian wisdom express itself toward God? self? others?   6/What is the source of temptation? What are two possible results? In what situations have you experienced these results?   7/How will you handle temptations you meet today? Why?

day 8   □   *James 1:16-27*

1/What characteristics of God are revealed in verses 17-18?   2/What gifts or endowments have you received?   3/How should God's righteousness manifest itself in you? Why?   4/What is the *implanted word*?

5/By what methods do you translate what you hear (sermons, Bible studies, etc.) into action?   6/What are you like today (v. 24)? How do you find out?   7/What will be the result of your quiet time today?

day 9   □   *James 2:1-13*
1/Toward what people or groups do you show partiality? What people does your church or group favor?   2/What should be your attitude? Why?   3/What reasons does James give that such partiality is absolutely wrong?   4/Contrast the distinctions made by *a*-man and *b*-God. 5/What should be your standard for action?   6/What is the law of liberty (cf. 1:25)?

day 10   □   *James 2:14-26*
1/Define *faith* and *works*. How are they related? How are both evidenced in your life?   2/Follow James' argument here. Contrast the beliefs of the demons, Abraham and Rahab. What is the additional quality in the belief of Abraham and Rahab?   3/With what image does James summarize his argument?   4/By what works will you demonstrate your faith today?

day 11   □   *James 3:1-12*
1/To whom is James speaking?   2/What is similar in each comparison he uses?   3/Describe an untamed tongue. What are the effects of its pollution? When have you polluted with it? experienced its pollution? 4/Contrast nature's predictability and the tongue's unpredictability. 5/How can you be *perfect* in what you say (cf. 1:26)?

day 12   □   *James 3:13-18*
1/List the characteristics of each type of wisdom. What are the results of each?   2/In what ways have you relied on these kinds of wisdom this past week?   3/Why is this passage especially applicable to teachers?   4/How can you obtain *wisdom from above* (cf. 1:5-6)?

day 13   ☐   *James 4:1-12*

1/What is the basic cause of wars among Christians? Why are they unnecessary?   2/What in your situation is a friendship with the world (consider your attitude toward material possessions, friends, study habits, work and leisure patterns)? If you are an enemy of God in any area, how can you restore your relationship to him?   3/Why must you not speak evil or judge your brother (cf. 1:22-25; 2:1-13; 3:8-10)? Who is the only true judge?

day 14   ☐   *James 4:13–5:6*

1/What qualification should you attach to any plans you make? 2/Why is it boasting if you ignore the qualification? In what sense is your life like a mist?   3/What responsibility does hearing God's Word bring?   4/Why is James so hard on the rich (cf. 1:10-11)? How do they make their treasures? What do they do with them?   5/For what purposes are you using your treasures?

day 15   ☐   *James 5:7-12*

1/What circumstances surround the brethren? Why is patience called for?   2/What are the circumstances you encounter in which patience is the only recourse?   2/What will patience accomplish? What is the result of impatience?   3/Recall the experiences of the prophets. 4/To what extent is your word trustworthy (cf. Mt. 5:33-37)?   5/What qualities of the Lord make patience tolerable?

day 16   ☐   *James 5:13-20*

1/What might prayer accomplish in each of these situations? What is the condition for an answer?   2/In what ways have you experienced the power of prayer in your circumstances recently?   3/Why is it so crucial to bring back a brother from wandering?   4/According to this letter, what areas do you need to be especially careful about in your Christian life? Why?

day 17   ☐   *Introduction to 1 Chronicles*

Chronicles (1 Chron. and 2 Chron. were originally one book) deals with the history of Israel as a religious community. It is written to a post-exilic audience who need to understand their history—what God has done to and for them and what tasks they are entrusted with. It draws from and supplements Samuel and Kings. *1 Chronicles 1:1–2:2* 1/Go through the genealogies, underlining the names you recognize. 2/Who is missing in verses 1-4 (cf. Gen. 4—5)? Why, do you suppose? 3/What nations were established by the descendants after the flood (cf. vv. 5-23 with Gen. 10:1-32)? Which do you recognize? 4/Trace the descendants of Abraham (cf. vv. 24-33 with Gen. 11:10-32; 25:1-16). Imagine the family constellations. How many generations were living at the same time? 5/Trace the descendants of Esau. What can you surmise about the ways of the Edomites (the line of Esau) from verses 43-54? 6/List the sons of Jacob (cf. Gen. 35:22-26). What name is out of sequence? 7/Is it important to you to know how God has dealt with your ancestors? Why?

day 18   □   *1 Chronicles 2:3-55*
1/List the members of the family of Judah (cf. v. 4 with Gen. 38). What resulted from the sin of Er? 2/What is the connection between God's concern for a person's own relationship to him and his concern for family history? 3/How many sons of Jesse are listed (cf. 1 Sam. 16: 10-11)? 4/How is Abigail related (cf. 2 Sam. 17:25)? Account for the difference. 5/What occupations are cited? Of what family lines? 6/How is the continuity of family lines assured? What is its purpose? 7/Compare or contrast our situation regarding family, sons and barrenness today. To what extent have attitudes changed? Why? Whose? 8/How do you fit into the line of history?

day 19   □   *1 Chronicles 3–4:23*
1/How many sons does David have (cf. 2 Sam. 3:2-5; 5:14-16)? Account for the difference. 2/Why does Solomon carry on the line? 3/When is the captivity cited in the genealogies? 4/Why do you think the lineage of Judah is repeated (here a collection of fragments having little connection with chap. 2)? 5/What special attention is given Jabez? 6/What occupations are cited? 7/What would you like to be

449

remembered for after you die? By whom?   8/Write out the epitaph
you would like.

day 20   □   1 Chronicles 4:24–5:17
1/Trace the descendants of Simeon.   2/What are some of their conquests? Why?   3/Trace the descendants of Reuben (cf. Gen. 49:3-4).
Locate their expansion on a map.   4/Where do the descendants of
Gad go?   5/What political and military structure is cited?   6/Imagine
you are a leader in one of the tribes. What are your concerns? How
will you be able to keep track of God's dealings with your people in the
past?   7/To what extent do you feel a part of history today? Why?

day 21   □   1 Chronicles 5:18-26
1/Who are involved in war here?   2/Why is this victory important?
What is their spoil?   3/How do you justify wars *of God*?   4/What
kind of people are the heads of the families of Manasseh?   5/Contrast
the behavior of the people in verses 20 and 25. How does God
respond? Why?   6/How can you remain holy to God in your culture?
7/What cultural values and practices have you absorbed into your lifestyle? Which coincide with God's values? To what extent are you concerned with those which do not? Why?

day 22   □   1 Chronicles 6
1/What is special about the Levites (cf. Num. 3:5—4:49)?   2/What are
their duties? How were they assigned?   3/Compare or contrast expected or assigned involvement in the church today.   4/Where do the
Levites live? How does this arrangement affect their ability to carry
out their duties?   5/Where do you live? Why?

day 23   □   1 Chronicles 7–9
1/List the sons of Jacob (cf. 2:1-2 with Gen. 49; Ex. 1:1-5). Which have
been accounted for thus far?   2/What clues does this account give
you about the daily life of the people?   3/What reason is given for
Judah's exile?   4/Note the care and precision involved in caring for

the house of the Lord. What characteristic of God does all this reflect? 5/What does it imply about the way your fellowship group functions?

day 24   ☐   *1 Chronicles 10*
1/Why does Saul commit suicide?   2/What further reasons are given for his death?   3/How do Saul's personal choices affect the whole kingdom?   4/How do you go about making decisions in your life? 5/Skim 1 Samuel 9—11. Contrast Saul's beginning with the epitaph given here. Could the same thing happen to you?

day 25   ☐   *1 Chronicles 11*
1/Why do the people now make David king?   2/What is David's response? Notice his preparation in 1 Sam. 16:1-13.   3/Why do you think David moves the capital from Hebron to Jebus (re-named Jerusalem)?   4/How does Joab become the military commander? What other job does he carry out?   5/What are the characteristics of David's chiefs?   6/What do you think of David's action in verse 18? 7/What does this chapter teach about leadership?

day 26   ☐   *1 Chronicles 12*
1/Notice that representatives of all twelve tribes of Israel are included among those loyal to David. Why do they choose to serve him (v. 18)? 2/What abilities do the various soldiers have which will be useful to David?   3/What gifts do you have to use in the service of your King? 4/Compare 1 Samuel 23:15-29 with the parade in verse 38. Imagine King David's feelings during the three-day celebration.

day 27   ☐   *1 Chronicles 13–14*
1/What is David's first official act as king?   2/What method is used to convey the ark to Jerusalem? Is this proper (cf. Num. 7:7-9)?   3/What is Uzzah's mistake (cf. Num. 4:5-6, 15, 19-20)?   4/How does David react to Uzzah's death?   5/Is the ark an instrument of blessing or curse (cf. v. 10 with v. 14)?   6/How did the events in chapter 14 help

to restore David's confidence?   7/Contrast David's way of making decisions (14:8-17) with Saul's and with yours.

day 28   □   *1 Chronicles 15:1–16:6*
1/Who are commissioned to bring the ark to Jerusalem?   2/What are they commanded to do in preparation for their task?   3/How does David prepare for the ark's arrival?   4/How is the procession described here similar to the one in chapter 13? How are they different?   5/What reason is given for the sacrifices?   6/What implications can you see here for the worship of God?

day 29   □   *1 Chronicles 16:7-43*
1/This psalm of thanksgiving is recorded again as Psalms 105:1-15; 96:1-13; 106:1, 47-48. What does it tell us about God's character? about his acts?   2/What do the verbs in verses 8-12 show about the various aspects of worship?   3/What key element do 15:15, 16:15 and 16:40 have in common?   4/What reasons are given here for praising God?   5/Think of some of the Lord's "marvelous deeds" which you have personally experienced, and take some time to give him thanks for them.

day 30   □   *1 Chronicles 17:1-15*
1/What is David's concern? Is it valid?   2/What advice does Nathan give initially? On what is it based?   3/Why does God say, "You shall not build me a house" (v. 5; cf. 22:8)?   4/What surprising alternate plan does God announce (v. 10c)?   5/Who is the most significant person to come from the "house and lineage of David"? Give praise today to the God who loved us enough to become one of us.

Month 47

day 1 ☐ *1 Chronicles 17:16-27*
1/What is David's action in response to the word of prophecy?
2/What do you think is his emotional response to *a*—God's negative
command and *b*—God's promise? 3/What requests does David make
in his prayer? Why these instead of others? 4/List the facets of God's
character for which David gives praise. 5/List the things about God
which you have observed in Scripture or in your own life. Praise him
for being this kind of God.

day 2 ☐ *1 Chronicles 18*
1/What kind of king is David? 2/Why does Tou send him gifts?
3/Who is responsible for his military victories? 4/What does David
do with the spoils of war? 5/What is your attitude toward *your*
possessions?

day 3 ☐ *1 Chronicles 19*
1/How is David's kindness in offering sympathy received? 2/How
does David show consideration for his embarrassed servants? Do you
show this kind of concern for others? 3/Why do the Ammonites go
to battle against David? 4/What is Joab's plan of defense? his attitude about the outcome of the battle? 5/Where do you think Joab's
faith is placed?

day 4 ☐ *1 Chronicles 20:1–21:13*
1/Why do you think David decides to count the people? 2/Why does
Joab object so strongly to this plan? 3/Why is God displeased with
David's action? 4/What is David's prayer concerning his guilt?
5/Of the three choices of punishment given to David, which would
you have chosen, and why? Which does he choose, and why? 6/What
does David's choice reveal about his relationship with God?

day 5   ☐   *1 Chronicles 21:14–22:1*
1/What retribution does the Lord's angel bring to Israel?   2/At what
point is the destruction halted?   Why?   3/What is David's reaction
when he sees the angel of God (vv. 16, 30)?   What is his prayer to the
Lord?   4/What glimpse is given of his shepherd's heart?   5/What do
Ornan's actions show about his attitude toward the king?   Why does
David refuse his gift?   6/How does God show David that he is forgiven?   What is David first required to do?   7/Write down what you
have learned here about the relationship of God's justice to his mercy.

day 6   ☐   *1 Chronicles 22:2–23:32*
1/What is David's reason for assembling materials for the building of
the temple?   2/Examine David's conversation with Solomon (22:
6-16).   What warning is given to the boy, and what encouragement?
3/What verbs comprise the commission given to the leaders (22:
17-19)?   4/What does the order of these commands imply for your
involvement in the Lord's work?   5/Which of the duties of the Levites
should you be carrying out in the worship of God?   Are you?   Consider
new ways you can do so.

day 7   ☐   *1 Chronicles 24–25*
1/What can your Christian group learn from the organizational planning described in these chapters?   2/Does the job described in 24:19
strike you as meaningless?   Why or why not?   3/What word is used
repeatedly to describe the work of the musicians (25:1-3)?   4/How
does God exalt Heman?   5/Consider the music to which you are
accustomed in worship. What does David's use of music suggest about
yours?

day 8   ☐   *1 Chronicles 26–27*
1/List the jobs mentioned in this section.   2/What explanation is
given about the census?   3/What characteristic did the gatekeepers
and stewards possess (26:6-9, 14, 30-32)?   4/Note that the listing in-
cludes even David's friends and the tutors of his children. Thus God
provided him with all the help necessary for the job he had to do.

What tasks has God given you, and what resources has he provided for their completion?

day 9   □   *1 Chronicles 28*
1/In speaking to the leaders of Israel, what does David say he wanted very much to accomplish? 2/Describe David's response to being denied this ambition. 3/What are the conditions for success taught here (vv. 7-8)? 4/What are the king's instructions to his son? 5/What aid is provided for Solomon (vv. 11-21)? 6/With what attitudes is the young king to serve God? 7/What is your motivation for serving him? 8/If you are weary of your responsibility in your Christian group, consider the encouragement verse 20 gives.

day 10   □   *1 Chronicles 29:1-9*
1/As David's reign draws to a close, what do you think are his top three or four priorities in life? What is the evidence? 2/Why does he say the job is a great one? 3/How does he initiate the free will offering? 4/What is to accompany the offering (v. 5)? 5/What is the result? 6/What is your attitude about giving of your substance? of your time and skills? Consider which of the demands being made on you are actually from the Lord. Plan your response to these demands.

day 11   □   *1 Chronicles 29:10-30*
1/Who receives the credit for the people's offerings? What reasons are given? 2/What requests does David make in his prayer? To what extent do you think these are answered? 3/What words and phrases describe Solomon's reign? What is the source of his authority? 4/How would you describe the prevailing mood of the scene recounted here? 5/Consider your place in the ongoing history of the people of God. Ask God to help you make a significant contribution to his purposes.

day 12   □   *Psalm 107*
1/List the areas of life from which God has brought deliverance

(vv. 4, 10, 17, 23).   2/What should be the response of those delivered? Why?   3/Characterize the pattern of man's turning to God and to sin. 4/How does God bring his people to repentance?   5/Relate verses 6, 13, 19 and 28 with 2 Chronicles 7:14.   6/Enumerate the *wonderful works* God does for his people.   7/What should the wise man consider?   8/How do you respond to the love of God? Why?   9/Summarize the psalm in a title.

day 13   □   Psalm 108

1/What is the significance of the repetition of Psalm 57:7-11 and Psalm 60:5-12 here?   2/For what is God worshipped? How do the people respond? What qualities of heart are awakened by God's revealed nature?   3/How dependable is God? Why?   4/Which verses indicate your personal experience of praise, trust, love and faith? 5/Summarize the psalm in a title.

day 14   □   Psalm 109

1/To what extent can you identify with the psalmist's situation here? How is he treated? Why?   2/To what extent does David request judgment on the accuser? On what basis? In what areas?   3/On what basis does David pray for deliverance?   4/What will be his response to the shame of his enemies? Why?   5/Have you ever been condemned to death?   6/Account for the extremes of the psalmist's desires. 7/Summarize the psalm in a title.

day 15   □   Psalm 110

1/What will eventually happen to David's enemies?   2/What is David's role in leading his people? What is the Lord's part?   3/What qualities of the Lord are revealed? What is his relationship to the nations of the world?   4/What is the Lord's relationship to David (cf. Gen. 14:17-24)? to *my Lord?* How will he be sustained?   5/How will the people respond to him? How do you respond to the Lord? Why?   6/Summarize the psalm in a title.

day 16   ☐   *Psalms 111–112*

1/What is the mood of these psalms (these psalms are special poems of praise with each phrase beginning with a different letter of the Hebrew alphabet)?   2/Begin an alphabetical list of events and provisions for which you can praise God.   3/Characterize the *works* of the Lord. How do they relate to his people? to his covenant?   4/Where does the praise take place? Why, do you think?   5/To what extent do you experience God's works personally? corporately?   6/List the benefits to those who *fear* and *delight in* the Lord.   7/Account for the response of the wicked man to the blessing of righteous men. 8/What are the attitudes and works of an upright man? To what extent are these true of you and your situation? Why?   9/Account for the wealth as well as the poverty of the righteous. Contrast the prosperity of the wicked with verse 10b.   10/How do you reconcile praising God in the midst of a world where the values and blessings cited here are often reversed?   11/When have you experienced God's graciousness, mercy and righteousness?   12/Summarize each psalm in a title.

day 17   ☐   *Psalm 113*

1/Characterize the glory of the Lord.   2/What provisions has he made for all mankind? for the poor and needy?   3/What is the extent of the Lord's praise? To what degree do you participate? 4/What were the emotional, social and economic situations of barrenness at the time this psalm was written? Compare or contrast with the situations and feelings today.   5/To what extent is God concerned with your joy? How do you know?   6/Summarize the psalm in a title.

day 18   ☐   *Psalm 114*

1/What event is especially significant in Israel's history? Why?   2/Do you treasure and appreciate a particular event that causes you to praise God? Why?   3/What supernatural incidents in Israel's deliverance are attributed to God? Why?   4/How does the earth respond to the *presence of the Lord*? Why? How do the people of Israel respond (cf. Ex. 14:21-30; 17:1-7; Josh. 3:7-17)?   5/How do you know the Lord is present with you?   6/Summarize the psalm in a title.

457

day 19   ☐   *Psalm 115*

1/Contrast idols and the Lord. What does each do? Why?   2/Relate the trust of the people with the worthiness of each.   3/How do other nations respond to the power of a country's god? Why?   4/What gods does your country claim? Why?   5/On what basis does Israel appeal for God's help? What is their confidence?   6/Assess the care of the sons of men for the earth.   7/What is your response to the Lord? Why?   8/Summarize the psalm in a title.

day 20   ☐   *Psalm 116*

1/Read this psalm aloud. Why do you love the Lord?   2/To what extent can you identify with the psalmist's situations here?   3/Relate the situations of life and death here (cf. Ps. 115:17).   4/How has the psalmist responded to God's preservation of him? Why?   5/Enumerate and relate the actions of *a*—the psalmist and *b*—God.   6/Relate the qualities of God and the relationship the psalmist vows toward God as a result.   7/How does the psalmist relate to God in the midst of trials? when he has been delivered?   8/What vows have you made to God? When and where have you paid them? Why?   9/Summarize the psalm in a title.

day 21   ☐   *Psalms 117-118*

1/Who are called on to praise God? For what reasons?   2/Can you say, "His steadfast love endures for ever"? Why?   3/How does God respond to those who call on him? to those who take refuge in him?   4/Characterize the actions of the surrounding nations on Israel. Relate the metaphors to Israel's history.   5/What is Israel's response to God in distress? in victory?   6/What is the condition for entry through the gate of the Lord (this psalm may have been used as a processional approach to the temple gates)? What is the promise for those who enter?   7/Contrast Israel's natural attractiveness (cf. Ezra 16:1-7) with God's honoring of her. What metaphor is used here?   8/In what ways has God given you *light*?   9/Summarize each psalm in a title.

day 22   ☐   *Psalm 119:1-40*

1/Find and define the synonyms of the law of the Lord.   2/What is the purpose of the law of the Lord? the result of keeping the law? 3/What is required to be blameless? How is it maintained before God? 4/How are *lips* and *eyes* related to keeping the law?   5/Why is God's Word essential for life? What is the result of forsaking the law? 6/Read these verses aloud as a prayer.

day 23   ☐   *Psalm 119:41-88*

1/How is God's Word described?   2/What questions will God's Word answer? Why?   3/How does the psalmist react to wicked men? What is his comfort? Why?   4/Who are your companions?   5/What is God's part in revealing his Word? What is man's part in understanding?   6/What is the benefit of affliction?   7/What is the value of God's law?   8/What is the purpose of your living?   9/Read these verses aloud as a prayer. To what extent can you identify with the psalmist's desires and situations?

day 24   ☐   *Psalm 119:89-136*

1/List the attributes of God which are also ascribed to his law. Compare the Word of God with the stability of the universe.   2/What are the *limits* of perfection? of God's Word?   3/What is involved in wisdom? in joy?   4/What contrasts are given here?   5/What are the prerequisites and consequences of keeping God's Word?   6/On what basis does God intervene in human affairs?   7/Which of these verses characterize your attitude toward God and his Word? Why?

day 25   ☐   *Psalm 119:137-176*

1/Characterize God's Word.   2/List the difficulties which have afflicted the psalmist in spite of his zeal for keeping God's Word. 3/To what qualities of God does the psalmist appeal? Why?   4/Summarize how the psalmist responds to God's Word. Why?   5/What actions are involved in keeping God's laws (underline the verbs)? 6/Summarize the benefits of understanding God's Word.   7/Which of these statements have you found true in your life?

459

day 26   ☐   *Psalm 120*
1/What is the psalmist's situation in this psalm?   2/What is needed for his deliverance? Why?   3/What recommends the Lord as an answerer?   4/When have you been involved in a similar situation? 5/How does the psalmist relate to his surroundings? Why?   6/Contrast his desires and those of his contemporaries.   7/What prompts desire for war? Compare or contrast the desires of your contemporaries. Which are involved in lies and deceit? Why?   8/Summarize the psalm in a title.

day 27   ☐   *Psalm 121*
1/What is the psalmist's answer to the question in verse 1?   2/When do you ask this question? What resources do you turn to for help? 3/Why is the Lord a sufficient helper?   4/Categorize and explain the specific ways the Lord helps. Under what circumstances is his help experienced?   5/When and in what ways do *you* experience specific help from the Lord?   6/In what areas is your confidence in God strengthened by this psalm?   7/Title this psalm.

day 28   ☐   *Psalm 122*
1/What emotions does the psalmist have when going to God's house? Why is this of significance to him?   2/Describe the city of Jerusalem. 3/Why do the tribes go to Jerusalem?   4/Analyze the connection between thrones of judgment and the city of Jerusalem (cf. 1 Kings 7:7). 5/To what does the psalmist dedicate himself? What are his reasons? 6/Title this psalm.

day 29   ☐   *Psalm 123*
1/What **inner** attitudes toward God does the psalmist discuss? Compare and contrast these with the attitudes you express in your prayers. 2/Analyze the way in which a servant would look to his master or a maid to her mistress.   3/What is the psalmist's problem? Describe the nature of his enemies. Why do they want to humiliate him (cf. Ezra 4:4-24; Neh. 2:17-19; 6:5-9)?   4/How does he handle this problem?   5/How do you handle scorn from non-Christians regard-

ing your personal life? regarding the body of Christ?   6/How do you
demonstrate honesty and trust when you approach God?   7/Title
this psalm.

day 30 □ *Psalm 124*

1/In what ways are the Israelites dependent upon God? What contrast does the psalmist make in verse 2?   2/Distinguish the four
images given (cf. Num. 16:31-35; Ps. 32:6; 22:13-20; 91:3).   3/What
real situations might the psalmist be recalling (cf. Neh. 6:15-16; Is. 37:
33-38)?   4/When have you experienced similar situations? Recall
your reactions.   5/In light of the whole passage, how have the
Israelites learned verse 8?   6/Title this psalm.

Month 48

day 1 □ *Psalm 125*

1/Describe the relationship between the Lord and those who trust.
What place do the words *for ever* and *evermore* have in this relationship?   2/Relate Mount Zion to the believers. In what historic sense is
this a spiritual truth for the believers as well as a beautiful simile (cf.
Ps. 78:68-69)?   3/In what sense is God like the mountains?   4/What
warnings should the righteous heed? Analyze the consequences of
sinful living.   5/Contrast the psalmist's solid trust in God with his
keen awareness of the dangers of sin. How can you experience this
balance in daily living?   6/Title this psalm.

day 2 □ *Psalm 126*

1/What relationship does this rejoicing have to the history of Israel
(cf. Ezra 3:10-13)?   2/What is the people's reaction to victory and
deliverance?   3/How do you react to good times in relationships,
character development, studies and work? Who gets the credit?
4/In what way does discouragement often follow great victories? How

is this true of the Israelites returning to their homeland (consider esp. the agricultural environment after 70 years)?   5/What was God's part in providing further victory? Explain the people's involvement. 6/How do verses 4-6 describe the law of consequences?   7/How might you follow the example of verses 5-6 in your personal witness? 8/Title this psalm.

day 3   □   Psalm 127

1/What two activities mentioned are done in vain? Why? What does this show about the integral relationship between God and man? 2/On what occasions do you find yourself laboring with anxious toil? 3/Analyze the contrast being made between the worker and the sleeper in verse 2. What does this say about the relationship between man's long hours and determination and God's giving?   4/In the light of these verses, what changes are necessary in your lifestyle? 5/Contrast the thoughts found here with those in Psalm 126:5-6. 6/What things are said about children? In what ways do they strengthen the community?   7/Contrast their position here with that in modern society.   8/Why do you want a family? Why not?   9/Title this psalm.

day 4   □   Psalm 128

1/What is the foundation of God's blessing?   2/List in your own words the blessings of God. Note the different aspects of life that are covered.   3/How can you *eat the fruit of the labor of your hands?*   4/What are the characteristics of a vine? What needs does it have? What does it produce?   5/In what ways can a lack of personal godliness lead a country to ruin?   6/What is the final by-product of the godly life? 7/Title this psalm.

day 5   □   Psalm 129

1/What has characterized the past history of Israel (cf. Ex. 3:7)? Describe the mood conveyed by this psalm.   2/Contrast the psalmist's thoughts regarding affliction in verses 2-3 (cf. Is. 51:23). What positive thought comes through?   3/What metaphors describe the present affliction of the nation? the activities of the enemy (the greetings in v. 8 are customary in the harvest field; cf. Ruth 2:4)? 4/What feelings are expressed? 5/What about God's character is seen through all these troubles? 6/How should this knowledge of God's character affect your feelings about your past? change your daily living in the present? 7/Title this psalm.

day 6 □ Psalm 130
1/What are the psalmist's concerns in verses 1-4? 2/Answer the question in verse 3. Outline his attitude toward sin and forgiveness (relate to v. 1). 3/What happens while he waits on the Lord? Why? What is involved in "waiting" in your life? 4/Describe the characteristics of God that lead the psalmist to have hope. 5/Contrast the beginning and end of the psalm. 6/How do you react when in the depths of sin and discouragement? What effect should God's character have upon your attitudes? 7/In what way does the extent of the psalmist's turning to God's love affect his influence on Israel? What effect do you have on others when you are in the *depths*? 8/Title this psalm.

day 7 □ Psalm 131
1/How does David describe his spiritual state? When do you feel this way? How often? 2/What positive action does he take? 3/How would you characterize his attitude toward himself? Analyze the relationship between this attitude and the calmness of his soul. 4/When does he begin to hope in the Lord? 5/Relate his hope to his own actions in Psalm 130:5-6 and here in verse 2. 6/How can you begin to demonstrate humility and honesty toward God? 7/Title this psalm.

day 8 □ Psalm 132
1/What has David done? 2/Explain his desire (cf. 2 Sam. 7). 2/How does he express his commitment to the task? 3/How do the people respond (vv. 6-7)? 4/What is God's response? 5/How is God's chosen dwelling different from David's conception (vv. 11-12)? 6/Analyze the relationship between the Lord and a physical locality. 7/Parallel verses 8-10 with 14, 16-17. 8/Title this psalm.

day 9   ☐   *Psalms 133–134*
1/What are the results of unity?   2/What metaphors describe it?
3/What happens to the oil after it is poured on the head (cf. Lev. 8:12)?
How does its influence spread?   4/What effect does dew have on an
area where rainfall is not plentiful?   5/What effect would real unity
have on your Christian group?   What specific attitudes and actions
would change?   List some personal changes that would help unify
your group.   6/What desire does the psalmist have in this psalm?
How can you bless God today?   7/Summarize the purpose and
themes of the Songs of Ascents (Ps. 120—134).

day 10   ☐   *Psalm 135*
1/Why is the psalmist praising God?   2/What memories of past victories are evoked?   3/How have the Israelites experienced the effects
of God's sovereignty and power?   4/As God's possession, what confidence do you have in God's active sovereignty?   In what ways do you
need God's power in your current situation?   5/In what ways is God
different from idols?   Contrast the fate of those who serve the living
God with those who trust in idols.   6/Summarize the reasons you
have for praising God.   7/Title this psalm.

day 11   ☐   *Psalm 136*
1/In what way does this psalm differ from the previous psalms of
praise?   2/What attributes of God provoke thanks in the psalmist?
3/What application would verses 2 and 4 have to the non-Christian
religions?   4/How does God demonstrate his understanding and
power in the physical universe?   5/Trace the work of God's hand
from creation through the deliverance of Israel. What can you learn
about the way God deals with people?   6/What attributes are suggested by the phrases *strong hand* and *outstretched arm*?   7/Correlate
verse 12 with the verbs describing God's actions. What prompts God
to action?   8/What is God saying in this psalm to those who may doubt
his love as the Israelites did at times?   9/Title this psalm.

day 12   ☐   *Psalm 137*
1/What emotions have the Israelites experienced during the captivity?

What methods of psychological warfare were the captors using? 2/Analyze the psalmist's response to the situation. To what extent is it justified?   3/What do you think is God's attitude toward the enemy? 4/When others do not take you or your faith seriously, how do you react?   5/As what priority is Jerusalem regarded? Why?   6/Title this psalm.

day 13   □   *Psalm 138*

1/List the reasons for David's thankfulness.   2/How did God answer his prayer? What is exalted as a result of this answered prayer? How does David demonstrate humility in receiving the answer?   3/What motivates the kings to praise God?   4/What paradox do you notice here?   5/Think of any lowly or haughty people you know. How does God respond to each type?   6/In what ways do adverse circumstances affect David's relationship with God?   7/Think about why he has the confidence expressed in verse 8. How can you derive assurance of God's fulfillment in your present situation?   8/Title this psalm.

day 14   □   *Introduction to Esther*

The book of Esther is the thrilling story of a Jewish girl whom God uses to save her nation. Esther is one of the Jewish exiles in Babylon. King Ahasuerus is Xerxes, king of Persia from 486 to 464 B.C. No mention of God is made in this book, probably indicating that the account is written at a time when it is dangerous to mention Jehovah. Read through the entire book in one sitting. *Esther 1*   1/What is the extent and wealth of Ahasuerus' kingdom? Describe life in the oriental court.   2/What kind of person is Ahasuerus? Memucan? Vashti? 3/Contrast the position of women in this court with the liberation of women after Christ.

day 15   □   *Esther 2*

1/How does Esther become a member of Ahasuerus' harem? Does she have a choice?   2/What is Esther's background? Characterize her from her conduct in this situation and from her relationship with Mordecai. In what ways can you identify with her? What can you learn

465

from her? 3/What kind of person is Mordecai? What do verses 21-23 reveal about loyalty?

day 16 □ *Esther 3*

1/What precipitates the tension between Haman and Mordecai? 2/Does Mordecai have a legitimate reason to refuse to bow down to Haman? 3/What insights do the events that follow give into Haman's character? 4/For how long does Haman plot revenge? 5/What reasoning does Haman use to convince the king of his plot against the Jews (history records the empire as impoverished at this time and Haman's offer is two-thirds the regular annual revenue)? 6/What is Haman's real reason for slaying the Jews? 7/How does the king's ready acceptance of this proposal comment further on his character and values? 8/What warnings do you see here against self-importance? 9/What are your basic values?

day 17 □ *Esther 4*

1/What immediate action does Mordecai take when he hears of pending disaster for the Jews? 2/Trace the steps in Mordecai's dealings with Esther to persuade her to take action. 3/What objection does Esther raise? 4/How does Esther respond to Mordecai's challenge that she is involved in an event larger than her self-interest? 5/How can you apply verse 14 to your present situation? Why do you think you are here today? 6/What does Esther's command to the Jews reveal about her faith and character?

day 18 □ *Esther 5-6*

1/What risk does Esther take in approaching the king? Imagine yourself in her place and culture, involved in this dramatic action. 2/Do you think she has a plan in the dinner invitation rather than approaching the king outright with her request? How does Esther's action mislead Haman? 3/How is the hand of God evidenced in the events of chapter 6? 4/List and explain the effects of Haman's character traits (esp. 5:9-14; 6:7-9, 12-13). What irony does he face in 6:10-11? 5/Contrast Zeresh and Esther. 6/What kind of woman/man are you? 7/What are the purposes behind your actions?

day 19 ☐ *Esther 7–8*

1/At the second feast, what request does Esther make? What are the benefits of her open identification with her people?   2/What series of events does the king set in action as a result of Esther's exposure? 3/How is the original decree made ineffective? What is the result in the Jewish community?   4/What are the *a*—risks and *b*—benefits of your open identification with Jesus Christ and his people?

day 20 ☐ *Esther 9–10*

1/What happens to the enemies of the Jews?   2/Why do you think the detail of 9:10, 15-16 is repeated?   3/What is the meaning of the Feast of Purim? How do you remind yourself of the mercies of God? 4/What can you learn from Esther's actions?   5/What are the outstanding features in Mordecai's character (esp. 10:3)? What is behind his moral strength? What can you learn from him?   6/Summarize the evidence of God's constant care for his people in exile through this book.   7/How has his care for you been evident in the last few weeks? in the last year?

day 21 ☐ *Introduction to Ecclesiastes*

Ecclesiastes deals with man's feeling of emptiness even though he has everything. *Ecclesiastes 1:1-11*   1/What is the background of the writer (cf. 1 Kings 3—4, 11)?   2/What are Solomon's intellectual, material, aesthetic and spiritual resources?   3/Is his situation more or less likely to foster a theistic view of life? Why?   4/Define *vanity* in this context. Does this word ever characterize the way you feel? 5/Does the writer have a circular or linear view of history? of nature? of life in general? Why is this important? Is it a Christian view? 6/Would you say that this initial passage is a view of life with or without a living God?

day 22 ☐ *Ecclesiastes 1:12–2:11*

1/To what extent is the search for knowledge for its own sake a legitimate pursuit for a Christian?   2/Is the search for meaning satisfied by knowledge?   3/Why is man restless when life seems to have so

little meaning? What does this tell us about man? about God's purpose for man?   4/Does real contentment come with ignorance?
5/What philosophy does the writer try in chapter 2? Is it the answer for him? Why?   6/To what extent is throwing yourself into your work, the arts or intellectual areas the answer?   7/How is the Christian supposed to use his mind?   8/To what extent does life offer the key to itself for this writer?

day 23   □   *Ecclesiastes 2:12-26*
1/To what extent does a man's status in life determine his degree of contentment?   2/Is there any redeeming value in wisdom itself? Where does true wisdom originate?   3/Does this passage suggest there may be another vantage point from which to view life?   4/What is the one event which happens to all men? How does this fact alter our view of life? of death?   4/What is man's relationship to the creation?   5/Why does man seem to have lost his enjoyment of the creation?   6/What moral element must be reckoned with?   7/How is God related to pleasure? to wisdom? to work?

day 24   □   *Ecclesiastes 3–4:3*
1/What are the dangers inherent in viewing life strictly from within the perspective of time?   2/To what extent does determinism give life meaning?   3/What control does man have over life?   4/Describe life in terms of the struggle between the issues of life and death.
5/What element in man makes him different from the world around him (v. 11)? How will eternity affect your life?   6/What difference does a moral sensitivity in man make?   7/Is it possible to deny the existence of evil in the world?   8/What are the implications of the fact that God is righteous and man is evil?   9/In what circumstances might death be better than life? Why?

day 25   □   *Ecclesiastes 4:4-16*
1/To what extent is the element of competitiveness inherent in man's nature?   2/What really drives you in your life? What goals beyond survival do you have?   3/What is the Christian position on competi-

tion versus the passive attitude of the fool?   4/How can you reconcile the motivation of doing what is good for your fellow man with the profit motive in our society?   5/Why do you think God has made man a social being?   6/What are the implications of a view of mankind as a single family?   7/What is fame's fatal flaw?

day 26   □   Ecclesiastes 5
1/Why is religion a part of even secular man?   2/In what ways do you seek to "use" God today?   3/How would you characterize the kind of religion described in the first few verses?   4/What is the degree of consistency between what you say you believe and how your life bears out that belief?   5/Why should we listen to God more than talk to him? How do you listen to God? When?   6/Compare or contrast the attitudes in civil and economic areas here with your views.   7/How should a Christian possess wealth?

day 27   □   Ecclesiastes 6
1/Compare and contrast verses 1-2 with 5:19-20.   2/What is the difference between riches as end and as means for the Christian?   3/If God has made man acquisitive and the earth productive, to what extent are diligence and thrift virtues in themselves?   4/What is the common end of all men?   5/What is the place of realism and dreaming in a Christian's life?   6/Who determines man's destiny?

day 28   □   Ecclesiastes 7
1/Enumerate life's perplexing problems.   2/To what extent can man avoid the fact of death? How does it alter your view of life today?   2/What possible good can come out of experiencing a great sorrow? How has sorrow affected you? What has been your response?   3/To what extent do you live in the past?   4/What is God's relation to prosperity and adversity? What is his purpose in each? What do you think are the chances that men would make God a vital part of their lives if they never face adversity?   5/What problems arise out of a purely moralistic view of life (that the good prosper and the wicked have problems)?   6/To what extent can we solve the riddle of life by

reason?   7/What do you think causes Solomon to write about women
as he does (cf. 1 Kings 11:1-11)?

day 29   ☐   Ecclesiastes 8

1/To what extent has God given man the capacity to understand his
situation?   2/What position do you take in civil affairs (cf. Jer. 27:12)?
3/What can be learned by voluntary submission to authority regardless of agreement with it?   4/How is slow justice unjust?   5/What is
God's intent in punishment (cf. Deut. 19—25)? Is it to be a deterrent?
6/To what extent are God's moral principles applicable for all time?
7/Why doesn't God punish sin immediately?

day 30   ☐   Ecclesiastes 9

1/How does the sovereignty of God lend meaning to your life?
2/What is the author saying about immorality in verses 4-5?   3/Does
the author advise living life wholeheartedly?   4/Characterize your
sense of urgency about your mission in life.   6/What is the meaning
of the parable about the king and the poor man?

Month 49

day 1   ☐   Ecclesiastes 10

1/What inclination of the heart is related to your ability to resist evil?
2/Why does folly always seem so much more powerful than wisdom?
3/To what extent can God's way be characterized as weak?   4/What
is recommended when we are confronted with evil in high places?
Why?   5/What is the wisdom of the proverbial statements?   6/Con-
trast the manner of a wise man and a fool. What are your responsibilities in balancing talk and action?   7/How does your view of the
Bible as God's words affect that responsibility?

day 2   □   *Ecclesiastes 11*

1/What actions are wise here?   2/To what extent do you act out of love, without concern for return? Why?   3/In what areas should you apply caution before taking a risk?   4/What is the danger inherent in delaying generosity?   5/What are the privileges or advantages of youth? What responsibilities toward God are involved?   6/Characterize the heart of youth without God.

day 3   □   *Ecclesiastes 12*

1/Have you resolved to follow God? Why or why not?   2/Why is it advisable to make such a decision early in life rather than waiting until later?   3/Since we were created in the image of God, what is our true element?   4/As your Creator, what rights does God have to your life?   5/As a created being, do you have any rights purely your own?   6/Do you think remembering God will come easier with the years?   7/What do the images in this chapter describe? To what extent is this a result of our fallen nature?   8/List your own and the author's conclusions about wisdom.   9/Summarize in your own words *the end of the matter.*

day 4   □   *Introduction to 2 Chronicles*

This is a continuation of the record begun in 1 Chronicles; the two were originally one book.   *2 Chronicles 1*   1/Re-read 1 Chronicles 28—29 quickly to recall how Solomon begins to rule all Israel. What advantages does he have?   2/What is the significance of the action in verses 2-6? What condition must be met (1 Chron. 28:9)?   3/Try to imagine yourself in Solomon's position in verse 7. What would be your request?   4/What does Solomon receive from the Lord in addition to the gift of wisdom?   5/Who will benefit most from the gift he has requested?   6/What gift would you most like to receive right now? Why?

day 5   □   *2 Chronicles 2*

1/What reason does Solomon give for wanting to build a house for God?   2/What testimony about the Lord is included in his message to

King Huram?   3/What can you surmise from the response about Huram's attitude *a*—toward Israel and *b*—toward the Lord?   4/How much can people learn about the Lord from your life and words? 5/Do you have purposes that exalt the Lord? Ask him to help you be a bold and consistent testimony to his greatness.

day 6   □   *2 Chronicles 3:1–5:1*

1/How long has Solomon been king before beginning to build the temple?   2/Note the attention given to detail. How would you describe the king's view of his task?   3/What is implied here about the importance of art? What might be some modern counterparts in daily life?   4/How does your activity in God's service compare with Solomon's with regard to time, care and quality?

day 7   □   *2 Chronicles 5:2–6:2*

1/Who have the task of moving the ark to the temple? Who takes part in this great parade?   2/What is inside the ark? Why?   3/What impresses you most about the chronicler's description of this scene? 4/Think about the history of these people—exile, wilderness wanderings, invasions, then the re-location and beginnings of a minority power. What emotional significance must the new temple have for each citizen?   5/What characteristics of God are most emphasized by the actions of the priests and the people? by God's own action here? 6/How does your worship of God reflect your awareness of his character? Praise him today for something about himself that you have not been aware of before.

day 8   □   *2 Chronicles 6:3–7:3*

1/Make an outline of Solomon's prayer to God in the presence of all Israel by titling each paragraph (RSV 6:12-42).   2/What repeated words or phrases can you find here?   3/What is Solomon's main request? What specific examples does he mention?   4/What results of sin are described?   5/According to Solomon's prayer, what precedes God's forgiveness of sin?   6/On what basis does Solomon dare ask all this?   7/According to his prayer, where does God dwell (6:21, 39; cf.

2:6)?   8/What two immediate events follow Solomon's prayer? How do the people respond? What is your response when you are aware of God's presence?

day 9   ☐   *2 Chronicles 7:4-22*
1/How long do the ceremonies and feasting for the dedication of the temple last?   2/What is their effect upon the people who were there? 3/What do you learn about God's character from his words to Solomon in verses 12-22?   4/How can you tell when you are being punished by God?   5/What promises does God make concerning Israel and her worship of him? Which of these apply to you?

day 10   ☐   *2 Chronicles 8*
1/What are Solomon's priorities as king as shown by the order in verses 1-2?   2/Note his consistency in adhering to these priorities amidst the pressures of administering the kingdom (vv. 12-15). Do you see a hint of inconsistency in verse 11?   3/In what areas of your life do you need to develop consistency? What are your priorities? 4/Note verses 13 and 14: "as the duty of each day required." Is there a duty required of you each day? If so, how can you perform it to the glory of God?

day 11   ☐   *2 Chronicles 9:1-12*
1/What kind of a person is the queen of Sheba (vv. 1-2, 4-6, 9)? 2/What does she want to know about Solomon?   3/What are her conclusions?   4/To what does the queen attribute the things she sees in Israel?   5/In your own mind, and in the view of others, who gets the credit for the good things and accomplishments in your life?

day 12   ☐   *2 Chronicles 9:13-31*
1/How does Solomon use God's gift of wisdom?   2/In what ways are the riches of Israel related to his wisdom?   3/To what uses does Solomon put the gold brought in tribute? Why do you think he does this? 4/List the gifts God has given you. How are you using them?   5/Read

1 Kings 11:1-3 to learn the rest of the story of Solomon. (Note again 2 Chron. 8:11, possibly the beginning of his disobedience.) What a sad ending to such glory! Pray that God will keep you true to himself. Resolve to keep him first in your life.

day 13   ☐   *2 Chronicles 10*
1/See 1 Kings 11:14-43 for a description of the opposition which arises toward the end of Solomon's reign and an explanation of verse 2. What is the complaint expressed by Jeroboam for the people of Israel? 2/From whom does King Rehoboam seek advice, and what answers does he receive?   3/Why do you think he seeks two opinions on the matter? Why does he choose the one he does?   4/How do the people of Israel react to the king's treatment of them? Compare this with their attitude toward Solomon in 1 Chronicles 29:23-25.   5/What glimpse is given here of the ongoing purposes of God? What parallels have you seen in your own experience?

day 14   ☐   *2 Chronicles 11*
1/What action does Rehoboam decide to take against the rebellious northern tribes?   2/What prevents him from doing so?   3/How does Rehoboam maintain control of the southern tribes of Judah and Benjamin?   4/What does Jeroboam's treatment of the Levites show about conditions in the northern territory?   5/What is the effect on the people of the ten tribes (v. 16)? on the "kingdom" of Judah? 6/What is the relationship of your patriotism or ethnic allegiance to your citizenship in God's kingdom?

day 15   ☐   *2 Chronicles 12*
1/What do you think causes Rehoboam to forsake God?   2/What is the result?   3/In what specific ways might Israel's unfaithfulness provide encouragement for her enemies?   4/What warning is given Rehoboam, and how does he respond?   5/Why do the king and princes make the statement in verse 6?   6/In what ways are verses 10 and 11 evidence for the general decline of the kingdom after Jerusalem's defeat?   7/What is the chronicler's general verdict concerning Rehoboam's reign? Upon what is his judgment based?

day 16 ☐ *2 Chronicles 13*

1/Compare the kingdoms of Abijah and Jeroboam with regard to their *a*—armies and *b*—royal families. 2/How are the priests selected in Jeroboam's northern kingdom? What are their gods? 3/Who are the priests in the south? 4/What is the main message Abijah calls out to Jeroboam and the people of the north? 5/Describe Jeroboam's battle tactics in your own words. Which side has the military advantage? 6/Who are the victors, and what is the decisive factor? 7/Think about what it means to have a God who intervenes.

day 17 ☐ *2 Chronicles 14*

1/Describe the prevailing atmosphere of Asa's reign (vv. 1-7). 2/Compare the size of Asa's army (men of Judah and Benjamin) with Zerah the Ethiopian's. 3/What statements does King Asa make in his prayer? What is surprising about his request? 4/How does victory come? What is the condition of the enemy after the battle? 5/Think of one or more situations in your life where the odds have been overwhelmingly against you. What can you learn from the way Abijah and Asa reacted in such situations? Apply this to one particular struggle you are in right now.

day 18 ☐ *2 Chronicles 15*

1/What specific reforms does Asa undertake in the spiritual life of his kingdom (14:2-5; 15:8-18)? 2/What encouragement does God give the king in these reforms? What promise does he make? Compare verse 2 with verse 15. 3/Is the emphasis of this covenant to be national or individual or both? What evidence do you find in this chapter for your answer? 4/What is required of the people in the oath sworn to the Lord? 5/What is their attitude toward this requirement? 6/Think about your relationship to God. Are you seeking him "with all your heart and with all your soul" (v. 12)?

day 19 ☐ *2 Chronicles 16*

1/Describe the new threat to Judah (v. 1) in your own words. 2/How does Asa deal with this threat?   3/In what way do Asa's actions in verses 2-3 differ from his policies in chapters 14 and 15?   4/What is the result of the king's misplaced confidence (15:19; 16:7-9)? 5/Why do you think he reacts the way he does in verses 10 and 12? 6/Compare Asa's way of dealing with his guilt with David's in 1 Chronicles 21.   7/When was the last time you realized you had disobeyed God on some point? How long did it take you to make it right?

> *day 20*   □   *2 Chronicles 17*

1/What specific programs does Jehoshaphat carry out as king? 2/Upon what is the teaching of the itinerant educators based? What do you think is the king's purpose in initiating this program?   3/What is the chronicler's evaluation of Jehoshaphat and his reign?   4/What is the source of the prestige and power Judah develops among the surrounding lands?

> *day 21*   □   *2 Chronicles 18:1-22*

1/Read 1 Kings 21:25-26 for background on Ahab.   2/Why would an alliance with Jehoshaphat be advantageous for Ahab at this point? 3/Why do you think Jehoshaphat responds as he does to Ahab's request?   4/How does Jehoshaphat show his perception of the spiritual decay in the northern kingdom?   5/Why does Ahab maintain a corps of 400 prophets?

> *day 22*   □   *2 Chronicles 18:23-34*

1/Why does Jehoshaphat not object to Ahab's action in verses 25-26? 2/Put yourself in Micaiah's place (vv. 12, 14-15, 17, 23, 25-26). How would you feel in each instance? Why do you think he gives the answer he does in verse 14?   3/What seems to be Micaiah's chief goal? Is he successful in achieving it? What is your chief goal?   4/What statements in this chapter show God's mercy in placing the responsibility for sin with Ahab rather than with the people of Israel?   5/Notice God's justice and the fulfillment of his purposes in Ahab's death (vv. 19, 33-34; cf. 1 Kings 21:17-19, 35, 38).   6/List some instances in which you have experienced *a*—God's justice and *b*—God's mercy. Ask him to keep you true to him in all your responsibilities.

476

day 23   ☐   *2 Chronicles 19*

1/Evaluate Jehoshaphat's action (18:3) in light of 19:2.   2/What basic attitude does Jehoshaphat have which prompts the statement "some good is found in you" (v. 3)?   3/Perhaps Jehoshaphat's stay in Israel has given him a fresh perspective on his concern for his own people. In any case, what new program does he initiate upon his return? 4/What is the purpose of the reformed system of justice (v. 4)? 5/Against what specific forms of corruption does he caution the judges? What is to be their attitude toward their job?   6/What additional responsibility is given the judges in order to prevent the system from becoming sterile and legalistic (v. 10)?   7/What attitude do you have toward your work?

day 24   ☐   *2 Chronicles 20:1-13*

1/What three things does Jehoshaphat do at receiving news of the new military threat?   2/How is the effect of his leadership evident? 3/How do you react in times of crisis?   4/List the elements in Jehoshaphat's prayer. Is the order surprising?   5/On what past events does he base his confidence?   6/Are you powerless in a certain situation? Make the last sentence of Jehoshaphat's prayer your own

day 25   ☐   *2 Chronicles 20:14-37*

1/If you had been present, would you have believed Jahaziel's announcement (vv. 15-17)? What is its source?   2/Do the people believe it? What are the two steps in their response?   3/How does God speak to you? What do you do in response?   4/What is the king's advice to the people as they are on their way to face the enemy? 5/What are the people of Judah doing while their enemies are destroying each other?   6/What results from this victory (vv. 25, 29-30)? 7/We have seen the concern for the people which Jehoshaphat and his father Asa have had (ch. 14—15, 17, 19). Yet what is said about the people in verse 33? Upon what (or whom) is your heart set?

day 26   ☐   *2 Chronicles 21–22*

1/What are the long-term effects of Jehoshaphat's decision in chapter

18 to make a marriage alliance with the house of Ahab (21:6; 22:3-5, 9-10)?   2/How does Jehoram draw others into his sin?   3/Where in this passage is leniency shown? Why? Where is it *not* shown? Why? 4/How do the people show their awareness of the good and evil leadership of their kings (21:19-20; 22:9)?   5/Through what means is the continuance of the line of David assured, in accordance with God's promise (22:11-12)?   6/Notice Jehoram's sad epitaph (21:20). Plan now to avoid such an end yourself. Determine some steps you can take now. Ask God to help you be useful to others and to him.

day 27   ☐   2 Chronicles 23

1/Between what segments of Judah's society is the alliance described here?   2/What is the purpose of this coalition? Who is instrumental in bringing it about?   3/What is the reason for the precautions that are taken for the king's safety (vv. 6-10)?   4/Write down in order the steps taken in the overthrow of the queen.   5/Athaliah still lives when Joash is crowned. What and why, then, are the people celebrating? 6/What is to be the underlying principle for the reign of Joash (vv. 16-17)?   7/Note that Jehoiada has been reluctant to go ahead with this course of action (v. 1). Re-read chapters 21—23. From your study of this section, would you say that forceful overthrow of a government is ever justified? If not, why not? If so, under what circumstances? Is there any indication of God's approval or disapproval of the events described here?

day 28   ☐   2 Chronicles 24

1/What major project is carried out while Joash is king?   2/How is this project financed?   3/What attitude do the people take toward the payment of this tax? How does it compare with your attitude toward taxes and that of people you know? What do you think accounts for the difference?   4/What is the relationship of the secular and religious life of the kingdom at this time (vv. 11, 14-15; cf. 22:11)? 5/What policy changes take place after the death of Jehoiada? How are they brought about?   6/How would you describe the character of Joash? What do you see as his greatest strength? his greatest weakness?   7/Compare vv. 23-27 with chapter 23 with reference to *a—*

existing political situation, *b*—leadership of the opposition, *c*—organization, and *d*—purpose of the conspiracy. Check your comparisons with your answers to question 7 of yesterday's study.

day 29   □   *2 Chronicles 25*

1/How does Amaziah seek to strengthen his position as king (vv. 3, · 5-6, 11-12, 17, 20-21)? 2/Compare the ways in which Amaziah responds to the word of the Lord in verses 7-10 and 15-16. What is his objection in the first instance? 3/How do you think he feels about the result of his obedience (v. 13)? 4/In what way may the first incident have led to the second? 5/How would you describe the relative power and prestige of Judah and Israel as seen in the relationship of the two kings? 6/How does Amaziah's death come about? Who are involved? 7/Compare this conspiracy to the ones in chapters 23 and 24 and also with 1 Samuel 26:8-11 and 31:4. What political attitudes do you see developing in Judah?

day 30   □   *2 Chronicles 26–27*

1/List the major accomplishments of Uzziah's reign. 2/What is the most important factor in the growth of his power (26:5, 7, 15)? 3/What effect does this political strength have upon the king's character? 4/Why is it wrong for Uzziah to burn incense to God? 5/How does he react to the correction given by the priests? What is the result? 6/In what ways has Jotham learned from his father's successes and mistakes? What weakness in his rule is noted by the chronicler? 7/Think about the principles in 26:5, 16a; 27:6 in relation to your own life and goals.

Month 50

day 1   □   *2 Chronicles 28*

1/What specific acts demonstrate Ahaz's faithlessness to the Lord (vv.

1-4, 16, 21-25)?   2/What is the result of the king's sin, and in what way
does it affect the lives of all the people?   3/In what way does the army
of Israel carry their legitimate victory to excess?   Who opposes them,
and how is the situation rectified?   4/How is God's continuing concern for both kingdoms shown in this passage?   5/Think of some
specific ways in which you can show mercy like that described in
verse 15.

day 2   ☐   *2 Chronicles 29*

1/What is Hezekiah's first priority as he takes the throne in Judah?
2/What first step is required of the Levites and priests?   3/Why do
you think they work so diligently now, when so recently King Ahaz
closed up the temple and promoted the worship of other gods? (But
notice a hint of something still lacking in v. 34.)   4/List the parts of
the rededication ceremony. Is there significance in the order?
5/What is the mood of the people at this sudden reform?   6/Has
the Lord ever helped you come back to him after a time away? If so,
what was your emotional response to the renewal of fellowship?

day 3   ☐   *2 Chronicles 30*

1/What is Hezekiah's role in the kingdom's changing attitudes? What
can you learn from him about living in a time of faithlessness and
spiritual bankruptcy?   2/Whom does Hezekiah invite and encourage
to come and keep the passover?   3/How would you expect the Jews
outside Judah, many living without spiritual leadership or a place to
worship, to respond to this offer? How did they respond?   4/What
does Hezekiah stress most in the message he sends by the couriers?
5/What exception is made to the requirements of the law of Moses?
Why?   6/What does this exception show about God's character?
What do *you* need in order to experience God's forgiveness?   7/Note
King Hezekiah's sensitivity to people in verse 22. Can you follow his
example this week?   8/What are two results of the two-week-long
worship service (vv. 26-27)?

day 4   ☐   *2 Chronicles 31:1–32:23*

1/What duties are assigned the priests and Levites?   2/How are they to be supported? How would you describe the provisions given to them? 3/In 31:20-21 Hezekiah's character is described. What is his chief goal? How does he know what is "good and right and faithful"? With what attitude does he pursue his goal? 4/Read the parallel account in 2 Kings 18:13—19:37. 5/What strategic measures does Hezekiah take to protect Jerusalem? 6/What does he do to give the people confidence? 7/Re-state the Assyrian propaganda messages in your own words. In what ways is this propaganda conveyed to the population of Jerusalem? 8/How does Hezekiah combat the taunts of the Assyrians? What causes their retreat and ultimate disgrace?

day 5   □   *2 Chronicles 32:24–33:25*
1/See Isaiah 38—39 for more information concerning Hezekiah's illness and the envoys sent from Babylon. What observations does the chronicler make concerning the king's attitude in his later years (cf. 31:21 with 32:25)? What activities occupy much of his time (32: 27-29)? 2/One is never too spiritual to fall into pride or materialism. Evaluate your own attitudes and goals at present. 3/List the specific abuses and wrongdoings of which Manasseh is guilty. 4/Which of these are commonly practiced today? According to the chronicler, what is the Lord's attitude toward them? 5/How are God's mercy and justice both shown in the way he dealt with Judah's sin (33:10-13)? 6/What indication do you find that Manasseh learns something from this experience? How would you characterize his "punishment"? 7/What lasting effect does the king's previous conduct have upon the spiritual life of the people? upon his family? 8/Determine now to live in a way that will help and not damage those around you. What step can you take today?

day 6   □   *2 Chronicles 34*
1/What element of Josiah's character results in his ruling so differently from his father and grandfather? 2/What verbs in verses 3-7 depict the thoroughness of his reforms? 3/What can you infer from verses 14-18 about the condition of the temple and the activity of the priests during the regimes of Manasseh and Amon? 4/How does

Josiah react to hearing the Law read?   5/Re-state God's specific message to Josiah in your own words. How does it differ from the general
prophecy concerning the kingdom?   6/How is the king's strong
influence over the people shown in verses 31-33? Are you in any position of leadership where you can exert influence for God? Pray for
Christian leaders in your community and in the government, that
their influence may be strong.

day 7   □   *2 Chronicles 35–36*
1/Compare this passover celebration to the one described in chapter
30. What similarities do you see? what differences?   2/What reason
could Josiah have for wanting to fight with the king of Egypt?   3/By
what means does God warn him against this battle? How can you explain the claims (and their apparent validity) of the Egyptian king?
4/What are the results of Josiah's actions *a*—for himself and *b*—for the
kingdom?   5/What descriptive words and phrases are used in connection with the regimes of Jehoahaz, Jehoiakim, Jehoiachin and
Zedekiah? During this unhappy era, what is God's attitude toward the
people?   6/In 36:20-21 re-read of the collapse of Judah. Look back
at King David (1 Chron. 29:26-28) and the international reputation of
King Solomon (2 Chron. 9:1-8) in the early days of the kingdom.
Since then it has split, the north has fallen to Assyria, and now the
south has fallen to Babylon. Re-read the warning God gave them
(2 Chron. 7:17-22). How important is it to you that you are obeying
God's commandments and walking before him day by day?

day 8   □   *Introduction to the Song of Solomon*
Some commentators believe the Song of Solomon is best interpreted
as a human love poem; others believe it is an allegory of the church's
love for Christ. Whether the poem is allegorical or not, it reveals principles of love, and a Christian can apply these in his relationship with
Christ. Interpretation will be suggested here on the level of a human
love poem, and application will be made on both levels: interpersonal
relations and the man-God relationship.   1/Read through the book
at one sitting, noting frequently repeated words, phrases and images.
2/When you have finished, scan it again and identify what seem to you

to be the main voices (or speakers) in this dramatic poem. 3/Spend some time reflecting on the relevance this work can have for your own life. What can it teach you?

day 9   □   *Song of Solomon 1:1–2:7*
(This study assumes that the poem has three main characters—a Shulammite girl, her shepherd lover and King Solomon—plus choral parts. Some interpreters think there are only two: Solomon and the girl.) 1/In 1:2-4, how do the women of Solomon's harem describe the king's love? 2/What conflicts arise between the Shulammite girl and these "daughters of Jerusalem" (1:5-8)? 3/Compare the images the king uses as he tries to win the girl's love (1:9-11, 15; 2:2) with those she uses as she resists him (1:12-14; 1:16—2:1). 4/How does the girl describe past delights she has enjoyed with her shepherd lover (2:3-6)? 5/What does 2:7 indicate about her reaction to 1:2-4? 6/Compare and contrast the harem's desire for Solomon, Solomon's desire for the Shulammite girl, and the girl's desire for her beloved. 7/What things are most likely to woo you from devotion to Christ? 8/What could you tell others about past delights you have had with him (cf. 2:3-6)?

day 10   □   *Song of Solomon 2:8–3:5*
1/The girl twice describes her beloved as "a gazelle or a young stag" (2:9, 17). What attributes does this suggest? 2/How does the beloved describe the girl? 3/How would you describe the Lover of the Church? 4/Why is it appropriate that lovely spring imagery fills the beloved's speech (2:11-15)? 5/In what ways does this imagery describe the return of the Lord Jesus (cf. Rev. 21:1-5)? 6/The girl several times calls her beloved "him whom my soul loves." How do what she has said and what she dreams of doing demonstrate this is true? 7/Have your words and actions ever demonstrated such love for another person? for the Lord Jesus? 8/Have you ever actively sought God in a time of "spiritual dryness" (cf. Ps. 42) and known the joy of restored fellowship?

day 11   □   *Song of Solomon 3:6–4:7*
1/Imagine (or draw) the picture of Solomon "coming up from the wilderness" on his litter (3:6-10). What words stress the magnificence of the scene?   2/Why would this splendor make it even harder for the Shulammite girl to resist Solomon's advances?   3/Read Matthew 4:8-10, and consider what the Lord Jesus Christ refused because of his love for the Father and the church.   4/In 4:1-7 (v. 6 may be an interruption) what human weaknesses is Solomon trying to exploit?   5/In what contexts is such expression appropriate?   6/Why is it destructive to another person when you arouse his or her emotions for selfish reasons?

day 12   □   *Song of Solomon 4:8–5:1*
1/Compare the first part of the shepherd lover's speech (4:8-11) with Solomon's (4:1-7) in intent, tone and imagery.   2/What does the shepherd say here about the effect the Shulammite girl has had on him? Is there any note like this in Solomon's speech?   3/The word picture in 4:12—5:1 centers around the image of a garden. How does the beloved describe his garden?   4/What does verse 12 tell us about the girl?   5/In verse 16, how does she respond to her beloved's exuberance?   6/Why is a desire for total self-giving appropriate in serious romantic love or in the marriage bond?   7/Reflect on Christ's feelings of love for the church. Do they inspire you to devotion and genuine self-surrender?

day 13   □   *Song of Solomon 5:2-8*
1/What joyful event is the girl dreaming about?   2/What delays her from responding to her beloved's knocking?   3/Read Matthew 25:1-3 and compare it with this incident.   4/How does this dream end differently from her earlier one (3:1-4)?   5/How might this ending reveal her fears and anxieties at this point in the story?   6/How do you respond personally to her statement "I am sick with love"? Is she wrong to feel this way? Consider her change from activity to idleness (cf. 1:6), as well as the pressures from Solomon and the harem.   7/Has she forgotten God? What role should God play in a situation like this one?   8/Have you ever been involved in an intense relationship which threatened God's place in your life?

day 14   ☐   *Song of Solomon 5:9–6:3*
1/In this section of dialogue, what is the first question the women ask
the girl?   2/What images does she use to describe the different parts
of her beloved's body?   3/What do you think is the significance of her
saying "this is my friend" (v. 16)?   4/What elements of friendship has
this poem already revealed?   5/Why is friendship a crucial part of a
permanent love commitment?   6/What is the women's second question, and how does the girl answer?   7/Do you find the Lord Jesus
Christ "altogether desirable" (v. 16)? In what ways is he your friend?

day 15   ☐   *Song of Solomon 6:4–7:9*
1/In 6:4-8 and 7:1-9 what images does Solomon use to describe the
Shulammite girl?   2/Why do you think the king this time describes
her as "terrible as an army with banners" (vv. 4, 10)?   3/Why do you
think he says, "Turn away your eyes from me, for they disturb me"
(v. 5)?   4/How does he flatter the girl in verses 8-10?   5/Verses 11-13
are difficult to interpret—might they be the girl's reminiscence of
being taken away by King Solomon's men?   6/Would Satan describe
you as "terrible as an army with banners"?

day 16   ☐   *Song of Solomon 7:10–8:4*
1/How does the girl again affirm her faithfulness to her beloved?
2/What good things does she want to give him?   3/What good things
can you offer the Lord Jesus?   4/Why do you think verse 4 has been
a continuing refrain in the poem?   5/Having studied the girl's character for several days, what qualities do you most respect in her?
6/Are these qualities strongly evidenced in your own relations with
people?   7/Are they strongly evidenced in your relation with God?

day 17   ☐   *Song of Solomon 8:5-14*
1/*The New Bible Commentary* suggests that the question in verse 5 is
asked by villagers as they see the girl returning home with her beloved. If this is so, how do her statements about love (vv. 6-7) and
about being a wall (vv. 8-10) relate to her actions in Solomon's harem?
2/How do verses 11-12 support the three-character interpretation of

this poem?   3/Why do you think the girl responds to her beloved's request as she does (vv. 13-14)?   4/Evaluate the comment that this poem "provides a wholesome balance between the extremes of sexual excess or perversion and an ascetic denial of the essential goodness of physical love" (*New Bible Dictionary*, p. 1206).   5/Considering what you have learned from the Song of Solomon, what should characterize your relationship to your spouse or to someone you are dating seriously? What characteristics would not make for an abiding relationship?   6/As these studies have mirrored your relationship with Christ, what strengths and weaknesses have you seen?

day 18   □   Introduction to 2 Peter
This letter, probably written by Peter shortly before his death, brings both warning and hope to the believers who receive it. False teachers are about; these are reminded that Christ will return to judge their wrongdoing. Believers can rejoice at the hope of Christ's coming; they must live lives worthy of him. Keep the perspective of eternity as you read this letter. Does your life day by day reflect your expectation of "new heavens and a new earth"?   *2 Peter 1:1-11*   1/Describe the author (cf. 3:1) and his readers. How are they *equal*?   2/What has God done for man? For what purpose? Through whom?   3/What is included in *all things* (v. 3) for you?   4/What should be your attitude toward the present world?   5/Why are God's promises given? What promises do you claim today?   6/What two thoughts are connected by the transition *for this very reason*?   7/How is man to respond to God's work for him?   8/In which of the supplements are you weak? Why? With what result?   9/Define and explain *shortsighted*.   10/Relate God's call and man's confirmation.   11/How do you know you will enter the eternal kingdom of God?

day 19   □   2 Peter 1:12-21
1/What is Peter's purpose in writing this letter?   2/If you are established in the truth, why do you need reminders?   3/What can you do for your Christian friends prior to your *departure*?   4/How does Christianity differ from mythology? To what facts does Peter refer? What do the facts prove?   5/What do you emphasize in your procla-

mation of Christ? 6/From what does a Christian gain spiritual knowledge? 7/What is the origin of prophecy? of interpretation? 8/How can you know whether the interpretation of Scripture given by various writers is true? whether your understanding of their interpretation is true?

day 20 ☐ *2 Peter 2:1-9*

1/Characterize false prophets. How extensive is their influence? 2/Relate their opinions to their standards of conduct. 3/What will be the fate of such persons? 4/Contrast God's past attitude and actions toward godliness and ungodliness. Will he act differently in the present and future? 5/What is the significance of *until* in verses 4 and 9? 6/How do you feel about ungodly people "getting away with" evil? 7/How do you relate God's judgment and mercy?

day 21 ☐ *2 Peter 2:10-22*

1/Characterize the false teachers as to their behavioral patterns, message and methods. 2/To what extent have they previously known the truth? 3/What is their fate? 4/Describe the kind of person affected by false teaching. 5/How can you resist false teaching? 6/What drives, habits, attitudes, people, etc., *overcome* you? 7/What is so attractive about evil that pulls a person back?

day 22 ☐ *2 Peter 3:1-10*

1/Who has predicted the coming of scoffers? 2/What specific point of false teachers strikes at the root of Christian doctrine and conduct? Why? 3/Where is the weakness in the scoffers' argument? 4/To what characteristics of God does Peter appeal? To what historical event? 5/Contrast the past judgment of water and the future judgment of fire. 6/When will *the day of the Lord* come? How? With what result? 7/What people do you hope will repent before the Lord's coming? How do you express your concern for them?

day 23 ☐ *2 Peter 3:10-18*

1/Describe the consummation of heaven and earth. What will be dissolved? What will exist? 2/What should be our response to this belief? 3/In what ways do lives of holiness and godliness hasten the kingdom's coming? 4/What is ironic about twisting the Scriptures to suit present desires? 5/How can you maintain your Christian stability? 6/Summarize Peter's exhortations to Christians and his warnings to false teachers.

day 24 ☐ *Introduction to Jude*
The warnings of 2 Peter are reiterated here, and believers are urged to live in purity instead of following the examples of immorality found even in the church. A man's faith should show in the way he lives. Does yours? *Jude 1-7* 1/Describe the difference in the author's relationship to Jesus Christ and to James. 2/How is Jude related to the recipients of this letter? By whom will mercy, peace and love be multiplied to them? 3/What is Jude's purpose in writing? 4/What is especially damaging about the false teaching of the grace of God? 5/List the specific sins mentioned from Israel's history (relate to those committed by the infiltrators). What is their punishment (cf. Gen. 18:16—19:28)? 6/Is anyone exempt from God's judgment? 7/What in your theology is a perversion? in your morality? 8/How can you *contend for the faith* in your situation?

day 25 ☐ *Jude 8-25*
1/Characterize the false teachers (cf. Gen. 4; Num. 16: 1-35; 22—24). 2/How is the action of the archangel Michael in contrast to these ungodly men? 3/How is the purpose of the love feast destroyed by their behavior? 4/What common attribute runs through the metaphorical descriptions? How do the consequences relate to the punishments? 5/What manifestations of this kind of life have you seen? 6/How are you to live in view of the ungodliness around you? What will victory in your life mean to God? 7/How should you and your fellowship act toward those involved in struggles with immorality or disbelief? Why? 8/How will you give praise to God for what he has done to keep you from sin? for what he will do in the future to protect you?

day 26   ☐   *Introduction to Daniel*

Daniel writes from captivity in a heathen country. He becomes a leading statesman, known for both his extraordinary wisdom and his resolute obedience to his God. His book teaches the sovereignty of this God over *all* nations and people. What conditions are you attaching to your obedience? Consider what God may want of *you* in a hard place. *Daniel 1* 1/What two spoils does Nebuchadnezzar take from Israel? 2/What type of young men does he want? Why? 3/What is Daniel's dilemma? How would the food defile him? 4/What risk does Daniel take? How does it reveal his trust in God? 5/Why do Daniel and his companions have favor before the king? 6/What is *a*—Daniel's and *b*—God's part in the exalting? 7/Name and consider some of the authorities that battle for your allegiance. 8/What do you risk to demonstrate your faith? Why? Whom do you set out to please? How does it find expression in resolutions?

day 27   ☐   *Daniel 2*

1/What is the cause of Nebuchadnezzar's insomnia? How does he regard his wise men? 2/Imagine Daniel's feelings as he hears about the decree. 3/Trace the progression of events. When does Daniel wait, pray, take initiative and commit himself? Why? 4/List the characteristics with which Daniel describes God. To what do these lead in his prayer? 5/Compare and contrast Daniel's conversation with the king with the wise men's (esp. vv. 11, 27-28). 6/What is the purpose of Daniel's interpretation? 7/What is to be the fate of Nebuchadnezzar and his kingdom? Why? Whose kingdom is to be established? 8/Upon hearing the interpretation, how does Nebuchadnezzar respond to Daniel? to God? 9/What are some situations in which you should prayerfully take the initiative? Why?

day 28   ☐   *Daniel 3*

1/What is Nebuchadnezzar's national decree? What do you think the image might have represented? 2/Describe the celebration. What is its purpose? 3/Contrast the young Jews' conflict here with that in chapter 1. 4/How has their response to the first conflict aided their response to the second? 5/What do Shadrach, Meshach and Abednego make clear to Nebuchadnezzar? How does the king react? 6/After their deliverance, what comments does the king make about these young men? To what extent has Nebuchadnezzar's knowledge of God increased (cf. 2:46-49 and 3:28—4:3)? Why? 7/What situations face you, forcing a decision between compromise and acceptance versus commitment and persecution? 8/In what ways can others see God acting in your life?

day 29   ☐   *Daniel 4*
1/What is Nebuchadnezzar's second dream? How is he described? What is to become of the stump? 2/What appeal does Daniel make? 3/Specifically how does a leader's ungodly life affect his people? 4/Compare Nebuchadnezzar's attitude and words before and after his humiliation. What does he have to learn? How has his attitude toward God changed? 5/How can you urge others to practice righteousness and mercy? 6/In what ways and areas of life are you proud? Ask for God's humbling and restoring now.

day 30   ☐   *Daniel 5*
1/Compare and contrast Belshazzar and Nebuchadnezzar. 2/Describe the condition of Belshazzar when the writing appears. 3/What does Belshazzar ask of and offer to Daniel? 4/What are Daniel's comments concerning Belshazzar's offer? Nebuchadnezzar? Belshazzar himself? 5/What is the message from God? How does the king respond? 6/According to chapters 4—5 what is man's basic problem before God? What response does God demand?

Month 51

day 1   ☐   *Daniel 6*
1/What is Daniel's position under this third king? 2/How do those around Daniel feel toward him? Why? What do they do? 3/How

does Daniel react to their plotting?   4/What are Darius' attitude and actions concerning Daniel? Why do you think he feels this way? 5/What happens to Daniel? What is his condition before God? before the king?   6/To what extent can you be blameless before God and men at the same time? Why?   7/How do you react when misfortune or ostracism results from godly actions on your part?   8/Summarize Daniel's faith and witness under the kings he has served. How have they responded to his God? Why?

day 2   ☐   *Daniel 7*
1/What issues are brought up in Daniel's dream? Who is the ultimate authority?   2/Why do you think God reveals the dream to Daniel? 3/Whom do each of the beasts have to face? Why does man have to answer to God for his actions?   4/What do the beasts represent? 5/How is God's kingdom to be established? Who is to reign ultimately? 6/As you participate in the establishment of God's kingdom, what situations, tasks and problems do you find personally tough? Are these primarily physical or spiritual difficulties?   7/In what ways does God reign victorious in your life?

day 3   ☐   *Daniel 8*
1/Having seen who is ultimately in authority, what revelation is given to Daniel in his second dream?   2/Who are represented by the symbols?   3/Describe these beasts or nations. What are the limits to their power? In what methods and actions do they engage?   4/How high does the little horn magnify itself? What are its purpose and actions toward things pertaining to God?   5/What is Daniel's reaction to what God shows him of the future?   6/Amid this turmoil and power, what is the effect on the Prince of princes?

day 4   ☐   *Daniel 9*
1/What is Daniel doing that seems to initiate his prayer?   2/Contrast Daniel's description of God and man.   3/What brings God's judgment and wrath?   4/On what ground does Daniel seek God's grace? What happens while he is praying?   5/How and why does God an-

swer prayer?   6/Wnat six things are going to occur? Note the difference between the positive and the negative acts to be accomplished 7/As a Christian, how do you seek God's wisdom, understanding and guidance?

day 5   □   *Daniel 10*

1/What is Daniel doing when he has this vision?   2/What does he see? To what extent are others affected by this vision? What is their response? How does Daniel respond?   3/Why are Daniel's words heard?   4/How is Daniel physically affected by the man's presence? Why?   5/How does the prophet receive peace and strength?

day 6   □   *Daniel 11*

1/What is revealed to Daniel? Who is revealing these things (cf. 10: 15-17)?   2/Describe the situation among nations.   3/What are some of the phrases describing the last ruler?   4/How does the ruler act toward God? Does he heed any god? What does he honor? What will his end be?   5/Who will be able to stand under such chaos and pressure? Why do God's people have to suffer? What is their responsibility during such times?

day 7   □   *Daniel 12*

1/Describe the time mentioned.   2/To what two ends will *those who sleep* awake? Describe these types of men. What responses are made to God?   3/In what two conditions before God are men today? What will be their respective outcomes? Why?   4/Does Daniel fully understand? What is he told to do? What is he promised?   5/Can you comprehend all of God's ways? How should you respond to what God *has* told or shown you?

day 8   □   *Daniel 1–12*

1/Briefly characterize the men in this narrative as to their situations and the way they end up.   2/Compare or contrast them with yourself.   3/Summarize briefly the discussions on nations and their

leaders. 4/What new things have you learned about yourself
through this study? about the Lord God? 5/Ask the God of Daniel
to make you a person faithful to him in situations of conflict and pressure. 6/Ask him who can change the hearts of kings to make you
spiritually influential in the lives of those around you. 7/Ask the one
whose kingdom will reign over nations to increase and strengthen
your faith in him.

day 9 □ Psalm 139

1/What relationship does the Lord have to the totality of David's life?
List the areas of his personality or life that God is acquainted with.
2/What does it mean for God to know his words altogether? What is
implied by the action of God's hand (cf. v. 5 with v. 10)? 3/What
responses does the psalmist have to God's knowledge of him? 4/Why
do you think David wants to escape the presence of God? Analyze
God's relationship to each of the possible places he might escape to.
5/What realization leads the psalmist to a sense of worship and freedom? 6/In what sense does his self-awareness grow during the
psalm (cf. vv. 2, 13)? 7/What kind of thoughts does God have toward
David? 8/Describe David's attitude toward God in these verses.
9/What characteristics of man are noted in verses 19-24? With what
attributes of God do you think the psalmist is identifying? 10/For
what things will you both praise God and request from him today?
11/Title this psalm.

day 10 □ Psalm 140

1/Describe evil men. 2/What is David asking God to do for him?
Why? 3/What qualities characterize David's personal relationship
with God? What connection do they have to his opening prayer?
4/What kind of actions characterize the wicked? What is David's attitude toward them? 5/What kind of enemies do you have? Why?
6/How does David express his confidence in God? 7/What is the relationship of verse 13 to the whole psalm? 8/Title this psalm.

day 11 □ Psalm 141

1/What emotions do you think David is feeling as he begins his prayer? How does he want God to receive this prayer?   2/What different aspects of his life is he concerned about in verses 3-4? What relationship do they have to each other?   3/What specific request does he make of God? Why?   4/In what way can you see humility in David's attitude? How open are you to the rebuke and correction of other Christians?   5/What dangers is he facing? What defense does he have?   6/How would you describe his attitude toward himself? toward God? toward enemies?   7/Title this psalm.

day 12   □   *Psalm 142*

1/How does David approach God when he is discouraged? Why do you think he emphasizes *voice*?   2/How can you develop this kind of honesty with God?   3/What are his enemies like?   4/Why does he cry to God? What is his problem? What does he expect God to do for him?   5/What two characteristics does David know about his persecutors (vv. 3, 6)?   6/In what ways do your problems tend to imprison you?   7/What qualities in God's nature recommend him as the solution to David's specific problems?   8/How can he have hope?   9/What do fellow believers have to do with the deliverance (contrast vv. 7b, 4a)?   10/Title this psalm.

day 13   □   *Psalm 143*

1/On what basis does David make his prayer?   2/What does judgment have to do with prayer?   3/What is David's understanding of the nature of man? How does this help him to lean on God in prayer?   4/Describe the condition of his inner life. What is the cause of this?   5/Analyze the verbs in verses 5-6. What progression do you notice? How does he go beyond mere mental assent to God?   6/What factors cause David to be thirsty for God?   7/How does God ask you to reach out to him? Why?   8/What four requests does David make in verses 7-8?   9/How does fellowship with God relate to the problem of being downcast? To what extent are you experiencing the reality of God in your life?   10/What is God's part in David's deliverance? What is David's part?   11/Summarize the basis for David's confidence that God would answer his prayer.   12/List the similarities of Psalms 142 and 143.   13/Title this psalm.

day 14   ☐   *Psalm 144*

1/What symbols does David use to describe God? Why does he think of God in these terms?   2/Think of one word that would describe God as he is seen in these verses.   3/To what extent does the worthiness of man determine whether God shows interest in him? How does God show that he is interested in man?   4/Contrast the power of man with the power of God.   5/What things characterize the enemy? Do you know people like this? To what extent are you concerned about lies and falsehood?   6/Account for the psalmist's singing. To whom does he direct his joy?   7/List, in your own words, the blessings David looks for. What different aspects of a person's life do they cover? 8/What is the result of such blessings? What relationship does this have to God the Lord? How does this apply to your country, city or group?   9/Title this psalm.

day 15   ☐   *Psalm 145*

1/Characterize David's relationship to God.   2/What confidence does he have regarding his own eternal life?   3/List the characteristics of God and his acts.   4/What is the people's response to these characteristics? What different ways are used to praise God in these verses? Which one might you use?   5/How can you reconcile God's attributes as seen in verses 8-9 with those in Psalm 144:5-6?   6/Who and what is included under God's compassion? How should this make a difference in the way you look at people?   7/Describe the kingdom and power of God. What is the extent of each? Why do all the saints talk about God's kingdom and power? To what extent is this one of your concerns?   8/What is God's attitude toward the downcast? What does he do? What people today fit in this category?   9/In what specific way is God the sustainer of the universe?   10/In what kind of people does God take a special interest? What does he do for these people?   11/What is the relationship between fear and love? 12/What is the end of the wicked?   13/What is David's response to this great God?   14/Title this psalm.

day 16   ☐   *Psalm 146*

1/To what has the psalmist dedicated his life? What is his stimulus?

2/What kind of men seem most worthy of trust? Are they (cf. vv. 4, 10)?   3/In what ways are you putting your trust in men?   4/What is the by-product of faith in God?   5/Why can the man who trusts God have confidence he will not be let down?   6/Think of an example for each of the oppressed or needy people mentioned.   7/What action does God take in each case? What does this tell us about his character? Compare this with the people mentioned in Psalm 145. 8/How is the eventual ruin of the wicked an encouragement to steadfastness and righteousness?   9/Title this psalm.

day 17 □ *Psalm 147*

1/Why is it *good* to praise God?   2/What aspects of his glory are seen here? How are these evident in God's relationship to Israel and creation?   3/What has God done with Jerusalem to merit praise (cf. Gen. 15:5)?   4/How does God provide for living things?   5/About what is God primarily concerned in his creatures? Why?   6/What about you pleases God? How do you know?   7/In what different ways has Israel experienced God's reality? How is his dealing unique to this people? 8/What overall picture of God do you receive from this psalm? How do you respond?   9/Title this psalm.

day 18 □ *Psalm 148*

1/What different aspects of the heavens are to praise God? For what reason?   2/Compare the references to God's Word in this psalm (vv. 5, 8) with those in Psalm 147 (vv. 15, 18-19).   3/What aspects of the earth and its inhabitants are to praise God? For what reason? 4/What does the nature and order of creation indicate about what God is like?   5/What is the scope, in creation, of the call to praise God?   6/What is the relationship of being near to God and praising him? In what ways can you more effectively praise God after studying this psalm?   7/How does verse 13 relate to the whole psalm? 8/Compare the overall picture of God you receive from this psalm with that you received from Psalm 147.   9/Title this psalm.

day 19 □ *Psalm 149*

1/What people have reason to praise God? What emotions charac-

terize their praise?   2/What different places are to be used for praising God (vv. 1, 5)?   3/What feelings does God have toward the believers?   4/What characteristic is linked to the victorious life? Why?
How does it relate to God's pleasure?   5/Think of a word that fits
the characteristic described in verses 6-9.   6/How is this psalm an explanation of Psalm 148:14?   7/Title this psalm.

day 20   □   *Psalm 150*

1/In what locations is God to be praised?   2/How can you praise him
according to his exceeding greatness?   3/What relationship might the
number of phrases that begin with *praise* have to the twelve tribes of
Israel?   4/For what aspects of God's nature are we to praise him?
5/Summarize the *mighty deeds* God has accomplished for Israel.
6/List the *mighty deeds* God has done that have specifically affected
your life.   7/How can you praise God today? What instrument will
you choose?

day 21   □   *Introduction to Revelation*

The Revelation (or Apocalypse) is an unveiling of something hidden.
John records his symbolic visions, allegories and exhortations between the time of the destruction of Jerusalem in A.D. 70 and the end
of Domitian's reign in A.D. 95. Inflexible hostility from Rome, persecution by the Jews and the pervasive influence for conformity to
heathen practices have subjected the Christians of western Asia Minor
to enormous pressures. This book deals with crucial questions such as:
When will Christ return to deliver his people? Is membership in the
church worth this suffering? How can any power resist the force of
Rome? Is God indeed the sovereign Lord over all nations? Although
first intended for the churches of Asia Minor, Revelation has relevance at every critical period of church history. *Revelation 1:1-8*
1/Follow the progression from person to person by which the revelation has come to the church.   2/What is John's place in this communication? What service has he rendered to the church?   3/Who are
to be *blessed?* Why?   4/How do you expect to become involved in this
revelation? Why?   5/To whom is the letter addressed?   6/Locate the
churches on a map of the times (cf. v. 11).   7/Who greets the

churches? 8/What qualities are attributed to Jesus? 9/List the truths mentioned here which will encourage the anxious and persecuted first-century Christians. Which encourage you? Why? 10/How are you a *priest* to God? Why? 11/What attribute of God is found in verses 4 and 8?

day 22 ☐ *Revelation 1:9-20*

1/How does John describe himself and his situation? 2/What is the setting for the vision he receives? What and whom does he see? 3/Compare other prophets' visions (Ezek. 1:26-28; Dan. 7:9-14). 4/How would you describe to others something you had never seen before? How important do you consider the physical description of what John sees? Why? 5/What impression do you get from John's description? Why? Imagine how you would respond. 6/How does Christ describe himself? What does he command? explain? 7/When have you been in Christ's presence? How do you know?

day 23 ☐ *Revelation 2:1-7*

1/Who is addressed here? 2/Who is the message from? 3/What characteristics are known and praised? 4/What is the claim Christ has against the church? How are they to correct the situation? 5/Relate the call for repentance and the promise to those who *conquer*. 6/How does Christ regard love? 7/Are false apostles a danger today? 8/How is your love for Christ shown? 9/What is the consequence of not repenting? Why, do you think?

day 24 ☐ *Revelation 2:8-11*

1/Find out about the history of Smyrna. 2/How does Christ's description of himself bring hope and comfort to the church there? 3/Describe the situation of the Christians in Smyrna. 4/How can they be *rich*? 5/What are they promised? Why? 6/Distinguish the first and second deaths. 7/In what ways are you poor? rich? To what extent are the people around you rich in this way? 8/What have you suffered for Christ? 9/How will the Christians at Smyrna *conquer* (cf. v. 7)?

day 25   ☐   *Revelation 2:12-17*

1/Investigate the political situation in Pergamum at this time (Augustus built a temple here for emperor worship).   2/How is Satan related to the city?   3/Characterize the *sword* (v. 12). What is its purpose?   4/Compare the Nicolaitan teaching with that of Balaam (cf. Num. 25:1-5; 31:16).   5/What temptations do they offer the people? What similar temptations face you today?   6/Contrast the results of hearing and not hearing the Spirit's words.   7/What is God's attitude toward sin?   8/What *things* might God have against you? Why?

day 26   ☐   *Revelation 2:18-29*

1/Describe the problem in this church. What does the Son of God predict for the prophetess, her lovers and her children? Why?   2/What sins do you tolerate in yourself? in your church?   3/To what extent are you responsible for others' sins?   4/What should the people in Thyatira *hold fast*? Why? What will be their reward (cf. vv. 7, 10-11, 17)?   5/How do future rewards influence your present life? Why? 6/Summarize the appearance and characteristics of the speaker in this chapter (vv. 1, 8, 12, 16, 18, 23).   7/What has the Spirit said to you in this chapter?

day 27   ☐   *Revelation 3:1-6*

1/What images are used here?   2/Distinguish the appearance and the reality of the lives of these people.   3/What admonition and what warning does Christ give them?   4/Which of your good works are *on the point of death*? Why? What steps will you have to take to revive them? 5/What characterizes a *worthy* person? What is his reward?   6/How do you think Christ will *confess* your name (cf. 2:17)? Before whom?

day 28   ☐   *Revelation 3:7-13*

1/List the references to Judaism. What is their significance?   2/Compare and contrast the *power* of the holy one and the Philadelphians (cf. 2:26-27).   3/How does Christ commend the church here? What is promised to them?   4/Whose names are cited here (cf. 2:17)? 5/Who might seize your crown? Why? How can you prevent such a loss?   6/Relate love and power.

day 29 ☐ *Revelation 3:14-22*

1/Summarize the characteristics of the speaker in this chapter (vv. 1, 7, 14, 21). 2/What images are used to describe the people of Laodicea? How do they view themselves? 3/What are the remedies for their situation? 4/What is the significance of the *white* garments (cf. 1:14; 2:17; 3:4-5)? 5/How does Christ relate himself to the people of his church? Why? 6/How are you related to Christ? Why? 7/What has Christ conquered? 8/In what areas and ways do you need .his help in conquering?

day 30 ☐ *Revelation 4*

1/Describe the scene here, noting characters, colors, images, intensity (cf. Ezek. 1:1-28; 10:1-22; 1 Chron. 24:1-19). 2/What is happening here? Why? 3/What is the reason for John's inclusion? 4/What is the point of reference for everything John sees? 5/What qualities of God are extolled? 6/What evokes the *worship?* 7/When do you respond in worship to God? Why? How? 8/How can you give God *glory and honor and thanks* today? 9/Can you join the singing of verses 8 and 11?

Month 52

day 1 ☐ *Revelation 5*

1/What additional objects and characters does John see now? 2/What is the problem here? Define *worthy.* 3/How is John affected? Why? 4/How is the problem solved? Why (cf. 3:21)? 5/Find the three songs. Who sing them? 6/What has the Lamb done for men? for God? 7/What will the Lamb *receive* (cf. 4:11)? From whom? 8/Relate *incense* and your prayers. 9/Consider how the Lamb is worthy of your praise. Worship him with the songs presented here.

day 2 ☐ *Revelation 6*

1/How is the Lamb's *worth* related to his opening the seals? 2/Describe the characters and objects in these dramatic scenes. What is each given? Why? 3/Identify the forces in the first four seals that are operative throughout history. In what ways have they been fulfilled in your lifetime? 4/To what extent do you think God is using these forces redemptively? judicially? 5/To what extent is history in God's control? 6/When will the gathering of brethren seen in the fifth seal be complete? What will happen then? 7/What event is John describing in the breaking of the sixth seal (cf. Is. 13:10; 34:4)? Enumerate the images. How would you describe such a happening? 8/How do men on the earth react to the cosmic disruptions? Why are they afraid? 9/Anticipate your reaction to this *day.*

day 3 □ *Revelation 7*

1/What are the responsibilities and purposes of the angels here? 2/Who will be *sealed?* What is the significance of the sealing (cf. Ezek. 9:4)? 3/In the numbering, which tribe is omitted? which is added (cf. Gen. 48—49)? 4/Distinguish the characters of the two visions. Who are represented in each group? Describe the appearance and origin of each. 5/What is the significance of the *white robes* in the later vision? 6/How do the people worship God? Define *belong.* 7/How will God and the Lamb care for the servants (cf. Is. 4:5-6; 25:8; 49:10)? Why? 8/To what extent will you need this care? Why? 9/What encouragement do you find here to help you manage living today?

day 4 □ *Revelation 8:1-5*

1/Contrast the earthly and cosmic reverberations of the previous six seals with the opening of the seventh seal. 2/What is the psychological effect? Imagine your response were you in John's place. What might be the significance of this response? 3/What actions break the spell? 4/Imagine the content and volume of *the prayers of all the saints* (relate 1900 years of prayers by the suffering church and the opening of the fifth seal). 5/To what extent will your prayers be included? For what purpose? 6/Contrast verses 1 and 5. Account for the difference.

day 5   ☐   *Revelation 8:6-13*

1/Compare and contrast the blowing of the first four trumpets with the opening of the six seals.   2/What images are used?   3/What is the state of the earth? the heavens? the men of earth?   4/To what extent are these catastrophes happening on earth now?   5/To what extent have they been portrayed in the Old Testament (cf. Ex. 7—10; Zeph. 1:3; Jer. 9:15; 23:15; Joel 2:1-11)?   6/What is God's purpose for the happenings here?   7/Evaluate your possessions and situation. What would last through such a devastation?   8/How does the end of "the good life" affect your daily living? Why?

day 6   ☐   *Revelation 9*

1/Define *woe*.   2/Identify the participants in the first woe.   3/How are the appearance and activities of the locusts here different from the insect locust?   4/What is the extent of their power? Upon whom? Why?   5/Compare the actions and influences of the locusts with what you know of the power of evil in your life.   6/Consider these images as a description of the loosing of the devil (Apollyon means Destroyer) and his angels on the world (cf. Joel 2:4-10; Lk. 8:31).   7/What is the scope and nature of the second woe? In what ways does it differ from the first?   8/Who are destroyed by the cavalry host? Why? Does the host accomplish its purpose?   9/Characterize those who remain. 10/Can you imagine a happening which might cause mankind to repent?   11/What has caused you to repent? To what extent?

day 7   ☐   *Revelation 10*

1/Describe this angel (cf. Rev. 1:7; Ezek. 1:26-28; Mt. 17:2). What messages about judgment does he dramatize?   2/What is the *mystery of God* (cf. Rom. 11:25-36; 16:25-27)? How have the prophets been involved in the mystery?   3/What is John's part in the revelation (cf. Ezek. 2:8—3:3)?   4/In what ways does your experience of revelation taste sweet? bitter? When?   5/What is the purpose of the delay before the mystery of God is fulfilled?   6/Contrast the worship of the elders and creatures (chap. 4—5) with the worship of mankind (9:20). 7/Contrast the idols (cf. 9:20 with Is. 40:18-26; 42:8; 44:6-20) with the Lord God Almighty (cf. v. 6 with 4:11).

day 8   ☐   *Revelation 11:1-14*

1/What and who will be protected while the world is in turmoil (cf. vv. 1, 5 with 7:3)?   2/What will be desecrated? Why (cf. vv. 2, 8 with Mt. 23:37-39)?   3/Characterize the two witnesses. What is the source of their authority (cf. 1:20 with Zech. 4:1-14)? How will they be conquered? When?   4/What will be the world opinion at their demise? at their resurrection (cf. Ezek. 37:5-14)?   5/Account for the different responses of the people in verse 13 and 9:20-21.   6/Consider what this passage would mean to first-century Christians (cf. chaps. 2—3). 7/To what extent does your church stand in the prophetic tradition of witness? Why?   8/Compare and contrast the experience of your church with the universal church here and the witness of Jesus Christ on earth (cf. Jn. 17).   9/In what ways are you influenced by world opinion of the church?   10/To what extent do you fear war with the beast? Why?

day 9   ☐   *Revelation 11:15-19*

1/Contrast the sights and sounds of the seventh trumpet with those of opening the seventh seal.   2/What is the significance of the verb tenses?   3/List the reasons for giving thanks to God.   4/What is the extent of God's *power* (cf. 4:11; 7:12 with Dan. 7:14)? Define *reign*. 5/Relate your thanksgiving to God's sovereignty.   6/What *destroyers* will be destroyed (cf. 6:3-8; 7:16; 8:7-11; 9:1-19)?   7/Who will be rewarded?   8/What in this hymn of praise will you affirm in faith today? 9/Summarize what has happened to mankind and the church before the vision of God's final reign here (cf. chaps. 6-11).   10/What is the significance of an open temple (review Ex. 34:6-16 for the original terms of the covenant)?   11/What is visible (cf. 1 Kings 8:1-12)?

day 10   ☐   *Revelation 12*

1/Characterize the combatants here. List he ways they are described (cf. Gen. 3:1, 14-15). Whom do they represent (cf. Mic. 4:10; Ps. 2: 7-9)?   2/Where does the action take place?   3/What indicates the power of the dragon? In what ways and areas is he thwarted (find the repeated phrase in vv. 7-12)? Why? Imagine his feelings.   4/What has made the coming of the kingdom possible?   5/Who has con-

quered (cf. 3:21; 5:5)? How?   6/What is the outcome of the conflict?
7/Compare and contrast the events of verses 13-17 with Israel's
exodus from Egypt (Ex. 14:5-31; 19:1-6).   8/What are Satan's feelings about the church? about you (vv. 12, 17)?   9/What weapons does
he have at his disposal for use against God? against the church?
against you? Why?   10/When will the people of God be safe from
Satan's power (cf. v. 6 with 7:1-8; 11:1-2)?

day 11   □   Revelation 13
1/Compare and contrast the two beasts as to origin, appearance, intent and actions (cf. 11:2 with Dan. 7:1-8).   2/Relate the beasts and
the dragon (chap. 12).   3/Relate the beasts' authority with God's sovereignty.   4/How are the people who do and do not worship the beast
designated (cf. vv. 8, 16 with 7:1-8)? In what ways is each group excluded by the other? What is the effect?   5/Account for the acceptance of the beasts' authority (contrast 11:11-13).   6/What three
falsehoods are promoted by the two-horned beast? How are these
falsehoods put into practice?   7/How can you be sure you will not be
deceived? How can you know which mark or seal is on you?

day 12   □   Revelation 14:1-5
1/Where is the scene now (cf. Heb. 12:22-23)? Who are participating
(cf. 7:3-4)? How are they identified (cf. 5:5-6)?   2/Compare and contrast the scene and sounds here and in chapter 5.   3/What is unique
about this new song?   4/Are you one of the redeemed?   5/Do you
think John is literally referring to celibates or symbolically referring
to purity here (cf. 2 Cor. 11:2)? Why?   6/Does marriage cause defilement?   7/Imagine your feelings when you are presented before God
as a virgin, chaste and spotless.   8/To what extent are you reserved
for God (cf. v. 4 with Jas. 1:18)?

day 13   □   Revelation 14:6-20
1/Contrast the voices and sounds of chapters 13 and 14.   2/What
messages are given? To whom?   3/What is the purpose of the messages (cf. v. 12 with 13:10)?   4/Contrast the eternal destiny of the

wicked and the righteous (cf. vv. 10-11 with Is. 34:8-10; vv. 1-6, 13 with 7:15-17). 5/To what extent are the elements of the *gospel* in verse 7 part of your experience? 6/Where do the last three angels come from (cf. 6:9-11; 8:1-5; 9:13; 11:1, 19; 16:7)? What are their actions (note the verbs; cf. Joel 3:13; Is. 63:3)? 7/Where will this action take place (cf. 11:8)? 8/Define *vintage*. How *ripe* do you think the earth is now?

day 14   □   *Revelation 15:1-4*
1/Skim chapters 15 and 16. How do verses 1-4 relate to the rest of these chapters? 2/How do the plagues affect God (cf. 6:16-17; 11:18; 14:19)? What is culminated? 3/Who are singing (cf. 12:11)? Where (cf. 4:5-6)? 4/What is the significance of *fire* (cf. 8:5; 9:17-18; 14:10, 18)? 5/How is the song identified? 6/Compare and contrast the exodus from Egypt (Ex. 15:1-12; Ps. 51:9-11) with eternal deliverance from the beast. 7/What attributes of God are extolled? 8/Worship God with this song.

day 15   □   *Revelation 15:5-8*
1/What is the source of the symbolism in this passage (cf. Num. 9:15; 17:7; Lev. 8:7-8; Ex. 40:33-38; Is. 6:4; Ezek. 10:4; 44:4)? 2/In what ways does the temple express the nature of God (cf. 11:19)? 3/How are the angels clothed (note esp. the adjectives)? 4/Who handle God's wrath? What is the significance of the containers (cf. 14:10)? 5/What qualities of the presence of God stand out in this vision? 6/Note what those who have conquered the beast say about God's strategy and tactics in judgment (cf. vv. 1-4). 7/To what extent do you pass judgment on God's judgment? Why?

day 16   □   *Revelation 16*
1/Try to imagine your feelings as an angel pouring your bowl. 2/How does one angel respond to God's judgment (cf. v. 6 with 6:10)? 3/Compare and contrast the seven bowls of wrath with the judgments of the seven trumpets. Which images and ideas are new? 4/Who or what experience the judgments? To what extent? What is their re-

sponse (cf. 9:20-21)? Why? Relate their response to their judgment and vice versa. 5/Describe the demonic spirits (cf. chap. 13). What is their goal? 6/What part of these spirits is encouraging opposition to God? 7/Who will participate in the final battle between God and evil? Who will be prepared for it? What will be *exposed*? 8/How is civilization destroyed (cf. 6:12-17; 11:19)? 9/How does your knowledge of the future influence your values in life? Why?

day 17   □   *Revelation 17:1-6*

1/How is the great harlot depicted? What is the setting? 2/What makes her attractive? Why is she repulsive? 3/With whom has she been involved (cf. v. 18)? 4/Whom does she symbolize (cf. Jer. 51: 7-14)? 5/Describe the beast. What is its association with the harlot? 6/What is God's response to harlotry (cf. Jer. 13:24-27; Ezek. 16: 23-43; Hos. 4:10-12; 5:4)? 7/Is your city and nation a harlot? What is the extent of corruption in your local, state and national governments? 8/How can you remain pure in the midst of your nation's *abominations* and *fornications*?

day 18   □   *Revelation 17:7-18*

1/How is the woman transported? 2/Add to the beast's description (cf. chap. 13). What is his history? his present activity? his future? 3/How do the people of earth respond to him? 4/What is the identification of the beast's seven heads? his ten horns (cf. Dan. 7:15-28)? 5/Relate the history of the beast and seven kings here with the healed mortal wound of the beast in chapter 13 (the Roman emperor Nero had died, but was expected to rise from the dead to fight against Rome). 6/What authority and power will the beast have? What is the fate of this alliance? What will they accomplish before their defeat? 7/Can you account for the beast's turning against the woman he has carried? 8/List situations and ways the Lamb and the faithful have conquered historically. 9/What indications do you see that God is active in the world when evil triumphs? To what extent is God active in your life when evil touches you? Why?

day 19   ☐   *Revelation 18*
1/What is the mood of this chapter? What music would suit the theme?
2/Examine the successive voices (cf. Is. 13, 21, 47; Jer. 50—51; Ezek.
26—27). What distinct emphases does each voice make? How has each
been associated with the woman (cf. chap. 17)?   3/Contrast the before and after pictures of the great woman (cf. 17:16).   4/Compare
and contrast the responses to her fall.   5/Read the chapter again,
picturing your favorite great city of modern civilization. Imagine your
reaction to her sudden catastrophic demise. What would be the political, social, economic, religious repercussions?   6/What cities do you
depend on? Why?

day 20   ☐   *Revelation 19:1-8*
1/Contrast the voices heard here with those in chapter 18. How is
this response to the harlot's fate different (cf. 18:20)?   2/What is the
focus of attention here? Why?   3/Do you think you will recognize the
exact modern empire and individual that finally culminate the suc-
cession of empires and individuals which have resembled these
prophecies? Why?   4/Will you join in the lament or the jubilation?
Why?   5/Who participate in the praise (cf. 7:9-12; 11:15-18; 15:2-4)?
For what reasons?   6/Imagine the feelings of the Lamb, the Bride
and the defeated rival as the marriage finally happens.   7/What is
your part in getting the Bride ready?

day 21   ☐   *Revelation 19:6-10*
1/What metaphors does John use to describe the sounds of jubilation?   2/What aspects of God's nature are portrayed by marriage (cf.
Hos. 2:2-23; 6:6; Jer. 2:2-3, 32-35; 3:1-13; 5:7-8; 13:27; Ezek. 16;
Eph. 5:21-33)?   3/Have you been *invited* to the marriage supper?
Why?   4/What is the angel's role? Why does he refuse worship?
5/To what extent do you worship the means by which the *true words
of God* come to you? Why?   6/To what extent do you prophesy? For
what reasons?   7/Worship God.

day 22   ☐   *Revelation 19:11-21*
1/List and describe the characters in this sweeping panorama of judg-

ment.   2/What are the names of the rider of the white horse? Recalling the persecuted believers to whom this book is addressed, how
is each name significant?   3/What is the rider's task (cf. 14:17-20;
Ps. 2:7-9)? What is his weapon (cf. 1:16; 2 Thess. 2:8)?   4/Imagine the
array of both armies. Where are you?   5/In what ways do you experience this war between the forces of good and evil in your daily living?
6/Who are "invited" to the *supper* here (cf. Ezek. 39:17-20)?

day 23   □   Revelation 20:1-6
1/How is this vision similar to others John has described (cf. 6:9-11;
9:1-2; 11:3-12; 12:9)?   2/Describe the place and duties of the martyrs
here. Compare and contrast their life on earth with their destiny
(cf. chap. 13).   3/How do you know you will not succumb to the political, religious and economic pressures of the beast?   4/What is *the
first resurrection* (cf. Lk. 14:14; 1 Cor. 15:20-26; Phil. 3:10-11; 1 Thess.
4:16)? What has nullified the power of *the second death* for those who
share in the first resurrection (cf. 2:11)?   5/Where is the beast during
this time? the dragon? Do you think men on earth will get along any
better with the deceivers out of the way? Why?   6/How do you relate
these visions with your time in history? Why?

day 24   □   Revelation 20:7-15
1/Who will lead the battle here (cf. Ezek. 38—39)? Why?   2/From
where will the forces come?   3/What is their target? How far do they
get?   4/What will be the final outcome? Why?   5/Imagine the scene
of the final judgment (cf. Dan. 7:9-14; Mt. 25:31-46). Who is the judge
(cf. Jn. 5:22-30)? Who will be judged? On what basis (cf. Jn. 3:16-21)?
6/What is the significance of *the book of life* (cf. 3:5)?   7/What is *the
second death*? Who will be involved (cf. 19:20)? Why?   8/To what extent do you fear the first death? the second death? Why?   9/What
do you think you will find out about yourself from the opening of the
books? What will you add to the books today? Why?

day 25   □   Revelation 21:1-8
1/Describe what John sees (cf. 3:12; Is. 60:11-22; 65:17-19; 66:22).

What are *new* (cf. 2:17; 3:12)? In what ways (cf. 7:15-17)? Why? 2/Find all the expressions of God's *will* (cf. Ezek. 37:27; Is. 25:8; 35:10; 43:19; 55:1). 3/Contrast the *former* and *new* things. 4/What prophecy will finally be fulfilled (cf. Is. 7:14; Mt. 1:23)? 5/How certain is the newness (cf. v. 5 with 19:11)? 6/Summarize the characteristics and nature of God which are apparent here. 7/Distinguish the participants and the different ends of all men (cf. Ps. 89:27-28; 1 Jn. 3:2).

day 26 □ *Revelation 21:9-21*

1/How are the Bride and the holy city related (cf. 19:7-8; 21:2)? 2/Describe the *glory* of the city. From what source does the city derive its character? 3/Compare and contrast other visions of such grandeur (cf. Ezek. 40:2, 5; 48:30-35; Dan. 2:35; Is. 62:1-5). How is the beauty described (cf. Is. 54:11-12)? How is it valued? 4/What is different about the heavenly city when contrasted with the tabernacle and camp of the Israelites (cf. Ex. 25—28)? with Solomon's Jerusalem (cf. 1 Kings 4—9)? with the cities of the Roman empire? with our modern cities? Why?

day 27 □ *Revelation 21:22-22:5*

1/Describe the atmosphere in the city. 2/Imagine you are being shown around. What impresses you most? Why? 3/What are the city's provisions (cf. 7:16-17)? For whom? 4/How will the city be related to earthly nations and kings (cf. Is. 60:1-3, 11-20; 52:1)? 5/What is the scope of its influence? Why? 6/What was the purpose of the temple (cf. 1 Kings 6:13; 8:1-30)? 7/What makes the separation of God and man unnecessary in this city (cf. Jer. 3:17)? 8/How will you worship God when you actually see his face? How do you worship him now?

day 28 □ *Revelation 22:6-15*

1/How does the angel explain the revelation to John (cf. 1:1-3, 17-19; 3:11-12; 10:8-11; 21:5)? 2/For whom is the revelation given (cf. vv. 3, 16)? 3/How can you *keep* the words of the prophecy (cf.

chaps. 1—3)?   4/What is the angel's title and occupation (cf. 19:10)?
With whom does he identify (cf. v. 3; 5:11-14; 7:11-12; 19:6-8)?
5/What will be the state of the world when the *time* finally comes
(cf. v. 11 with 1 Thess. 5:1-10; 2 Tim. 4:8)?   6/What will be the reward of those who are ready (cf. 7:14-17; 21:25; 22:2; Is. 40:10; Gen.
3:22)?   7/How can a person *love* falsehood? What is his lot (cf. 21:8)?
Why (cf. 19:11)?   8/To what extent is the Lord Jesus *the Alpha and the
Omega* of your days? of your life? of the history of the world?

day 29   □   *Revelation 22:16-21*

1/How does Jesus describe himself (cf. 5:5; Num. 24:17; Is. 11:1-10)?
2/Why is John entrusted with this revelation?   3/To whom is the appeal directed in verse 17? in verse 20? For what reasons?   4/Who is
warned? Why is the completeness of this revelation so important?
5/What plagues have been described in this book?   6/What can you
say with certainty about the second coming after reading Revelation?
7/To what extent do you join the assent and appeal of verse 20? Why?

day 30   □   *Revelation 1–22*

1/Imagine that your church has received this letter from John, has
read it, passed it around and discussed it.   2/For what reasons was
the letter written? To what extent do they apply to your church?
3/To what extent is your church persecuted? Why?   4/What aspects
of *a*—God's nature and *b*—Satan's nature and power revealed here
need to be emphasized in your church? in your society?   5/How can
you join in the praise of God when Satan is finally defeated? To what
extent is such praise part of your church worship now?